DOING BUSINESS IN CHINA

By the same author

THE RAMPANT DRAGON
SYNERGY: JAPANESE COMPANIES IN BRITAIN

DOING BUSINESS IN CHINA
THE LAST GREAT MARKET

GEOFFREY MURRAY

ST. MARTIN'S PRESS

© Geoffrey Murray 1994

All rights reserved. For information, write:
Scholarly and Reference Division,
St. Martin's Press, 175 Fifth Avenue,
New York, NY 10010

First published in the United States of America in 1994

Printed in England

ISBN 0-312-11682-9 (CLOTH)
ISBN 0-312-11683-7 (PAPER)

Library of Congress Cataloging-in-Publication Data

Murray, Geoffrey, 1942–
    Doing business in China : the last great market / by Geoffrey Murray.
        p. cm.
    Includes bibliographical references and index.
    ISBN 0-312-11682-9. -- ISBN 0-312-11683-7 (pbk.)
    1. United States--Commerce--China. 2. China--Commerce--United States. I. Title.
HF3128.M87 1994
330.951'059--dc20   94-13029
                                                                 CIP

Contents

Foreword xi
Acknowledgements xiv

1. THE DREAM OF 1.2 BILLION CONSUMERS
   - *Key Points*
   - The Dragon Awakes 1
   - Socialist Market Economy 8
   - Flaws in the System 9
   - Losing Land to Development 11
   - Feverish Inflation 13
   - Monetary Taps – On or Off 16
   - Summary 19

2. REFORM MAY TAKE 100 YEARS
   - *Key Points*
   - Socialist Modernization 22
   - Socialism Plus Capitalism 23
   - Socialist Market Economy 28
   - Restructuring State Planning 30
   - Reforming the Public Sector 34
   - Hybrid Problems 43
   - Chain of Debt 45
   - Featherbedding 47
   - Smashing the Iron Rice Bowl 49
   - Private Business 52

3. THE COAST WILL GET RICHER FIRST
   - *Key Points*
   - Special Economic Zones 56
   - Shenzhen 59
   - Xiamen 62
   - Shantou 66
   - Hainan 68
   - Zhuhai 70

- Economic & Technological Development Zones   70
- Guangzhou   71
- Shanghai   73
- Tianjin   77
- Dalian   79
- Other Cities   80

4. DEVELOPMENT AND INVESTMENT PROSPECTS
   ELSEWHERE IN CHINA
   - *Key Points*
   - Yangtse Strategy   86
   - Yangtse River Economic Development Co.   88
   - From the Delta to Tibet   89
   - Revival for Wuhan   91
   - Jiangxi and Hunan   94
   - Sichuan Province   96
   - Swords to Ploughshares   98
   - Yellow River Revival   102
   - Qinghai Mineral Treasures   105
   - Border Trade   106

5. FOREIGN INVESTMENT: WHO, WHAT, WHERE AND HOW?
   - *Key Points*
   - New Market   110
   - The Overseas Chinese   115
   - Taiwan   121
   - The United States   124
   - Japan   126
   - South Korea   132
   - Europe   134
   - Infrastructure Prospects   136
   - The Chinese Multinationals   139

6. THE MAIN OPTIONS FOR INVESTING IN CHINA
   - *Key Points*
   - Representative Office   143
   - Joint Ventures   145
   - Understanding the Operating Rules   152
   - Finding the Right Partner   153
   - Shared Goals Essential   158
   - More Cautionary Tales   161
   - Bureaucratic Barrier   163
   - Envelope Business   165
   - Finding a Place to Stay   167

Contents ix

- Mistakes on Both Sides — 171

7. CASE STUDY: THE AUTOMOBILE INDUSTRY
   - *Key Points*
   - China's Slow Start — 175
   - Japanese Latecomers — 176
   - China's Strategy — 179
   - Cautious Expansion — 180
   - Contrasting Fortunes — 185
   - Other Foreign Players — 188
   - Beijing Jeep — 192

8. THE CHINESE ART OF SALESMANSHIP
   - *Key Points*
   - The Chinese Consumer — 195
   - Consumer Influence — 198
   - Import/Export Rules — 203
   - Copyright Problems — 208
   - Distribution System — 209
   - Sales Promotion — 212
   - The Media Scene — 216
   - Buying News — 218
   - Street-level Promotion — 220

9. NEGOTIATING SKILLS REQUIRED FOR SUCCEEDING IN CHINA
   - *Key Points*
   - The Meaning of a Contract — 222
   - Patience and More Patience — 223
   - Beijing Jeep — 226
   - The Chinese – by the Chinese — 228
   - The 36 Strategems — 233

10. MANAGEMENT AND LABOUR
    - *Key Points*
    - Management Contrasts — 243
    - Labour-Management Relations — 248
    - Trade Unions — 253
    - Social Security — 254
    - Finding Staff — 256
    - Job Hunting — 258
    - Job Switching — 262
    - Training Costs — 265

x   Doing Business in China

11. CHINA'S FINANCIAL SYSTEM
- *Key Points*
- Banking Structure   269
- Foreign Banks   276
- Borrowing from Chinese Banks   277
- Revival of Stock Exchanges   279
- Accountancy Reforms   286
- Future Markets   288

12. TAXES AND TAXATION POLICY
- *Key Points*
- What do I Have to Pay   291
- Past Tax Structure   295

13. THE CHALLENGES THAT LIE AHEAD
- *Key Points*
- The Cement Crumbles   300
- Whither Democracy?   305
- The Diplomatic Equation   309
- Hong Kong's Future   313
- Resolving Trade Worries   314
- Converting the Yuan   316
- Long Way to Go   318

Appendices

1. An Introduction to the Chinese Government Structure   325
2. China's Banking System   327
3. Law of the People's Republic of China on
   Foreign-Capital Enterprises   331
4. Procedures for the Registration and Administration of Resident
   Representative Offices of Foreign Enterprises in China 334
5. Contract for Employment of Chinese Employees   337
6. Major Overseas Agreements Signed by Chinese Investors,
   1990–93   341
7. Learning Mandarin in China (where to go)   342
8. How Reliable Are Chinese Statistics?   343

Bibliography   344
Index   345

Foreword

ALTHOUGH I have spent almost thirty years working in Asia, it was not until 1990 that I had my first opportunity to visit the People's Republic of China. From 1969 to 1984, I had been exposed to some aspects of Chinese culture as exported to Japan over the centuries. The peripheral Chinese experience then continued through a five-year sojourn in Singapore. Nevertheless, it is hard to explain the exalted feeling of 'finally coming home' that swept over me as I drove into Beijing from the capital's airport on a beautiful, crisp and sunny autumn day in 1990. I have always felt comfortable in the East, and found the rhythms of life in China, even the obvious harshness, extremely appealing. There was nothing more satisfying than leaping onto my ancient, incredibly heavy Flying Pigeon bicycle and joining the throngs battling through the capital's congested streets morning and night, or turning off and exploring the tranquil world of the few remaining 'hutongs' (traditional alleyways) of old Beijing; sadly, these are gradually crumbling before the wrecker's ball through the insatiable demand for new highways and skyscraper blocks of flats and offices to bring the city into the modern world.

I had been invited to pass on some of my accumulated experience as a foreign correspondent to young Chinese journalists coming to grips with the demands of the country's dash for a market economy and increasing exposure to the concepts and manners of the outside world. The first visit lasted six weeks and made a profound impression. There was no hesitation, therefore, in accepting an invitation to return to China for nine months in 1991. Out of that long stay came my first book on China, *The Rampant Dragon*. Returning to Beijing in March 1993, I was staggered at the amount of change that had occurred in less than two years. It was not simply the new highways and buildings that had sprung up, but also the mindset of the people with whom I came into daily contact. There was more money around. That much was obvious in the thronged appearance of luxury department stores ablaze with lights, colourful fashions and the latest electronic equipment which would not have caused a raised eyebrow in London, New York or Tokyo, but were certainly a startling change for the better in China, where drab, utilitarian state-run stores manned by the world's surliest sales assistants used to be the norm. For virtually everyone, the main source of conversation was: how to make money; how to get a second or even third job to supplement the meagre returns from the first one. Communism was hardly ever mentioned, other than in lip service.

Reading the *China Daily* every morning, one was bombarded with headlines announcing new government initiatives to open up the economy, encourage more foreign investment in previously-closed sectors, allow more freedom for private business, permit young men and women to find their own jobs etc., etc. There was a strong sense of excitement, of irrevocable change taking place on a mammoth scale. Out of this was conceived the idea of a fresh and detailed look at the whole process of economic reform, and, in particular, how it is affecting the climate for foreign investment.

I have set out to write a book that, hopefully, will appeal to a wide audience. Obviously, I want to provide the foreign businessman with as much information as possible on the rules and regulations covering business activities in China, the procedures for establishing a company, whether wholly-owned or a joint venture, dealing with Chinese bureaucrats, establishing an understanding with local managers and workers, and getting on with the bank manager. I have also tried to provide a snapshot of the investment possibilities available in individual cities, special economic development zones, provinces and autonomous regions. At the same time, I feel it is essential for any foreign businessman to understand the *context* in which he is working. Hence, I have described the process of economic reform, how capitalism is being married with communism, and what the Chinese authorities mean – or seem to mean – when they talk about creating a 'socialist market economy'. China is engaged in a unique experiment which is still in the preliminary stage. There is some confusion; officials find themselves in blind alleys and have to retrace their steps. It is a fluid situation and I have tried to capture the essence of that fluidity. In this respect, it is hoped that the book will also be of some value to those whose interests lie in the wider parameters of contemporary China studies.

There are great opportunities today for doing business in China. But, despite a warm affection that I have for the Chinese and for their country, I hope that I have not painted too rosy a picture, and that anyone going into China having read this book will be well prepared for the many difficulties that still exist, and are likely to continue doing so for some time.

LIVERPOOL
February 1994

Acknowledgements

I RECEIVED help on this book from a wide range of sources, some of whom cannot be mentioned by name. There are, for example, several Chinese who provided me with essential information on the financial and economic structure who did not wish for any acknowledgement out of fear that this would be misconstrued as revealing state secrets to a foreign agent. There is, alas, still a great deal of paranoia in high places in China that stifles legitimate contact between Chinese and foreigners. There were also a number of foreign businessmen who were willing to share their views and their anecdotes on doing business in China but did not wish to have themselves or their companies identified. For those people who can be named, I wish to express my thanks to the British Embassy in Beijing for its encouragement of this project and the China-British Trade Group in London. Audrey Perera in Singapore provided considerable assistance by interviewing a number of Singaporean businessmen whose opinions are quoted in this book. Finally, there is one person who provided valuable suggestions for improvement, a careful proof-reading service and enthusiastic encouragement when the strains of finishing this manuscript under tight deadline pressure became rather onerous. I wish to dedicate this book to Tai-Yu, my inspiration.

1 The dream of 1.2 billion consumers

> **KEY POINTS**
>
> In this opening chapter, I want to sketch out some of the elements that will be explored in more depth through the rest of the book. This will involve looking at:
> - The explosive development of the Chinese economy which has transformed the lives of the bulk of the Chinese population in one way or another.
> - The key statistics that support China's claim to have 'astonished the world'.
> - The role China is expected to play in the much-heralded Pacific Century.
> - How big is the Chinese consumer market likely to be?
> - The thrust of China's overseas economic diplomacy.
> - Basic flaws in the system.

THE DRAGON AWAKES

PROCLAIMING the foundation of the People's Republic of China to cheering multitudes crammed into Tiananmen Square in the heart of Beijing on 1 October 1949, Communist Party Chairman Mao Zedong declared: '. . . the 475 million people of China have now stood up'. In retrospect, he was probably a bit premature, The real awakening of China – with a population more than doubled – only occurred after the Chairman's death three decades later when his long-time comrade-in-arms, and more recently ideological foe, Deng Xiaoping, began to dismantle the centrally-planned Stalinist-style economy and let in the fresh air of the free market. China's economic performance since then has brought about one of the biggest improvements in human welfare ever recorded.

In his personal testament on economic reform – issued in March 1992 under the official title of Central Committee Document Number 2 – Deng declared: 'The people are pleased and the world has been astonished' by China's development during the previous decade. He was not exaggerating.

A visitor to China today is greeted by an economic boom that is awesome in its breadth and depth. The great cities along the southern and eastern seaboard, starting from Guangzhou (formerly Canton) – now almost a twin city of its neighbour Hong Kong, due to return to Chinese control in 1997 – and working north through Hangzhou, Shanghai, Nanjing, Tianjin and, slightly inland, to Beijing itself, are bursting with obvious prosperity. Luxurious department stores are crammed with shoppers buying consumer goods, especially costly Western-designed ones. Streets are clogged with traffic belching fumes into increasingly smoggy atmospheres. The air is gritty with dust rising above new factories, office blocks, homes and new highways which are being built at a feverish pace by construction crews working round-the-clock.

An American writer who travelled through the Pearl River delta of southern China, in a giant arc from Zhuhai through Guangzhou to Shenzhen, in 1993 gushingly wrote: 'It is one vast construction site with factories, apartment complexes and shopping plazas sprouting everywhere. There may never before have been so much construction in one place in history. The headlong rush for profit can be felt in every town and city.'[1]

The country now has more than a million millionaires (calculated in the local currency). While the average annual per capita income rose above 2,000 Yuan for the first time in 1992, some entrepreneurs in Shenzhen had reached the 10 million Yuan plateau. The China News Service said many of the nouveau riche were on waiting lists for China's new golf courses, with annual membership fees as high as $42,000.

The prosperity radiates out from the coastal enclaves into the hinterland, where newly-rich peasants have taken full advantage of the opportunities allowed by economic reform to develop a life-style often superior to that of city dwellers. A forest of television aerials dominate village rooftops, and until they were declared illegal in 1993, satellite dishes were becoming an increasingly common sight. In the richest villages, the latest status symbol is a brand-new Mercedes parked in the driveway.

The sprawling industrial cities of the interior – like Chongqing and Wuhan, both larger than greater London – lack the sparkle of their coastal counterparts (drab streets under a huge pall of industrial pollution), but they, too, are jammed with traffic, shops crammed with eager shoppers, their markets, restaurants and night-clubs abuzz with activity.

The transformation has been rapid and remarkable. 'In 1981, each 100 urban households in China averaged less than one colour television set among them; ten years later it was 70. In 1981, there were six washing machines for every 100 city households, in 1991 more than 80; in 1981, 0.2 refrigerators, ten years later almost 90.'[2]

Life may still be harsh in some of the remoter rural areas (three-quarters of the population remain on the land), but it is still a vast improvement on conditions that prevailed within living memory of most peasants. Before the reforms, at least 30 per cent of the population lived in abject poverty and starvation was not uncommon. As many as 46 million people may have died in the great famine that followed Chairman Mao's mad 'Great Leap Forward' in the late 1950s, when he sought to transform China from an agricultural to an industrialized state virtually overnight and failed disastrously.[3] There may still be about 10 per cent of the population officially regarded as absolutely poor, but the benefits of trickledown economics are finally reaching out even to them.

Napoleon was supposed to have said, 'Let the Chinese dragon sleep, for when she wakes she will astonish the world.' Undoubtedly, China has woken up after a long sleep and is beginning to return to the position of pre-eminence it once occupied. For many centuries, Chinese science and technology, productivity and incomes were the world's best. But in the past 500 years, as the West grew rich and strong, China first lay torpid and then, for most of this century, was convulsed by revolutions, war and famine, tyranny and anarchy.

However, just a generation from now, one of the world's weightiest questions may be how to handle a self-confident (and possibly aggressively xenophobic) China presiding over the biggest economy on earth. By 1994, China's economy was four times bigger than 1978, when the economic reform programme began. By 2002, there is every prospect that it will be eight times bigger. At that point, China will have matched the performance of Japan, Taiwan and South Korea during their fastest quarter-centuries of economic growth.

Economists at the Manila-based Asian Development Bank now describe China as the 'engine of growth' for the rest of Asia, and predict continuing rapid economic growth, possibly held back only by 'emerging bottlenecks' – in transportation, energy and raw-material production – and continued tight monetary policy. William Bodde, Executive Director of the Asia-Pacific Economic Cooperation (APEC) secretariat – a body set up to formulate a regional version of the European Common Market – predicts China will play the major role in the much-predicted Pacific Century that is said to have dawned.

The World Bank, meanwhile, envisages the emergence in the next decade of a new economic powerhouse centred on 'Greater China' to challenge the regional domination of Japan and its place on the global economic stage. The bank looks at mainland China, Hong Kong and Taiwan as one unit and, linking it with the powerful overseas Chinese business communities in Southeast Asia (about 80 per cent of the investment that has poured into booming southern China in recent years has come from Taiwan, Hong Kong, Singapore and Thailand), sees the emergence of 'a fourth growth pole in of the global economy' after the US, Japan and the European Community.

It estimates that the Chinese Economic Area will rank far ahead of both Japan and Germany in gross domestic product (GDP) within the next nine years and will be approaching that of the United States (although in per capita terms it will obviously be much smaller). A bloc comprising mainland China, Taiwan, Hong Kong and Singapore would currently generate exports of some $350 billion, which would just about equal Japan. At the same time, vast amounts of capital are flowing out of China, Hong Kong and Taiwan into Southeast Asia to join hands with local Chinese businessmen in challenging Japan's long domination in the region.

In terms of domestic product, the 1991 World Development Report of the World Bank, calculating on an exchange rate basis, listed China ninth in the world in 1989. In 1993, a World Bank and

International Monetary Fund estimate showed that when calculations were pegged to purchasing power parity, China's economic strength ranked third in the world after the United States and Japan.[4]

Between 1953 and 1990, China's gross national product (GNP) rose by an annual average of seven per cent, ranking it third in the world. The figure was lower than the equivalent rates of 8.4 per cent for Singapore and 8.1 per cent for South Korea, but just ahead of the 6.9 per cent average for Japan. The 1980s marked the peak economic development when the GNP increased at an average rate of 9.2 per cent, second only to South Korea's achievement of 9.7 per cent. Between 1979 and 1991, China's per capita GNP increased at an annual average rate of 7.2 per cent, compared to a global average of 1.2 per cent.[5]

Although per capita GNP in 1992 was only about US$370, placing China firmly among the poorer Third World states, the figure was distorted by a drastically weaker exchange rate of the Yuan against the dollar. In fact, Chinese generally now enjoy a life-style equivalent to many middle-income economies. The figure is further distorted by the great differences between rural and urban areas. 'Per capita GDP in [Beijing] is already over $1000 and in Shenzen in Southern China almost $2000. Residents in some of China's most affluent areas may already enjoy similar purchasing power to average Thais, Malaysians or Indonesians. Indeed, recent re-evaluations based on purchasing power parity also suggest the country's GDP may be higher: IMF figures calculated in this way put per capita GDP at US$1450.'[6]

The GDP grew 13.2 per cent in 1992 and, although the government had originally predicted a more modest eight per cent for 1993, the final figure was, a repeat of the previous year. If that growth is sustained, China by the year 2010 could have a bigger economy than the United States.

China has entered the top ranks in many key industrial and agricultural sectors, if the figures presented by the State Statistics Bureau can be relied on. In 1950, output of steel was 610,000 tons, putting China in 26th place in the world; by 1991 it had climbed to fourth place (70.57 million tons). Coal production in 1950 was 43 million tons, ninth in the world, climbing to 1.1 billion tons (top) in 1991. Output of crude oil in 1950 was 200,000 tons, for a world ranking of 27th, but by 1991, China was in fifth place with annual production of 139 million tons. Cement output rose from 1.41 million tons (8th position) to 248 million tons (top) during the period under review. The Chinese also claim to have taken the lead in several areas of agricultural production, including cereals, rapeseed and pork.[7] Again, if the growth can be maintained at current levels, The World Bank believes China's output in 2020 could equal about 80 per cent of the total output of the rich nations who comprise the Organisation for Economic Cooperation and Development.

Economic reform has also had a significant impact on trade patterns, both exports and imports. The share of trade in GNP rose from just under 10 per cent in 1978 to over 35 per cent in 1991. Since 1980 exports have increased fivefold to more than $90 billion, and almost 80 per cent of this comes from manufactures. Increasing domestic affluence has also led to an upsurge in imports. Originally, the government had predicted imports totalling $300 billion in the period 1991-95. But towards the end of 1993, the predicted figure was drastically raised to $350 billion.[8] Overall, China's foreign trade has grown from $21 billion in 1978, when the economic reforms began, to $170 billion in 1992 – an impressive achievement when one considers the economic lethargy prevalent in the rich countries that provide its main markets. By 1995, the nominal value of this trade could approach $300 billion.

So, is this the mouth-watering market of 'one billion consumers' that Western businessmen have dreamt about for years?[9] Well, perhaps not quite. A more reasonable figure would be a target consumer population for foreign goods somewhere in the region of 65 million at present. However, this is likely to exceed 200 million by the end of the century[10], putting it on par with the United States or the EC. A study by McKinsey, the US multinational consultancy organization, in 1992 estimated that by the turn of the century China will have a market for consumer durables that is, in terms of purchasing power and population, larger than most of the East and Southeast-Asian markets of today.[11] By 2025, many foreign car manufacturers believe that there could be at least 450 million Chinese capable of owning their own vehicle (compared to only a handful at present; most vehicles currently on China's roads are state-owned).

There is, therefore, great scope for the foreign businessman to aim for. Indeed, it is the nature of and opportunities within this potentially huge market which form the centrepiece of subsequent chapters in this book. The object will be to examine the strength of the Chinese economy, and the long-term goals which the political leadership are trying to achieve through an expanding programme of reform. Where is the Chinese economy going? Is it safe to invest in what remains a very volatile market? What are the prospects for social and political stability, especially after the departure of the present ageing leadership in Beijing? Which industrial sectors and which geographical areas offer the best investment opportunities for the foreign businessman? How does one break into the Chinese market and how does one survive once in? What are the main regulations covering the operation of a foreign company in areas such as financial reporting, taxation, land use, hiring and firing local workers and welfare provision? All will be dealt with in turn.

But as a preliminary and to dampen down any excess of euphoria generated by the rosy statistics and future growth predictions already referred to – it should be stressed that whatever direction China takes in the foreseeable future it is unlikely to make the rest of the world feel completely comfortable. Chinese leaders do not pretend to share the West's values and are often at odds with it in foreign-policy objectives.

Beijing authorities make no secret about the basic thrust of their diplomacy. They want advanced technology, finance and managerial experience, but not the West's cultural values – dollars, not democracy; profits, not political pluralism. The official media is untiring in its effort to explain to the Chinese people why they should welcome foreign businessmen into their midst. The *Workers Daily*, for example, explained: 'In order to win superiority over capitalism, socialism must boldly assimilate and adopt all the fruits of civilization created by human society.' But with an eye to reassuring comrades who feared this came close to introducing capitalism, the newspaper added: 'People have not [assimilated it] before because of fear of total Westernization. They need not fear. We are not blindly copying.' Shanghai's *Liberation Daily* took this theme further. Letting in foreign companies would, it conceded, mean allowing capitalism on to Chinese soil, but it would be a weak child and could be strangled in the cradle. 'Wage labour and exploitation exists in foreign firms but such enterprises have to be managed by us. [. . .] We can learn management from them and gain profits from taxes. Meanwhile, power will remain in our hands.'[12]

This attitude is perfectly understandable – after all, Chinese civilization has been able to survive for so long as a unique entity because of its genius in assimilating foreign creeds and subordinating them to its own purposes. At the same time, reliance on foreign investment and Western-funded joint ventures has spread wealth through much of Asia in the past 30 years. And many non-communist countries in the region have been just as concerned as China not to become 'Western' in their search for prosperity.

In the Chinese case it is a bit more complicated, because helping it also strengthens the ability of the government to maintain the core values of socialist civilization which could, in Western eyes, become a destabilizing influence in the years ahead. Indeed, the twin pillars of China's current resurgence are powerful material drives coupled with formidable xenophobia. The gamble for both sides, of course, is that the capitalist child might prove a lusty infant that defies strangulation.

SOCIALIST MARKET ECONOMY

The Chinese Communist Party's 14th National Congress in October 1992 set the seal on Deng Xiaoping's legacy, the 'socialist market economy', [to be discussed in more detail in Chapter two] which was hailed by speaker after speaker in the Great Hall of the People as a stunning theoretical breakthrough which had created a socialist dogma far more complete than anything offered by the classic Marxist thinkers from Marx himself through Lenin, Stalin and even Mao Zedong. Delegates were sent out with an exhortation to spread the message to the farthest corners of the land – the market is in, long live the market.

Farms and factories, schools and service industries throughout the country are encouraged to 'put themselves on the market', to honour the principle of Adam Smith neatly refashioned in a socialist suit of cloth. To ensure its success, the party bosses of Guangdong, Shandong, Shanghai and Tianjin were elevated to membership of the party Politburo. By bringing them into the inner sanctum, the Beijing leadership obviously wanted to make sure that they did not stray too far from orthodoxy.

None of the congress delegates, however, appeared to have recognized the other side of the market, as a cruel, impartial arbiter of man's economic fate. They also seem to have forgotten that socialism originally developed as a response to the tyranny of the market during the industrial revolution. This consideration did not stop Party Secretary General Jiang Zemin from saying that simultaneous prosperity for everyone was not possible, and the country had to allow and encourage some areas and individuals to grow rich first – a veritable heresy to the Marxist purist. Jiang also conceded that the price of reform in the state sector could be unemployment – a chief source of concern as far as social stability is concerned – but this could be mitigated by the state speeding up the establishment of a social insurance system and urban housing reform.

Deng Xiaoping's stated goal for some years has been to prove that communism does not have to mean stagnation and inefficiency, and that it can beat capitalism at its own game. Soviet leaders like Nikita Krushchev used to make the same extravagant claims which proved to be empty. The Dengist formula, however, is that while the state will retain overall control, it will emancipate the people's productive energies and redistribute resources to where they can be used most effectively. The 'all-directional reform', in which foreign investment is the magic weapon, will win public support and quell restlessness among the country's many minorities, especially strategic Tibet and equally remote Xinjiang (where a significant Muslim minority has become increasingly restless).[13]

FLAWS IN THE SYSTEM

Any businessman entering China today should be aware that a lot can still go wrong in the country. The political balance could once again swing back towards the defenders of the status quo, especially in the potential power vacuum following the death of Deng. Someone could panic over the rapid pace of change – as happened in 1989 – and order out the army (although the PLA lost a great deal of face with the people over its involvement in the Tiananmen Square massacre; in addition, the military, like most arms of the government, has important entrepreneurial interests and a large stake in the success of the economic reforms). The Beijing leadership is haunted by the memories of hyper-inflation in 1988, when shoppers swept everything off the shelves and stampeded banks to withdraw their savings as inflation touched 40 per cent. The brakes were applied and the economy came to a shuddering halt. This generated public discontent and unrest culminating in the events of June 1989.

There are many flaws in the system that cannot be overlooked. The Chinese system continues at the stage of quasi-reform, with many inherited defects that will not disappear overnight. It is still, essentially, a planned economy. The key sectors are still state-run and respond to administrative decision rather that the market dictates of supply and demand.

'State-owned industry accounts for 40 per cent of GNP [. . .] a considerable reduction since 1978 when the share was almost 80 per cent, and reflects important changes in the economy as it moves away from Soviet-style central planning towards more market-oriented systems. However, about a third of State-Owned Enterprises (SOEs) operate in the red and much of their productive effort is channelled into the accumulation of unsaleable inventory. It is estimated by some analysts that without the protection of artificially low cost raw materials and energy as many as 70 per cent of all SOEs would be unprofitable.'[14]

Cooperation between provinces is poor – and the impression is of competition between them growing as they struggle for a bigger piece of the economic pie created by the open door policy – which makes it hard to take advantage of economies of scale.[15] This is in line with the ancient lessons of Chinese politics: 'mouth the line but go your own way'; or, 'the mountains are high and the emperor is far away'.

The plus factor in the fierce inter-provincial rivalry generated by the decentralization of economic power is the growth of competition overcoming the former lethargy of centrally-run monopolies. All have been galvanized by the success of Guangdong Province, adjacent to Hong Kong, which has boomed under a comparatively laissez-faire, pro-business government which has encouraged the growth of a strong non state-run sector. Each province is trying to outdo its neighbours not only in attracting foreign investment but also in developing new models of reform that go beyond those being promoted by the centre.

On the negative side, however, is the growing evidence of regional and even provincial trading blocs being built up that encourage internal protectionism. For example, Sichuan Province keeps out many products from beyond its borders despite their good quality, in the interests of local products – arguing that this is necessary to ensure good after-sales service. The poor interior provinces which supply raw materials to the prosperous coastal areas for processing generate income by taxing the flow in both directions. Farmers coming to Beijing from the south to sell their products on the free markets complain bitterly of the numerous roadblocks they have to negotiate at provincial and district borders, all of which extract their ounce of flesh. This is reminiscent of the situation that prevailed during the warlord era as China fragmented after the collapse of imperial rule – although it should be emphasized that, for the moment at least, I am speaking in economic more than political terms. But it is a worrying trend for the rulers in Beijing as they tried to hold a giant country together when so many elements, especially on the fringes, are pulling in different directions.

Reflecting this worry, the central government in mid-1993 ordered provincial and municipal officials to abide strictly by the economic measures laid down by Beijing. But many economists doubted the order would be obeyed as the regions have been increasing their economic power and circumventing existing regulations to fight for their own interests. From village up to provincial level, it is a dog-eat-dog fight for a bigger share of the booming economic pie – the frantic pace perhaps partly generated by fears that it may not last. According to one economist '. . . the regional economies have evolved into warlord economies. The central government is losing its grip'. One key concern for the centre is that no matter what its own economic priorities, the regions are increasingly determined to go their own way, channelling funds into their own pet industrial projects, often duplicating the efforts of other areas and ensuring that no-one makes money.

LOSING LAND TO DEVELOPMENT

Typical are the development zones [to be discussed in more detail in chapters three and four] being set up the length and breadth of

China to attract foreign investment through what the Chinese call 'the two exemptions and three deductions' – meaning they enjoy a tax holiday for two years and reduced taxes for the next three – as well as other long-term special concessions (eg: reduced land-use fees and utility charges). But the problem is that, dazzled by the well-publicized success of the four SEZs – Shenzhen, Zhuhai, Shantou and Xiamen – followed by coastal cities like Shanghai and Tianjin, virtually every local government official throughout the land decided that foreign investment is the answer to all their problems of overcoming economic backwardness.

Eventually, the central government decided this was not beneficial to anyone in China and might end up deterring foreign investors. SEZs, officials in Beijing warned, were eating up precious farmland and contributing to a highly damaging wastage of scarce financial resources. In 1991, official statistics showed China had only 117 special development zones. By late 1992, the number had risen to 1,951. But, the Ministry of Agriculture calculated that if various rural development zones were included, the number was actually 8,700, while the official weekly magazine *Outlook* was even more bullish, asserting that there were more than 10,000 such zones by the end of 1992.

According to Chinese law, changing the use of any piece of arable land larger than 0.67 square kilometres and non-arable land in excess of 1.3 sq.kms. requires the approval of the State Council (ie: cabinet-level) in Beijing. But in the scramble to get on to the foreign investment gravy train, local authorities apparently ignored the rules. Some defy logic. The small city of Guanghan in Sichuan Province, for example, covers only nine sq.kms, but planned to build an industrial development zone of more than 20 sq.kms. Typically, local authorities create a development company and start to build in the hope of eventually selling off the industrial parks, apartment complexes and other facilities to outsiders. The results do not always justify this careless optimism. It is probably fortunate, therefore, that few of the projects have so far even got to the building stage. According to government officials, all but two per cent of the zones actually existed only on paper. If they were all suddenly to come on stream, demanding state investment in basic infrastructure, it would literally break the bank. All that has been achieved is that a few more peasants have been chased off the land and, in many cases, added to the vast force of jobless migrant labour roaming around the country, or, increasingly, seeking to smuggle themselves into foreign lands of opportunity like the United States.

Vice Premier Zhu Rongji (the former Mayor of Shanghai brought into the central government in October 1992 as a dedicated economic reformist and a few months later given wide-ranging powers to bring an overheated economy under control) warned that the excessive opening of development zones would drain the country's investment in other vital projects, lead to hyperinflation and loss of a significant amount of farmland. He estimated that if all the announced zones were to be developed by government investment it would cost a staggering $790 billion, and even if all the proposed annual investment in infrastructure were diverted to these projects it would still take six years to complete them. Mr Zhu said that about eight per cent of the country's farmland had been lost in the rush for industrial development, as farmers were tempted to give up their traditional occupation: 'This could have immense impact on the healthy development of agriculture and the normal supply of food.'

In a bid to hold down inflation, the authorities in Beijing set an economic growth target for 1993 of between eight and 10 per cent (fairly modest given the economy's performance in preceding years). By June, this had to be raised to 14 per cent (the final figure was about 13 per cent). One of the chief reasons for the revised figure was that provincial authorities totally ignored the centre and openly went all out for a boom-at-any-cost strategy. This, in part, stems from the desire of local officials to feather their nest and build up their own fiefdoms after years of having to toe the party line.

FEVERISH INFLATION

The feverish pace of economic growth immediately triggered the inflationary explosion Beijing had feared. In the first half of 1993, inflation in the major cities tripled to an annual rate of around 20 per cent. This coincided with a central government decision to finally abandon all grain coupons and other subsidies to the urban work-force which had helped cushion low wages. Compensatory pay increases were pushed through for the State sector, but with the economy awash with money, and more being printed, the consequences were inevitable. Although the government grimly clung to the official exchange rate for the local currency, the Renminbi (RMB: literally, people's money), the people were not interested. The exchange rate on the semi-official foreign exchange 'swap markets' where most of the real deals are done these days, effectively created a 100 per cent devaluation of the RMB. The black market thrived, with every petty trader trying to get his or her hands on precious US dollars. The Foreign Exchange Certificates (FEC), the artificial money which foreign tourists are required to use in all their transactions, suddenly enjoyed a revival in fortune after months of predictions that the dual currency system was to be abolished. Some hotels in Beijing, for example, unashamedly put up signs in their restaurants warning patrons – mainly locals it should be added – that there would be a 50 per cent surcharge on the bill if they wished to pay in RMB.

Alarmed by the inflationary trend, and demonstrating a distinct lack of trust in the ability of the leadership to bring it under control, consumers immediately went on something of a panic buying binge reminiscent of 1988, emptying shops of colour television sets, refrigerators, radios and stereo equipment. Prices soared as a result. In one Beijing department store, a Japanese television set that had been selling for 11,000 Yuan jumped 15 per cent in price overnight and no-one blinked an eyelid. In fact, sales increased sixfold.

The Chinese economy has an alarming propensity to seesaw between boom and bust. Twice in the 1980s, the brakes had to be slammed on the rapid economic growth because of dangerous inflationary pressures. In a typical cycle, there is a rapid expansion of credit, money supply, investment and consumption – which is followed by tighter control of credit, investment and prices. In the past, this has quickly led to budgetary pressure because of the subsidies necessary to prop up the chronically loss-making state industries and prevent unemployment. Then, the cycle starts all over again. Economic reform inevitably leads to these severe cyclical swings because the transition from a planned to a free economy is not easy and the reformers are anxious to avoid social chaos.

The difference with past booms, however, is that the one witnessed in 1993 seemed less amenable to control. Central bank officials admitted that they could neither control the money supply or credit creation. The classic method of raising interest rates was tried and produced not the slightest ripple. Given, the inflation rate, potential investors saw no reason to put their money into bank accounts which would only lead to shrinkage. Vast amounts of money, therefore, were awash in an uncontrolled system seeking speculative investments that further undermined official control. This, frustratingly for China, is one big difference with Japan's early post-war experience, when industry benefitted from the disciplined savings habits of the populace to lay the foundations for the global economic successes of later years. In 1991, bank savings totalled 911 billion Yuan, representing a 43-fold increase since 1978. But there is a lot more money hidden away that the government does not know about and has not got the apparatus available to bring it back into circulation and use it efficiently. 'If all this money was put into the market at one time, it will cause horrific damage to the economy.'[16]

In desperation, the central leadership launched a new 'unified strategy' to try and restore some control, including strengthening of macro-level supervision and control over the economy which seemed likely to introduce even more contradictions into the move towards a market economy. A State Council circular ordered banks throughout the nation to stop lending to businesses which raised funds in violation of state regulations, or had diverted loans for real-estate development and stock purchases. And, in view of the shortage of funds, it ordered the concentration of lending in areas where it was most needed – the agricultural sector, some of the key state-run businesses and national priority construction projects.

Finance Minister Liu Zhongli said sternly that spending would be drastically cut on the building of fancy hotels, flashy department stores and shopping malls, and the manufacture of consumer products such as television sets whose market had become saturated. Other cost-saving measures included trimming the bloated bureaucracy and reducing the purchase of luxury cars for official use. Economic and Trade Commission head Wang Zhongyu, given the task of supervising the macro-economy, meanwhile, announced that the government would deal sternly with any authorized capital-raising activities, and also planned closer regulation of the property and stock markets, especially in dealing with the appearance of illegal exchanges and futures markets beyond the officially-permitted ones in Shanghai and

Shenzhen (typical example: a stock exchange set up by a hospital in Chengdu, capital of Sichuan province, which attracted tens of thousands of customers to buy and sell shares. Finance Minister Liu ordered provincial authorities to close the exchange, but admitted that this would have to be a 'gradual process' because so many people were involved: 'If this market is allowed, you will see that each province will want to have a stock exchange and that will cause chaos.'

There had been excessive duplication in many manufacturing industries evidenced by the fact that in the first quarter of 1993 alone, fixed-asset investment had increased by an astonishing 70 per cent compared to the same period of the previous year. Giving these figures, Mr Wang complained it was placing an intolerable strain on the infrastructure, particularly energy and transportation, and leading to record losses in the state sector. A senior government economist, Mr Yang Peixin, admitted that the situation had become so bad that many state factories had been forced to shut down because of lack of operating capital, having already drained the resources of the nation's banks to such an extent that virtually all were running at a loss.

MONETARY TAPS – ON OR OFF

One of the problems is that China's monetary taps have only two positions: on and off. Merely trying to slow down money growth does not work because banks will ignore directives and the unofficial market will thrive. If there is going to be any central bank control, the tap has to be turned off completely, which will cause considerable repercussions throughout the overstretched economy. In most countries, the central bank decides lending and interest rate rules for the banking community in line with official policies on inflation and money supply.

But although it has been a centrally-planned economy, China surprisingly has opted for a grass-roots system in which the provincial banks submit their requirements for funds to the People's Bank of China, which then works with the State Council guidelines and specialized banks to finalize the national plan for the coming year and submit the proposals to the State Council for approval. Not surprisingly, regional banks, who are more interested in promoting their business by making big loans than in playing a role in the grand plan, exaggerate their needs and the likely end benefits in order to get as much money as possible.

Thus, Beijing's decisions are based on false premises and its grip on money supply is weakened. The answer, of course, would be to strengthen the autonomy of the People's Bank so that it can use its muscle through its regional branches to detect any dubious dealings by provincial governments working hand-in-glove with local banks. Alternatively, of course, there is a market-based solution: making the local banks commercially responsible for profits and losses, with no central government bail-out in case of trouble, which would make them a bit more careful about where they placed their money.

On a more personal level, the Chinese man-in-the-street was also for the first time asked to play his part in reining in the runaway economy and restore shaky government finances through the introduction of personal income tax and a far-reaching Value-Added Tax. Although the tax on individual income was designed to address the widening gap between rich and poor, assurances were given that people would still be able to accumulate wealth. Officials stressed it would begin with a very high threshold so that the poor would not face an additional burden. In the corporate sector, foreign and Chinese enterprises would be treated the same, everyone paying a flat 33 per cent tax. More of the tax money would be distributed to local governments, achieving the goal of channelling money from the rich coast to the poorer inland areas and from manufacturing to basic industries.

Amid all these announcements in mid-1993, a fierce struggle appeared to be underway within the leadership over whether there should be a halt to the economic reform programme for at least a year or two while the various contradictions were sorted out and some semblance of discipline restored among a populace that, in the words of the army newspaper *People's Liberation Army Daily* had abandoned itself to a 'spirit of mammonism'. Vice Premier Zhu was accused of possessing a 'Great Leap Forward mentality', but he was adamant there was no turning back. And he was bolstered by many authoritative economists who warned the government against any slowing down, saying that applying the brakes now, in the words of one of them, Professor Wu Jianlian, would mean 'China's economic development walking into a cul-de-sac'.

Macro-economic reform – making the overall economic system more efficient is going to be the key challenge for China's planners in the years ahead. There is, for example, a need to revamp the banking structure, giving banks the freedom to make the loans to whom they want and at competitive interest rates (rather than the present system where there is still a great deal of government-directed lending to the ailing state industry dinosaurs). Macro-economic control, however, is becoming increasingly more complex through the rapid growth of private sector industry and rural enterprises operating on commercial rather than state-directed lines. The existing administrative structure simply has not caught up with these changes.

The economy's most pressing need is for flexible, responsive – and rich – capital markets. At the moment, funding is largely fed to industry through a banking system that works along political lines; firms looking for investment money must curry favour with government agencies that hold the purse strings. State-owned companies, whether they lose money or not, usually have first call. The central bank is not autonomous and exerts no control over the money supply; [in 1992] for all of Beijing's pro-market rhetoric, state enterprises received over $60 billion in bank loans, up 20 per cent from the previous year; private firms are generally denied loans. Though banks can provide foreign firms with such simple services as letters of credit and traveller's cheques, they play a relatively inconsequential role in those companies' financing plans.

'[in 1991] Beijing took an important step towards creating a market for government bonds. [In 1992], however, speculation by underwriters nearly destroyed the system. A variety of underwriters, including state banks and financial institutions, were given $7 billion in government debt to sell. Speculating prices would improve, the underwriters held on to the paper – and lost heavily when the value of the issue plunged. [In 1993] the government reverted to past form and simply ordered local governments and state enterprises to buy up $6 billion worth of debt.'[17]

While a great deal has changed in the past decade of economic reform, a great many of the basic structures and fundamental tenets on which the socialist state is built remain untouched. The Chinese leadership is effectively trying to mate two totally unrelated animals – the free market and state control – in a way that has no proven track record of success. Wang Bingqian, the hard-headed finance minister for 11 years, repeatedly warned over a period of several years of the inherent dangers in continuing the system of funnelling billions of dollars into inefficient state industries simply to preserve their ideological role as the backbone of the socialist economy. In 1991, this led to a budgetary deficit of almost $3 billion, with a similar performance expected in 1992 – due to what Mr Wang described as '. . . loose management of expenses for overstaffed departments, sightseeing and banquets with public funds, too many subsidies and bonuses'.[18]

Actually, the real extent of the damage is disguised by the fact that under China's peculiar accounting system, foreign and domestic debt is counted as income and not as a deficit. If these items were added, the deficit would be well in excess of $7.5 billion. This continued budgetary haemorrhage is weakening the central government's ability to carry out the programme of change in a well-structured manner. A lot of very hard decisions are going to have to be made shortly on the key issue of industrial restructuring and the relinquishing of state control. Allowing the market free rein will create individual hardship and sources of social tension – a prospect that the leadership may shrink from. But without these changes, the foundations for long-term economic growth will be undermined.

Looking at the issue from the viewpoint of foreign investors, China's biggest drawbacks are a lack of corporate law and the fact that the overall legal structure as a whole is rudimentary. Because of lack of legal redress, forming relationships of trust with individual Chinese remains critical to the success of any business venture. In the present confusion between the powers of central and provincial governments, it is often difficult for a foreign investor to know who has the authority to sign a contract or participate in a deal. And, as the political climate is in a state of flux, conditions which apply for one deal may not apply for another months later. Thus, there is a large fund of international business goodwill towards China which could disappear if joint ventures start to go wrong because of these various structural weaknesses or because of other factors as yet unimagined.

SUMMARY

In this chapter, I have attempted to set down some of the

parameters for the discussion that will be developed in subsequent chapters. There cannot be any dispute that China has achieved remarkable economic expansion in an extremely short period (even more remarkable when one considers the periods of political turmoil, such as the decade of the Cultural Revolution 1966-76, with its slogan of 'make revolution not production', that brought economic activity almost to a standstill). What can possibly be disputed are the rosy predictions for the years ahead for they depend on high levels of political pragmatism – a commodity that has not been seen in abundance for much of the life of the People's Republic of China. Yet, if all goes well, China is bound to be an extremely important player in the twenty-first century global economic structure.

I have tried to set out some of the challenges facing the Chinese leadership in achieving this goal. One constant theme is the importance placed on foreign cooperation. Foreign investment in the Chinese economy seems to have become self-sustaining if there is no turning back. Nevertheless, as I will elaborate in subsequent chapters, the Chinese market is not one for the fainthearted. It requires detailed knowledge, bargaining skill and, perhaps above all, flexibility to ride the inevitable bumps. It is the sort of market where one can just as easily lose a million as make one – as seen by some of the people who will be quoted in this book who have learnt the hard way.

FOOTNOTES:
1. *Newsweek*, 5 April 1993.
2. China Survey, the *Economist*, 28 Nov. 1992.
3. Figure quoted by the late Harrison Salisbury in *The New Emperors*, London, HarperCollins, 1992. pp167-8.
4. Quoted in *Beijing Review*, 16-22 Aug. 1993. 'China's Comprehensive National Strength'. pp22-5
5. Ibid.
6. Briefing Paper from British Embassy, Beijing, August 1993.
7. Beijing Review.
8. *China Daily*. 10 Sept. 1993.
9. It is a dream that has beguiled Western companies since the nineteenth century Industrial Revolution, when one British writer declared: 'If we could only persuade every person in China to lengthen his shirttail by a foot, we could keep the mills of Lancashire working round the clock.' – Quoted in *Beijing Jeep* by Jim Mann, New York, Simon and Schuster, 1989.
10. British Embassy Briefing Paper.
11. A Fresh Look at China. McKinsey Quarterly No.3, 1992.
12. Quoted in the *Sunday Telegraph* 1 Nov. 1992.
13. Geoffrey Murray. *The Rampant Dragon*, London, Minerva Press, 1993. pp173-5.

14. British Embassy Briefing Paper.
15. Even within provinces, cooperation can be poor. On a tour of Henan and Hubei provinces in mid-1993, for example, a group of Western reporters passed through a succession of small towns each with its own cement factory. Officials admitted that because of this costly duplication of effort few were profitable. But each community stubbornly hung on to its own factory as a talisman of future prosperity as the construction boom edges inland from the fringes.
16. *Financial Times* 21 Sept. 1992.
17. *Time* magazine. 10 May 1993.
18. Reuters news agency quoted in the *Financial Times*, 3 Sept. 1992.

2 Reform may take 100 years

KEY POINTS
In this chapter, I wish to examine the shape and possible future direction of the Chinese economic reform programme, as well as its philosophical and ideological underpinnings. The key questions:
- What do the leaders in Beijing mean when they talk about 'socialism with Chinese characteristics' and the creation of a 'socialist market economy'?
- What role does capitalism have to play in achieving this goal?
- How long will it take to achieve a fully-fledged socialist market economy?
- What will be the future role of central planning as more control and responsibility is handed over to individual industries and enterprises?
- Will the government be able to persuade entrenched bureaucratic interests to relinquish their total control over every business decision in the public sector?
- How can the government overcome the inherent weakness of state-run industries and make them competitive? What are the key elements of the ongoing enterprise reform programme?
- How does the 'contract responsibility system' work for state industries?
- What does the government mean when it announces plans to 'smash the iron rice bowl'?
- What future is there for the private sector?

SOCIALIST MODERNIZATION

THE GOAL of the 'socialist modernization' was set out by the 12th National Congress of the Chinese Communist Party in 1982:

'The general objective of China's economic construction for the two decades between 1981 and the end of the century is, while steadily working for more and better economic results, to quadruple the gross annual value of industrial production – from 710 billion Yuan in 1980 to 2,800 billion Yuan or so in 2000. This will place China in the front ranks of the countries of the world in terms of gross national income and the output of major industrial and agricultural products; it will represent an important advance in the modernization of her entire national economy; it will increase the income of her urban and rural population several times over; and the Chinese people will be comparatively well-off both materially and culturally. Although China's national income per capita will even then be relatively low, her economic strength and national defence capabilities will have grown considerably, compared with what they are today. Provided that we work hard and in a down-to-earth manner and bring the superiority of the socialist system into fuller play, we can definitely attain our grand strategic objective.'

The current message to the masses, therefore, is that once-vilified capitalism is good or, at least some parts are good. But what do the Chinese mean by capitalism and how can it flourish in a shotgun marriage with central planning?

What is clear is that even the Chinese are not exactly sure what they mean by these various terms or what they want to achieve in the long run. The definitions are constantly being redefined; new ideas are tried out and abandoned if they do not produce the expected results relatively quickly. That can be just as confusing for the provincial bureaucrat trying to ensure he or she is always following the correct 'line' as it is for the foreign businessman trying to develop a strategy to work within the system. And for the latter there is also the dismal prospect that this situation may prevail for some considerable time: in line with the Chinese inclination to take the long view, the current party leadership is predicting it may be 100 years before the reform process is complete and a fully matured socialist economy is achieved!

SOCIALISM PLUS CAPITALISM

For the Chinese Communist Party, 'socialist' and 'socialism' indicate a system in which government owns all the means of producing wealth and is devoted to the common prosperity of all the people. To a capitalist, the same words may mean a system in which central control stifles initiative, damages productivity, and does not reward fairly those who make the greatest contributions to a nation's economy. 'Capitalist' and 'capitalism' on the other hand, are usually, in Chinese contexts, merely code words implying exploitation, unbridled individualism, corruption and class division. In a Western context, the words tend to imply freedom of action, opportunity for creativity and initiative, and substantial rewards for risk-taking and entrepreneurship. China's reforms are essentially an attempt to combine socialism and capitalism — but by taking only the Chinese concept of socialism and the Western concept of capitalism.

There was a time — recent enough to be vividly remembered by Chinese in their early 30s — when to speak in favour of capitalism could lead to instant denunciation and possible death. These days, even conservative party ideologues speak in positive terms about many elements of capitalism.

On 23 February 1992, the *People's Daily*, mouthpiece of the Chinese Communist Party, published a front-page article that not only praised capitalism's historic role but called for '. . . adequately developing the capitalistic economy inside China'. It was the first time anyone could recall the word being officially approved in communist China. Within weeks, Deng Xiaoping visited southern China to declare that the whole country should concentrate on making money and stop worrying about whether what they were doing was capitalist or socialist.

Premier Li Peng, regarded as a hardliner in the ongoing battle to defend the dominant role of socialism in China, has declared: 'We must further reform and open up to the rest of the world. The principal criterion for judging the success of reform and the open policy is whether they help develop the productive forces of our socialist society, increase our country's overall strength and raise the people's living standards. In carrying out our reform and opening to the outside world we should emancipate our minds, seek truth from facts and boldly explore new ways. We should not hesitate to draw on the achievements of civilization the world over and to assimilate . . . any advanced technology of other countries, including the developed Western countries, and any advanced methods of operation or techniques of management.'[1]

Party General Secretary Jiang Zemin caused surprise when, meeting 100 senior college students in Beijing in May 1992, he told them that the party noticed only the adverse side of capitalism while neglecting those aspects China could learn from for its 'socialist construction'. The weekly magazine *Beijing Review* commented: 'It seems to be the first open admission of its kind by a Chinese leader'. Jiang said a key goal for China was to learn all the good and advanced ideas from overseas, including capitalist countries, to speed up China's economic development. "Socialism is a brand-new social system," he said. "We should inherit and make use of all the social productive forces and all the excellent cultural achievements made in capitalist society when constructing socialism."'

Later the same year, Jiang followed this up at in a policy speech to the National People's Congress (China's essentially rubber-stamp parliament) in which he stressed that to achieve superiority over capitalist countries, socialist states should not hesitate to adopt from abroad, including the developed capitalist states, any advanced methods of operation or management techniques related to modern production and the commodity economy. 'Foreign funds, resources, technology and skilled personnel, along with privately-owned enterprises that are a useful supplement to our economy, can and should be put to use for the benefit of socialism. That will not harm socialism but help it, since political power is in the hands of the people, and since we have a strong public sector.'

In discovering the merits of capitalism, the Chinese leaders can be said to be returning to their roots, for Marx himself believed that capitalism was an inevitable stage on the road to the creation of a socialist utopia.

But the end product is still to be a 'socialist' state with distinct 'Chinese characteristics'. Deng spelt out the policy in 1985 when he told a congress of scientists: 'All our policies concerning opening to the world, invigorating the domestic economy and structural reform are directed towards developing a socialist economy. We allow private businesses, joint ventures with Chinese and foreign investment, and wholly-owned foreign enterprises to grow in China, but we see to it that socialist public ownership always remains the mainstay. The goal of socialism is common prosperity for all the Chinese people, not class polarization. If our policy results in polarization then we have failed. If it produces a new capitalist class, then we have really taken to evil ways.'

The phrase 'socialism with Chinese characteristics' was first used by Deng in 1982, and over the years it is has been a subject of much debate over its definition because of its ambiguity (by being ambiguous, of course, the government can switch direction without appearing to do so). But this is very much in keeping with the entire Chinese revolutionary experience. In the crises of the early days, the Communist Party strove to find socialist revolutionary paths suited to China's conditions by refining and reinterpreting socialist principles in the light of these conditions. The result has been an ongoing debate as to the meaning of socialism itself.

A resolution at the Twelfth Central Committee in 1984 enunciated seven characteristics of socialism, including some 'Chinese characteristics': abolition of systems of exploitation, public ownership of the means of production, remuneration according to work, a planned commodity economy (the classic socialist economy would not include a commodity aspect, nor would it allow the competition implicit in the idea of a commodity economy; more on this later), political power in the hands of the working class and other labouring people, highly developed productive forces and labour productivity eventually overtaking capitalist countries, and socialist ethics cultivated under the guidance of Marxism.

Under Mao Zedong, it was claimed that socialism in China had reached a highly advanced stage. This assertion has now been dropped in favour of one that, in fact, China is only at the preliminary stage and there is still a great deal to do in developing socialist economic theory. At the same time, economists have discarded the traditional idea that only an economic system built on the imaginary social model conceived by Marx is socialism and that only the Soviet model of three-quarters of a century ago is out-and-out socialistic. There might be many economic models leading to socialism and a socialist economic system should not be one that defies all change.

It is recognized that total central planning is not possible. Equality is fine in principle, but it is permissible for some to get rich before others.[2] At present, so long as the public sector predominates it may be supplemented by collective, private, foreign and other sectors, with companies under the same or different types of ownership allying themselves together or even merging with one another. It is erroneous, the reformers argue, to believe that at this stage China will be more socialist if the size of production units is larger or the degree of public ownership is greater.

Because increasing productivity is a goal of socialism it is not only permissible but often desirable to contract or lease state enterprises to motivated entrepreneurial managers while the state retains actual ownership. The theory that ownership and management must be combined shackles productivity. It is necessary to combine planning with a commodity economy incorporating market mechanisms. It has been realized that a planned economy with an excessively high degree of centralization is not the only form of socialist economy.

To lay the base for development, China must go through a very long primary stage to accomplish industrialization, commercialization and modernization of production which many other countries have achieved under capitalist conditions. In the primary stage it is understandable that within the developing socialist economy there should be an element of capitalism. Such elements as there may be in China's reforms are not subject to criticism as being counter-revolutionary but are in fact desirable and necessary for achieving the socialist goal of enhancing productivity. Therefore, the two can cooperate within the socialist economy just as in other countries workers and capitalists often cooperate for mutual advantage.

Jiang Yiwei, Editor of the bi-monthly magazine *Reform* and a research fellow of the Chinese Academy of Social Sciences argues that '. . . socialism [in China] is still at the primary stage and the economy is underdeveloped, [hence the need for] tolerance of capitalism. Starting from this perspective, we can well understand the many concrete reform measures, such as co-existence of the publicly-owned mainstream enterprises with individual economic entities, private enterprise and enterprises with foreign investment; multiple forms of public ownership; encouragement of the shareholding system and the issuance of stocks; separation of ownership from management; state-owned enterprises leased by collective management or transferred to individuals; integration of the policy of ''. . . remuneration in accordance with work performance and efforts. . ." with other forms of distribution; and the policy of "one country, two systems", a policy which means that the capitalist systems of Hong Kong, Taiwan and Macao will remain unchanged for quite some time [after reabsorption by the mainland].'[3]

SOCIALIST MARKET ECONOMY

Gong Yuzhi, former deputy head of propaganda for the Chinese Communist Party Central Committee in charge of theoretical work, sought to clarify the meaning of a 'socialist market economy' as 'the practice of a modern market economy under the circumstances of socialism'. China will let market forces, under the macroeconomic control of the state, serve as the basic means of regulating the flow of resources. Instead of the past highly centralized planned economy that operated in accordance with administrative instructions – and resulted in long-term stagnation – market forces are now given an increasingly important role.[4] As Jiang Zemin told the party faithful: 'The practice of reform proves that wherever the market forces are given rein, the economy becomes more vigorous and the economic situation well developed.'[5]

The concept has evolved gradually. Shortly after the Third Plenary Session of the 11th CPC Central Committee in 1978 the phrase '. . . ensuring the leading role of the planned economy and making the market economy as an adjunct. . .', by definition implied the abandoning of Mao's adherence to a total 'planned economy' and heralded the advent of economic reform. The Third Plenary Session of the 12th CPC Central Committee in 1984 then confirmed that the socialist economy is a 'planned commodity economy'. This broke away from the conventional ideology that the commodity economy conflicts with socialism and the planned economy. This represented another great leap in the thought processes of the party.

But, according to Gong Yuzhi, '. . . it should be admitted that at that time and during quite a long period thereafter, the question of whether the commodity economy should be operated mainly by planning or regulated by the market had not been answered. The confused ideology about this resulted in hesitation in taking steps to develop a market economy. The idea that the "market economy is peculiar to capitalism" had not been cleared up and was still sometimes in vogue.'

However, in early 1992, Deng Xiaoping made his famous inspection tour of South China, during which he said: 'A planned economy is not socialism – there is planning under capitalism, too. And a market economy is not capitalism – there are markets under socialism as well.' The reform floodgates were flung wide open.

Nevertheless, there were still those who worried that this headlong dash for development would also lead to another aspect of capitalism – namely, privatization. Gong provided an important reassurance: 'What we stand for is a market economy based on the maintenance of public ownership as the leading role, supplemented by private ownership. It is not a market economy based on privatization, or in other words, an economy with private ownership as the dominant factor. People used to think the market economy is closely connected with private ownership. All misunderstandings, both at home and abroad, stem from this. The misunderstanding holds that China's emphasis on giving rein to market forces and the introduction of a market economy means privatization and an adoption of capitalism.

'We must confess that in the past we indeed linked social public ownership with the planned economy and that the market economy was connected with the capitalist system and private ownership. Now we are opening up a new way which is different from the market economy with private ownership as its basis and also distinguished from the planned economy with public ownership as its basis, as practised by our predecessors.

'Our way is to combine socialist public ownership with the market economy. For this purpose, it is necessary for us to change the old, unitary structure of public ownership into one where the public economic sector remains dominant and diverse sectors of the economy enjoy common development. This also requires us to change the current forms of public ownership, turning the public-owned (or mainly public-owned) enterprises into independent economic entities operating on their own and assuming responsibility for profit and loss. This means reforming the structure of public ownership rather than practising privatization.'

But diversity was there. Gong stressed, proceeding from the reality that China is still at the initial stage of socialism and, therefore, should not practise a '. . . unitary socialist public-owned economy. We must develop an economy with diverse forms of public ownership as the dominant part, supplemented by individual, private and foreign-invested sectors. We should set up an economic structure under which the various economic sectors can co-exist for a long time to come, develop in an all-round way and bring their own initiative into full play'.

But is it possible to combine a market economy with socialist principles? The party ideologue was sure that it was – because the market was not exclusive to Western-style capitalism. 'The market economy, as an economic means and operating mechanism, basically has similar functions under socialism and capitalism. It should be recognized that the market economy was first developed under capitalism and accumulated a lot of experience. At present, it is still developing in depth. We regarded the market economy as a product of capitalism in the past [so] we rebelled and limited its development. As a result we have paid a high price in our economic development. Being a means and method of regulating the flow of resources, the market economy is the common product of modern civilization, a result of the economic development of the modern world. It is neither of a capitalist nature, nor peculiar to capitalism. Socialist countries can certainly take it, study it and make use of it.'[6]

Pointing out that China is vast, heavily populated and suffering from poor communication, an official recently observed: 'It is impossible under such conditions to include all socio-economic activities in the state plan and to use administrative orders alone to direct production... It is precisely for these reasons that China's planned economic system needs to be improved so as to let the market forces play a role in regulating production.'

Nevertheless, the state must keep a fairly firm hand on the tiller. To illustrate this point, the party faithful often use an analogy provided by party elder (and conservative) Chen Yun: 'A bird cannot be held too tightly in one's hand because that would kill it; it must be allowed to fly. But it must only be allowed to fly within its cage; without the cage it will fly away. If the bird represents economic revitalization, then the cage represents state planning.'

RESTRUCTURING STATE PLANNING

In line with its determination to decentralize and free the economy, as well as to maintain public ownership and control of all key production, China ostensibly has been using two different types of plans for some years. There is the mandatory state plan through which the state controls essential materials and regulates production, while at the same time using economic rather than administrative means to direct production of less critical items under the guidance plan. Mandatory planning involves the state deciding allocations of raw materials and ensuring their supply at a fixed price, output levels, price of finished products, as well as designating end-users.

In recent years, the government has permitted an excess of mandatory plan products to be produced and sold at the manufacturer's discretion in many cases, but here the latter is on his own – finding his own source of raw materials or parts and having to negotiate a price for them. The same applies to customers. Since the late 1980s, more and more mandatory plan products have become available in this way. The majority of rolled steel, for example, and most of the cement is no longer allocated or subsidized by the state.

The second method of state control has been the guidance plan, covering a vast range of goods and services not considered crucial, and where enterprises will compete and have direct contact with the market. 'The guidance plan,' said the *China Daily*, sets 'targets for manufacturers, which may or may not be met, based on market conditions.' Somewhat contradictorily, it added: 'The manufacturers, however, bear the responsibility for failing to attain targets.' The state may (or may not) assist in reducing taxes on a manufacturer or a product by providing raw materials, and 'by raising or lowering prices'. Prices continue to have a secondary regulatory role, even in the new market-oriented economy, though price is a fundamental element of a market. Services at the level of daily life and most agricultural products have not been covered by either plan.

Pricing has become a key area where the state has finally begun stepping back and letting the market take over. One example: 'In some places, cinemas are free to set prices, which have been regulated for 40 years by the state.'[7] According to the State Pricing Administration, 97 per cent of all retail goods were bought at prices set by the government in 1978, the first year of reform. Among agricultural and sideline products purchased by the state,

92.6 per cent were sold at fixed prices, 1.8 per cent at government-guided prices, and 5.6 per cent at market regulatory prices. By 1991, the percentage of retail goods sold at prices fixed by the government had fallen to 20.9. Government guidance plans covered 10.3 per cent of retail prices and 68.8 per cent were subject to market regulation.

Explaining government thinking, Ling Bing, senior economist with the State Pricing Administration, said it was generally agreed that '. . . future price reforms should focus on the establishment of a socialist market pricing system. This will by no means create a laissez-faire system, but rather one in which prices are subject to government guidance and macro-control. The prices of most commodities and labour services will be decontrolled, while those of a small number of products directly related to non-renewable resources, public utilities, products often in short-supply and those having a close bearing on the national economy and the livelihood of the people will continue to be determined by the government.

'The government will primarily rely on economic means for macro-level price regulation, including making adjustments to the interest rates, exchange rates and salaries, in an effort to minimize the range over which prices may float and create a steadily developing economy. In short, the relaxation of prices is an important prerequisite for the establishment of the market system. However, the practice does not automatically result in a market system. The price system in the Chinese market should unite government macro-control with market regulation to accelerate the development of the country's socialist market economy.'[8]

Elaborating on this concept, Gao Shangquan, vice-chairman of the State Commission for Restructuring the Economic System, explained that the main functions of government control over economic activities in future would be: '. . . maintaining an overall balance, defining proportionate relations of the economic structure, curbing inflation and guarding against major fluctuations in the market; formulating industrial policy, making timely readjustments in accordance with market changes, issuing information and demands in the world and domestic markets, guiding enterprises to adjust product mix and promoting a rationalized economic structure; formulating financial and monetary policies as well as policies dealing with imports and exports in accordance with the nation's industrial policy and using such economic levers as interest rates, tax rates and foreign exchange rates in a coordinated manner to achieve the state's economic development goals and to realize a reasonable and equitable distribution of income; enacting laws and regulations for standardizing the behaviour of investors and managers as well as the market and circulation order so as to ensure the sustained, steady and coordinated development of the national economy'.[9]

According to Jiang Zemin, through macro-control a socialist country can integrate the '. . . people's immediate interests with their long-term interests and the interests of some with the interests of all, exploiting the advantages of both planning and market forces. [. . . .] When the state makes plans, its main tasks should be to set rational strategic targets for national economic and social development, to forecast economic development, control total supply and total demand, to readjust the geographical distribution of industries and of productive forces and to muster the financial and material resources necessary for the construction of important projects – all for the purpose of speeding up economic development by employing all economic levers'.[10]

On the development of the market, Jiang declared: 'We should continue our efforts to develop commodity markets, especially for capital goods, and build up financial markets [including] bonds, stocks, and other negotiable securities, and markets for technology, labour, information and real estate, so as to form an integrated national market system open to all. We should strengthen market rules and regulations, dismantle the barriers between regions, prohibit embargoes and prevent the formation of monopolies, so as to promote competition on an equal footing.'[11]

Competition is a relatively new concept in the People's Republic. Extolling its virtues, a book published in Beijing in 1988 pointed out that '. . . the market creates competition, setting one enterprise against another in securing orders, the goodwill of customers and their repeat business. There are numerous stories of buyers changing suppliers because of shoddy products, of enterprises upgrading their products, of small producers besting larger ones by providing special services and so on. For example, factories which thought themselves in a favourable position because of the scarcity of their products formerly refused to sell replacement parts, forcing customers to buy completely new ones; today they are glad to sell spare parts.

'Competition forces management to improve its operating practices in order to improve profits, and to spend more in research and innovation, thereby meeting additional needs and creating growth for their companies. For example, an electric fan manufacturer had for years been content to coast along simply meeting its quotas rather than upgrade its old facilities, improve its designs, and increase production. When the state ceased buying the factory's entire output, the factory was forced to change its ways.'[12]

REFORMING THE PUBLIC SECTOR

Although a significant amount of private economic activity now exists, state-owned enterprises remain the centrepiece of Chinese-style socialism. There is little movement towards privatization allowing the firms to sink or swim at the dictates of the market; the main government stress is on reviving the vitality and profitability of the public sector, separating the relationship between ownership and management of enterprises, giving them more autonomy in the day-to-day running of their business operations. On an experimental basis, the more prosperous state firms have been converted into '. . . legal entities responsible for their own decisions about their own operations and expansion and for their own profits and losses'.[13]

Under classic Soviet-inspired central planning, production targets are first set for major goods and commodities and the required material and energy inputs determined. Only then is need for consumer goods considered. What is not planned for simply does not get built, and there is no point in shopping around for it. An overlooked need, or a new one – whether can-opener or computer chip – may not find its way into the master plan for years, if at all. Because Chinese economic planning originally followed the Soviet pattern, the emphasis was nearly always on substantial growth in heavy industry with only secondary attention to other parts of the economy. For example, '. . . at some periods, the machine-building industry produced machine tools but insufficient equipment for agriculture, food processing, manufacture of consumer goods etc. Steel mills produced semi-finished products that light industry was not equipped to process further, but produced no materials for steel window frames or wire and nails. Heavy industry received large appropriations for new facilities and products, while light industry could secure little in the way of materials, funds or facilities'.[14]

Specialized ministries deal with each industrial sector, with various subordinate administrative units dealing with specific aspects of the business, such as finance, materials, labour.[15] For many key products, there are a minimum of six levels of authority each of which is required to rubber-stamp the decisions taken at factory level. According to a case reported in the official press, one major industrial project required the seals of 860 offices at central, provincial and local level before final approval could be achieved.

At the bottom of the ladder are the individual enterprises, which have tended to receive insufficient attention because the administrative units above have their own interests, as well as other enterprises to worry about. Obviously, the individual enterprises have little status, and the director of even a fairly large factory, for example, may be unable to spend as little as 100 Yuan ($13) without permission of higher authority. The director of a large Shanghai research institute once complained that he did not 'have the right to decide to buy a packet of tea'.

When centralization is pushed to the extreme, there is a tendency for managers and workers to care nothing for quality, market needs, sales potential, or profits and losses. Since they have no influence, it is pointless for them to care. Their only concern is meeting state quotas for their products, which their ministry is obliged to purchase from them and offer to consumers whether the products are actually usable or not. The economist Huan Xiang summarized the situation thus: 'The consequences of over-centralization are: the more centralized the more rigid; the more rigid the economy, the lazier the people; the lazier the people, the poorer they are; the poorer they are, the greater the need for centralization, forming a vicious circle.'

Factory managers also faced further official interference at shop-floor level. From 1956, when the Communist Party began to extend its grip to all aspects of daily life, a party committee was installed in each enterprise to which its directors were responsible. The committee had to approve all decisions, meaning in effect that it was the in-house party secretary who controlled the enterprise not its director. The problem with this system, however, was that while the former might be skilled in political manoeuvring he did not necessarily have much idea about how to run a business. Ideology – and preservation of the status quo – therefore, tended to triumph over business common sense.

By 1980, it became obvious that economic reform could not achieve its full potential if this system remained in force and Deng Xiaoping launched the idea of giving the factory director full responsibility for the day-to-day running of the enterprise, relegating the party secretary to a secondary role. But it was not an idea that gained instant approval, especially from bureaucrats and party activists who would see their power diminished. Hence, it took four years before the Factory Director Responsibility System (FDRS) gained sufficient support to be introduced on an experimental basis in six cities – although it was rapidly adopted throughout the country.

The official media jumped on the bandwagon with enthusiastic articles reporting how tens of thousands of factories were formally operating under FDRS with great success. One typical example involved the Taishan Iron and Steel Corporation (TISC), in central Shandong Province, a medium-sized conglomerate specializing in the production of iron and steel, building materials, electric power and chemicals. In the mid-1990s, it was a highly profitable company, but less than a decade earlier it had been an absolute disaster, '. . . a virtual ruin overgrown with weeds and filled with rusting equipment. In May 1984, when Wang Shoudang, now general manager, took over the shambles, he inherited nothing more than two 55-cubic metre blast furnaces of little value.

'From 1971 to 1981, Wang, 53, a former furnace workshop chief, had witnessed day-to-day operations, the decline and eventual closing of the complex. While the directorship changed hands seven times, no significant improvements were made. On the contrary, the ironworks accumulated a 46 million Yuan deficit and was a heavy burden on the local government. The result was bankruptcy. Upon assuming the general manager's post, Wang asked not for financial support from the state bank or the local government, but instead for decision-making power. Thus, in 1984, the local government granted Wang the still rare privilege of autonomy to manage enterprise affairs.

'The first difficulty facing Wang was funds shortage. The

recovery of only one furnace required well over three million Yuan, a sum unavailable from either the local government or banks, since they, too, faced a tight money supply. Undeterred, in May 1984, Wang journeyed to Shanghai, where he signed the reborn corporation's first cooperative agreement with the Shanghai Metallurgical Industrial Bureau and the Shanghai Metal Products Company to carry out compensatory trade. According to the agreement, the Shanghai partners invested the three million Yuan for furnace recovery, while in return TISC would supply 30,000 tons of pig iron at a state-planned price over a four-year period. TISC raised an additional 30 million Yuan by signing similar cooperative agreements with 11 enterprises and departments in various provinces. The influx of funding not only allowed the corporation to refurbish the second furnace but to build a new 100-cubic-metre furnace. The end result was that annual pig iron output rose to 180,000 tons. In February 1993, TISC repaid its debts and its new steelworks, with an annual production capacity of 100,000 tons of steel ingots, went into operation'.[16]

A remarkable recovery indeed. But the TISC success story, notwithstanding much of the media enthusiasm, in general proved to be somewhat overblown, for serious problems were reported in the system's operation. The State Economic Commission, for example, found that only 20 per cent of work units were using FDRS satisfactorily, as bureaucrats were refusing to delegate powers and party secretaries were rigorously resisting the factory directors' supposed new authority. In September 1986 the Central Committee and State Council jointly issued three sets of regulations attempting to define the roles of factory directors, party committees and 'workers' congresses' in state-owned industrial enterprises. But it left a lot of grey areas and loopholes exploited by those opposed to change.

It was not until April 1988, after almost nine years of preparation and in the face of stiff opposition by entrenched special interests, that an Enterprise Law was passed which declared that a state-owned company would in future be 'an independent accounting unit' (i.e.: responsible for its own profits and losses and not receive state support for operating deficits). In relation to each enterprise, the state would observe 'the principle of separation of ownership and managerial authority'. The law reaffirmed FDRS under which the factory director would occupy the central position in the enterprise and 'assume overall responsibility for its material and cultural progress'.

Nevertheless, the director still was not given complete freedom. A clause in the law said that the director was criminally liable if because of undefined 'faults in his work' he 'causes the property of the enterprise or the interests of the state and the people to suffer heavy losses'. The waters were further muddied by a provision that '. . . the grassroots organizations of the Chinese Communist Party in an enterprise shall guarantee and supervise the implementation of the guiding principles and policies of the parties and the state in an enterprise'.

In addition, the law declared that '. . . an enterprise shall ensure that its staff and workers enjoy the status of the masters [of the enterprise] and shall protect their lawful rights and interests. An enterprise shall practise, through the staff and workers' congresses and other forms, democratic management. The trade union in an enterprise shall represent and safeguard the interests of the staff and workers and conduct its work independently according to law'. These various provisions had the effect of partially negating any improvements in business management brought about by the introduction of FDRS.

Other experiments in individual management responsibility have also been conducted in recent years. The most prevalent is the contract responsibility system, widely used since mid-1987, which requires specific economic commitments from factory managements. According to the official press, some agreements '. . . may be based on increasing profits, some on decreasing deficits (for the money-losing factories) and some on cost and value output indexes'. Either a factory as such, an individual factory director, or a group of individuals who manage the factory may be contractors, with the state in all cases the opposite party. A contract is drafted through negotiations.

A clever manager with good negotiating skills can use the contract responsibility system to his advantage. He will try to negotiate the best terms possible with the bureaucrats which he knows are well within the capabilities of his company. Having committed himself to hand over to the state a specific amount of profit, the manager can then go away and try to ensure profit levels much higher than the commitment. This excess can be pocketed and, in the words of one unhappy senior bureaucrat, 'spent in ways that run counter to the state's interests' (e.g.: stock or foreign-exchange speculation).

Some economists now claim the contract responsibility system is no longer capable of motivating state firms to do better and instead favour expansion of a shareholding system to maximize efficiency (see below). But this view is opposed by conservatives who see the contract as a means of retaining at least a modicum of control. In this respect, they are loud in their praises of Shougang (Capital Iron and Steel Works), a far-flung complex on the outskirts of Beijing, once China's leading steelmaker, turning out 5.7 million tons annually, but more recently struggling with massive debts caused by many of the factors already outlined. The company adopted a contractual agreement with the Beijing authorities that specified the annual profit level it must hand over to the state, rising 7.3 per cent per year, in addition to tax payments. Excess profits are retained to fund expansion and modernization.

In return, Shougang was allowed to bypass state trading firms and deal directly with foreign companies. It set up its own commercial bank and gave managers the freedom to make investments without government approval in projects worth as much as $35 million. With these reforms, as well as with updated technology and offers of incentives to workers for improved performance, earnings rose 35 per cent to $550 million in 1992.

The official media heaped praise on Shougang for its performance – motivated, perhaps, by the fact that the company relieves the state of a considerable welfare burden. It provides its 250,000 workers with various services including housing, schools, groceries, hospitals, recreational centres and buses for outings. Employees, for example, can send their children to one of 50 company-run kindergartens which only charge a token fee.

Nevertheless, some economists saw the contract responsibility system as merely a transitional device on the road to a full-fledged socialist market economy. 'It has played a positive role in our economic reform and development,' conceded Zhou Shulian, Industrial Research Centre director at the Academy of Social Sciences. 'But it will increasingly become unsuitable for the establishment of a socialist market economy. Although contracts are signed on an equal and voluntary basis, at the end of the day the system still fails to change the subordinated role of enterprises to their administrative authorities.' Zhou also argued that under the system the ownership of assets could not be clearly defined, and the goal of making enterprises responsible for their own profits and losses would be difficult to realize.

Leasing has also become an increasingly common way for provincial and local governments to withdraw from involvement with tens of thousands of small enterprises. Lease terms generally have these standard features: first, the leasee is required to turn over to the state an agreed-on amount or proportion of earnings; second, the leasee must make a substantial personal investment in the enterprise. Leasing is generally used only in connection with smaller enterprises, but nevertheless it can be relatively profitable.

In the final analysis, however, liberal economists in general stress the fact that the only answer, especially in resolving the issue of assets ownership, is to press ahead with the experimental share-holding system introduced in a few cities like Shanghai for the larger companies in the public sector. Answering the fears of conservatives who see this as the forerunner to mass privatization, Beijing University economics professor Dong Furen said: 'There is no need to worry about the occurrence of capitalism because a large part of the shares can go to public legal persons and state-owned enterprises can be allowed to purchase each other's shares,' His colleague, Professor Li Yining, agreed. 'The shareholding principle should be promoted on the basis of public ownership. State-owned enterprises should be encouraged to purchase each other's shares, form partnerships or exchange some of their shares at equal value. [And] more pilot enterprises can be selected to sell shares to their own workers and to individuals of various social sectors.'[17]

The Beijing leadership is careful to distinguish between Western-style shareholding and the version it is now developing to suit Chinese needs. As Vice Premier Zhu Rongji, explained: 'We are making use of the mechanisms of a market economy [but] I would never think of that as capitalism. In the primary stage of socialism we do not exclude the existence of development of a private economy. We only require that public ownership be its mainstay. In the shareholding system we are adopting, we will limit the percentage of privately-controlled stocks. People want to buy stocks, and this is a good means of collecting money for our industry and promoting good management. Socialist or capitalist, either system can issue stocks and bonds.' By early 1993, Zhu said, there were about 3,700 'shareholding enterprises' in the country, and 70 companies had their shares listed on either the Shanghai or Shenzhen Stock Exchange.

In a related step, the government began establishing stock-based enterprise groups with an eventual goal of about 100. The enterprise groups differ from existing economic alliances because they are linked by holding companies and subsidiaries which buy each other's shares. Liu Jipeng, who helped draft the rules for the groups in 1991, said the idea was '. . . to promote coordination among member companies, with each specialized in large-scale production of component parts of a product in order to keep costs to a minimum. The new conglomerates, by coordinating and concentrating their resources on developing new technologies and products are expected to be competitive on both the domestic and overseas markets'. Liu termed the new practice 'shareholding system of public ownership' as stocks would not sell to individuals. 'Such a system serves as a link between public ownership and the commodity economy China is trying to develop.'

The core of such conglomerates will be large industrial or commercial enterprises, or pure holding companies with abundant capital. Although closer-circle member companies remain independent businesses, they will either turn into subsidiaries or be leased to holding companies, or the management of their fixed assets entrusted to the holdings of the state. Top decision-makers of the corporations, either boards of directors or a management committee, will represent the groups in drafting unified development plans, borrowing and repaying loans, carrying out foreign trade, conducting transactions of their fixed assets and appointing managers to member companies. The new group's inner-circle members will be placed under separate government plans, which means they may enjoy more privileges in output quota, investment, allocation of materials and labour, wage issue and accounting.

Specialized financial companies will be created to raise funds, including the issue of bonds and shares. They will also be permitted to export their products and import technology, equipment and raw materials. (Until recently, Chinese firms have had to sell their goods to special companies that are authorized to deal in foreign trade, although there has been a lot of illegal bypassing of official channels.)

Liu said China's economy had been suffering from imbalances in product mix, industrial make-up and enterprise organizational structure: 'Administrative command will not work in this regard. They have to be achieved through transactions on a capital market. To do this, enterprises have to evolve from pure producers into independent investors that expand businesses and improve efficiency through well-chosen investment activities.'

This is a significant switch in direction compared to the past, when each factory was independent in almost all its operations. Specialization was very low. Production projects, dispersed and duplicated, were unable to reach the expected economic scale. In 1989, for example, the automobile industry had 757 companies established by different government departments and local authorities to manufacture vehicles or various components. With one or two exceptions, they had an annual average output of only 4,000 vehicles, while some could only turn out 100 cars a year on handicraft-type production lines. That is now changing. Under the new enterprise strategy, the Hubei No.2 Automobile Plant, one of the few with a large production capacity, which is now part of the Dongfeng Automobile Group, spread out across the country encompassing 300 enterprises in 14 different industries.

'Members of the group have undergone a reshuffling and technical reform. Each has a target of a special field of production, such as assembly, spare parts manufacturing, special-purpose car production, bus production or provisions of other labour services. This type of business adjustment enables them to make most of the group by taking advantage of each other's specialities. As a result, most have managed to hold on to a stable share of the market. After entering the group, some enterprises suffering losses or on the verge of bankruptcy have turned the corner and become 'small giants'. When the No.2 Automobile Plant reduced its output of spare parts for five- and eight-ton lorries, letting other co-operators share the work, it was able to produce main parts for lorries. As a result of this cooperation between enterprises with different specialities, [it] was able to increase its annual output of five-ton lorries from 85,000 to 140,000 during the Seventh Five-Year Plan (1986-90). [It] provides a good model for all Chinese industries.'[18]

HYBRID PROBLEMS

But behind all the glitter of the booming coastal economy and the genuine success stories, there is a far more complex reality that remains a major headache for the Beijing leadership. The economy currently being created is very much a hybrid of the good and the bad. The cream on the economic cake is a relatively efficient light-industrial sector which powers the impressive export growth figures, assisted by relatively cheap and semi-skilled labour. But beneath it there remains the ponderous, state-owned sector of heavy resource and manufacturing industries similar to that which represented the economic core of the old Soviet Union.

China counts about 11,000 large and medium-size state firms (2.5 per cent of total businesses) that make steel, machinery, textiles and other industrial goods, holding two-thirds of the fixed assets and contributing an equal amount of state revenue through taxes and profits. But this is offset by subsidies paid out to prop up the many 'basket cases' which soak up 17 per cent of government spending and contribute to the annual budgetary deficits.

During the Seventh Five-Year Plan (1986-90), the output value of state-owned industries increased at an average rate of 7.3 per cent, compared to 17.6 per cent for collectively-owned industries and 74 per cent for Sino-foreign joint ventures. In 1990, the output value of foreign-funded enterprises grew by 56 per cent while that the state firms could manage only 2.9 per cent.

For all the inroads of the free market, the state sector still accounts for 55 per cent of industrial output (compared to 76 per cent at the beginning of the 1980s) and employs more than 70 per cent of the 148 million urban workers. The enterprises are virtual mini-societies, providing social-welfare benefits for their 106 million employees; guaranteed lifetime employment, subsidized housing, free schools for workers' children, generous pension plans and free health care. According to one Chinese expert: 'The state enterprises are the basis for socialism. Without them, what is socialism?'[19]

Like the old Soviet plants from which they drew inspiration – and often blueprints and capital equipment – the state industries in the main are dilapidated, over-manned more than 10 per cent and produce shoddy goods that have little appeal. It might well make sense to close them and start again. Transforming them into viable players in a free market is the real challenge of Deng's economic reforms, whose success or failure will determine whether China emerges as a true economic giant in the next century.

The scope of the problem may be illustrated by a report from the State Statistics Bureau which said 33.8 per cent of state-owned industries under the budget-recorded deficits during the first four months of 1993. 'Since 1990, no significant improvement has been made in this regard. Money-losing firms occupy a third of the state-owned industrial sector.'[20]

Professor Li Yining of Beijing University listed five factors which were holding back the state sector: (1) Firms were still relying too much on the state rather than seizing the chances offered by the various management responsibility systems; (2) producers were slow in reacting to the market; (3) bureaucrats remained reluctant to give managers full responsibility to make individual decisions which would allow factories to take effective steps to reduce stockpiles and production cost; (4) the market mechanism could hardly act in China's economy because the state enterprises were not really businesses but welfare societies; (5) firms had to exercise self-restraint and workers should accept that wages and bonuses were not a divine right but linked to performance.

This latter aspect reflects the government's longstanding fear of social instability. Urban residents in particular have long enjoyed a highly subsidized existence – with homes largely provided by their employers, and staple food and other necessities of daily life supplied under a ration coupon system at prices way below production costs. Between 1991 and 1993, these subsidies were steadily phased out and the urban population was required to pay market prices in decades. To offset the inevitable increase in the cost of living, which could have triggered riots, workers were given substantial wage increases. Regardless of the performance of individual enterprises, workers' incomes benefited from state largesse. In the first four months of 1993, the State Statistics Bureau reckoned these wage increases pushed up the production costs of state enterprises by 11.8 per cent.

Under a pricing system which even many Chinese officials agreed was irrational, the prices of the raw materials purchased by the state sector – previously kept artificially low (one reason why the oil and coal-mining industries have consistently operated at a loss; the price of crude oil in China in 1993 was still only a third of that sold on the world market) – were allowed to rise to find their market level. The rise was also encouraged by a supply shortage caused by the heavy demands of rapid economic growth. But at the same time, many industries have not been able to pass these increased costs along to the end users due to the low prices dictated by the central planners. Despite all the noise about reform since 1978, these complaints were being aired as the reality prevailing in 1993!

CHAIN OF DEBT

Financially, a chronic problem for state enterprises has been breaking the 'chain of debt' in which many have been hopelessly enmeshed. Take the example of the Shanghai No.5 Steel Works, which owed its suppliers more than 500 million Yuan and had no way of paying the debt. How could it when customers like the bearing factory in Wafangdian, Liaoning Province, could not pay its 10-million Yuan bill? But the Liaoning factory had its own problems. It was spending considerable time and money – 200 people at a monthly cost of 200,000 Yuan – to collect 200 million Yuan in debt. Caught in this chain of debt defaults, the steel works has been unable to collect on 670 million Yuan and therefore unable to meet its obligations. It also was having difficulty buying raw materials, paying for utilities and meeting its 8-million Yuan monthly payroll. The steel works was not alone. Nationwide, the amount of debt in arrears among enterprises rose from 100 billion Yuan in 1989 to 150 billion Yuan in 1990.

Trying to stem this growth industry, the government launched a new campaign in Northeast China in June 1991 to break the chain of debt. Most of those involved were large and medium-sized state enterprises producing means of production for fixed customers, who, even though they failed to pay their bills for years on end, often continued to be supplied because that was part of the plan.

The links of the debt chain are clear. Mainly, it starts with projects of capital construction and technological transformation. They default on the enterprises producing equipment, who default on steel works or other manufacturers of raw and semi-finished materials who default on coal producers . . . and so it goes. The government identified five factors which it believed accounted for the growth of the debt defaults: (1) projects of capital construction and technological transformation whose budget estimates are so ambitious that they must defer payment to creditors, and in some cases, default on payments; (2) enterprises that incur debts are incapable of paying for the goods they buy; (3) the failure on the part of the government to allocate enough funds to enterprises which it is obliged to subsidize out of policy considerations, and thus reducing these enterprises' capabilities to pay their debts; (4) some firms, whose products are unmarketable, have to default on their suppliers in order to survive; (5) due to disorder in commodity exchange, slack discipline in settling accounts and a blunted sense of credibility, some enterprises purposely defer payment to their suppliers, believing the practice can generate economic returns.

In March 1990, the State Council announced a nationwide campaign to tame debt defaults and set up a group of leading businessmen and bureaucrats to deal with them headed by Vice Premier Zhu Rongji. This drive cleared 160 billion Yuan in debt defaults which helped ease the capital squeeze felt by large and medium-sized State enterprises and shored up plummeting industrial growth. But the general understanding of the major source of the chain of debt defaults was far from perfect.

For some time, the government concentrated on providing premium bank loans, which cleared up old debts merely by creating new ones. In 1991, the government came up with a new strategy, which, while emphasizing the need for the clearing up of old debts, also stressed the need to avoid new debts. Government officials toured the country working their way on the chain of debt for 319 targeted large and medium-sized enterprises, and within weeks claimed to have collected 4 billion Yuan. In September 1991, the government introduced a system of fines for failure to meet payment deadlines, and warned managers that 'more serious punishment' was contemplated if they did not mend their ways. A system of economic courts was established to deal with debt disputes. Sceptics, however, felt this was merely tinkering with the carburettor when a complete engine overhaul was desperately needed. Certainly a lot of longstanding bad debts were eliminated. But the problem recurred in 1993 when the government imposed a credit squeeze.

FEATHERBEDDING

Turning to the labour side, fear of idle hands being led into mischief (i.e.: challenging authority particularly through street protests) has been a key factor behind two of the biggest headaches for the state sector: featherbedding (too many workers doing too little work) and the maintenance of enterprises whose poor performance in any other society would have mercifully been terminated through immediate cessation of business activities.

In 1986, Beijing passed a ground-breaking law that authorized bankruptcy for state firms – taboo in the heyday of Maoism – and ordered some closures, but the programme stalled in the conservative backlash that followed the 1989 Tiananmen massacre and only began to be pursued again with some vigour in 1992 (when over 350 firms, a third of them state-owned, declared bankruptcy, resulting in 1.4 million urban workers losing their jobs). In the past, bankruptcy was only allowed in the state sector if another company was willing to take over responsibility for the entire work-force. These days they are either transferred to service companies set up by the state-owned firms or merely given a severance package.

The closures can be explosive in social terms. A report by the Chinese Academy of Social Sciences in early 1993 warned of possible disturbances in the cities, citing the prospect of rampant inflation and eventual job losses at state enterprises. In 1992, about 2,500 workers, half the staff, at the government-owned Seagull Watch factory in Tianjin went on the rampage, smashing equipment after they were laid off. 'Liaoning Province, in the Northeast, reported 276 incidents over a period of seven months in which factory managers and supervisors were beaten up by resentful workers, and police now protect senior factory cadres. The academy found that more than half the city-dwellers it polled were upset with reforms that mandated higher rents and health-care fees.'[21]

Summing up the thrust of 'enterprise reform'', Gao Shangkun, vice-chairman of the State Commission for Restructuring Economic System, noted: 'Since the introduction of reforms, some state-owned enterprises have been dynamic, achieving good economic returns and high market share for their products. It is clear, however, that township and foreign-funded enterprises are more vital and their equity positions sounder than state-owned enterprises. They are independent economic entities, responsible for business risks and profits and losses. Using flexible management methods, township enterprises can easily implement useful business decisions and eliminate those practices found to be detrimental. In the past two years, over 600,000 (three per cent of the total) township enterprises have closed down; three million farmer-turned-workers returned to their villages to do farm work or become self-employed. This constant promotion of practices advantageous to business and the elimination of practices which prove detrimental has optimized enterprise structure and boosted production as well.

'State-owned enterprises, however, lack such flexibility. Even when enterprises suffer losses, workers and staff members still receive wages and bonuses. Moreover, lack of profit does not deter factory directors and managers from travelling on official business and staying in luxury hotels. The change in enterprise operating methods should be based on the general goal of establishing a new planned commodity economic system and combining the planned economy with market forces by the end of this century and plans for this change made in accordance with the outline of the Ten-Year Programme and the Eighth Five-Year Plan (1991–5).

'[The changes] can be roughly divided into the following five stages and five types of enterprises. State-owned enterprises in the special economic zones and development zones and shareholding enterprises whose shares are held by legally-entitled persons may be considered among the first group of enterprises to complete operational changes. Since these enterprises are endowed with a favourable external and internal environment, it is easier for them to change their methods of operation. These can be followed by State-owned enterprises for which production and business activities are basically geared to the market, and then by those whose production and business activities have not yet been geared to the market, but which have a balanced supply-and-demand for products are among the third group. The few key state enterprises with important, mandatory tasks and operating methods which cannot be changed quickly will form the fourth group. Enterprises of a monopoly nature and those with restricted resources may not yet be able to manage their own affairs independently or assume sole responsibility for their own profits and losses, but they should still be prepared for eventual exposure to the market.'[22]

Nevertheless, there is some evidence that the pace of reform has slowed down, especially in relatively conservative regions (such as the Northeast), because of resistance from local cadres. Ostensibly, the resistance stemmed from qualms about massive layoffs if the state sector was exposed to full market forces. But there are other factors. 'Many government officials feel it is a matter of course to direct enterprises and institutions – like a babysitter with an infant – and do not feel it their duty to offer services to them.'[23] 'Some local government departments are reluctant to part with the powers which they should pass on to the enterprises under them. As a result, many decision-making powers continue to rest in the hands of local governments and fail to reach the producers. Some government departments have been reorganized into companies, but only in name. They, in effect, still function as government departments. [. . .] Some enterprises are playing wait-and-see. They want to know if the delegation of powers is real and are reluctant to make an effort to improve their management on the strength of the regulations.'[24]

SMASHING THE IRON RICE BOWL

After 'liberation' in 1949, the new Communist regime was deeply concerned about the possibility of disaffected elements in the cities who might stir up social instability. This can be partly explained by the peasant background of Mao Zedong and many others in the leadership which made them uncomfortable with and even suspicion of 'city slickers'. Thus was created the 'iron rice bowl', the system whereby urban workers were guaranteed a job for life regardless of performance, with dismissal only possible for ill-defined 'gross negligence'. With this went other heavily subsidized perks regarding housing, food, clothing, medicine and education. In the spirit of egalitarianism, much prized in New China, wages were equal regardless of the job done, and there was little differentiation between management and labour. Thus, there was little incentive for a worker to seek promotion or to do a better job other than an excess of revolutionary zeal – and that soon palled for most people. All one had to do was to clock on in a morning to be guaranteed a day's pay. Very often, there was not enough work to go round, especially as the state's monthly quotas could often be taken care of in a few hours. The more conscientious might stay on the premises, finding a quiet corner to sleep; others would slip away to take care of household chores like shopping or dealing with the many bureaucratic demands governing urban life.

Maintenance of this system proved to be a terrible drain on government finances, as well as tending to defeat any efforts to promote greater production efficiency. Thus, in 1991, the decision was taken: the iron rice bowl would be completely smashed by the end of the century.

Experiments began with a labour contract system, giving management some control over hiring and firing. A worker now signs a contract with his employer covering a specified number of years, after which it has to be renewed, enabling enterprises for the first time to get rid of inefficient or redundant staff. Labour Ministry statistics issued in mid-1992 showed that about 13.5 million workers nationwide had signed such contracts, 14 per cent of state employees, along with 1.58 million employees of foreign-funded businesses. Many companies were enthusiastic about the idea and claimed it had resulted in an immediate increase in productivity and profits. But others, after a period of trial, decided to revert to the old system and grant 'permanent employee' status to contract workers once again.

A brewery in Zhejiang attracted considerable attention in 1993 when it reintroduced the concept of lifetime employment having experimented with the contract responsibility system. Critics claimed it was sticking the shattered pieces of the iron rice bowl back together again, and was trying to take the easy way out rather than persevere with the current uncertainties of the reform process. The management of the Qianjiang Beer Group, however, insisted that what it was doing was in the spirit of reform and was designed to enhance productivity through greater worker security.

The perceived secret of success is that the status of lifetime employment has to be earned. Workers have to put in nine years of uninterrupted service before being considered for permanent employment. Then, the entire work-force will consider their suitability – based on a number of factors, including their work record and contribution to the company – for elevation to lifetime employment. Once elevated, the worker becomes eligible for the various perks such as medical care, social insurance and housing.

Each year, the Workers' Congress will undertake a performance review and unqualified employees can have their title removed once again. The management emphasized that only three to five per cent of the work force would be able to gain the honour.[25]

Explaining the split verdict on the employment reforms, the China Labour News said: 'Permanent employment has some advantages as it gives employees a sense of security and honour and maintains the attraction of the enterprise to its employees. It also enables firms to train employees systematically and government to transfer employees from one place to another according to the needs of economic development and construction. But the system today is no longer suited to the development of productive forces as it runs counter to the requirement of the planned commodity economy. For one thing, it protects lazy employees and dampens the initiatives of the whole, For another, enterprises adopting the permanent employment system cannot make use of the labour market to meet their needs. In addition, there are too many unwanted employees on the payroll while there is often a shortage of the skilled people that are really needed.'[26]

At the same time, wage reforms are being implemented in the state sector which seem to have dealt a death blow to the principle of egalitarianism. After the People's Republic was formed in 1949, all workers were paid the same wages regardless of individual productivity or creativity. But as part of ongoing economic reforms, the government has determined that wage levels should more accurately reflect individual merit and output. Zhu Jianzhen, Deputy Minister of Labour, told a conference in Beijing that more than 41 million workers in state-owned enterprises – more than half the total work force – currently have their income tied to performance which has greatly raised their enthusiasm and boosted productivity.

But problems remain. According to Liu Zhifeng, Vice-Director of the State Commission for Restructuring the Economy, the present system involves a differentiation between wages and bonuses on the one hand, and free medical care and other forms of welfare on the other. The reforms currently cover only wages and income, while welfare payments continue to be distributed among workers equally regardless of individual performance. Thus, the principle of payment according to one's work [rather than the old way of according to one's need] has not been completely carried out, Liu said.

'To smash egalitarianism completely, enterprises should combine the two categories and distribute both according to individual performance and skills. Enterprises should adopt wage distribution measures that improve economic efficiency and raise workers' enthusiasm for production. Firms will enjoy full autonomy in income distribution, without government interference, said Liu, although the State will practise macro-control over their total payroll in light of each company's management, economic efficiency and success in the market.'[27]

PRIVATE BUSINESS

Another aspect of economic reform is the emergence, with official blessing, of private businesses. They were anathema in Maoist China, where work for hire was considered a form of capitalist exploitation. Virtually none existed up to 1976 when the decade of chaos known as the Cultural Revolution ended. (A private entrepreneur would be have been hauled before a kangaroo court as an incorrigible 'rightist' and would have been lucky to escape with his life.) Nowadays, the official position is that private businesses are appropriate in a country such as China that is still in the preliminary stages of socialism, and where they constitute only a small percentage of total investment and business volume.

They are divided into two groups: individual businesses, which employ seven or fewer workers, and private enterprises, which employ eight or more. Most of the former are one-person or family operations – retail stalls or small shops, restaurants, repair or transport services etc – while the latter may be larger versions of the same kinds of business or may be involved in light industry or some other fields. In the middle of 1993, official figures indicated there were about 15 million individual businesses and 154,000 private enterprises, although this probably understates the true situation somewhat.

'The private sector is playing a more and more important role in the market economy. It now turns over to the state an annual average of 20 billion Yuan in taxes, about 7.8 per cent of the total state revenue from commerce and industry. In the economically backward regions private businessmen have become the mainstay of the local economy and the main source of financial income. They have also become a driving force in the state's efforts to develop the tertiary industry. [and] as the reform of the labour system deepens in the state-owned enterprises, more and more surplus workers from state enterprises are turning to the private sector; about 700,000 such workers as well as other unemployed people are employed annually in this sector.'[28]

As an example of this, the nonferrous-metal industry in mid-1993 announced plans to trim its 1.01 million work-force by at least a third before the end of the century to enhance productivity, sales and profits. The China National Non-ferrous Metals Industry Corporation (CNNC) said redundant workers would be 'encouraged to run private businesses'. In another significant move, 'surplus staff' in the Communist Party and government departments, as well as retired cadres, were told they could become private entrepreneurs if they left their jobs. A confidential document circulated within the party in 1992 urged public bodies to start up private sideline businesses which would be free of any government interference. At that time, at least 200,000 of the 50 million party members had already registered as entrepreneurs.

A constitutional amendment giving private businesses the right to exist was passed at the 1988 National People's Congress, and a few months later the State Council issued new rules 'to provide legal protection' for them. And in 1993, Vice-premier Zhu Rongji told an international conference in Shanghai: 'China will continue to allow and support the development of private and foreign-funded enterprises, which will compete with publicly-owned enterprises on an equal footing.'

But despite these protestations of support, private businesses face a number of problems which suggest they are far from achieving equality. It is very seldom, for example, that they can obtain bank loans (some local governments actually forbid banks under their jurisdiction to make such loans). A 1993 survey of the private sector discovered at least 40 per cent of firms citing this as their biggest difficulty. Some government departments have also issued regulations to limit privately-made products entering State-owned stores.[29]

This would seem to be one of the factors involved in the increasing cross-fertilization, creating a mixed economic of state, collective and privately-owned enterprises. After they reach a certain level of basic capital accumulation, some private companies decide that their future lies in some form of alliance with a larger concern in the public sector, giving them access to relatively advanced technology, advanced equipment, often under-utilized skilled workers, bank loans and friendly bureaucrats, while still retaining control of management and operations. In return, state-owned or collectively-run enterprises can put their idle equipment to work with private firms while still retaining property rights.

According to Zhang Ping, an economist at the Institute of Economics of CASS, '. . . such grafting can improve the allocation of labour forces, funds, technology and resources and introduce go-for-profit management strategy into state-owned enterprises',[30] But, to his sorrow, many private firms have impure motives when they seek an alliance with a state-run enterprise. What they are after, purely and simply, is protection: 'Private entrepreneurs are worried that their property cannot be protected under existing laws. The new businesses usually donate money to public works such as building bridges, schools and roads in their home town to pacify their fellow villagers [motivated by what the Chinese call 'red eye disease', or jealousy]. They are leaving leeway for themselves at the rustle of the leaves in the wind [. . . .] because discrimination towards the private economy still exists.'

Given the history of ideological U-turns in communist China, this caution is readily understandable – even if it is frustrating for liberals pressing for an all-out dash to a full market economy.

FOOTNOTES:
1. Report on the work of the government delivered to the National People's Congress on March 20, 1992.
2. 'We must allow and encourage some areas and individuals to grow rich first, so that more and more areas and individuals will do so until common prosperity is eventually achieved.' – Jiang Zemin, addressing the NPC 12 Oct. 1992.
3. Speaking at a meeting of 40 top economists in Beijing March 1992.
4. Interview.
5. Policy speech to the NPC plenary session 12 Oct.1992.
6. Interview.
7. 'Market plays dominant role'. *Beijing Review* 23–29 Sept.1992.
8. Ibid.
9. Article contributed to *Beijing Review* 15–21 June, 1992.
10. NPC speech 12 Oct. 1992.
11. Ibid.
12. *Changing China. The New Revolution's First Decade, 1979–88* by James M.Ethridge, Beijing,

New World Press, 1988, pp98-9.
13. Jiang Zemin reporting to the NPC, 12 Oct. 1992.
14. *Changing China*, p83.
15. By the early 1990s, there were at least 100 separate central government departments employing 40 million people. An organizational reform programme adopted in March 1993 called for a reduction to 41 ministries and commissions and 18 affiliated institutions, and a 20 per cent staff cut, by the end of the year. *Beijing Review* 16–22 Aug. 1993.
16. Beijing Review 6 Sept. 1993.
17. Interviews.
18. *Beijing Review*, 11 May 1992.
19. Quoted in *Time Magazine*, 10 May 1993.
20. *China Daily*, 2 June 1993.
21. *Time Magazine* 10 May 1993.
22. 'Enterprise Reform – New Operating Mechanism.' *Beijing Review*, 15–21 June 1992.
23. *China Daily*, 18 June 1993.
24. Editorial in *China Daily*, 20 August 1993.
25. Xinhua News Agency 7 April 1993.
26. Translation published in *China Daily*, 7 July 1992.
27. Xinhua, 8 May 1993.
28. Ibid., 22 May 1993.
29. *China Daily*, 5 May 1993
30. Interview.

3 The coast will get rich first. . . .

KEY POINTS

This chapter will examine two key planks of the economic reform programme:
- The five Special Economic Zones, intended to act as lightning rods to conduct the so-called white heat of foreign technological advancement to the entire country.
- The 14 coastal cities opened to foreign investment in the mid-1980s, and given specific roles in agricultural and industrial modernization and export trade development as part of a policy of letting the coast get rich first and pulling the interior along in its slip-stream.

The main questions:
- Have these concepts worked in the way in which they were originally intended?
- What do these economic zones have to offer that is not available elsewhere?
- Have they possibly created more problems than they have solved?

SPECIAL ECONOMIC ZONES

ONE HOUR'S drive north of Hong Kong lies Shenzhen, a communist experiment in capitalism which the entire country wants to emulate. In 1980, it had a population of 30,000, consisting almost entirely of duck farms and was regarded as one of the poorest localities in the country. A decade later, it had become a sprawling urban jungle of two million people and covering 200 square miles, gateway to Guangdong province, home of a good many of the country' new millionaires, and with a per capita income more than seven times the national average.

Foreign business know-how and money combined with Chinese cheap labour and abundant land to turn the entire city into a giant building site. Skyscraper office blocks sprouted almost overnight out of the former farmland. Restaurants are today filled with business executives shouting into their mobile telephones between mouthfuls of exotic food undreamed of under the old regime of politically correct austerity. Traffic jams abound and luxury hotels teem with prostitutes in defiance of repeated crackdowns by a puritanical central government. There are theme parks, discos, golf courses and even a racing track (horse racing was banned under the communists and was only allowed back in a small way at the start of the 1990s).

Shenzhen is the best known of the original four 'Special Economic Zones' – along with Zhuhai, Shantou and Xiamen – established in 1980 as the cutting edge of the economic reforms. Given the presence of many sceptics, if not opponents, within the party leadership, care was taken to stress that this was an experiment that could be abandoned if it went wrong. Creation of the SEZs had the advantage of confining any dangerous developments within defined geographical boundaries which would limit the risk of contagion. Barbed wire and guard posts, giving the impression that one was entering a foreign country (which in one sense visitors were), ensured that this would be so. The choice of sites also seemed deliberate. Shenzhen is close to the border with Hong Kong, Zhuhai adjacent to Macao, while Xiamen and Shantou face Taiwan. Thus, the four zones could also be justified as smoothing the way for reunification of the three 'lost territories' with the motherland.

In April 1984, the government, having positively evaluated the achievements of the SEZs, decided to open a further 14 cities forming a string of pearls along the extensive coastline – Beihai, Dalian, Fuzhou, Guangzhou, Lianyungang, Nantong, Ningbo. Qingdao, Qinhuangdao, Shanghai, Tianjin, Wenzhou, Yantai and Zhanjiang. They were granted special privileges generally, but a particularly favourable climate was to be created for investors in Economic and Technological Development Zones, which established in each city.

The original SEZ concept called for Shenzhen and Zhuhai to be multi-purpose zones fostering a wide range of industries, including agriculture, animal husbandry, residential housing, off-shore oil-field support and tourism. Xiamen and Shantou, meanwhile, were to develop processing for export and tourism as their major sources of income. In 1988, however, the government re-examined its overall coastal strategy under which the SEZs were to concentrate on high technology industries, while the 14 coastal cities were to focus on improving the quality of existing products and developing new ones for export, particularly in machine building and electrical goods. From then on, the rest of the coast was gradually opened up and encouraged to give priority to the developments of township enterprises and agriculture and to establish contact with foreign companies in the hope of building up business in processing for export. At the same time, Hainan island, in the far south facing Vietnam, was elevated to the country's 31st province and made the fifth SEZ.

The government's aim in creating the SEZs was not just to duplicate the 'processing zones' and 'free trade zones' found in other countries – although all three offer favourable tax and other conditions to investors and are export-oriented. Nor was it just a way of creating jobs and generating foreign exchange. Rather, the objective was to build from the ground up, completely modern cities that would be comprehensive economic development areas, with a high proportion of technology, knowledge and capital-intensive enterprises. From them, skills and technology would eventually flow to the rest of China. Production for export was the primary objective of the SEZs, but they were also seen as an important, if limited source of advanced products for the domestic market.

For investors, the attractions started with low wages and geographical location: all have temperate climates, excellent water transportation, and passenger airline and helicopter services. In addition, however, SEZs offered many economic pluses such as enterprise income tax and other taxes possibly being waived or reduced for several years after profits begin; export taxes waived; import duties and some business taxes waived on a wide variety of imports needed to establish or operate an enterprise; land available on favourable terms; after-tax profits allowed to be repatriated without penalty; reduced welfare contributions to cut labour costs; raw materials and equipment available at preferential prices based on charges to state-owned enterprises;

and, under some circumstances, special zone products allowed to be sold in the Chinese market. In addition, decentralization of decision-making power allowed local authorities to cut through much of the old bureaucratic red tape, with pragmatism and flexibility the watchwords.

The zones are generally hailed as great successes by the Chinese, even though they have been less attractive to foreign investors than expected[1] and have not become major centres of high technology. Until 1986, the SEZs ran a serious foreign trade deficit, but there was a distinct improvement in 1986 when the zones cut back investments in low technology and non-productive projects. Nevertheless in 1993, when the five SEZs were said to account for 15 per cent of China's foreign trade, imports exceeded exports by about $450 million (although the main contributor to this red ink is Hainan alone).

Shenzhen leads the way with a foreign trade volume three times that of Shantou. Most of its workers are employed by Hong Kong-based businessmen turning out toys, textiles, shoes, electronic goods and chemicals. In fact, in all four of the original SEZs the bulk of the investment has come from Chinese businessmen in Hong Kong, Macao and Taiwan partly escaping from rising labour costs at home. Other foreigners have often been deterred from investment by the lack of advanced infrastructure to match the ambitions of local and central authorities. Only in the mid-1990s was the problem finally being tackled, with local and foreign-borrowed money being poured into upgrading overstrained road and rail systems, port facilities and telecommunications networks. In Shenzhen, a new container port is being developed at Yantian, its first phase, costing $75 million, being owned and funded 70:30 by Hong Kong investors and a Shenzhen-owned company.

SHENZHEN

But how successful has Shenzhen been in achieving the government's long-term objectives, and where does it go from now? These were the questions examined in June 1993 when the city leadership met to discuss the SEZ's future. On the plus side, it was agreed that as a testing ground for reform, Shenzhen had been very successful. With price controls lifted and mandatory production goals abolished, the incompatibility of the planned and market economies became glaring and could only be resolved by strong measures in favour of the latter. Shenzhen pioneered the concept of letting state-owned enterprises go bankrupt if they failed to meet the grade in management efficiency or marketable products; the successful ones were given their head to adopt shareholding systems and even become limited liability companies listed on the local stock exchange. Only because Shenzhen demonstrated the success of the drastic break from the worst aspects of the socialist past, so the argument goes, was the rest of the country allowed to follow suit.

Nevertheless, it was also pointed out that '. . . Shenzhen was to be one of the points where the Chinese economy intersects with the world economy and a window from which the world could peer at China's new market-driven economy. [It] was to be the point of contact with dialogue with Hong Kong, as well as the mainland's vantage point in working with and competing against the British colony'. But, Hong Kong is now returning to the fold; all of China has become one large development zone, and many areas, led by Hainan and Shanghai, are more open and flexible. Shenzhen, it was admitted, had lost many of its advantages.[2]

Despite Shenzhen's ambitions to become China's main export and foreign-exchange earnings centre, and a base for advanced technology, banking and finance, up to the time of writing there was little sign that foreign investors viewed it as a good location for high-tech industries; most of the investment, as already noted, has been in simple assembly rather than original manufacturing or research and development.

And many of the industries already in the SEZ are packing their bags. Like migratory birds, many enterprises are now moving out of the supposed business paradise in search of better nesting spots. In mid-1993, the Shenzhen Municipal Government released what were described as 'incomplete statistics' which showed that about 40 per cent of the businesses set up in the special zone had either moved out or were planning to do so. Of the new enterprises established in the Shenzhen area in the 1990s, some 70 per cent were outside the zone.[3]

This migration is not necessarily unwelcome, illustrating the classic progression of any economy through agriculture to industry and on to services. (In recent years, real estate and finance have become the leading industries in Shenzhen.) In the past, the city was the 'factory' and Hong Kong 'the shop', but many local officials wanted it to become the shop as well, with some of the factories being moved elsewhere.

Many of the departing managers complained that '. . . work efficiency is falling and preferential policies are now fewer in Shenzhen compared with some inland cities. Business had become more difficult, they said. For instance, the procedures for the establishment of a new project, which needs only one day in Huizhou and three days in Pudong [Shanghai] usually take more than half a year in Shenzhen. As various development zones are flourishing throughout China [. . . .] many companies feel they have lagged behind and are not sure if Shenzhen is capable of taking the lead in the economic development of the country. With increased cost of labour and materials in Shenzhen, many enterprises have taken steps to seek locations with lower production costs. Cities around Shenzhen, such as Bao'an, Dongguan, Huizhou, and Zhongshan, in fact, can provide cheaper labour, water, power, transportation and land'.[4]

A survey of those who had chosen to leave Shenzhen in 1993 found that nearly half said their production and operating costs would be much lower by relocation, 35 per cent cited more flexible government policies or more efficient bureaucracies elsewhere. When asked 'What is your view of Shenzhen's investment environment?' 60 per cent said there were too many hindrances and efficiency was often low, 30 per cent said the city was too densely populated and its basic infrastructure – especially energy and transportation – was inadequate; in addition, other parts of the country offered a larger potential market and a greater return on real-estate investments. Another problem cited was that because of intense competition among enterprises in a similar trade, the market in Shenzhen had become smaller and profits lower.

The current favourite location is Bao'an, a new district set up in 1993 with jurisdiction over eight towns and one large farm, located west of the SEZ and containing the local international airport as well as being traversed by two expressways linking Shenzhen with the provincial capital Guangzhou. It is supposed to concentrate on the production of automobiles, motorcycles, bicycles, extra-thin fibre, state-of-the-art compact-disc players, high-class glazed tiles and vegetable and fruit-juice processing.

The old industrial buildings and sites being left behind by the exodus are getting a new lease of life as shops, restaurants, financial businesses and real-estate projects. Dasheng Electronics Industrial Company, for instance, turned its old building into a large restaurant, and also planned to build a high-rise shopping centre on the site. Huafa Electronics Industrial Company, meanwhile, planned to turn its old work-site into a hotel after moving to the suburbs.

Such plans, however, may run counter to Shenzhen's desire to finally achieve some semblance of order after a decade of disorganized, often chaotic development, which has siphoned off investment funds for potential duplicative building programmes. For example, of the 1,700 investment plans approved in 1993 totalling almost $6 billion, more than a third went into construction programmes – and half the amount was for building more office blocks, commercial residential buildings and hotels.

Much of this development was described as irrational by one senior planning official. Qun Ti, Director of the Investment Planning Division under the Shenzhen Planning Bureau, announced that, in future, the city would strictly control the scale of capital investment, limiting the annual amount spent to no more than $2.25 billion; strictly control the erection of commercial buildings and high-rise buildings, '. . . avoiding construction of similar tertiary industry programmes and restrict the construction of hotels'; tighter surveillance of bank loans to ensure that demand for key construction programmes is met and priority given to development of transport, communications and energy facilities.[5] Both Shenzhen and Zhuhai felt the pinch induced by the central government's tightening of monetary policy in mid-1993 to try and cool down the overheated economy – resulting in a significant number of idle, half-developed, building sites.

XIAMEN

Up to the mid-1970s, at the approach of important national holidays, an official announcement was routinely heard on radio that the mainland would suspend shelling the Taiwanese-held islands of Jinmen (Quemoy) and Matsu. Although the mutual shelling eventually tapered off into a war of words, the military tension blocked development of Xiamen (formerly Amoy), a city less than 10 miles from Jinmen, which Western visitors as recently as 1985 recall as a dead city with no street lights and few productive industries.

In fact, all of Fujian Province opposite Taiwan was turned into a front line preparing for a possible invasion of nationalist troops seeking to retake the mainland. Partly as a result, the province, with a population of 30 million, was one of China's poorest areas. However, since China shifted the focus to economic reform, the artillery exchanges have been replaced by a growing flow of business across the Taiwan Straits. This has benefited Xiamen immensely. It has evolved from a closed frontier city into an increasingly internationalized economy since being designated an SEZ. The investment spree gathered particular momentum after the central government in 1989 and 1992 approved three areas outside the city proper to be zones specifically targeted at Taiwanese investors.[6]

In 1992, Xiamen's per capita GDP had grown more than fivefold from a decade before and was three times greater than the national average. By the end of March 1993, the city had approved 1,754 foreign-invested enterprises with a capital commitment of $5.7 billion. Out of this, Taiwan business had launched 717 projects involving $1.8 billion in investment, concentrated in electronics, engineering and petrochemicals. However, at least half of the investment has come from Hong Kong and Macao, while Chinese investors from Southeast Asia also have established an important niche. Around 40 per cent of the city's industrial output is sold overseas. Exports have increased 20-fold since 1980. Nine of the city's foreign trade enterprises ranked among China's top 500 enterprises.

According to Wu Jie, Director of the local Foreign Investment Office, Xiamen had decided to shift its focus to larger overseas companies in a bid to establish more capital and technology-intensive businesses, and hoped to steer foreign businessmen into the development of transportation, port construction, plane and ship repair, and large tourist facilities.

Despite official optimistic pronouncements, however, Xiamen has had to fight hard to establish its credibility as an SEZ. The investment environment has often been compared somewhat unfavourably with its rivals in neighbouring Guangdong Province. In 1991, the city suffered considerable embarrassment when foreign investors constructing a new hotel taped a meeting at which land officials sought and accepted bribes. Since then, the city's conservative mayor has been replaced and officials have endeavoured to improve their image. In March 1993, it was announced that the zone's constituent regions would be granted greater autonomy to approve foreign investment. Much is also being made of infrastructure development programmes underway or planned which, it is claimed, will overcome most of the city's existing deficiencies in port facilities, road and rail links, and telecommunications. And, with the direct passenger traffic now allowed between the mainland and Taiwan (the Beijing government has designated Xiamen, Shantou and Shanghai as the official entry/exit points), the pot of gold at the end of the investment rainbow may finally be in sight.

Until 1993, Xiamen port had only four berths capable of handling primarily coastal freighters up to 10,000 tons capacity, along with one container dock. This was a serious bottleneck, resulting in a significant portion of the city's exports being transhipped through Hong Kong. At the time of writing, a new 30,000-ton freighter wharf had been commissioned, and three further large berths for coal, grain and general use were slated for completion by the middle of 1994 with the help of World Bank loans. Funding also came from a Hong Kong company which become the first foreigner to invest in Chinese port ownership, rather than management, with an 80 per cent stake in one of the new berths. Through these developments it was claimed that by the end of 1994 the port's annual handling capacity would have increased from 6 million to 9.5 million tons, and container capacity quadrupled to 400,000 standard units. Another Hong Kong company has become the first foreigner to invest in Chinese port ownership, rather than management, with an 80 per cent stake in a berth.

Road haulage is constrained by a poor highway network, typified by the fact that it usually takes twice as long to drive to the adjacent Shantou SEZ in Guangdong as it does from Shantou to Hong Kong, which is almost twice the distance. A $70 million upgrading of roads within Xiamen began in early 1993 for completion by the end of 1994. Barring delays, a new expressway will be opened to the provincial capital Fuzhou during 1995, which should reduce travelling time from the present gruelling six-and-a-half hours by car to about one hour. A contract was exchanged in early 1993 for a new 25-mile highway to the inland city of Zhangzhou, but at the time of writing the project was in doubt as the foreign investor involved was under investigation by Hong Kong securities officials.

Rail links are also inadequate, and electrification of existing lines has done little to improve travelling times. This should change, however, with the construction of a Japanese-style 'bullet train' link between Xiamen and Fuzhou, with construction costs estimated in excess of $2.1 billion. The Japanese are supposed to provide 70 per cent of the finance plus all the technology for the 170-mile line which the trains will cover in just over one hour. Air links have been established with Hong Kong, Manila, Singapore, Penang, Kuala Lumpur and Jakarta and a $45.7 million three-year expansion of the airport got underway in 1993 aimed at lifting passenger capacity to five million from the predicted two million in 1993. The runway is also being extended to handle Boeing 747s.

Most of the money for infrastructure development has been provided by the central and local governments, apart from World Bank assistance for port expansion, a low-interest loan from Kuwait for the airport improvement, and Japanese government loans for new telephone equipment. But central government funding is becoming more difficult to obtain, mainly because, as discussed in Chapter Two, Beijing has to bail out loss-making state industries leading to a budget deficit. Xiamen, therefore, is also having to compete for funding and low-cost loans with other coastal areas, especially the Pudong development in Shanghai – to be discussed later. Xiamen officials conceded they would increasingly have to seek new sources of funds. Following the example set by Guangdong, where Hong Kong businessmen have built roads and power stations, investors from the colony took a 30 per cent stake in a new 1.2m KW coal-fired power station near Xiamen. Taiwanese investors, who have language and often family ties with Fujian, prefer to invest in processing industries rather than infrastructure projects, which are generally seen as too risky because of Taiwan's continuing political rift with the mainland and the lack of investor protection agreements between the two sides.

Xiamen has tried to overcome its perceived weaknesses

compared to the other SEZs by offering more favourable terms for foreign investors and stressing that start-up costs remain significantly lower than elsewhere and there is a large pool of semi-skilled workers due to a liberal policy on the importation of labour from other parts of China. But it remains weak on labour for high-tech enterprises. But the city is battling with an image problem. Western firms in particular have not yet perceived any compelling reason for locating in Xiamen, which boasts no specific technical expertise and little in the way of local raw-material sourcing.

Some of its difficulties are encapsulated within half-an-hour's drive from the city where one of the largest infrastructure developments on the mainland's eastern seaboard is taking shape. Haicang, which planners estimate will cost $885 million to complete, is being hailed as China's 'ethylene city', with plans for deep-water berths to unload oil and for factories to convert it into a host of downstream plastics and chemicals. Despite considerable construction activity, Haicang had at the time of writing not signed up any of the foreign petrochemical companies it was designed to attract. Xie Tingmu, a Haicang official, was confident foreign investors would eventually be knocking on his door – but only when the infrastructure is ready. Haicang neatly illustrates the difficulties faced by China in coordinating rapid economic coastal growth with the limitations of the infrastructure. While Haicang runs before it can walk, the area's ports, roads and telecommunications limp along behind, unable to keep pace with double-digit growth.

SHANTOU

This city, with a 1993 population of about 800,000 lies close to the border between Guangdong and Fujian and is the ancestral home of many of the Chinese who now make their home in Hong Kong, Singapore, Malaysia, Indonesia, Thailand and the Philippines. Foreign investment has come largely from this source, notably from Hong Kong.

The zone itself covers 33 square miles and is divided into two areas of approximately equal size – Lunghu which borders the eastern edge of the city proper and Guanggao a little further out, the former designated for light industry, the latter for heavy industry, electrical power and perhaps petrochemicals. Major industries at the end of 1988 included agriculture and food processing (export of high-quality foodstuffs such as prawns, shrimps and eels), textiles, and arts and crafts.

Shantou boasts it can compete with Shenzhen and the other zones on the basis of costs and on the flexibility of its bureaucracy. Factory rents are a third of Shenzhen's and labour costs are also lower. It appears to be succeeding and boasts a bewildering array of products, ranging from video equipment to perfume.

The current location of Shantou was silted up from the sea about 450 years ago. Commerce gradually developed and in the nineteenth century it was designated one of the 'treaty ports' open to overseas trade. It became an industrial and trade centre during the early 1930s. In 1933, the city's seaport handling capacity ranked third in the country after Shanghai and Guangzhou. But the local economy plunged and trade withered in 1938 when Japanese troops occupied the city. The Chaozhu-Shantou railway, China's first privately-run line, was dismantled, never to be restored, and thousands of residents were forced to move to the hinterland. Although Shantou was resuscitated into east Guangdong's political, economic and cultural centre after the founding of the People's Republic, it failed to see substantial development before the 1980s because of insufficient investment.

In 1981, the central government allocated a small piece of land to establish a SEZ, hoping to take advantage of the city's extensive overseas ties to boost local development (it is estimated that for every 10 Chinese living abroad, one is from Shantou). The SEZ was expanded to cover the whole urban area in November 1991. Apart from investing heavily, overseas Chinese have responded by donating $300 million since 1979 to develop public facilities, including a local university.

Shantou is promoting the merits of Nan'ao Island, where it has spent over $1000 million on infrastructure construction to turn it into a 'commercial and tourist paradise' where 'more favourable and flexible policies will be adopted'. The government sold use rights of 1,330 hectares of land to a Taiwan businessman for $180 million, and also contracted the construction of a five-mile bridge connecting the island with the city to another Taiwan company.

A railway and a motorway to connect Shantou with Guangzhou were due for completion in 1995. But the city has yet to solve the biggest problem – its traffic, among the worst in China. The streets are narrow and packed with automobiles or all sorts, along with tens of thousands of motorcycles, causing some residents to complain that the deafening din during the rush-hour had turned the downtown area into '. . . a video-game battlefield. Motorists change lanes wantonly, blow horns when signs forbid them to do so, and turn a blind eye to traffic lights'.

HAINAN

The Chinese government has said it wants to turn Hainan Island into a 'second Hong Kong', although this is not an attempt to copy the territory's political system, but only to introduce the sort of effective business practices which made the British colony such a regional economic powerhouse. Hainan, in fact, has ambitions to challenge Guangdong as the leader in China's go-go economics.

'The seven million Hainanese supposedly generate 80 per cent of their output from agriculture. But the 400,000 residents of Haikou [the provincial capital] have little memory of the pastoral life. The streets are lined with shops chock-full of the good things that the modern world has to offer, many of them imported from Japan. At 9 o'clock on a Sunday evening, you have to fight your way through the crowds sizing up the Christian Dior and Yves Saint Laurent displays in the hard-currency shop. They are not just window shopping. A nice non-designer blouse can cost 200 Yuan, roughly a month's salary for a secretary. Foreign bosses report that their secretaries nonchalantly turn up in such gear all the time. Those who tire of shopping can refresh themselves in Haikou's plentiful karaoke bars, which become hard to squeeze into within an hour after they open. The customers do not arrive on foot. The main roads boast perpetual traffic jams. It is said 300 new Mercedes cars prowl Haikou's streets.'[7]

Much of Hainan's wealth until now has come from property and finance, although this has proved a rather precarious base. In early 1992, the provincial government opened stock market trading in four property companies and one import-processing firm. The island did not have central government permission for this and the market was quickly closed. But under-the-counter deals continued.

'Frustrated would-be investors can always turn to the property market. Nobody any longer keeps track of the number of 30- and

40-storey office buildings being put up by round-the-clock construction crews. Luxury flats and villas are being built at a similar pace. One banker says the cost of land for office buildings has more than doubled in the past year. The land on one prime site, bought four years ago for 200 Yuan a square metre, is now worth around 2,500 Yuan a square metre.'[8]

Billions of pounds, including a high percentage from foreign investors, has been poured into creating an advanced infrastructure in transportation, cargo handling, telecommunications and electric power-generating capacity. The island's main airport in Haikou is now the country's seventh largest in handling capacity, with international links to Hong Kong and Southeast Asian capitals. Other incentives include a very modest 15 per cent corporate tax rate and virtual freedom to import, especially if the things brought in are to for reprocessing as exports. But, as yet, many of the towering office blocks remain unfilled, and the new infrastructure hardly tapped by industrial users.

The main hope for takeoff rests with Yangpu, a derelict piece of land on the north-western tip of the island, where a 20 square mile development zone has been carved out around a natural deep ocean harbour. The free trade bonded area for export-oriented advanced industries is surrounded by rich deposits of natural gas and oil, salt and titanium suitable for development of a petrochemical industry, brown coal, oil shale, fine quality quartz sand and limestone, which can be exploited for energy and building materials industries. The island produces 300,000 tons of iron ore per year from reserves estimated at 400 million tons. It is also rich in tropical produce such as rubber, coconuts, pepper, coffee, cocoa, tea, pineapples, sugar cane etc. It is the largest producer of natural rubber in China, accounting for more than 70 per cent of total production. The Yangpu peninsula, however, is considered unsuitable for any form of agriculture, hence its allocation for industrial use.

In 1988, the Hong Kong subsidiary of one of Japan's biggest construction companies, Kumagaya Gumi, signed a contract with Hainan to lease the development zone for 70 years. It then put together a development enterprise group comprising major enterprises from Japan, South Korea and Hong Kong to raise the billions of dollars needed to develop the site. This was followed by a programme of developing the site for a mix of light, heavy and tertiary industries which by the time it is completed early in the next century will have transformed an agricultural area with a population of only 26,000 into an advanced urban centre of at least 250,000 people.

Hainan officials stressed that Yangpu was different from the other SEZs. Elsewhere, creation of the infrastructure required a major injection of state funds. At Yangpu, the land-use rights have been leased out to foreign businessmen who then have to create the infrastructure with their own funds. When this is completed, the state will invest through the development of its own industries.

The project ran into early trouble when certain sectors, with some media backing, began to grumble that it was an infringement of China's sovereignty. But Deng Xiaoping quickly silenced the opposition by declaring that 'this rare chance to develop Yangpu should not be delayed'. In May 1990, Party Secretary General Jiang Zemin toured Hainan and announced: 'The introduction of foreign capital to develop land is purely a commercial action. We exercise control over administration of justice and public security there; it will not infringe upon China's sovereignty.' The Chinese media quickly fell into line and began eulogizing the Yangpu development as the way ahead.

ZHUHAI

Zhuhai, bordering on the old Portuguese colony of Macao, is the smallest of the SEZs and has commanded the least attention. It has good port facilities capable of handling 30,000 ton vessels, but its land links are far from perfect. Road links to Guangzhou, 88 miles away, are difficult, although these problems should eventually be overcome when the New Pearl River expressway reaches Macao.

The zone was originally intended to be the service centre for an offshore oil industry, but the failure to find sufficient oil meant this role never materialized. It has, however, succeeded in developing a thriving trade in agricultural produce and has attracted some light industrial projects to ensure that the SEZ has not been a failure.

ECONOMIC AND TECHNOLOGICAL DEVELOPMENT ZONES

As already mentioned, the central government, having favourably assessed the performance of the four pioneering SEZs, decided to open up further areas of the country to foreign investment through the creation of Economic and Technological Development Zones (ETDZ), which have become known as the '14 coastal cities'. Most of them had a history of commerce and trade and many were the old treaty ports established in the nineteenth century as a persistent West knocked on the door of isolationist Imperial China. The rationale for the establishment of the ETDZs was that the cities involved enjoyed a number of advantages, including a more skilled and better educated work-force, better communications, better industrial infrastructure and a tradition of commerce. Premier Li Peng told the NPC in 1988 that the coastal areas must speed up the growth of an export-oriented economy. Their prosperity will stimulate the economic growth of the whole country.'

Originally, the idea was that the interior would supply raw materials and semi-finished products to the coastal areas for processing and export. But when the inland provinces objected strongly, saying this smacked of old-style colonialism, the policy was modified to allow the interior to become master of its own industrial fate. The coastal areas, meanwhile (according to Li Peng) would make full use of '. . . their abundant and low-cost labour resources, carry out a policy of importing raw or semi-finished materials and exporting finished goods, encourage both labour-intensive and labour/technology-intensive processing for export and participate in international exchange.'[9]

How the cities carried out this task will be considered mainly by looking at the experiences of the most famous cities involved – Guangzhou (Canton), Shanghai, Tianjin and Dalian. The remaining cities will be dealt with more briefly in order to avoid needless repetition.

GUANGZHOU

Guangzhou is the undisputed political, economic and cultural capital of Southeast China. It is a vibrant, fun-loving city as different from austere Beijing as chalk is to cheese. Streets are jammed with horn-blowing vehicles from dawn until long after midnight, and lined with neon-decorated shops, glitzy restaurants, karaoke clubs and bars. All are filled with businessmen and women preoccupied, it would seem, with seeking new ways of making money. Situated at the head of the Pearl River Delta (and forming a triangle with Hong Kong and Macao), the port city has a long trading history since the first European merchant adventurers – the Portuguese followed by the British – landed there centuries ago. Until the mid-nineteenth century, it was the only Chinese port permitted by imperial decree to trade with the foreign 'barbarians'. For the Manchu emperors, this proved to be a mistake. Finding it hard to provide the silver bullion needed to buy much-desired Chinese silk and tea, the British resorted to payment in opium, grown in its Indian colony of Bengal. That led to the first Opium War and the ceding of Hong Kong to Queen Victoria. Guangzhou then came under strong British and, to a lesser extent, French influence until the Japanese occupation during the Second World War and the subsequent Communist liberation in 1949.

During the worst years of Maoist rule, when China was generally closed to outside influences, Guangzhou retained its old imperial role as a window on the world – especially through its twice-yearly trade fair. Since the open door policy was announced, it has once again fallen under the sway of Hong Kong and grown rich on the investment and processing work from the colony through a strong network of family connections that have survived the imposition of artificial political boundaries. The city has a broad industrial base, with particular strength in the light-industrial sector, including textiles, electronics, pharmaceuticals and food processing, and is also a major centre for oil exploration in the South China Sea. Its ETDZ is located in the historic Huangpu (Whampoa) district about 20 miles downstream on the Pearl River from the city centre, where new port facilities have been built with World Bank assistance. The ETDZ has been among the most successful of its kind as a result of substantial investment, notably from Hong Kong, centred on food processing, canning, textiles and the assembly of electronic components.

Guangzhou is the capital of Guangdong Province, China's richest thanks to the additional presence of three of the SEZs, which has ambitions to become Asia's fifth 'little dragon' (the nickname given to Hong Kong, Taiwan, Singapore and South Korea because of their explosive economic growth in recent years). The province is allowing more foreign banks to set up offices and subsidiaries and encouraging its own financial institutions to explore overseas business aggressively, with the aim of attracting another $140 billion in foreign investment by the end of the first decade of the twenty-first century.

SHANGHAI

It is fitting that Shanghai is now being given a larger role in the economic reform process. History weighs heavily on the second biggest city in China, with a population of more than 13 million, and its gateway to the world in the past two centuries. Westerners and Chinese were drawn to the cosmopolitan environment that bred wealth in the nineteenth and early twentieth centuries. By the end of the 1940s, Shanghai, with approximately one per cent of the national population, contributed a fifth of industrial output and handled two-thirds of the foreign trade.[10] It was also Asia's financial centre, dwarfing Tokyo and Hong Kong.

The liberation in 1949 cost it dearly. The Communists forced one million skilled Shanghaiese into exile in remote parts of the country, while hundreds of thousands fled abroad, mainly to Hong Kong and Taiwan, where, ironically, their financial and business expertise helped the two places become economic powerhouses on which mainland China now depends heavily for its revival. Until the mid-1980s, Shanghai's municipal government was required to hand over 90 per cent of its revenues to the central government, and even though there has been some relaxation since, it still contributes about one-sixth of the state revenues. When the open-door policy was introduced, Shanghai fell far behind Guangdong.

Shanghai's original success was based on light industries, but these were taken away when the Communists took power. By 1979, heavy industry accounted for half its industrial output, and most of it is state-owned (an estimated 940 large and medium-sized enterprises). As a result, Shanghai was crippled by all the appalling inefficiencies of the public sector outlined in chapter two (one example was the local state-run textile industry, the biggest hard currency earner at the time, which was driven to the verge of bankruptcy by the success of new township enterprises in neighbouring Jiangsu and Zhejiang).

The city also had to bear a heavy political burden. because of its strong capitalist traditions and pervasive foreign influence before

1949, it was singled out for particularly nasty treatment during the Cultural Revolution nightmare. It was an important power base for the infamous 'Gang of Four' – one of its members, Wang Hongwen, being made Mayor and ensuring that all his ultra-Maoist henchmen were inserted into all the key bureaucratic positions. It took some time to eradicate these influences, but the city's fortunes began to revive when first Jiang Zemin and then Zhu Rongji headed the local administration before moving on to greater things at the centre. With an easing of the heavy hand of central government and a massive inflow of foreign investment, plus a revival of its old financial role, the Shanghai is regaining some of its lost glory.

The signs are there for all to see. For more than a century, Shanghai was the commercial hub and a beacon for traders. In 1992, consumer retail sales in the city reached $8.7 billion, top in the nation. Shoppers flock to Nanjing Street, which claims an average daily flow of some 1.5 million people. Industrial output in 1992 exceeded $42 billion. Some of China's biggest domestic and foreign-invested firms are located here – household names such as the Baoshan Iron and Steel Complex, Shanghai Petrochemicals, Shanghai Volkswagen Automobile Company, Shanghai Bell Telephone Equipment Manufacturing, Yaohua Pilkington Glass. Its best known products have included cotton, silks, carpets, bicycles and sewing machines, but it has diversified into chemicals, petrochemicals, metal products and shipbuilding. Local shipyards have full order books from overseas; the locally-built MD83 passenger aircraft is being exported to the United States from where its design originated; Shanghai-made satellites orbit the earth, carried aloft by Shanghai-made rockets. Meanwhile, the famous Bund overlooking the Huangpu River has been restored to its former glory and is once again crammed with foreign banks and other financial institutions – names like Chase Manhattan, Citibank, Hong and Shanghai, Standard Chartered, Bank L'Indochine, Mitsui, Sumitomo.

Three economic and technological development zones were established in the 1980s after Shanghai got the green light for a re-opening to the outside world. Processing industries were allocated to the Minhang zone; the Hongqiao zone focused on finance and foreign trade, and was a pioneer in implementing the land rights transfer scheme; Caohejing, meanwhile, became the base for high-tech development, testing, production, operation, training and service.

Moving into the 1990s, attention switched to development of the Pudong New Area, a new town of more than one million people being developed on partly-reclaimed land across the Huangpu River (the Yangtse's final tributary on which the port is built) from the main city area, and bigger than the original four SEZs put together. Existing plans for its development indicate that the process could take up to 30 years and cost in excess of $10 billion. Premier Li Peng described Pudong as 'the focus of China's efforts to attract foreign investment'. China's aim is to create a high-tech manufacturing base as well as a strong service sector, especially banking and other financial services. In order to make it more attractive to outsiders, foreign businesses are being allowed to open department stores for the first time and foreign banks were permitted to set up branches, as opposed to the more restricted 'representative offices' previously allowed, with their activities covering the whole of Shanghai. A number of banks have taken advantage of this relaxation, while the Japanese supermarket chain Yaohan and upmarket department store Isetan have broken new ground with a Pudong store in a joint venture with local interests. By the middle of 1993 more than 1000 foreign-funded projects with a total investment exceeding $4 billion had been approved, most in the high-tech sector and involve microelectronics, chemicals, medicines. aviation, telecommunications, precision and measuring instruments, micro-biology and automobile parts. But they have been swamped by Chinese firms who have flocked in from even the most remote areas of the interior to take advantage of the preferential treatment on offer. Pudong wants to double the number of foreign-funded projects by 1995.

Looking at the queue of potential tenants, Huang Qifan, the area's administrative vice-director anticipates that Shanghai in general and Pudong in particular will have attracted 100,000 trade-related companies by the end of the century, creating a '. . . vast market of securities, future trading, call loans, retail and wholesale trading and gold and foreign exchange'. By 1995, there will be five major futures markets operating, covering grain, coal, cotton, crude oil and other materials, as well as country's largest stock exchange.[11]

In 1991, the city was given greater powers to approve projects and raise funds without central government approval, an important step away from the rigidity of central planning. During the rest of the current decade, domestic and overseas funding will be sought for five development zones in Pudong covering mainly industrial uses, export processing, transit trade, services including banking, real estate, information and consultancy, and science and education, high technology and new industries.

To help finance the development, Shanghai set itself a target of raising around half a billion pounds annually through the issue of Pudong construction bonds, and selling off shares in state-run companies on domestic and overseas markets. To help revive the enterprises, they have been given permission to handle their own imports and exports, rather than having to work through centralised agencies as before.

Among the areas being developed is the Jinqiao export processing zone, within which is the Fujita Industrial Zone being developed with Japanese capital and aimed specifically at Japanese manufacturing companies. The 100-hectare project is being jointly developed by the Fujita Corporation of Japan and the Jinqiao administration for completion by the end of 1995. Top priority is being given to attracting investors in fields such as industrial robotics, optical fibre telecommunications, genetic engineering, facsimile machines and office automation equipment.

Within Pudong, Jinqiao is complemented by the Waigaoqiao Free Trade Zone, which has been so successful in attracting industry that the Shanghai authorities had to bring forward the second phase of development by a couple of years and almost double the area of land being requisitioned for development. A third prong is the development of the Zhangjiang advanced technology zone, which is supposed to concentrate on information processing, biotechnology, new materials, space and aeronautics technology and marine oil and gas production – although the top priority will be trying to create a domestic computer industry to rival that of Japan. Finally, there is the Lujiazui banking and trade area, where architects from Britain, France, Italy, Japan and China were invited to design separate blueprints which were later combined to form a skyscraper complex that would not look out of place in New York or Hong Kong. By 1995, more than 100 high-rise buildings (at least 30 storeys) are supposed to be open for business. A 1,300- foot television tower was due to be completed and operating by May 1994.

Pudong has to be seen as part of a broad Chinese strategy which calls for massive economic development all along the Yangtse River which travels nearly 3,500 miles from the Tibetan plateau before reaching the sea near Shanghai. Some officials use an archery analogy, with the coastal region around Shanghai as the bow and the Yangtse as the arrow aiming into the heart of some of the most heavily populated areas of China; others refer to Shanghai as the 'dragon's head', conveying the idea of goods and services funnelling through Shanghai to, and from, the rest of the world. The Yangtse valley holds nearly 15 per cent of the entire population and currently provides about 40 per cent of the country's total output value. But it has been lagging behind because of central government attention on the coastal development zones. The giant Japanese 'sogo shosha' (trading firms) have not been slow to see the potential and three of the biggest, C.Itoh and Co., Mitsui and Marubeni Corporation have established wholly-owned companies to handle entrepot trade an d import and export business. This will become increasingly important as more modern container ports are developed along the Yangtse and the river developed to handle larger cargo ships. (To be discussed in more detail in the next chapter.)

TIANJIN

Shanghai's desire to regain its position as the pearl of the Orient is not going unchallenged. Further up the coast, Tianjin, known as the 'gateway to Beijing' with a population of nine million, is trying to take advantage of its geographical location to enhance its role as a communications hub linking Northeast Asia and Europe and the rest of the world. It has ambitions to become the first SEZ in North China as well as its biggest international commodities transfer centre. It has also been fiercely lobbying the central government to become the third stock exchange after Shanghai and Shenzhen by playing on its role as an international port. As a preliminary, it set up a securities trading centre dealing in treasury bonds and funds, and 22 local firms were a llowed to experiment with a shareholding system (largely internal, although one chemical products manufacturer has managed to be listed on the domestic and Hong Kong stock exchanges).

In 1991, the city government launched a 10-year programme to upgrade 100 existing enterprises through adoption of new technology, merging or closing down factories that do not make the grade. It is also developing a comprehensive petrochemical and chemical industries base, building an iron and steel complex, a seamless steel pipe plant and moving towards becoming a major light-duty truck and compact car producer (target: 300,000 trucks annually by 1995). Other key industries to be developed include ethylene, polyester, automated telephone systems, video-recorder manufacturing, copper metallurgy, chemical fertiliser plants and cement.

Tianjin has played up its advantages of 'low taxes, cheap land and cheap labour' to attract investment to the Tanggu Economic and Technological Zone set up on saline-alkaline land unsuitable for farming. By mid-1993, 1,300 Sino-foreign joint ventures had been set up with total investment of over $2 billion, and had been joined by more than a thousand Chinese firms. The target now is attract $2.5 billion in additional funds by the year 2000. The biggest effort has gone into persuading big corporate names from Japan, Taiwan and South Korea to put their money into the city to create the so-called Bohai Economic Rim [see next chapter], but Tianjin has also been working hard to establish joint ventures with EC members to ship semi-finished products back via a rail 'bridge' that now links the eastern Chinese coast with Western Europe. At present, half of the foreign investment has come from Hong Kong, and has largely gone into light and heavy industry. But the balance is shifting towards more investment in the service sector, such as transport, finance, consulting services, tourism and trade.

Befitting its proximity, South Korea is emerging as an important player in Tianjin's future. In early 1992, the Seoul government announced plans to build an industrial park in the city for small Korean companies involved in such labour-intensive industries as textiles and electronics. This industrial park is expected to house 100 companies eventually. Tianjin is currently the site of the single largest corporate investment by a Korean company in China so far – a 50/50 joint venture between Samsung Electronics and Tianjin Telecommunications and Broadcasting producing video cassette recorders and components, with a target of 600,000 machines a year by 1997. meanwhile, Taiwanese entrepreneurs have been offered their own exclusive section of Tanggu, with the emphasis on light industries.

Since the economic reform programme began, Tianjin claims to have spent more than $5.2 billion on city planning and infrastructure development. As a result, traffic congestion is rare and access to Beijing and other nearby cities is easy via a network of expressways. In 1990, the port opened China's first international sea-land container terminal, which remains the country's largest. More berths are being added to the original seven to boost handling capacity from 400,000 to 700,000 standard containers by the end of 1995. Regular shipping services link it with 70 ports around the world. Tianjin Harbour Container Company is also pioneering container transfer stations in the inland provinces to help the landlocked areas expand their foreign trade. Stations have been opened in Beijing, Taiyuan in Shanxi Province, Zhengzhou in Henan Province and Yinchuan in Ningxia Hui Autonomous Region, where the goods are loaded into containers, and all the paperwork handled, before being shipped by road or rail to the port and waiting ships. Other areas to be targeted include Inner Mongolia, Shandong, Sichuan, Shaanxi, and Heilongjiang Provinces.

DALIAN

Dalian, at the tip of the Liaodong Peninsula , was once known as Port Arthur and until 1945 was part of Japanese-colonized Manchuria and had a Japanese population of some 300,000. Many of the older generation speak Japanese because they were forced to do so at school, but the city's university continues to produce more graduates in the language than anywhere else in China. The city of some five million people is often referred to as 'Little Japan' because of a strong concentration of Japanese industry – around 100 currently economically active. But with the Japanese now showing more interest in developments further south, such as Shanghai's Pudong zone, Dalian's international profile is changing. The South Koreans are moving in, while Hong Kong investors have established more than 1000 firms and are showing increasing interest in developing the city's infrastructure.

Dalian's opening to the outside world began at the turn of the century after the Japanese humbled Tsarist Russia in a brief land and sea war. Its second opening occurred in 1945 under the terms of the Yalta Agreement at the end of the Second World War. Now, it is enjoying a third flowering of international interest, playing on its advantages as the only major ice-free port in the area and the second largest harbour in China after Shanghai. City authorities believe that Dalian must play to its strengths by following Hong Kong's example in developing entrepot trade based on its ports – which, in turn, will help open up the whole of the relatively backward Northeast region (in the process stemming the flow of cash and young talent which is heading south and thus widening the economic gap between the two). The old port can handle 60 million tonnes a year, but a new port at Dayao Bay has added a further potential 100 million tonnes of capacity. A new international airport was opened in the 1980s; there are good rail links with Beijing and Harbin and there is a modern highway linking the port with the provincial capital of Shenyang.

The city's development, however, faces two major handicaps. First, as is the case throughout the Northeast, there is a predominance of old and money-losing state firms, whose continued debts contribute heavily to a chronic deficit in city finances. There are many pivotal firms, such as Dalian Shipyard, Dalian Steel Works and Dalian Locomotive Plant, which are crying out for more independence and a say in their production and management. In the foreign sector, meanwhile, most of the firms are processors whose products are largely exported. But these have exacerbated the second major problem for Dalian – a water shortage. As a result, the city authorities have decided to readjust the industrial balance to give more emphasis to the service sector – which, it is hoped, will contribute 45 per cent of GDP by the end of the century.

OTHER CITIES

In the final section of this chapter, I would like to look briefly at some of the other cities involved in the coastal opening.

Qingdao (formerly Tsingtao) is well known among beer drinkers for its local tipple first developed by the Germans, who took over a small village at the beginning of this century and built the present attractive city with a splendid harbour (ranked fourth nation-wide in the amount of cargo it handles). Sea breezes and cold currents make the city a desirable refuge during the baking summer heat in North China. The ETDZ was established on Huangdao Island in 1985 and by the end of 1992 had attracted 650 firms, about a fifth of them foreign. Part of the island is allocated to a high-tech industrial estate designed to attract research institutes, and by June 1993, 160 firms had moved in. Apart from beer, Qingdao's traditional industrial mainstay has been textiles. But diversification has brought in heavier industries such as petrochemicals, rubber and shipbuilding. Much of the industry has been shifted out of the old city because of growing pollution and transportation bottlenecks. A necklace of small industrial districts have been set up along the coastline, all engaged in cut-throat competition for overseas funds. There has been a major construction boom, especially in new housing funded largely by foreign funds (primarily from Hong Kong). There is a very strong South Korean business presence in Qingdao – more than 130 firms representing about one-third of Korean's entire investment in China.[12]

From Qingdao, there are good road and rail links with Yantai, a popular tourist resort on the tip of the Jiaodong Peninsula in Shandong Province, which has established an ETDZ about six miles from the city with an adjacent deepwater harbour. Its main industries are food processing, machinery, chemicals, textiles and building materials.

In the same general area is Qinhuangdao, famous as the place where the Great Wall runs down from the mountains to its northern terminus at the Bohai Sea, as well as the site of the former military airport from which then defence minister Lin Baio tried to flee to the Soviet Union after his alleged failed coup attempt in September 1971 (only to die when the plane crashed, apparently after running out of a fuel, in Mongolia). Nearby is Beihaide, the summer resort where the Chinese leadership relaxes when the heat becomes too oppressive in Beijing. The port is China's third busiest, handling much of the coal and oil on which the economy of adjacent areas is built, and as a result it has concentrated its efforts in attracting foreign investment primarily on import-export trade-related ventures, financial services and shipping. Rail links with the interior and with Beijing and Tianjin are excellent.

Ningbo, the second largest city in Zhejiang Province lying across Hanzhou Bay from Shanghai, claims as its most famous former citizen the Hong Kong billionaire Sir Y.K.Pao. Its chief attraction is the deepwater Beilun Harbour, where freighters berthed at a 100,000-ton-class wharf continually offload Australian iron ore for trans-shipment to the giant Shanghai Baoshan Iron and Steel Complex. This is one of 14 existing wharves – including one capable of handling 150,000-ton oil tankers, and a 50,000-ton general purpose berth. In 1993, a new 200,000-ton wharf was being constructed. Near the harbour is the Ningbo ETDZ established in October 1984. One interesting feature within the Zone is the Xiaoshan Industrial District, being developed exclusively by funds from Hong Kong entrepreneurs. The city provided water, power and transport facilities, but remaining development is the responsibility of the investors. Elsewhere, there is the Ningbo Free Trade Zone, which not only enjoys all the preferential policies granted to the SEZs and ETDZs, but claims even more leeway, including total freedom of import and export trade, circulation of foreign currencies, entry and exit of personnel and no administrative control over business scope.

The Zone hopes to have 2000 firms resident by the end of the decade. Ningbo residents living abroad have already invested £130 million in setting up enterprises in real estate development, wool processing, textiles, garments and shipbuilding. Up to June, 1993, approval had been given for 266 ventures involving foreign capital totalling more than a billion pounds, including:

- A £660 million petrochemical project involving the American Concord Group which will develop a five million-ton oil refinery, a 300,000-ton ethylene plant and a 45,000-spindle chemical fibre factory.
- The Beilun Steel Plant, with an initial production of 1.5 million tons annually, jointly built by the Concord Group, the Baoshan Iron and Steel Complex and the Ningbo Development Zone. Total investment is expected eventually to reach about $2 billion.
- The China National Paper Industry Company, with Indonesian involvement, will plans to invest at least $1000 million to build a one million-ton copperplate printing paper project.

There is no doubt that the central government envisages a large role for Ningpo in the ongoing development process. But there are problems to be overcome, notably a transportation bottleneck. Neither road nor rail facilities are good enough to take full advantage of the highly-efficient harbour once goods have been landed. A double-track railway and an expressway linking it to key cities like Shanghai and Hangzhou are due to be completed by 1995 to ease the strain.[13] The goal, provincial officials explain, is to link the railway to Pudong as part of the 'Yangtse Strategy' to be discussed in the next chapter, whereby Ningpo and Zhejiang Province in general becomes the processing and shipping base for Shanghai and cities all along the river.[14]

Also adjacent to Shanghai is Nantong, a trading port on the northern side of the Yangtse River estuary which has long been famous for its textiles and silk. The third largest port on the river, its handling capacity is being expanded fourfold the end of the century. The small ETDZ is primarily aimed at light industries.

Fuzhou, one of the most attractive cities in the country and ancestral home of millions of overseas Chinese, faced many problems after the foundation of the People's Republic due to its proximity to Taiwan. But times have changed, as they have for its near neighbour Xiamen (already discussed in the section on SEZs) with which it will soon be linked by a modern highway slashing journey times sixfold. Improved road links, as well as the presence of an efficient harbour, and a major railway line to Shanghai and Beijing, have helped enhance the attractiveness of the Mawei ETDZ a few miles from the city centre. The major industries so far attracted have been iron and steel, machine building, electronics, chemicals, foodstuffs, textiles and shipbuilding. Fuzhou also has a Free Trade Zone which went into operation in January 1993 – and claimed to have attracted 100 letters of intent from Chinese and foreign companies even before the Zone's creation was publicized.

The other ETDZs tend to be rather small and have not yet achieved their full potential, particularly in attracting foreign investment. All, however, insist they are making rapid steps to catch up.

FOOTNOTES
1. In fact, Chinese companies have flocked to the Zones to take advantage of such privileges as their relative freedom in exporting and the right to retain foreign exchange earnings.
2. *People's Daily* Overseas Edition. 29 July 1993.

3. *China Daily*, 15 May 1993.
4. Ibid.
5. Ibid.
6. The Cheng Shin Rubber Industry Co. located in Xinglin investment zone for Taiwanese businesses, is the largest and probably among the most successful Taiwanese enterprise on the mainland. It produces bicycle tyres, 99 per cent of which were exported in 1992, although in 1993 the company planned to sell 30 per cent domestically. It also planned to start making automobile tyres. [*China Daily* 29 May 1993]
7. *Economist*, 5 Sept.1992.
8. Ibid.
9. Quoted in *China Perspectives*, Arthur Anderson & Co, Third Edition May 1989.
10. *China Daily*, 21 June 1993.
11. Futures are a key part of Shanghai's plan to become the country's modern business capital and an Asian financial force. The existing Shanghai Metal Exchange was used for the first such trading experiments. As China's economy begins to expand rapidly it is becoming a key player in many of the commodities traded in the futures exchanges worldwide. The Metal Exchange in May 1992, for example, began trading spot contracts in copper, aluminium, lead, zinc, tin nickel and pig iron as a first step. Hu Yuezheng, Vice President of the Metals Exchange explained: 'We want Shanghai to be the Asian metal trading centre, with our opening hours fitting the gap when London and the United States markets are closed.'
12. The Qingdao Economic and Trade Commission predicted the total would reach 200 by the end of 1993. [*Beijing Review*, 18 June 1993]
13. *Beijing Review*, 6 Sept. 1993.
14. *China Daily*, 28 Aug. 1993.

4 Development and investment prospects elsewhere in China

KEY POINTS

This chapter will look at the development activities and potential of the rest of the country. This will include:
- The Yangtse Strategy to bring prosperity to the entire length of China's most important river.
- The role of the Yangtse River Economic Development Company, a Shanghai-based collectively-run conglomerate, that is showing how regional rivalries can be transformed into cooperation.
- A province-by-province breakdown of development plans and investment opportunities.
- The key cities in the programme to develop the river basin as an area of high technology and scientific research and development.
- The transformation of the defence industry, largely located in the interior, into thriving civilian companies that have attracted considerable foreign investment.
- The opportunities for foreign companies to invest in, operate and manage major infrastructure projects throughout the valley.
- The rejuvenation of China's 'birthplace', the Yellow River, with large injections of foreign cash, especially in resource exploration and mining.
- The late flowering of the border regions where most of China's ethnic minorities reside.

YANGTSE STRATEGY

IF NATIONAL and international attention in the 1980s was focused on China's SEZs and the coastal development zones, it is now shifting to the 'heartland provinces' centred on the mighty Yangtse River. 'The bow is shaped and it's time to sharpen the arrow,' said Tong Yizhong, Vice-Director of the Foreign Investment Administration, referring to the 'bow and arrow' development strategy designed in the early 1980s to bring China into the international market – the bow being the coastline and the Yangtse River valley, stretching inland some 3,500 miles from Shanghai to the Tibetan plateau as the arrow. The strategy now is to combine the 'Gold Coast' with the 'Golden Waterway'.

This is a highly significant development in the open door policy. The inland region previously was closely guarded since it accommodated most of China's defence and heavy industrial base built during the 1960s against the danger of a possible invasion from the Soviet Union or the United States. The region includes Anhui, Hubei, Junan, Jiangsu, Jiangxi, Sichuan and Zhejiang provinces, covering an area of 1.1 million square miles and responsible for 40 per cent of the nation's gross industrial and agricultural output. The Yangtse delta contains China's largest processing industrial base, and a string of important riverside cities as far as Sichuan province replicate this industrial structure, with a growing emphasis on machinery, electronics and precision instruments. The predominance of defence industries has created a large talent pool in advanced research institutes as well as skilled labour. In between the cities, the valley is one of the most important areas for the production of agricultural commodities, including grain, cotton and edible oil. Rural enterprises have also prospered, currently representing 39 per cent of total national output in this sector. The region boasts a large proportion of China's mineral resources, especially non-ferrous metal mines, and the government has been considering ways to let overseas investors join in their development.

The Yangtse itself is a valuable asset, representing 36 per cent of the country's water resources. The river, along with its various tributaries, has an estimated hydro-energy potential of 270 million kilowatts, part of which will be tapped through the ambitious Three Gorges Dam project near Yichang in Hubei Province, which both the central and local leaderships expect will generate a vast amount of fresh industrial activity all along the middle and upper reaches of the Yangtse, and hopefully control the floods which have been so disastrous for the region in the past).

These heartland provinces received little foreign investment in the 1980s and were jealous of coastal success. The first step was taken in 1992, when the river port cities of Zhangjiagang, Zhenjiang, Nanjing, Wuhu, Jiujiang, Wuhan, Yueyang and Chongqing were declared open to foreign ships after a 40-year hiatus. The central government also designated Chongqing, Jiujang, Wuhan, Wuhu and Yueyang as open cities enjoying the same preferential treatment as those on the coast. In the same year, the final decision was taken to go ahead with the Three Gorges Project – to be completed by 2009 – setting the pattern for the full development of the Yangtse River Valley.

Like the powerful currents of the river itself, there was an immediate rush to invest. 'Foreign-funded enterprises have sprung up in Jiangsu province at the rate of 10 a day since the beginning of 1992. In Wuhan, capital of Hubei province, the establishment of 300 foreign-funded enterprises was approved during 1992, more than the total for the previous 10 years. Projects involving energy resources, telecommunications and transportation command the greatest amount of attention. In Chongqing, on the upper reaches of the river, over 300 foreign-funded projects were approved in the first 10 months of 1992. Similar trends can be seen in Anhui, Jiangxi and Hunan provinces.'[1]

In order for the inland areas to catch up, however, massive investment is required in ports, bridges and highways beyond local or even central capabilities. As a result, foreign businesses are being allowed to invest in and bid for contracts for several major construction contracts, which they will then be able to manage and operate for a 15-year contracted period before ownership reverts to the Chinese. 'Under the policy, foreign capital can be introduced in the construction of power plants, railways, high ways, ports and postal facilities [throughout the valley]. This means China will concede to foreigners parts of markets formerly highly monopolized by the Chinese authorities. Since most infrastructure projects are low in profits, China will also allow foreign businesses to take part in some related projects, such as commercial real estate and advertising schemes alongside expressways and railways.'² Among the high-profile infrastructure projects underway or planned are a new Beijing-Kowloon railway line on an inland route, updating of the southern section of the existing Beijing-Guangzhou railway along the coast, a Beijing-Shanghai bullet train with speeds up to 250 kph, a network of railway lines throughout the Yangtse Delta to link up various ports and the interior; new deepwater berths in Shanghai harbour giving it an additional handling capacity of 2.4 million tons, six deepwater berths at Ningbo with a handling capacity of 3.5 million tons, and an additional 19 million tons of capacity to be created along the Yangtse through construction of 24 new berths; new highways linking Shanghai with Nanjing, Ningbo and Hangzhou; expansion of the Grand Canal in Jiangsu; and fibre-optic cable communications links between Nanjing, Wuhan and Chongqing.

YANGTSE RIVER ECONOMIC DEVELOPMENT COMPANY

A key role in turning the river into the envisioned 'golden waterway' has been given to the Yangtse River Economic Development Company, a Shanghai-based collectively-run conglomerate claimed to be the country's largest. Many cities along the river have benefited from its allied development strategy.

The company created a stir when it was launched in September 1992 because it was the first cross-regional shareholding company founded by several city governments (Shanghai, Nanjing, Wuhan and Chongqing joining forces with the Bank of Communications). According to company director Gu Chuanxun, many cities along China's longest river agreed to break regional economic blockades and cooperate closely. Founded with a registered capital of 650 million Yuan, the conglomerate's shareholders include 31 city governments, the Bank of Communications and its 28 branches, and 386 large and medium-sized enterprises. It was also trying to sell its stock to individuals. Subsidiaries handle international trade, real estate. commerce, industrial affairs and deal in raw materials and petrochemicals.

Since its establishment, the company has helped pool capital for constructing the Ningbo Commercial Centre, as well as launch the Science and Technical Industry Investment and Development

Company, the Yangtse River Shipbuilding Company and the United Yangtse River Economic Development Company International (a joint venture in which Taiwan-based enterprises hold a 60 per cent share). It is also financing the building of commercial and office blocks and factories designed to attract foreign companies in Wuhan and Chongqing and in key economic development districts such as Shanghai Pudong New Area, Nanjing New and Hi-Tech Development District, Nanjing New Port Area and Changzhou ETDZ. With its support, Ningbo was able to start a $35-million project which combines a three-star hotel with an amusement and shopping centre. Similar commercial and industrial projects were also being built or planned in Shanghai, Wuhan, Chongqing, Suzhou, Nantong and Wuhu. Its regional company in Wuhan is involved in a joint venture with American interests producing light helicopters, while the Chongqing regional company spent $1.4 million on four Russian hydrofoils to ferry passengers along the Yangtse.

FROM THE DELTA TO TIBET

Inevitably, the prosperous delta region – long known as 'the land of fish and rice' – will play an important role in promoting economic expansion for the rest of the river, as well as its entry into the international economy. Shanghai's efforts to regain its former predominant trading role were described in the last chapter. Surrounding Shanghai is Jiangsu Province, which has seven major cities and 37 counties along the Yangtse River, The general goal for provincial development is to link up with the Pudong to create a powerful industrial base that also relies heavily on high technology and information processing. Jiangsu wants to make full use of the Yangtse's transportation potential by establishing industries which have a large transport volume and consume much water – petrochemicals, energy, iron and steel, building materials and shipbuilding. By the turn of the century, the seven riverside cities want to achieve an annual industrial output between them of $168 billion, based on an average 15 per cent increase per year.

Foreign investment has a big role in achieving these ambitions. In fact. foreign enterprises form a third of all firms in the province, with Suzhou the most popular site (more than 5,100 on the city's books by June 1993 - although only 2,481 were in actual operation - with investment of over $7 billion, accounting for two-thirds of the city's exports). Leading industrial sectors in the city have taken the lead in forging close links with a number of world famous transnational corporations. The city's electronics industry, for example, joined hands with Philips of the Netherlands to establish China's first development and manufacturing centre for colour televisions. Other big names which have been attracted to the city include Du Pont of the United States and Japan's Mitsubishi Corporation. Suzhou, a charming garden city built around numerous narrow waterways and known as the home of silk, is currently forging close links with Singapore. In mid-1993, an agreement was signed for the construction of a Singapore Industrial Park, the first phase of which will cover about five square miles, which will complement the four industrial and tourist development zones already set up around the city. Suzhou is also creating separate development zones funded by outside counties and cities, and small industrial districts operated by local townships.

Rural areas of neighbouring Anhui Province traditionally have been among China's poorest giving rise to a mass migration of hungry peasants to the cities. Because of this, Anhui girls dominate the nursing and domestic service professions in Beijing. Nevertheless, Anhui is not without its pockets of prosperity and these are steadily expanding. It ranks first in East China for mineral deposits with proven reserves of about 90 minerals and ores including coal, iron, copper, ferrous sulphur, porcelain clay, limestone and quartzite, plus considerable reserves of oil and gas. The province has established a strong industrial presence in non-ferrous metals, petrochemicals, textiles, building materials, mechanical and engineering centred on the Maanshan-Anqing region. The recently opened ports of Anqing, Chizhou, Maanshan, Tongling and Wuhu have regular freighter services to Hong Kong, Japan and Singapore.

Anhui has been looking outwards since the central government granted the provincial capital Hefei and Wuhu preferential policies similar to those enjoyed by the coastal open cities. From the beginning of 1992 until mid-1993, this resulted in agreements being signed with 1,300 foreign enterprises. Despite the images of rural deprivation, Anhui actually has a strong scientific and technological research and educational base. Hefei, for example, is the site of the Chinese University of Science and Technology. The province was one of the first in the country to export technology and this is now an important part of its overall foreign trade activities. Hardware and software technology have been exported to some 40 countries, including Britain, Canada, Germany, Japan and the United States, according to province officials.

REVIVAL FOR WUHAN

The Yangtse flows some 660 miles through Hubei Province, where development centres on the provincial capital Wuhan, a sooty city of rundown factories and oppressive summer heat (urban population three million, with another seven million in linked satellite areas). It was China's great inland industrial power in pre-revolutionary days and retains some of that even today. Hubei is dominated by heavy industries, such as steel, cars and shipbuilding, but under communist control these have been almost entirely under state control, their inefficiency impoverishing the host. To try and escape from this morass, the central government agreed to give Wuhan some of the privileges and autonomy the coastal areas have enjoyed for some time. It is a natural choice. The city lies at China's cross-roads, halfway up the Yangtze, and halfway between Beijing and Guangzhou on the main north-south railway line.

With at least a third of the city's state-run factories operating in the red and many others on the borderline, local authorities have been keen to encourage foreign interests to take over and introduce some much-needed managerial reforms. In this regard, Wuhan Cityford Dyeing and Printing Industry Company, manufacturing cheap, brightly-coloured clothing for export, has become a model for the future. In 1992, the city offered various loans to persuade the Hong Kong-based Hongtex Company to invest capital in refurbishing the Cityford plant and provided seed capital for a joint venture. The Hongtex management were given complete control over the hiring and firing of workers – an unknown phenomenon in Wuhan since liberation – agreeing to pay unemployment benefits and undertaking to find new jobs for those laid off. The new managers eventually laid off 70 per cent of the 2,400 workers and also set about dismantling the decades-old system of guaranteed wages and benefits. The city's communist leadership even acquiesced in stripping the company union of any say in the proceedings. According to reports of the event, '. . . the prime function of the union today is to organize banquets for its members'.[3]

Within 10 months, the new management was reporting a profit of just over $1.5 million, and an enthusiastic Wuhan Vice-Mayor was able to declare: 'The Cityford phenomenon could become a model for the future, opening the way for the transformation of large and medium-sized state enterprises.' He wanted at least 100 companies to follow the 'Cityford model' within three years, with an eventual goal of merging at least half of Wuhan's state-run firms with foreign businesses. But the central government quickly threw a spanner in the works with a programme to curb runaway inflation by restricting the ability of cities and corporations to issue unauthorized stocks and bonds as a means of raising cash. Beijing officials maintained that the high interest rates being offered were fuelling inflation and draining the monetary supply. Combined with burgeoning unemployment that threatened to bring labour unrest (capitalist methods of operation in Wuhan alone could potentially cost several hundred thousand jobs), Wuhan's leaders conceded they would not be able to grant the same concessions to other companies that had been granted to Cityford.

When chief reformer Deng Xiaoping visited Wuhan at the start of 1992, Hong Kong's leading tycoons got the message. In the 18 months that followed the Deng visit, the city authorities approved more than $4 billion in foreign investment, mostly from Hong Kong businessmen for grandiose infrastructural and property projects. In stark comparison, only $114 million was committed in the previous year.

Wuhan's future is closely linked to a container terminal to be built by Wharf Holdings, a Hong Kong property company, which envisages using Wuhan as a collection point for raw materials and industrial output from central China, as well as an entry point for its imports. Departing goods would clear customs at the city's container port and then be carried by rail to Hong Kong for transhipment. This should be seen as an insurance policy by Hong Kong investors, who see the development of modern ports all along China's coastline as a distinct challenge to the British colony's dominance of the container trade. Therefore, Hong Kong has to develop new road and rail links with the interior to maintain its premier trading role. There is talk of a new 340-mile superhighway into Hunan similar to the one that Hong Kong tycoon Gordon Wu has built in Guangdong Province. Peter Woo, head of Wharf Holdings, has already promised $1.5 billion by 1996 to develop a railway line between the Wuhan container terminal already mentioned and Hong Kong. However, all these projects remain on paper and much of the development capital pledged in recent years has still to be spent.

Foreign involvement in container terminals like the one at Wuhan are very much part of a trend. Peninsula & Orient (P & O) Steam Navigation joined forces with Swire Pacific of Hong Kong to purchase 50 per cent of a container terminal at Shekou in the Pearl River Delta at a cost of $80 million. It also took a controlling stake in another terminal in the Yangtse River port of Zhangjiagang for $50.25 million. At the time of the second purchase, P & O said it was looking at a number of other port investment opportunities along the Yangtse and in north-eastern China.

Apart from the numerous Hong Kong investments in Wuhan, the city hosts several global industrial companies such Philips and Japan's NEC which are involved in separate fibre-optic cable ventures with Chinese partners. But the biggest single investment is the $1000 million required for the construction of a car manufacturing plant involving the French car-maker Peugeot. This plant, however, will not be open before 1996 at the earliest (see chapter seven for more details of the Chinese automobile industry).

Looking at the rest of Hubei, the province has nine 'economic development zones' apart from Wuhan. These are at Huangshi (centre of the province's metallurgical sector), Huanggang, Ezhou, Xiaogan, Shashi, Jingzhou, Yichang, Xiangfan and Shiyan. Yichang is only 25 miles from the controversial Three Gorges Dam Project aimed at providing not only flood control but also water supply, navigation and power generation. When completed, the generating capacity is supposed to be 18,200 megawatts to make the Yichang-Chongqing (Sichuan Province) region 'the largest hydro-energy base in China'. Riverside areas along the middle and upper reaches of the Yangtse will then develop their building materials, metallurgy, machinery and electronics sectors drawing on the strength of their existing industries. Localities in the reservoir area are due to commence work soon on a network of railways and top-grade highways alongside the Yangtse, while communications links will be upgraded through an optical-fibre cable along the river between Wuhan and Chongqing. The State has granted 19 cities and counties in the reservoir area preferential policies to promote local economic development.

Typical are the development zones being established just across the border in Sichuan Province at Fuling and Fengdu primarily to service the migration of local industries as well as public facilities following the construction of the dam. A third of Fuling's downtown area and the whole county seat of Fengdu will be under water when the water level of the planned reservoir surface reaches 525 feet above sea level. The unprecedented migration project provides them with a sound reason to rebuild their industries in well-planned development zones.

JIANGXI AND HUNAN

The river city of Jiujiang forms the portal through which backward Jiangxi province is opening up to the outside world. Development is concentrated on a 75-mile corridor stretching from Jiujiang to the provincial capital Nanchang, within which foreign businesses have been given carte blanche to establish any type of industry; they have also been given access to the tertiary sector in real estate, trade, information processing, consultation, tourism and advertising. Setting itself a goal of becoming a high-tech city offering comprehensive services by the turn of the century, Jiujiang has created the Balihu Development Centre (2.4 square miles) and Yanjiangdu Free Trade Zone (1.2 square miles). The Nanchang-Jiujang Region will also accelerate the tapping of agricultural resources to turn the area into a major base for marketable farm produce and a foreign-currency earner.

Yueyang in Hunan Province plays an important role in the take-off of the interior. The city is trying to develop itself into the second largest economic and trade hub in the middle reaches of the Yangtse behind Wuhan by throwing open its doors to the outside world. The Chenglingji ETDZ, the South Lake China Dragon Boat Culture Development Zone and the Lakeside Food Industry Development Zone were set aside for foreign investors, although at the time of writing some of the areas are still largely vacant lots. More than 7,000 overseas Chinese of Yueyang origin have been encouraged to introduce foreign capital into the city; liaison offices have been set up in South Korea, Japan, Commonwealth of Independent States (CIS) and Western Europe; and overseas banking tycoons, managers and technological experts have been engaged as the city's economic or investment advisors. The aim from now, according to Mayor Ouyang Song, is to guide foreign investment into high-tech industry and resource development and technical renovation of existing enterprises. To secure an ideal investment climate, the city launched 10 capital construction projects, including two 5,000-ton foreign trade docks and a new railway station.

Since the mid-1980s, Yueyang has ranked first in Hunan in economic growth, and particularly in foreign-related investment. It has forged economic and technological links with 28 countries and regions and has endorsed 242 foreign-funded projects with $675 million of committed foreign investment. Situated at the juncture of the Yangtse and Beijing-Guangzhou Railway, Yueyang has emerged as the largest petrochemical base in central-south China. The output value of its petrochemical products makes up 63 per cent of the total output value of industry in Hunan, and this could be further enhanced if oil exploration in the vast Dongting Lake area is successful. This region is also continuing to develop its agricultural potential while at the same time creating a broad industrial base around an economic zone comprising the cities of Changsha, Xiangtan and Zhuzhou.

Hunan, with a population of 62 million, is strategically placed with five major railways and seven national highways passing through the province linking North with South and East with West. It has developed considerable trading ties with the outside world, the import and export volume increasing 13-fold between 1978 and 1992. Sixteen of the 400 foreign enterprises within its borders are ranked amongst the top 500 trading firms in the nation. In 1992, the province granted permission for the establishment of 782 Sino-foreign joint ventures, cooperatives and wholly foreign-owned firms, double the number approved in the previous 13 years. By the middle of 1993, another 697 projects had been approved. At the same time, Hunan has been developing its own overseas enterprises and has already established 55 companies in locations such as Hong Kong, Macao, Thailand, Japan and North America.

Deputy Governor Tang Zhixiang set out Hunan's goals in the coming years as tapping abundant local resources to develop high-quality agricultural products for export particularly high-yield varieties of various grains, cotton, oil crops, fruits and sugar-bearing crops; comprehensive development of timber resources; development of high-quality aquatic products; promoting the smelting of ferrous and non-ferrous metals and related processing industries; promoting the technological transformation of existing light, textile and food-processing industries; development of a high-profile petrochemical industry, products to include butyl rubber, special lubricating oil, oil additives and various synthetic materials; development of chemical products, including agricultural products and medicines 'currently unavailable in China'; transformation of the machine-processing industry into an integrated producer of advanced machinery, electronic products and industrial instruments; priority to be given to developing new industries such as those related to computers, micro-electronics, new materials, and biotechnology.[4]

SICHUAN PROVINCE

Almost 1,700 miles from the mouth of the Yangtse lies Sichuan province, the most populous in China (equivalent to France and Germany combined). But although it contains one-tenth of the country's 1.3 billion population, it only commands 6.5 per cent of its gross national product and six per cent of its farmland. Development of an already substantial industrial base is essential both to soak up surplus farm labour but also to boost living standards. The peasant riots of mid-1993 are a warning of what could happen if this is neglected.

There is prosperity in patches, however. Chengdu, the provincial capital, boasts its first underground shopping centre, and a subway is planned under its boulevards. The streets of Chongqing (which has become China's biggest city, with 14 million people to Shanghai's 13 million) are clogged with traffic - because it is built on steep hills, the city has few bicycles. A subway is also planned, with Hong Kong funding. Meanwhile, across the Yangtse River at the Chongqing Economic and

Technological Development Area, and the New and High Technology Development Zone on the Jialing River, the new China is being built at a feverish pace. Plots are being cleared for factories, even if much of the building actually in progress, including villas for expatriates, is for residential use. Some 150 enterprises involving foreign participation have signed up for the zone, with $360 million of foreign money committed, and the city has set itself a goal of attracting a minimum of $2.7 billion to establish an export-oriented, high-production economy. Typical is Chongqing Vehicle Plant, which has put its 1995 production target at 250,000 minivans and two million motorcycles (the city already turns out a third of China's annual motorcycle output).

Chongqing, however, has paid a high environmental price for its past industrial pre-eminence. Due to combination of high humidity and little wind to blow away the smokestack emissions, it has for years been known as the acid-rain capital of China, where environmentalists claimed that 'metal is eaten faster than anywhere else in the world'. It was also called the fog capital (240 photochemical smog days recorded in 1990, for example). The municipal bureau of environmental protection forced industries within the city to raise the height of their smokestacks to reduce the toxicity of acid rain falling on residents, but officials admitted that all this did was to transfer the pollution elsewhere. A new thermal power station with not only taller chimneys but also a $30-million desulphurization plant was commissioned in 1993 to ease the problem, along with an emphasis on attracting cleaner high-tech industries.

In Chengdu, meanwhile, a high and new technologies Development Zone contains an 'incubation centre' that is to serve as a greenhouse for premature but promising high technologies. Fan Shibin, deputy manager of the Brilliant Development Corporation which has overall management of the zone, explains that it will incubate not only pioneering industries for the city, but also new mechanisms for enterprise management as well as government performance. Most local governments now demand that enterprises in such zones get rid of the 'iron wages' (inflexible wage scales), iron rice bowls (life-time employment with perks) and 'iron armchairs' (permanent leading posts), pillars of the employment system under the planned economy. In place of this outdated thinking, according to Fan, most zones are promoting contract employment and shareholding systems to explore the scope for the transfer of enterprise management patterns.

SWORDS TO PLOUGHSHARES

Sichuan province is also the site of an ongoing experiment in converting the gargantuan defence industry to production of civilian goods. In order to prepare for national defence in the 1960s, when China seemed to face a threat from all directions, led by the Soviet Union and the United States (plus the US-backed Nationalist forces on Taiwan), the best talent, the most advanced technology and equipment, with unlimited funds was concentrated on establishing a complete defence industry in the remote mountainous areas of inland provinces, notably Sichuan, Hunan, Yunnan and Guizhou. Meticulous government planning used to guard military manufacturers from worries such as supply of materials, funds and market conditions. But as the threat of war eased in the 1970s, the central government decided to put an end to the war-time footing of the military and in the early 1980s the decision was taken to trim one million soldiers from the bloated People's Liberation Army (PLA); the result of this decision was that orders for weapons and ammunition fell sharply, and, to survive, much of the defence industry was told to forget the guns and start thinking about producing something more mundane – like refrigerators and colour television sets.

The government conversion strategy was to set up so-called 'window enterprises' in the SEZs and other coastal economic development zones during the 1980s to introduce foreign technology and capital for the development of a limited range of 100 products. These window enterprises then became information centres and bridgeheads for the inland ordnance enterprises to develop an export-oriented economy. The changeover seems to have worked. Over the past decade, the defence industry in south-west China has manufactured four million motorcycles, nearly 500,000 refrigerators, about 700,000 cameras, over 100,000 minibuses and 1,000 heavy trucks.[5] It is reported that 70 per cent of China's defence plants are now turning out products for civilian use. The industry as a whole has a target of manufacturing civilian goods valued at 10 billion Yuan (or about $1.75 billion) in 1995.[6]

The military-to-civilian transformation has contributed to the current prosperity of military factories and also pushed them to the forefront of local economic development. In Mianyang, a remote city on the northwest edge of the Sichuan Basin, for example, there are 28 backbone military research institutes and enterprises. Their 20,000-plus technical talents include some of the country's best in electronics, astronomical and nuclear technologies. Because of the military connection, they were artificially isolated from other parts of the city. Contacts were rare between the military and local government which had little interest in defence.

Mianyang is now seeking to end its isolation. Though the city is currently known as China's Silicon Valley for a host of backbone high-tech research institutes with links to the military, lack of publicity has been one of the heaviest fetters to the city's opening ambitions. Like many towns in the interior it is now engaged in a major exercise in self-promotion (typified by a slogan in a workshop of the Fuling Cigarette Factory in Sichuan exhorting workers to 'scramble for fame and profit'. Under Mao, the Chinese were educated to despise both, the goal of production being to 'serve the people'). Mianyang is so proud of the 80,000 technical personnel in its 450,000 population, and its 200-plus research institutes, that it is staging an annual Science and Technology Festival and inviting the rest of the world to attend. The central government chose Mianyang as a pilot city to facilitate the military-to-civilian conversion of local defence research institutes and enterprises. It is estimated that 70 per cent of the enterprises approved so far by the High and New Technology Development Zone have a military background.

Meanwhile, more than 600 miles away in Chongqing, municipal authorities also decided to move military factories from nearby mountains into its development zones. The former Mayor of the city, Sun Rongchuan, used to refer to powerful defence industry as 'a tiger sleeping in the remote mountains'. Chongqing officials have now turned that round to describe the current transformation as involving a 'tiger leaping down the mountains'.[7] There have been no shortage of foreign takers given the loving care lavished in the past on companies in the military sector. At least 20 joint ventures have been created, primarily in vehicle manufacturing.

When Chen Zisheng and his colleagues decided to manufacture trucks and sewing machines in the late 1970s, they were largely driven by an instinct to survive. 'It was a last ditch struggle,' explained Chen, director of the Jianshe Manufacturing Plant. The gun maker had been forced into the corner by a steep drop of military orders and did not realise that, by turning to the production of trucks and sewing machines, they were paving a way that was destined to be followed up by the nation's war industry. Jianshe, however, was lucky to establish a link with the Japanese Yamaha motorcycle company, which has been a lucrative partnership for both sides. Yamaha continues to pour big investment into the venture to build new assembly lines.

Jianshe is now the country's second biggest motorcycle producer, lagging only behind another Chongqing-based company, Jialing, which was hived off from the Norinco (China North Industries) arms manufacturing group and was able to form a technical cooperation agreement with the leading Japanese manufacturer Honda. Jialing now plans to double its current output to one million machines a year by 1997.

Norinco, one of the country's biggest military suppliers, has diversified so much that 70 per cent of the output of its 300 units and subsidiaries is civilian goods. It has even brought the amusement arcade concept to war through the operation of a unique weapons range north of Beijing where paying customers can shoot everything from hand guns to anti-tank rockets. Now it is looking for foreign joint-venture parts for at least 200 projects in advanced machinery, motor-vehicle assembly, optical, electrical and chemical products. An official of its development planning department ackowledged that Norinco was hindered by having many of its manufacturing plants located in remote interior regions, but this could be overcome by moving them to central or coastal areas.

The transition from swords to ploughshares, however, has not always been smooth. Ni Runfeng, director of the Changhong Machinery Plant, a military radar producer in Mianyang, recalled how he was caught in a vice between senior officials demanding he convert to civilian production and military workers who refused assignments to new workshops set up to produce television sets. But that is now a distant memory. Nearly two decades of cooperation with Japan's National Panasonic

Corporation has laid a solid foundation for Changhong's technological upgrading. Their self-designed colour television production line introduced in 1989 as the first of its kind in the country is regarded as equal to the quality of imported lines. Having won a firm footing in Southeast Asia and Eastern Europe, Changhong is now planning to set up a joint venture in Indonesia to produce 300,000 television sets annually. It has been turned into a stock company – Changhong Electric Appliances Company – and with two new colour television assembly lines added to the existing six, the company ranked first in production and profits in the nation's electronics industry for four successive years (1989-92).

At the Hunan Dongting Rubber Plant, long monopolized by the army green of rubber-soled shoes and raincoats of the military, workers are now making colourful sneakers, air cushions and nylon raincoats for export. But there are still headaches. Plant officials complained that they had to face restraints peculiar to the military industry (eg: it still has to rely on an administrative company affiliated with the army's Central Logistics Department whenever it deals with foreign customers, rather than dealing direct).

Looking elsewhere, Guizhou (abutting both Sichuan and Hunan provinces) had the third largest concentration of military industries, located in remote mountain gullies, surrounded by high walls and 'keep off' signs. By the end of 1992, however, the changed climate had resulted in 37 joint-venture or cooperative agreements being signed with businessmen from Hong Kong, Macao, Taiwan and the United States for the manufacture of such products as light trucks, coaches, computer diskettes and floppy diskette cases, rubber sealants, plastic and rubber products and aluminium foil. Officials recall, however, that the early days of transformation were hard. Factories were forced to 'find rice for the waiting pan', as the old Chinese saying goes. They produced whatever they could lay their hands on, such as electric fans and blankets, meat grinders, kitchen utensils, desks and chairs. Most of the products were low quality, low-grade items with little output value. A number of enterprises which were unable to find a suitable product to manufacture contracted their work-force to highway construction and other projects. It has been a long learning process, but the results are beginning to show. One major step forward was the relocation of many enterprises to more accessible locations along railway lines.

In 1985, newly-settled in a high-tech development zone in Ziunyi City, Jiangnan Aviation Industrial Corp. pioneered the use of imported parts from Japan's Toyota Motor Co. in 1985 to assemble a 1.25-ton, multi-passenger lightweight truck. In the following three years, the corporation developed and manufactured its own vehicles under the Hangtian trademark, including mini-vans, ambulances and police cars. Today, 80 per cent of the vehicle parts are produced domestically. Meanwhile, the Guizhou Aviation Industrial Corp., re-established in a development zone in the provincial capital Guiyang, moved away from the manufacture of military aircraft to become a major player in the automobile parts market. It has developed a range of over 800 components, and a truck-sealing compound developed at one of its factories has captured 60 per cent of the domestic market.

Looking ahead, a senior defence official in Beijing said the industry aimed to step up its expansion into civilian production, 'moving into everything from space technology and shipbuilding to petrochemicals and textiles'.[8] The industry had some of China's most advanced technology, more than 1,000 firms with three million experienced workers and 300,000 researchers in defence-related science and technology institutions. China demonstrated to the world how successfully it had made the switchover at the 1993 International Exhibition on Peaceful Use of Military Technology in Hong Kong. More than 300 mainland firms showed off a wide range of products from satellite launch rockets to door locks. A total of 79 deals worth $2.52 billion were signed, along with 99 verbal agreements valued at more than $975 million.

YELLOW RIVER REVIVAL

Moving further north, 'China's birthplace' the Yellow River is also being reborn with large injections of foreign cash. Three thousands years ago, the Yellow River was the most developed area in the world, the Chinese say, and for a long time it was the political, economic and cultural centre of the empire. For various reasons, development slowed in the nineteenth century and its economic progress was gradually outstripped by the other major valleys further south. In the past few years, however, the number of overseas enterprises attracted to the provinces lying along its banks from Henan, through Gansu and Qinghai, as well as the Ningxia Hui and Inner Mongolia autonomous regions, has doubled and redoubled, along with a considerable input of aid from foreign governments and international organizations.

Minerals will fuel its recovery. Three of China's four largest coalfields lie along the river, as well as four of the important oilfields. There are eight large hydroelectric power stations. Some 140 kinds of mineral ores have been detected along with large reserves of bauxite for processing into aluminium, as well as gold. China has embarked on a drive to open up its mining industry to much-needed foreign investment. Following a comprehensive review of resources policy, the government began speeding up the creation of legislation covering both the exploration and exploitation of the country's vast mineral reserves by foreign mining companies. At a mid-1993 conference staged by the Ministry of Geology and Mineral Resources, Vice-Minister Zhang Wenju said China faced an urgent need to encourage an influx of the latest technology and foreign capital as the mining sector was lagging badly in the country's economic modernization drive (due to outdated technology and inefficient mining methods, per capita yields of most minerals in China are estimated by experts to be only half the world average). Priority would be given to copper, lead, zinc, iron ore, coal, diamonds, rare earths and uranium.

Previously, the minerals sector was highly sensitive, with the old mining regulations being described by foreign mining firms as 'strongly nationalistic' and providing little incentive for major investment. But all that is supposed to change under the government's 'Prospecting Treasure Plan'. Zhang promised the new regulations would 'shape an attractive mineral investment climate' while protecting China's economic interests.

Draft regulations indicated the government would permit both companies and individuals to seek exploration and mining permits. Ventures could be cooperative, Sino-foreign, or wholly foreign-owned. Companies seeking an exploration permit will be restricted to a maximum area of 625 square miles for oil, gas and coalfields and 62.5 square miles for all other minerals. An exploration permit will be valid for five years with renewal allowed for a further two years. A mining licence will be valid initially for 20 years, with a further 10-year renewal available.

For the first time, Chinese gold mines were also opened to external investment in 1993, although officials admitted that foreigners would only be allowed a slice of low-grade mines or those which were hard to dig (the major low-grade mines are located in Yunnan, Guizhou and Sichuan provinces, and in Guangxi Zhuang Autonomous Region). Previously, the only foreign involvement was in the provision of technology and equipment to the industry. American, Australian, Canadian and South African gold companies immediately expressed interest, encouraged by a further reform which brought Chinese gold prices into line with international levels, ending the system of artificially low government-set prices.

After years of procrastination, the Chinese also began throwing up the doors to increasing exploration for oil both on and offshore. Again, a booming economy placed a heavy strain on existing production and it was estimated that by 1995 China would become a net importer of oil.[9]

Much is expected of the vast and inhospitable Tarim Basin in Qinghai province in the remote northwest, where, based on fairly vague seismic data, experts reckon there are reserves of up to 100 billion barrels of oil and 8,300 billion cubic metres of natural gas. Even if it eventually turns out to contain only a fraction of this amount, the region could still become one of the world's biggest oil and gasfields. Exploration contracts have been signed with several major oil companies, predominantly Japanese (backed by Tokyo government loans so far amounting to some $75 million), covering several huge tracts of territory. Exploration and development is also being accelerated at three areas in Xinjiang-Tulufan, Turpan-Hami and Junggan Basins.

A major impetus for the exploration programme was a government decision in 1993 to finally begin freeing up prices of domestically-produced oil and gas and allow them to float in line with world market trends. Chinese oil producers traditionally sold their output to the state at prices set by the latter which bore no resemblance to international indicators. This became a significant discouragement for the producers who found it increasingly difficult to meet the rising costs of equipment and technology. Typically, the government began timidly, introducing a payment system to 14 medium and small oilfields at something close to world market prices, while most of the country's oil output was kept at mandatory levels. The industry supervisory body, the China National Petroleum Corporation, however, indicated that pricing reform would proceed gradually.

Faced with declining production in old oilfields, the government also decided to transform the CNPC's 21 oilfield administrations into enterprise groups by 1995. While pressing ahead with new exploration, the policy included measures to encourage redevelopment of some of the older fields – with the new enterprise being allowed to retain any profits rather than being handed over to the State as in the past. Also being reviewed is the system whereby the fields had to hand over virtually all their output to another corporation – Sinopec – for refining and processing into petrochemicals.

This would certainly benefit the country's largest oilfield at Daqing in the northeast province of Heilongjiang which has 20,000 productive wells. It was a vast wilderness until 1960 when Mao Zedong sent 70,000 demobilized soldiers and workers to dig for oil. Eating frozen potatoes and rotten cabbages in shabby rammed-earth houses, the work-force suffered great hardships and made so many sacrifices that Mao coined the slogan: 'In industry, learn from Daqing'. The city became an epitome of toughness. Today, it is a prosperous city of one million people, enjoying one of the highest standards of living in the country. But if it is to remain so it will have to diversify into downstream activities. Once it becomes an enterprise group in 1995, Daqing is eager to cooperate with foreign firms to develop a petrochemicals capability.[11]

QINGHAI MINERAL TREASURES

Raw material development is also the main hope for Qinghai which is adjacent to Tibet and has an area one-and-a-half times the size of France but a population of little more than four million. The province is the source of both the Yangtse and Yellow Rivers, and huge falls in their upstream river courses offer rich hydroelectric potential (six large stair power stations are already planned for the upper reaches of the Yellow River). Going into the twenty-first century, Qinghai sees itself as a major energy- and minerals-processing base for China. The Longyangxia hydroelectric project near the province's eastern border has already enabled the establishment of a group of large energy-consuming industries for the smelting of aluminium, magnesium, silicon and iron ore.

The Qaidam Basin in the middle of the province is described by local officials as the province's 'treasure bowl', containing vast proven oil and natural gas reserves, as well as 4.5 billion tons of mostly high-quality coal with low ash and sulphur content. Under the Kunlun and Qilian mountains are large proven caches of iron, manganese, chromium. vanadium, copper, lead, zinc, nickel, tin, molybdenum, antimony, mercury, gold, silver, platinum, beryllium and selenium. The iron reserves are estimated at 2.2 billion tons, and the province claims the country's largest lead and zinc mines, and is a primary producer of asbestos.

In the south of the Qaidam Basin lies the Qarhan Salt Lake, China's largest supplier of soluble potassium chloride (potash fertilizer) and magnesium chloride. The lake holds virtually all of the nation's discovered potassium chloride, reserves now being tapped by the Qinghai Potash Fertilizer Plant, a joint venture with Israel's Dead Sea Works Ltd. China has a critical shortage of potash fertilizer. Annual demand currently exceeds two million tons, which has to be imported apart from 200,000 tons coming from Qinghai. This will be eased by new investment by the joint venture partners to add an additional 800,000 tons of productive capacity.

This is the largest foreign-funded project in the province at present. But it is early days yet. Having been given State Council permission to grant foreign investors the same favourable terms as those available in the SEZs and coastal zones, Qinghai began luring businesses to its newly-established industrial development zones in the provincial capital Xining only in 1992. A year later, it was able to report 50 signed agreements.

BORDER TRADE

China has land borders of over 12,500 miles, most of which are inhabited by ethnic minorities, which constitute just over eight per cent of the total population. Of the 55 recognized minorities, at least 20 belong to the same racial group as people in the neighbouring countries or regions. In the past, this has been a cause of some concern in a security-obsessed government, but is now becoming a source of economic strength as cross-border trade flourishes. Trade more than doubled in the period between 1989 and 1992.

Yunnan Province, located in the southwest with some 20 ethnic minorities, was the first, in 1985, to undertake reforms, allowing easy movement over its 1,900-mile borders with Vietnam, Laos and Myanmar (Burma) and designating 17 ports and 90 other areas as areas where border trade could be conducted freely. Large quantities of commodities made in Southeast Asia flow in, while Chinese-made goods such as machinery, electronic products, building materials, textiles and articles for everyday use flow in the opposite direction. In 1992, two-way trade was worth more than $375 million.

The central government has ambitious plans to integrate the economy of the southern border regions with that of the neighbouring states. A proposed road from Yunnan to the Burmese coast, reminiscent of the 'Burma Road' lifeline of Second World War fame, would give the region access to the deepwater port of Rangoon.

The Guangxi Zhuang Autonomous Region in the southeast adjoining Vietnam removed all border customs posts and lifted restrictions that had limited Vietnamese businessmen from travelling more than 12 miles into China – permitting them, instead, access to seven border counties and cities. Entry and exit formalities were also simplified for both Chinese and Vietnamese engaged in business. All this was made possible because in 1991 the countries finally resolved the political differences that led to a nasty border war 12 years earlier (in which the PLA got a bloody nose and the Vietnamese reckoned they were the winners) and, hopefully, ended centuries of mutual antagonism.

Although a latecomer to border business, the Inner Mongolian Autonomous region has caught up fast. Along boundaries of over 2,500 miles it has opened up 11 land, water and air ports. Barter markets have been established in a number of towns bordering the CIS and independent Mongolia. In May 1992, China and the CIS set up a joint closed 'mutual trade market area' in the town of Manzhouli. Along the Ergun River, Chinese and Russian ships loaded with basic products like cement and timber shuttle back and forth. As with Vietnam, this is a sharp contrast with past antagonism which resulted in occasional border clashes between Chinese and Russian troops.

The longest border is in the Xinjiang Uygur Autonomous Region, populated by the majority Han people, as well as Uygers, Hui, Kazakh, Mongolian, Tajik, Uzbek, Tartar, Russian and other ethnic groups. Xinjiang really came into its own with completion of a railway line between the regional capital Urumqi and the Alataw Pass, completing the Eurasian Transport Corridor between Lianyungang on the Yellow Sea and the Western European rail system. To promote business, Xinjiang has opened up various border markets, and sent delegations to the neighbouring countries of Central Asia to discuss economic cooperation and development of trade. And, to further promote its products, a department store, the Urumqi Industrial and Trade Centre, was opened in Alma-Ata, capital of Kazahkstan.[10]

Border trade has also flourished between Tibet and Nepal. In 1992, the Chinese and Indian governments signed an agreement to open trade outlets, restoring traditional border trade which had been suspended for 33 years due to various disputes which led to at least one war.

At present, the trade in most of the ethnic minority areas remains mostly at the barter stage. It is primitive, but in the absence of much foreign exchange, it makes sense. At markets, deals like the exchange of 10 eggs for four handkerchiefs or two electronic watches for five embroidered shirts are common. At some of the ports in Xinjiang, trucks full of grain, edible oil and garments, cross over into the CIS, and bring back chemical fertilzer and cement of equal value.

There is a strong feature of reciprocity, especially in the northeast. On the Chinese side of the border, there is a relatively large population with a relatively developed industrial base. But the infrastructure is backward and raw materials, advanced technology and equipment are in short supply. In the Russian border areas, meanwhile, the population is sparse, but raw materials are abundant, supporting a strong mining and heavy industrial structure. There is, however, a shortage of labour, and agriculture and light industries, especially textiles, are also in short supply. The upsurge of border trade, therefore, has been mutually beneficial and is officially recognized as such in both Beijing and Moscow. A freer climate has also resulted in a large-scale labour movement. In recent years, an estimated 50,000 labourers have been sent from Heilongjiang Province to the CIS. New joint ventures in manufacturing and infrastructure development on the Chinese side of the border have also seen the presence of Russian workers.

FOOTNOTES:
1. *Beijing Review*, 15 Feb. 1993.
2. Ibid. 28 June 1993.
3. United Press International quoted in the *South China Morning Post*, 13 July 1993.
4. *Beijing Review*, 20 Sept. 1993.
5. Xinhua News Agency, 21 July 1993.
6. Ibid.
7. Ibid.
8. Chen Dazhi, Director of the Integrated Planning Department of the Commission of Science and Industry for National Defence, quoted in *China Daily*, 28 Aug. 1993.
9. In 1993, it was producing 2.8 million barrels a day of which about 400,000 barrels were exported.
10. *Beijing Review*, 22 March 1993.
11. Oil firms in countries such as Russia, India, Burma and Argentina have already shown strong interest in cooperating, the *Business Weekly* reported in September 1993.

5 Foreign investment: who, what, when, where and how?

KEY POINTS

In this chapter we shall be considering the growing involvement of foreign capital in Chinese business. The key elements:
- Why foreign businessmen decide to invest and why China wants and needs investment.
- The steps the Chinese have taken and are thinking of to improve the investment climate, including the opening up of previously-closed sectors, relaxation of the entry procedures and a devolution of decision-making powers to the provinces
- A breakdown of the main foreign investors – who is doing what, where and how.
- A look at China's key players.

NEW MARKET

FOR MUCH of the period since the 1949 Communist takeover of China, foreigners have been treated with suspicion. The country had rediscovered its national pride and was determined to be self-dependent and self-sufficient (apart from some initial help from the Soviet Union and other socialist states). There were constant reminders of the humiliations of the nineteenth century when Western powers exploited the weakness of fading Imperial China to gain unfair trading concessions and even broad swathes of Chinese territory. In splendid, prickly isolation, Communist China slipped further and further back, its ageing economic structure creaking and groaning at the seams, until Deng Xiaoping came along with the only rational solution – a reopening to the outside world, particularly the affluent West.

Since 1979, there have been several 'gold rushes' as foreign businessmen have pushed their way in to gain a toehold in the market, only to retire battered and bewildered in many cases by the twists and turns of the economic reform process. There have been peaks and troughs, the most recent following the government's crackdown on the pro-democracy movement in mid-1989 which led to widespread if temporary sanctions against China by outraged Western governments. Within a couple of years, however, the tide began to build up again.

Just how much foreign investment China has attracted so far, and how many foreign companies are operating in the country in one form or another, remains subject to some dispute. It illustrates some of the difficulties of dealing with Chinese statistics. Official figures showed that in the first three-quarters of 1993, $15 billion was actually invested by foreigners and another $82.5 billion pledged in new contracts – a 171 per cent increase over the previous year. Utilized foreign investment since the doors were opened in 1979 stood at $52.5 billion.[1] Some 40,000 foreign-funded enterprises have gone into operation, directly employing six million people and providing at least 17 per cent of China's exports; foreign capital comprised 10 per cent of China's total investment in fixed asset, and provided 8.5 per cent of its industrial output value.[2]

Caution is needed in dealing with such numbers. Although the Chinese announce astronomical figures for contracted investment, only a fraction of it is actually committed for a variety of reasons. The Chinese like to announce big numbers in the hope this will encourage others to jump on the seemingly unstoppable investment bandwagon. Equity from the Chinese side is often included in the value of the project inflating the size of the apparent inflow.

Despite a record number of contracts announced in 1993, the government finally admitted that very little of the money had actually been committed by the foreign investors. Official figures showed that only 18 per cent of the promised funds had actually been supplied. In 1992, the figure was 19 per cent. There has, in fact, been a steady decline in the contract/realization rate ever since the mid-1980s. The Chinese did take some of the blame.

'Fund shortages on the Chinese side used for setting up joint ventures, due to the government's tight credit squeeze [imposed to control an overheated economic boom], are partly to blame', conceded a senior economist. The squeeze also made it more difficult for foreign businessmen to exchange their local earnings into foreign currency. But some officials also conceded that a growing problem was the fact that many of the announced projects were actually fraudulent. Some Chinese companies set up phoney joint ventures to take advantage of the favourable tax treatment on offer. Bribes were paid to the relevant authorities to turn a blind eye to these illegal activities, the officials admitted.

Nevertheless, there is no doubt that there has been an explosion of foreign interest and a significant inflow of capital. A survey of 1,067 American companies conducted in June 1993 by the American Chamber of Commerce, for example, found that 63 per cent of the firms without a current presence in China intended to make an initial investment within five years, while 89 per cent of those already established were planning additional investments in the same period. There is hardly a single important Japanese corporation which does not have some form of trading or manufacturing presence in China today. The same increasingly goes for the South Koreans and the Taiwanese; most of the region's ethnic Chinese captains of industry are pouring money into huge projects. Singapore is planning to build whole cities. Western statesman make high-profile visits to Beijing with large business delegations in tow and come away with contracts worth hundreds of millions of pounds.[3]

Indirect investment is growing through the listing of Chinese companies on the Shanghai and Shenzhen stock exchanges, as well as Hong Kong, New York and Sydney. A plethora of 'China Funds' have sprung up in the West to cash in on the feverish investor interest. But given the nascent state of the Chinese stock exchanges, and the country's company law and accounting methods (see chapter 11), direct participation in the marketplace is likely to remain the dominant form of foreign investment for some years to come.

Vice-Premier Li Langqing, in charge of foreign trade, said China had two advantages over other countries in the Asia-Pacific region in attracting foreign investment – low labour costs and a vast market. The latter argument certainly finds favour with Tan Yik

Fay, a executive with Motorola (China) Electronics Ltd, which produces portable telephones, radio pagers and semiconductors at a plant in Tianjin: 'China is the only potentially lucrative market in the world now where telecommunication equipment can be enlarged to profit-making levels.' Y.S. Hahn, President of a Korean sports shoe manufacturing plant in Tianjin, echoed the point: 'Low taxes and a skilled but inexpensive work-force helped, but the increased purchasing power of the Chinese consumer was what finally clinched the decision to come here.'

Chinese officials, however, concede that there is still a lot of room for improvement. Top priority, for example, is being given to meshing China's policies with the rules of the General Agreement on Tariffs and Trade (GATT), membership of which is being assiduously pursued by Beijing.

For a start, foreign-funded enterprises are slowly being placed on an equal footing with domestic concerns, ending the restrictions on the purchase of raw materials, price-setting and sales in the Chinese market; many have to export most of their output, having also paid high import duty on vital components needed due to difficulties in obtaining them locally. This has also been necessitated by a Chinese insistence that the firms have to earn enough foreign exchange to meet any costs involving foreign currency payments.

'We should allow [the firms] to sell all their products in China – provided they are advanced and needed by the domestic market – as well as giving them foreign trade rights,' said Ms Jiao Sufen, Director General of the Foreign Investment Administration at the Ministry of Foreign Trade and Economic Cooperation (Moftec).[4] She also advocated strong support for foreign investment in export-oriented agricultural projects. Investors in this sector have up to now found it difficult to export their products which are under strict government quota restrictions. New regulations were being drawn up, she said, to encourage more transnational corporations to establish investment companies within China. They would have to be major investors already before applying for the new business. The purpose would be not only to establish new businesses, but also provide them with a focused export/import service and foreign exchange facilities. One of the first to take advantage of the concession was Philips, which had already invested some $975 million in a dozen factories in China. As a further step, Ms Jiao said the government would adopt further preferential policies to encourage transnationals to establish their Asian or Asia-Pacific regional headquarters in China. Capital or technology-intensive businesses would be able to sell part or all of their output on the domestic market, '. . . and the government will help them balance their foreign exchange needs'.

Reviewing prospects for 1994 in an interview with *Business Weekly*, Lin Kun, Deputy Director General of Moftec's Foreign Investment Administration, revealed that foreign investors would be able to run joint-venture airlines with domestic partners on a trial basis for the first time. They would also be encouraged to invest in the country's commercial airports, 'except for their air traffic control systems', as well as being able to set up joint ventures to run railways and highways.

Trade Minister Wu Yi, meanwhile, promised that the banking, commerce, tourism and real estate sectors would be gradually freed for foreign investment. Foreign firms in all sectors would be given more legal protection, including intellectual property rights; local governments would be given more power to approve foreign projects, to simplify procedures and hold decision-making power in export and import.[5] Miao Fuchun, Moftec spokesman, stressed that '. . . our general objective is to create a fair competitive environment according to the principle of the market economy. To ensure this, we must give equal treatment in such areas as taxation, tax rates, exchange rates, transport, communications and work procedures'. Improvement of the legal framework and greater transparency of regulations were important in bringing Chinese practices closer to international standards, he added.[6]

But it looked for a while as if there would be a high price to pay for more access to domestic markets. Moftec officials indicated the government wanted to change the current preferential tax policies for foreign-funded ventures to bring them into line with those applied to their Chinese counterparts. Most State enterprises have had to pay 55 per cent of their profits as income tax each year, while foreign enterprises benefited from tax-preferential policies at both national and local level and in many cases pay only 15 per cent, although the average is 24 per cent. But the State Taxation Administration insisted there was no plan to erode the favourable treatment under the tax reforms planned for 1994 which called for the two rates to be equalized at 33 per cent. Tax officials stressed that foreign firms would be given a rebate to bring them back to the former level (see chapter 12 for a more detailed discussion on the tax structure).

As noted in the previous chapter, the Chinese are also allowing more foreign involvement in major infrastructure projects using a new type of investment vehicle known as BOT – build, operate and transfer. The foreign side of the venture handle the construction project, operate it for a set period (normally 15 years) and then hand it over China. BOT has already been adopted for a railway line in Zhejiang and a port in Hubei. However, Western companies have been somewhat cautious about the BOT formula since it means having assurances about revenue streams in areas where price controls still exist.

For the really big players at the top end of the market in financial and technology terms, the government is dangling a golden carrot of participation in its three most important projects for completion by 1998 combining telecommunications and computers. These are the 'Golden Bridge Project'. for the establishment of a national public economic information network; the 'Golden Customs Project', for the establishment of a national economic and trade information network, and the 'Golden Card project' designed to promote the nationwide use of credit cards (a former symbol of capitalist decadence that has only penetrated as far as a handful of the country's nouveau riche so far).

The Chinese are also looking for massive injections of funds and technology to overcome a bottleneck in its railways network, backbone of the national economy. Other backbone industries, particularly the iron and steel sector, also need a major overhaul that will have to come from capital injections from either world leaders in the industry like the Japanese or Americans, or from international pension funds. Optimistic officials in Beijing and the more upbeat of the foreign businessmen believe that despite the amazing upsurge in investment in recent years, the best is yet to come.

THE OVERSEAS CHINESE

In 1992, official Chinese figures show the bulk of 'actual' foreign investment came from Hong Kong and Macao ($7.7 billion).

Taiwan was next, although a long way behind ($1050 million), followed by Japan ($670 million), the United States ($510 million) and South Korea ($112.5 million). All continued to make substantial capital injections in 1993. But others are catching up, notably the countries comprising the Association of Southeast Asian Nations (Asean), where millions of 'overseas Chinese' have accumulated great wealth from their managerial and entrepreneurial expertise.

There are estimated to be at least 55 million ethnic Chinese living outside the mainland borders, including 21 million in Taiwan and the six million in Hong Kong. Of Asia's 'four tigers', only South Korea is not Chinese. Another four Southeast Asian countries with tigerish ambitions – Thailand, Malaysia, Indonesia and the Philippines – have Chinese minorities that account for an astonishing share of their economies. Indonesian Chinese, only four per cent of the population, are reckoned to control 17 of the country's 25 biggest business groups. In Thailand, an ethnic Chinese minority of between eight and 10 per cent owns 90 per cent of commercial and manufacturing assets and half of the capital of the banks. Malaysia's Chinese, who make up around a third of the population, have a much larger share of economic power. The Malay-controlled government tried for 20 years to whittle down this influence by enforced transfer (often faked) of Chinese-owned company shares to Malays, but has finally admitted defeat because of the damage this was doing to the national economy.

Overall, the 1990 gnp of Asia's overseas Chinese was estimated at a minimum of $337 billion, a quarter greater than the figure for mainland China. Worldwide, they probably hold liquid assets (not including securities) worth $1125 billion to $1.5 trillion. For a rough comparison Japan recorded bank deposits in 1990 totalled $2.25 trillion. This capital has been accumulated and is deployed through a distinctive form of social and business organization. 'One Chinese writer described Japan's homogenous society as a block of granite and Chinese society as a tray of sand. Each grain in the tray is not an individual but a family. They are held together not, as in America, by law, government and public ideals, nor, as in Japan, by a concept of national solidarity, but by personal acquaintance, trust and obligation. The result has been a highly decentralized business structure based on secretive, entrepreneurial, family-owned firms that are run autocratically but cooperate smoothly and informally with each other, often across national borders.'[7]

The return to their roots by the overseas Chinese, is described by Kitti Dumnernchanwanit, president of a Thai industrial conglomerate, in these words: 'I am Chinese but was born in Thailand. I always realize that for a human being it is a must to bring progress and prosperity to his country of origin.' He is overseeing a $1005 million forestry, pulp and paper project in Guangdong Province.

Another typical example is Indonesian businessman Liem Sioe Liong, one of the wealthiest overseas Chinese in the region, who decided to return to his ancestral roots in Fujian Province by teaming up with two state-controlled Singaporean companies to develop an industrial park costing $187 million in the first phase. Singapore also has close links with the province, home of people speaking the Hokkien dialect still widely used in informal conversations in the island republic. Directly and indirectly (through companies with whom he is connected) Liem held 70 per cent of the equity, while the two Singaporean companies, Singapore Technologies and Jurong Environmental Engineering, each had 10 per cent. The project involved creating a commercial, industrial and commercial complex to attract light and medium-sized industries from Taiwan, Singapore, Hong Kong and Japan. It is designed to be a low-cost export manufacturing base acting as a springboard for further trade and investments inside China. A Singapore investment analyst described the project as an example of '. . . the Singapore Inc. approach – cash-rich government companies linking up with well-connected private interests to exploit an opportunity'.

Liem is involved in many other projects, including water treatment and power plants to supply industrial estates and towns. Another Indonesian, Mochtar Riady, billionaire head of the Lippo Group, which ranks among the top five conglomerates in his country, also plans to develop an industrial park, supported by a port and power plant, in Putian, the Fujian town which is his ancestral home. In Beijing, a distinctive landmark is the office, conference and hotel complex known as the World Trade Centre, in which Robert Kuok, a Malaysian Chinese tycoon is a partner. His Shangri-La hotels are in several

Chinese cities, and he is heavily involved in projects in his ancestral town of Fuzhou.

The headlong rush by Singapore Chinese businessmen to invest is typified by the agreement signed in May 1993 to develop an industrial township in Suzhou (see previous chapter). This called for the creation of a 45-square-mile new town – dubbed Singapore II by the island's press – using the republic's integrated planning approach as a model. An eventual population of 600,000 is envisaged to take advantage of a hoped-for overseas investment windfall of around $20 billion. Under the terms, Singapore and Suzhou municipal government formed a joint venture, with the former holding 65 per cent of the equity. On the Singaporean side the lead role was taken over by one of the island's best known conglomerates, Keppel Corporation, which brought, and then put together a consortium of companies offering a wide range of skills to build the town.

'China Fever' had been rampant in the republic since former Prime Minister Lee Kuan Yew visited China in 1992, returning to chastise Singaporeans for their lack of entrepreneurial zeal in failing to match their Hong Kong and Taiwan counterparts investment in mainland projects. The message was heeded with an immediate upsurge of investment. Within months, Singapore companies had injected some over $900 million in 742 separate projects – more than the entire amount invested between 1979 and 1991.

There was no such hesitation early on by Chinese-run companies in Thailand. Between 1979 and 1992, the Chin Tai Group, for example, established 48 joint ventures with Chinese interests from Sichuan in the south to Liaoning in the far north. It began by investing in poultry, livestock and aquatic production and fodder processing, branching out into motor and machine manufacturing, and latterly on to real estate and banking, before moving in Shanghai's Pudong New Area with an oil refinery and soybean-product factory. Another big investor is the Charoen Pokphand Group, an agriculture-based conglomerate founded by Chinese immigrants in the 1920s, whose holdings in China include 30 feed mills, a motorcycle plant and 30 other firms, which in 1992 reported revenues of over $495 million. Providing an important support service is Bangkok Bank, Thailand's largest, founded in 1944 by Chinese gold merchants and traders, which has opened a branch in Shantou, a city from which many of Thailand's large Teochew community hail.

Johnny Lau left his native Guangzhou as a young boy to live with an uncle in Macao, eventually venturing into selling electronics in, successively, Singapore, Malaysia and Hong Kong, and finally setting up a one-man trading company in the latter city in 1975. Specializing in audio components, he carried his samples around in a paper bag. Lau might have remained just another small businessman if he hadn't recognized the promise of China before a lot of other people. In 1981, he established a small factory in the Pearl River delta town of Zhongshan at a time when, as he recalled, 'there was no electricity and the people knew nothing about business'. Today Zhongshan is a resounding success and so is Tomei, Lau's company, supplying audio equipment to Sony, Philips and RCA among others in the field. Lau employs nearly 26,000 people at 12 plants in southern China, which he describes as a 'paradise for manufacturing'.[8]

In these ways, the prosperous elements of the Chinese diaspora are bonding together with the mainland to create something akin to a nation without borders that, linked by blood, ambition and hard work, may bid fair to challenge Japan some day as the pre-eminent economic power on the western rim of the Pacific Ocean. This should be a sobering thought for those Western businessmen who have hesitated to enter the Chinese market because of the perceived risks involved.

This world-wide network of Chinese entrepreneurs is likely to continue to play an important role in China for at least the next two decades, according to Singapore's Lee Kuan Yew.[9] 'At even half the present growth rate, China will become a considerable economic weight in 20 years. As China's economy grows, major investors from America, Europe and Japan are renewing their China interests. The value of the investments from these industrial countries will dwarf that of the overseas Chinese. But China will not forget that it was Hong Kong, Macao and Taiwan Chinese who demonstrated between 1989 and 1992 that investments in China can be successful with *guanxi*' Mr Lee noted that entrepreneurs from the three bustling economies had, through their investments – especially after the imposition of Western sanctions following the 1989 democracy crackdown – inspired other Chinese in Southeast Asia to follow suit, thus enabling the

Chinese economy to get back on track and revive Western interest in doing business with the mainland.

Mr Lee contrasted the attitudes of Western and ethnic Chinese businessmen towards China's supposed weaknesses, especially the lack of rule of law and transparency of rules and regulations. He cited a study, *Chinese Business Strategies*, by Nigel Campbell and Peter Adlington of the Manchester Business School, which stated:

'During periods of strong rule, imperial power reached into the furthest corners of the Chinese Empire. The exercise of this power was arbitrary and brutal: the Mandarin was both prosecutor and judge. A separate judiciary was never established, and hence the ordinary person never looked to the law to settle his grievances. Traditionally, he would take the law into his own hands. The modern equivalent of this situation is that the bureaucrat interprets central regulations to suit the conditions of his own province and city. Family ties and a closely-knit peasant society have lent value to personal relationships. Where there is not enough to eat, not enough room on the bus or not enough steel for the factory, personal relationships are vital. They provide the lubricant which smoothes away anarchy. *Guanxi* is the asset value of personal relationships built up from family, village schoolmates and so on. In short, Chinese law is flexible and open to interpretation by officials, whilst Western law is rigid and can be interpreted only by the courts.

'What ethnic Chinese from Hong Kong, Macao and Taiwan did was to demonstrate that *guanxi* through the same language and culture can make up for a lack in the rule of law and the transparency in rules and regulations. This *guanxi* capability will be of value for the next 20 years at least, until China develops a system based on rule of law and with sufficient transparency and certainty to satisfy foreign investors.' Mr Lee insisted there was nothing wrong with *guanxi*. Networking was a fact of business life and the was no need for ethnic Chinese '. . . to be apologetic about wanting to maximise benefits through contacts and access to opportunities'.

Nevertheless, the former Singapore prime minister warned, it was necessary for ethnic Chinese in 'sensitive' countries in Southeast Asia [he presumably had Indonesia and Malaysia particularly in mind] to take care that they do not neglect investment opportunities in their native countries which might give rise to accusations of disloyalty. Increasing investments in China could affect race relations and the problem should not be underrated. 'If relations turn sour between any Asean country and China, those ethnic Chinese who have invested in [their ancestral home] will be accused of disloyalty.' He pointed to the reaction of some indigenous media to such investments. Indonesia's Merdeka had dwelt on the 'capital flight' possibly rising to a level that could undermine development of the Indonesian economy. Other local press had questioned the loyalty of the ethnic Chinese who were investing capital in their 'home villages' in China when their own countries from which they had derived their wealth needed this capital. [Indonesian Chinese were treated with great suspicion after an abortive Communist coup in Jakarta in 1965.]

He suggested that one way to mitigate this was for China to use its links with ethnic Chinese in Southeast Asia to invest in Indonesia, Malaysia and Thailand in particular, where energy resources such as gas and oil were abundant and labour costs low. He cited a steel rolling plant near Kuantan in Malaysia which was a joint venture between the Malaysian Government and Shandong Province. 'More such joint ventures in Asean will offset the impression that the flow of investments is one way.'

TAIWAN

It was not so long ago that PLA sentries patrolled the beaches of Fujian province trying to prevent would-be asylum-seekers swimming across the narrow straits to Taiwanese territory. Now, the flow is in the other direction. Combining the mainland's rich manpower resources with Taiwan's vast capital reserves, technology and economic network, it is now being argued, will ensure that China's labour-intensive industries enjoy competitive strength internationally for years to come.

The fact that China's rulers can display this level of pragmatism towards an old political foe in the interests of economic development is at least a partial answer to those who are reluctant to invest in the mainland because of fear that, as has happened several times in the past, the rulers in Beijing at some time in the future will again turn back the revolutionary clock.

Since the early 1980s, Taiwanese businessmen have poured billions of pounds into the prosperous southern provinces mainly through Hong Kong, and the government in Taipei is now seeking a higher profile in the British colony before its handover to China in 1997. Typical of this was the permission given in August 1991 for three state-run banks to open offices in the territory to help fund the drive to retake large swathes of the mainland at least economically. 'Hong Kong is like a pair of gloves. Taiwan wears one and China wears the other so that they can shake without really touching,' explained Kenneth Lai, Managing Director of the Taipei Trade Centre in Hong Kong. 'It is not openly stated, but Taiwan wants to gradually expand its influence in China through trade, investment and free ideas,' added Lee Yee, editor of a Hong Kong-based political monthly, Nineties.

This stands in stark contrast to the former policy of 'Three Nos' – which outlawed negotiation, compromise and even contact with the communists. After China opened the doors to the outside world in 1979, Taiwanese businessmen who wanted to take advantage of this had to brave the threat of prison sentences at home. Deals were mainly struck in Hong Kong and no Chinese visas were ever stamped into the passports of visitors from the island. Since the accession of a more liberal, Western-educated leadership in the mid-1980s, a gradual relaxation began. The 1949 pledge to retake the mainland was quietly dropped; in 1987, travel restrictions to the mainland were dropped (although travel must still be done via Hong Kong) and in mid-1992, Taipei took a further important step by allowing local banks to deal directly with their local counterparts in such areas as letters of credit and foreign exchange remittances, rather than having to deal through foreign banks. However, the ban on Taiwanese banks setting up branches on the mainland was retained.

Once given their head, however, there was no holding Taiwanese businessmen. Investment in mainland projects totalled $300 million in 1990, and tripled the following year and by 1993 had reached almost $2.5 billion. The forecast for 1994 was at least $3 billion.[10] These are the official figures. Some analysts believe that they understate the true position by at least 150 per cent. The Taipei government estimates that around 4,000 of the island's companies have invested across the Taiwan Straits, including about a fifth of the 260 firms listed on the local stock market.

In the beginning, the Taiwanese mainly invested in labour-intensive enterprises promising quick returns such as plastics, textiles, garments, shoes, electronic toys and bicycles. By 1993, the electronic toy industry had almost entirely moved to the mainland. At the time of writing, however, investors had begun to edge into heavy industries, including iron and steel and machine building. Many Taiwanese computer producers moved their research institutes to major cities such as Beijing and Shanghai.

Winston Yang, whose father heads the island's foremost conglomerate Formosa Plastics is adamant that this is an unstoppable wave. 'We have to go to China. In my opinion our future direction is mainland China. We have to be close to our customers.' This was a widely-shared view, leading to growing pressure on the government to lift all restrictions. The government, however, believed this would accelerate a business exodus, draining investment away from Taiwan itself and jeopardizing the island's future prosperity and weakening it politically. The brakes, therefore, remained halfway on, with companies forbidden to obtain loans from Taiwanese banks or by raising equity on the stock exchange for mainland investments; listed companies also had to obtain approval from their shareholders for any moves towards the mainland.

Business leaders like Winston Yang, however, argued that the business environment on Taiwan had become less convivial due to rising land and labour costs. For the petrochemical industry, there was also the growing presence of environmental groups whose pressure has held up key projects. Nan Ya Plastics, the group company which Yang heads, produces pvc and polyester products for use in manufacturing a range of consumer goods such as handbags, shoes and rainwear. In the late 1980s, it was quietly exporting 10 per cent of its output to the mainland; by 1993, that had risen to 60 per cent. 'Our customers are urging us to set up factories in China. If there is a market you must go to it,' Yang stressed, adding: 'If private market reform would prevail one day along with burgeoning entrepreneurship, the mainland would offer a fabulous potential to accommodate many competitors.' Such arguments do not offer much comfort for the independent-minded Taipei government.

On the mainland side, there has also been some relaxation with a decision taken in October 1993 to allow limited direct trade with Taiwan. New regulations designated the coastal ports in Fujian, Guangdong, Shandong and Zhejiang Provinces, as well as Shanghai to handle the trade in which mainland firms who have obtained approval from the Ministry of Foreign Trade can import Taiwanese goods or export to the island in tightly controlled quantities. But Taiwanese goods cannot carry a label referring to the country of origin as the 'Republic of China', which is what the Taipei government calls itself.

THE UNITED STATES

By the end of 1992, 50 of the 500 largest American companies had invested in China, and the total US capital contributed was $6.3 billion, second only to Hong Kong and Macao, although only about one-sixth of the latter's input. All the big names are there. In a touch of exquisite irony, the Tiananmen Square mausoleum of Mao Zedong, guardian of socialist revolutionary purity, is guarded on two sides by branches of America's global fast-food leaders McDonalds (whose Guangzhou restaurant holds the firm's world record for customers through its doors on day one) and Kentucky Fried Chicken (first into China with its Beijing store in 1988).

Walt Disney is also present, in a comics-publishing joint venture with the Post and Telecommunications Press. Disney tried to produce a Chinese-speaking Mickey Mouse and Donald Duck for the first time in 1987, but pulled out in 1990 in protest at counterfeiting of its comics and products. In 1993, with the passage of China's first copyright law, the company decided to have a second go. An initial print run of 60,000 for a Mickey Mouse comic was snapped up overnight at a price equivalent to $0.30 each. Nevertheless, it was made clear that the behaviour of the Disney characters would have to be both politically and socially correct so as not to set a bad example to Chinese children.

'Excluded from the Chinese editions [. . .] will be a sequence in which a lad eating an ice cream and leading a dog pursuing a cat becomes entangled in a tree with the ice cream smeared across his face. "Since, in Chinese cities, it is not allowed to raise a dog, not to mention a dog led by a small boy, we didn't want to run counter to the regulations so we dropped the story," said Mr Zhao

Wenyi [a senior editor with Disney's local partner]. Also banished from Donald Duck's family will be his money-worshipping Uncle Dagobert, whose habit of bathing in piles of dollar bills is not deemed appropriate for a Chinese audience – never mind that people have been told for the past 10 years that "to get rich is glorious".[11]

The Disney experience symbolizes many of the problems the United States faces in China. From the nineteenth century, Americans have tended to regard China as their special preserve (typified by the vicious row, and search for scapegoats, in Washington political circles after the Communist victory in 1949 over the issue of who had 'lost China'). The 1950–53 Korean War and the subsequent cold war rhetoric put paid to any hopes that the US could have any influence with the new regime in Beijing. Only after resumption of diplomatic relations in 1979 were American businessmen able to begin streaming back into China with dreams of megabuck deals. But relations have never been smooth, with the issue of alleged Chinese human rights violations repeatedly surfacing as sand in the oil of diplomatic niceties. In an attempt to force the Chinese into better treatment of its dissidents, Washington has repeatedly used the threat of withdrawing China's Most Favoured Nation (MFN) trading status which would be a heavy blow to China as the United States is one of its most important export markets. Each year the threat is made and heated debate heard in the US Congress, but so far the MFN arrangement has survived. This is further exacerbated by American irritation over a widening bilateral trade gap in China's favour, and alleged Chinese large-scale arms sales to Third World countries – prompting repeated threats from Washington to impose trade and other economic sanctions unless there is a change of heart in Beijing.

This, however, is a two-sided weapon as the Chinese have not been slow to point out. Anything that damages Sino-US trade could end up hurting American firms in China more than their local counterparts – a point that President Jiang Zemin made most pointedly when, during a visit to the United States in November 1993, he visited the Boeing Aircraft Company in Seattle. China has been one of Boeing's best customers in recent years. President Jiang was equally blunt in his meetings with President Bill Clinton, telling the United States to keep its nose out of China's domestic affairs. At the same time, the Chinese issued a new collection of the works of Deng Xiaoping (119 speeches and essays between 1982 and 1989) designed to send a coded message to the Americans. The official media made much of remarks Deng made to former President Richard Nixon in October 1989, that it was up to the United States to take steps to improve relations. 'China cannot take the initiative. That's because the United States is a powerful country and China is a weak one. China is the victim.' For China to beg was impossible, Deng stressed. 'It doesn't matter if sanctions last 100 years. The Chinese people will never beg for them to be lifted. If any Chinese leader makes a mistake on this issue he will fall from power. The Chinese people will never forgive him.'[12]

The United States and Japan are currently locked in a struggle for who is going to lead the Pacific into the twenty-first century – with China playing an increasingly large role whether the other two want it or not. For the United States, a possible vehicle is the Asia Pacific Economic Cooperation (APEC), founded in 1989 at the suggestion of the then Australian Prime Minister Bob Hawke, and also including Canada, China, Hong Kong, Taiwan, and the six countries of ASEAN, with a small secretariat established in Singapore. APEC is the latest in a series of attempts to establish closer economic cooperation between the countries comprising the world's most dynamic region. Gross domestic product of East Asia, around $4.5 trillion, is within striking distance of the US; the two areas are trading on a scale unimaginable only a decade ago, a scale that can grow exponentially if some kind of loose customs union can be established. But these hopes seem somewhat premature given Asian reservations about American leadership claims.

JAPAN

The Japanese began rather cautiously in China, but the pace has picked up dramatically in the 1990s. The first investments were made in tourism and expanded outwards to encompass textiles, electrical appliances, food and chemicals. Liberalization of the service sector then began to attract major supermarket operators, with two of the biggest, Yaohan and Daiei, opening large-scale joint ventures in several big cities. The globe-spanning Japanese trading firms began moving into the export-import sector now that they have been able to set up local branches with legal status equal to that of Chinese firms. Other growth sectors from now on are seen as agriculture, transportation, energy and communications. In 1993, for the first time, Japan became China's largest trading partner supplanting the United States, while in the reverse direction the Chinese moved up from fifth to second.

Japanese investment in Asia first went to the four tigers – Hong Kong, Singapore, Taiwan and South Korea – and then moved on to Thailand, Indonesia and Malaysia. But as investment in these areas reached saturation point in the late 1980s, Japanese companies began to look seriously at China. Originally, they viewed it only as a giant market, and it was some time before it began to appear as a production and potential export base. Initially, most companies only wanted to cooperate with small and medium-sized companies, the inference being that the dinosaurs in the state sector were too inefficient and consistently lost too much money. State involvement was also another reason for shunning Beijing and its environs for a long time and setting up shop in provincial areas, where governmental interference would likely be much lower (although, conversely, approval for projects could take a frustratingly long time partly because the local enterprises did not have enough decision-making autonomy).

According to Chinese data, the first investment from Japan was made in 1979 and in that year the total capital involved was $10.5 million. Before that, there had been too much fear of the political climate and the possibility of nationalization. Even as China began to open up, the Japanese proceeded with their customary caution, the big companies leaving it to the small fry to test the waters first and help iron out any local difficulties in the investment climate. There were only 27 projects worth $55 million established up to the end of 1983.

The pace picked in 1984-5, before a downturn in 1986-87 when an overheated domestic economy persuaded the government to adopt an austerity programme, and political turmoil (party Secretary General Hu Yaobang was removed and there were major student demonstrations) undermined confidence of foreign investors because the situation was unclear. The investment curve turned upwards again in 1988, although the Chinese were far from happy with what they perceived as a lack of Japanese enthusiasm. This was summed up by Chu Baotai, Vice Director of the Foreign Investment Bureau in the Ministry of Foreign Trade, who declared: 'Some Japanese asked why should we use our own capital and technology to train, support and accommodate our competitors? This is a wrong attitude. Japanese companies in China can achieve profit levels on their products around 20 times higher than if they had stayed in Japan.'[13]

In 1988, Japanese Prime Minister Noboru Takeshita visited Beijing to sign an agreement protecting investments and giving companies equal treatment with Chinese ones. This started what became known as the 'high tide' of Japanese investment, especially in the area of telecommunications, household electrical appliances. The first big name in the field was National Panasonic, which established a joint venture in Beijing to manufacture videotape recorders, followed by NEC, which decided to produce integrated circuits and digital telephone exchange systems in Beijing and Tienjin. In 1988 and the spring of 1989, the Japanese and Chinese governments held many discussions which led to the signing of a bilateral investment protection agreement and the establishment of a non-governmental Sino-Japanese Investment Promotion Organization. But after the unhappy events of June 1989, foreign investment went into drastic decline. China, anyway, was on an austerity drive. But, for political reasons, the Japanese thought it too risky to break ranks with its Western allies who were imposing economic sanctions in protest at the crackdown on the democracy movement. In 1990, however, the Chinese Government began a strategy of using Tokyo to break the Western sanctions, setting off a fresh wave of Japanese capital movement.

Up to 1991, however, the chief characteristics of the investment were that it was concentrated in the Special Economic Zones to gain preferential treatment; most of the money went to the non-manufacturing sector (in other Asian countries, the proportion of Japanese money in manufacturing averaged 38.4 per cent, while in China, non-manufacturing accounted for almost 80 per cent); most of the businesses were medium and small sized (in 1989, a Japanese investigation found that 37.9 per cent of the investments were lower than $750,000, while 30.6 per cent were between that figure and $2.25 million); in the manufacturing sector, there were 34.6 per cent of the businesses employing less than 50 people, and 28.4 per cent with 50 to 100 employees (only one enterprise employed more than 1,000 employees and that was a Beijing colour television factory run by Matsushita.[14]

Before 1987, investments were concentrated in the hotel and services sectors. The Japanese initially were reluctant to put money into manufacturing because China's policy then required 70 per cent of the output to be exported back to Japan or to a third country, and only 30 per cent could be sold within China (and with product quality a headache in the early days, there was no guaranteed foreign market available). Running a hotel offered no such difficulties. But, the Japanese investment led to distortion of the Chinese economic structure by contributing to a glut in hotel rooms. In fact, oversupply became so bad that the State Council in 1989 barred the construction of any more five-star hotels in the capital. One worry was that the Chinese had to match any Japanese investment in the joint venture, which meant that with money in short supply anyway, too much of it was being siphoned off from more productive industrial sectors.

The bulk of the early manufacturing investments were from migrating industries in highly competitive but generally low technology sectors searching for ever-lower production costs. Textiles is a typical example. Japanese firms first moved out of their home base to South Korea and Taiwan where labour costs were lower. Then, when wages began to rise in these two countries, the factories were closed and the companies moved on to China. This kind of investment had no technology, so it could not possibly meet China's main requirements in seeking foreign investment, some Chinese officials grumbled.

According to one source: 'In order to attract the Japanese investment, China had to provide a basic infrastructure, roads and the best possible factory facilities, which cost a great deal of money. So, although we could recoup some of this investment by earning foreign exchange, the presence of the Japanese was still somewhat damaging to us. We provided the facilities but they did not provide any kind of technology, so the benefits are very limited. If the Japanese hadn't come and invested in the low-technology areas – textiles, shoe pads – we could have made our own. Their presence reduced the opportunities for our domestic firms. Without them, we could have heightened our research and developed our own technology to make the same excellent products which we could have exported and even occupied the Japanese market. But they used our cheap labour and they made money. And although they sold the products back to Japan it's us who lost the export chance.'[15]

Even when they received Japanese technology, the Chinese complained that it tended to be old and low-grade which could do little to modernize or upgrade its industries. The Japanese were accused of being unwilling to reveal their advanced techniques to a potential competitor. This was particularly true in the automobile industry, where the Japanese were happy to sell as many vehicles as China could take, but held back from investing in manufacturing joint ventures. The Chinese Government countered this reluctance with a warning that 'if you do not come, then we will invite others'. That did the trick – as will be discussed in detail later in relation to the motor industry.

The investment pattern throughout, however, has been characterized by a careful, long-term strategy. A typical example is Dalian, the town nicknamed 'Little Japan' in the northeast which was discussed in the last chapter. There, the big trading companies established offices in the early 1980s. At that time there was not much money to be made, but the initial groundwork was laid. Later, they were able to become important players in helping new companies to establish operations and to import and export their goods. The trading companies were followed by the banks, and together they were instrumental in the construction of modern office buildings, apartment houses and hotels. By taking care of major concerns, such as financing and location, as well as important details such as installation of electric plugs that are compatible with Japanese voltage, they were able to ease the transition pains of the many firms already in Dalian and ensuring that more would follow.

The peak in Japanese investment does not yet appear to have been reached, especially with an ever increasing number of companies being forced by an appreciating currency and high labour costs to cut down domestic production and relocate their manufacturing operations elsewhere in the world. The pace began to pick up in 1992. In that year alone, the big five in the electronics industry – Hitachi, Matsushita, Mitsubishi, Sony and Toshiba – between them invested more than 100 billion Yen ($937 million).[16] Matsushita, better known under its brand name of National Panasonic, has become one of the biggest foreign employers in China and its Beijing factory is a key supplier of colour picture tubes to the Chinese television industry. It has opened 12 factories in China, the latest being one in Dalian to manufacture components for videotape recorders. Ten of its ventures make products for the domestic market, making Matsushita unusual even among Japanese companies. In 1992 Toshiba opened a $90 million factory in Dalian to produce electric motors and television components for other parts of the company's empire overseas; it also took a 78 per cent share in a joint venture in Hangzhou, Hangzhi Machinery and Electronics, manufacturing a whole range of products from photocopier cables to telephone handsets. Honda Motor Company expects to be building one million motorcycles a year at various Chinese factories by the end of the century. Canon, the leader in photocopying, established two wholly-owned, for-export-only factories, one in Dalian to recycle copier cartridges, and the other in Zhuhai, Guangdong province, to make lenses and cameras. Its next objective was a joint venture to build and sell copying machines domestically.

At the same time, the Japanese Government continued to provide substantial development aid to cement the alliance. Tokyo gave $93 million in 1993 and was scheduled to match the amount in 1994. Since 1979, the Japanese have pledged an estimated $15.6 billion in government preferential loans for China's economic reconstruction, although it has not all been utilized yet for a variety of reasons. Japan supplied more loans and donations than any other economically-developed country, a senior Moftec official declared.[17]

All this activity has helped improve the atmosphere between the two neighbours who have had a curious bitter-sweet relationship stretching back almost two millennia. Much of Japan's culture and traditional values came from China, but unlike other Asian states, the Japanese refused to kow-tow to the Chinese emperor or send tributes. As China went into decline and Japan rose in the mid-nineteenth century, relations steadily deteriorated and Japan's brutal occupation of vast tracts of the mainland in the 1930s and 1940s left a bitter legacy that has been hard to eradicate. The Chinese never tire of reminding the world of Japanese war-time atrocities, although apologies at imperial and prime-ministerial level finally seem to have cleared the idea. Nevertheless, the Chinese and Japanese can hardly be described as brothers. They need each other for the moment and so they make the best of it. But there are a lot of people on both sides who foresee an eventual economic conflict erupting as China begins to challenge Japan's dominance of the Asian economy.

SOUTH KOREA

China sided with the communist North in the Korean War and was for many years its main political and economic backer. But the Chinese have become more pragmatic about separating economic and political issues. Ignoring the ideological bonds as well as Pyongyang's obvious unhappiness, the first unofficial contacts were made with South Korea in the late 1970s. Despite the lack of diplomatic relations, non-governmental trade soared from a minuscule $12.7 million in 1979 to an estimated $10 billion in 1993. Only the United States and Japan currently sell more goods to China. Steel, cars, electronic appliances and heavy industrial goods are most in demand, while the Chinese mainly supply raw materials in return.

The two countries signed an agreement giving each other MFN status for investment and business ventures in 1991, and in August the following year diplomatic ties were finally established. By the end of the year, more than 900 South Korean projects had been approved. China is now South Korea's fourth biggest trade partner and its number three favourite investment spot. The bulk of the investment has gone into chemical fibre, garment, electronic, machine building, toy, farm produce and food-processing industries, with just over a third of the money going to set up solely Korean-owned concerns.

In the late 1980s, the Seoul government formulated a development programme for its backward western coast facing China, and proposed the creation of a Yellow Sea Economic Zone encompassing the Shandong and Liaodong peninsulas and the eastern coast open cities. The opportunity was eagerly seized by Qingdao (see chapter three) at the tip of the Shandong Peninsula, which quickly became one of the most popular investment spots for South Korean enterprises, especially now that direct flights can link Seoul and Qingdao in an hour (alternatively, passenger ferries run twice a week).

In Yantai, on the other side of the peninsula, Jin Suk Young bought an existing factory and hired 150 workers, mainly women, to assemble precision parts at a quarter of the wages paid to their counterparts at home. The venture was an immediate success, prompting Jin to declare: 'We'll be moving all our production over here. The corporate headquarters will remain in South Korea, along with our technical, marketing, quality control and trade departments. But manufacturing will be transferred here within two or three years.'

Gradually, the investment tide has moved south (as far as Guangdong Province, where 19 joint ventures have been established). In August 1992, the two countries signed an agreement to establish a huge industrial complex in Tianjin, giving South Korean companies rights to 130,000 sq.m. in the city for 50 years. The state-run Korea Land Development Corporation will manage the construction of an industrial complex due for completion by the end of 1994. Chinese officials predict major Korean investments in the Yangtse Valley covering steel, cement, machinery, electronics, power-generation and automobiles. This will mark the second phase of Korean economic involvement in China, moving away from the labour-intensive and raw materials-processing sectors into capital and technology-intensive and even infrastructural projects. In the latter category, a major Korean construction company Dong Ah is involved in a $3 billion deal with Beijing municipal authorities to build a motorway, an underground railway and cement plant in the city, while Hyundai Engineering and Construction, part of the country's biggest industrial conglomerate, was hoping to win a contract for a $3 billion dam project on the Yellow River.

This is part of another trend where, after letting the small fry initially test the waters (resulting in capital injections of no more than $630,000 in most cases), the major corporate names in Korea – Daewoo, Hyundai, Lotte and Samsung, for example – are finally moving in and discussing a whole range of major programmes involving big money. Daewoo Heavy Industries, for example, joined a venture to produce an 'Asian airbus' by 1998, with the strong possibility of Singapore and India also becoming involved. In Seoul, government officials enthuse that closer collaboration between the two countries typified by the rapid upsurge in investment dea ls will 'create a twenty-first century Asia-Pacific economic miracle'.

EUROPE

With the furious investment pace being set by the countries already mentioned, there is a danger of European companies being left out in the cold. Individual companies have done quite well, and all the major corporate names are represented in various parts of China. But there is not the same sense of opportunities being grasped as with, say, Japan, Taiwan, Singapore and South Korea.

Speaking at a London conference[18] on the future of Hong Kong, Victor Fung, Chairman of the colony's Trade Development Council, warned that Europe ran the risk of missing the boat, because the opportunity Asia offered investors would not wait while the members of the European Union resolved their complex economic problems. He feared Europe would continue to look inward to the single European market, with the bulk of investment and executive time devoted to forging links with the emerging economies of eastern and central Europe. 'Will these priorities keep investment and management out of Asia – or at least on the margins – at a time of unparalleled opportunity?'[19]

Countries like the United States and Japan, however, were grasping the opportunity with both hands. Fung cited the initiative being taken by President Bill Clinton to promote the Asia-Pacific Economic Forum as a vehicle for closer American involvement in the booming region (see above). Japan, too, was seeking to play a key role in the predicted shift in the economic balance from West to East. The Hong Kong businessman said that in raising the alarm he was not acting purely out of philanthropic motives, '. . . because we in Asia will also pay a price if European companies are not fully engaged in the region. As leaders in innovation and high-tech production in many sectors we need the stimulus European companies would bring'.

Despite these fears, the fact remains that Britain, France, Germany and Italy are all rated by the Chinese in the top 10 investors. Britain's relations with China have been bedevilled with difficulties over the 1997 handover of Hong Kong, and there is little argument that the trade relationship has been affected (the Chinese hinting that life for British businessmen would be far easier if only their government would stop trying to introduce democracy into the soon-to-be former colony). Nevertheless, British companies did pledge almost $100 million to 130 Chinese projects in 1992, significantly ahead of Germany, about the same as Italy, but less than half that of France. And although no specific figures were provided, both the British and Germans were reported to have increased their capital input sixfold in the first half of 1993 compared to the same period in the previous year.[20] At the same time, Sino-British trade more than doubled between 1986 and 1991, and the increase was more than fourfold if trade via Hong Kong was included. Using the broader calculation, two-way trade passed the $3 billion mark for the first time in 1991 and continues to grow.[21]

In contrast to Britain, Germany has maintained a low profile and managed to avoid political problems in its relations with China. The Germans have one of the biggest investments in the automobile sector, for example, through the two Volkswagen factories, including one in Shanghai where the capacity was being increased from 100,000 to 150,000 by the end of 1993 (the VW plants will be discussed in more detail in chapter seven on the Chinese automotive industry). Other German firms are also establishing a strong presence. Daimler-Benz, through its subsidiary Deutsche Aerospace, had ambitions for collaborative ventures in satellite technology, solar collectors and other electronic components. A consortium including Siemens and AEG is involved in building a 11-mile stretch of underground railway in Guangzhou, while a Siemens subsidiary was trying to persuade the Chinese to buy its ICE high-speed train system. Siemens also penetrated the power plant market with a joint venture to make instrumentation and control equipment (vital for increasing the reliability, cost-effectiveness and service life of power plants while cutting fuel consumption and waste emissions) at a factory in the Nanjing Economic Development Zone. It also had high hopes of major telecommunications contracts in transmission systems and digital mobile telephones. Other companies, meanwhile, are seeking contracts for container ships to be built in former East German shipyards on top of an existing deal for eight ships signed before reunification.[22]

INFRASTRUCTURE PROSPECTS

Greater opportunities for European companies, in particular heavy equipment suppliers, could open up in the years ahead, especially with the Chinese government announcing grand plans for as much as $120 billion to spend on upgrading the country's transport and service infrastructure. The plan calls for the total length of railways to be extended from the present 33,000 to 44,000 miles, offering opportunities for suppliers of premium-grade rails such as British Steel and a 20 per-cent increase in rolling stock. Some of China's diesel and electric locomotives are now being supplied by GEC Alsthom of France, but because of a strong domestic industry Asea Brown Boveri, the Swiss-Swedish Group, believes the best opportunities will lie in supplying sophisticated components rather than complete foreign-made vehicles. ABB is already involved in a joint venture to produce signalling equipment. There is also a road-building programme designed to add about 125,000 miles to the country's inadequate highway network. Only about 3,750 miles of the national roads are classified as highway, properly paved and consisting of more than one lane each way. Another part of the government programme calls for a doubling of the number of ports to 600 to ease a situation where at least half of the ships calling at cargo-clogged ports have to wait days for unloading. Detailing these moves, an official announcement said that '. . . while continuing to use loans provided by the World Bank and foreign governments, China will welcome foreign investors to run joint ventures or solely-owned ventures in the construction of railways, highways and civil aviation facilities other than air-control systems. Meanwhile, the country will encourage localities and enterprises to construct docks, roads and railways for their own use.'[24]

Given China's acknowledged energy-supply deficiencies, power demand is estimated to exceed supply by at least 20 per cent nation-wide; 120 million peasants still live without electricity, while brownouts and blackouts bedevil the major cities. According to Chinese officials, nuclear energy will have an increasing role to play (although only as a supplement to thermal and hydroelectric power) with several plants planned for construction by the end of the century. At the time of writing, feasibility studies were underway in the provinces of Liaoning, Hainan, Jiangsu and

Shandong, and foreign partners were being sought for the construction. China has two operating nuclear power plants at Qinshan in Zhejiang Province and at Daya Bay near Hong Kong, the latter involving the French company Franatome. The Chinese have also indicated that there will be wide-ranging possibilities for foreign companies to become involved in the Three Gorges Dam project referred to earlier.

For years, foreign businessmen in China have gnashed their teeth over the difficulty of making telephone calls around the country. Ironically, international connections are often far easier to get than domestic ones. Some Japanese executives, for example say that in trying to call one of their factories in another part of the country the best way is often to pass a message through their head office in Japan. The Posts and Telecommunications Ministry calculated as recently as the early 1980s that the capital's ancient telephone exchanges were so overloaded that at least one-third of all calls never got through. This spurred a cartoonist to depict an old man trying to put through a call while his son and grandson waited. The old man says: 'If I cannot get through, my son can; if my son cannot, my grandson can'. Even in the early 1990s, it was reported that foreign businessmen had turned down cooperation offers from a county only 30 miles from the city centre because there was no way they could telephone their head offices.

Twenty per cent of the country's total telecommunications revenue currently is generated by one city, Guangzhou, which in 1989 became the first city to have more than one million 'phone lines. A year later, Shanghai became the first metropolis to adopt seven-digit numbers because its six-digit system could no longer cope with demand – with 450,000 applicants on a waiting list for connection. By the end of the century, the government hoped that every family in Beijing, Shanghai, Tianjin and all the provincial capitals would have a home telephone. In 1992, it was estimated that 2.4 million urban households had their own telephone, compared to 1,000 in 1980, of which two-thirds were in Shanghai. Nevertheless, some parts of the country still have no telephones at all. At present, there are 1.6 fixed wire telephones per 100 persons. But under a 10-year (1991–2000) telecommunications plan, the government determined to bring this down to one in five. To achieve its objectives in Beijing alone, however, requires the creation of another 2.5 million telephone lines.

In order to meet its target, the government opened the door to foreign telecommunications firms for joint ventures to expand production capacity and improve product quality. Hakan Jansson, president of Ericsson AB of Sweden, estimated that by the turn of the century China would represent 15 to 20 per cent of the world public telecommunications market (the sector absorbed more than $3 billion between 1991 and 1993). The country's largest manufacturer, China National Post and Telecommunications Industry Corporation (PTIC), for example sought foreign partners to help revitalize all of its 28 subsidiary factories, many of them set up in the 1960s and 1970s and hopelessly obsolete. In the decade from 1984, it had signed deals for 18 technological renovation projects covering digital program-controlled telephone exchanges, optical-fibre communications systems, digital microwave systems, telephones, fax machines and mobile communications. In 1993, it gained permission to import foreign production lines in four of its factories. These included expansion of capacity for producing mobile telephones – the most treasured possession of the new Chinese yuppie – with equipment provided by the American firm Motorola. In Beijing, almost all radio pagers and mobile phones are said to be Motorola products. The company's business has expanded so rapidly it frequently runs recruitment ads in mass-circulation Chinese newspapers.

A second PTIC factory, meanwhile, was importing computer-controlled switching system technology from Northern Telecom of Canada. And a French company, Alcatel, was the prime candidate to supply the production lines for mainframe distribution systems that form part of digital telephone exchanges. Alcatel has a joint venture in Shanghai which was in the process of expanding its capacity of telephone switches from 300,000 to one million a year. The Swedish firm Ericcson, which first provided telephones to China 100 years ago, now accounts for a fifth of the market in digital switches. Meanwhile, the American giant AT & T is involved with the State Planning Commission in a 'Long-Term Comprehensive Partnership' involving cooperation in manufacturing advanced program-controlled switching systems, setting up r & d facilities, and transferring microelectronics, manufacturing and research technology and developing mobile telecommunications networks.

THE CHINESE MULTINATIONALS

Finally in this chapter, I want to look at the Chinese companies who are becoming the powerhouse of the country's economic revolution both at home and overseas and the leader in China's own increased foreign investments. Foreign banks and financial institutions are queuing up to lend money to China International Trust and Investment Corporation (CITIC), widely considered to be the closest thing to a Western-style company in the country even though it is under direct control of the State Council (China's Cabinet). It was set up to act as China's investment arm overseas, and as far as the government is concerned its prime role is to assist in the modernization of the national economy through investments primarily internationally that encourage a transfer of technology and managerial know-how to the mainland. But CITIC has also taken full advantage of the move towards a market economy to pursue domestic business opportunities, including a role in some of the country's most ambitious infrastructure development projects. They include a sea bridge linking Ningbo, Zhejiang Province, to Daxie Island, in which the company planned to invest $6 billion over 10 years as part of a plan to turn the island into an export-oriented economic zone and port.

CITIC portrays itself as a 'Socialist conglomerate engaged in production, technology, finance and services.' One of its major subsidiaries is China International Economic Consultants Inc. (CIEC) which is of particular importance to foreign investors and traders as a gateway both to China and to other CITIC group companies. It publishes various books on foreign investment including the China Investment Guide, a valuable work of reference, and also offers introduction services to potential partners, key ministries and regulating bodies, as well as feasibility studies and market research. Two subsidiaries of CIEC offer legal and accountancy services. Other arms of CITIC include companies involved in import/export trade, travel, real estate development, investment in high technology industries, and one which, in close collaboration with the PLA, imports and exports defence equipment and technology. As indicated by its title, CITIC is an important non-banking financial institution. The most important are attached to key government organs with the role of raising capital internationally and from non-governmental sources at home to promote projects sponsored by their parent ministries. Many provinces have their own ITIC, each with a keen eye on business opportunities – typified by the one in Guangdong Province which is the materials supply partner in a highly profitable McDonald's hamburger outlet.

The original driving force behind CITIC was Rong Yiren, who was rewarded for his efforts by promotion to one of China's vice premiers in mid-1993. New chairman, Wei Mingyi, outlining his plans soon after taking over, said the company would establish securities, insurance and futures companies to take advantage of opportunities in China's booming service economy. He also saw promising opportunities in the crumbling of the state's long-standing monopoly in the petroleum, telecommunications and aviation sectors. Further international borrowings, especially in Japan and Singapore (where demand for Chinese bonds is particularly strong), seemed likely as CITIC sought to raise its capital base from the current $9 billion to $22.5 billion by the end of the century.

The Beijing-based company, established in 1979, sits on top of a corporate pyramid that also includes CITIC Industrial Bank and the wholly-owned CITIC Hong Kong. The latter, in turn, has a 45 per cent stake in CITIC Pacific which held significant equity holdings in some of the biggest corporate names in the Hong Kong and is now reckoned to be its 10 largest companies in its own right. The holdings include Cathay Pacific (12 per cent), with which it then set up Dragon Air (taking a 46.2 per cent equity share) that flies to the mainland and to other regional destinations; Hong Kong Telecom (12 per cent) and Macao Telecom (20 per cent). CITIC Pacific also has wide-ranging interests in retail and import/export businesses and a major property holdings. It is, for example, cooperating with one of Hong Kong's biggest companies, Swire, in the development of new shopping malls and office complexes along the railway line leading from Kowloon into southern China. And from Hong Kong, through various subsidiaries, CITIC Pacific is also investing back into the mainland, especially in food processing – using the booming Special Economic Zones like Shenzhen as a launch pad to open up new product markets in the rest of the country. In the wider world, CITIC has stakes in real estate, timber, pulp, paper, aluminium smelting and other major industries in Australia, Canada and the United States

Established at the same time in 1979, the China National Aero-Technology Import & Export Corporation Group (CATIC) has grown into a powerful conglomerate of 12 domestic subsidiaries and 39 overseas representative offices, controlling 130 enterprises. Although designed primarily as a window of investment and trading opportunities with the Chinese aerospace industry, it has diversified into a wide range of activities including the manufacture of mechanical and electrical products, labour services, real estate, hotel management and materials development.

Through CATIC, China plans to become more aggressive in the aviation markets of Africa, Asia and Latin America. 'Zhao Mingqi, Group Vice President, said improvement and renovation of Chinese-made civilian planes was being made with the export market in mind. Chinese planes, mainly light and small passenger and cargo aircraft, were competitive in price and reliability, he said. In the past, China has exported 650 planes, mostly military models. The export of civilian planes began in 1986 when six Yun-12s were sold to Sri Lanka. According to the Group's goals, imports and exports of aircraft will reach $1 billion by 1995 and double by 2000.'[25]

Another important window on the outside world is China Everbright Holdings, set up by the State Council in 1982 and incorporated in Hong Kong. It has offices and subsidiaries in Beijing, Tianjin, Guangzhou and Wuhan, and its principal business activities are described as 'co-production, joint ventures, investment, finance, tourism, labour export, import and export, compensation trade and consultancy.' In 1985, the State Council also set up the China Industry and Commerce Development Corporation (INCOMIC), whose main remit is trade development.

FOOTNOTES:
1. *Financial Times*, 18 Nov. 1993.
2. Taken from various sources, including *China Daily* and *Beijing Review*.
3. German industrialists accompanying Chancellor Helmut Kohl signed some 20 contracts and letters of intent in Beijing worth $1.6 billion. Among the deals was an order for six A340 long range Airbuses. *Times* and *Financial Times*, 16 Nov. 1993
4. Interview given to *Business Weekly*, 22 Aug. 1993.

5. *Beijing Review*, 26 July 1993.
6. *Financial Times*, 18 Nov. 1993.
7. *Economist*, 18 July 1992
8. *Time Magazine*, 10 May 1993.
9. Addressing the Second World Chinese Entrepreneurs Convention in Hong Kong, 22 Nov. 1993.
10. Ministry of Economic Affairs statistics.
11. *Financial Times*, 5 July 1993.
12. Associated Press, 3 Nov. 1993.
13. *People's Daily*, 6 Nov. 1988
14. Based on an interview with a researcher with the State Economic Commission who wished to remain anonymous,
15. Ibid.
16. Figure provided by the Electronics Industrial Association of Japan.
17. Chen Kongming, Deputy Director General of the Foreign Financing Administration, quoted in *Business Weekly*, 31 Oct. 1993.
18. 10 November 1993.
19. Writing in the *Financial Times*, 11 Nov. 1993.
20. *Beijing Review*, 18 Aug. 1993.
21. HM Customs and the Census and Statistics Department, Hong Kong.
22. *Financial Times*, 12 Nov. 1993.
23. It supplied 10,000 tonnes of such materials in 1992. [*Financial Times*, 26 Nov. 1993].
24. Xinhua News Agency, 24 Nov. 1993.
25. *China Daily*, 27 Aug. 1993.

6 The main options for investing in China

KEY POINTS

Having looked in some detail at the current principal players in the China market, let us now consider the practicalities of establishing a presence there. In this chapter, therefore, the issues to be considered are:
- The choice of the right business model – joint venture, representative office or wholly-owned enterprise.
- The essential Chinese legal requirements for each type of business.
- The underlying principles governing the relationship between China and foreign businessmen.
- The difficulties in choosing the right Chinese partner.
- Essentials to keep in mind before investing, especially the need for a clear definition of business objectives.
- What can go wrong – the disappointments on both sides of the fence as expectations sometimes fail to materialize.

REPRESENTATIVE OFFICE

THERE ARE three business models which have been declared acceptable for foreigners by the Chinese authorities – joint venture, wholly-owned company and representative office. Basically, if a company wants to get involved in manufacturing, then a joint venture is regarded as the proper approach. If it merely wants to sell imported products in China, then a representative office is the best choice. Alternatively, if both aspects are involved, then the option of a wholly-owned subsidiary may be feasible in some circumstances. A representative office, however, is not allowed to do business directly, but can only, in the words of the official jargon, 'build relations and provide technical support'. Most companies set up a representative office in one or more of the major cities such as Beijing, Guangzhou, Shanghai and Tianjin, or one of the SEZs. The representative office is responsible for appointing distributors, and providing technical support and training.

Representative offices are primarily covered by the Interim Regulations for Control of Resident Representative Offices of Foreign Enterprises in China, issued in October 1980, and the 1983 Procedures for the Registration and Administration of Resident Representative Offices of Foreign Enterprises in China (which, among other requirements, insisted on a non-profit role, as well as re-registration annually). Representative offices for banks and other financial institutions were covered by separate regulations in the same year. On top of these central regulations, some municipal and provincial governments have their own rules covering specific areas.

But although, I have stated that representative offices cannot sell anything, clever businessmen have found ways to get around the restriction. So much so, in fact, that in 1993 the government issued a memorandum to foreign businessmen which said in effect: 'You are reminded that foreign company representative offices in China are not allowed to earn revenue. However, we know you all do it so we are going to tax you on this income.'

Under an overhaul of the administrative structure, the Ministry of Foreign Trade and Economic Cooperation (MOFTEC) has become the sole supervisory government agency for representative offices, although certain industry-specific businesses, such as financial services, still have to be approved by the relevant authority. But in other areas there are still many irritants created by a plethora of local regulations. There is, for example, no nation-wide duty-free import policy. Thus, while representative offices in Beijing can no longer import a car duty-free – as they could before 1990, Tianjin allows two vehicles and Dalian has no restrictions whatsoever.

In order to establish a representative office, a foreign company needs a local sponsor, which is often an enterprise with which it has had business dealings in the past, but could also be one of the consultancies set up by government departments such as MOFTEC or FESCO (Foreign Enterprise Service Corp., the traditional source of local labour). Applications have to be accompanied by legal documents sanctioning the firm's business activities in its home company, memorandum and articles of association, a complete list of the board of directors, the most recent balance sheets and profit/loss accounts from the home head office and financial statements from the firm's main bank. Within 30 days of approval being received, the company has to register with the municipal or provincial bureau of the State Administration for Industry and Commerce (SAIC), again presenting all the documents previously mentioned along with the approval certificate. After the registration approval is received, the final steps are to open a bank account with the Bank of China, register with the Public Security Bureau, the Customs and the Tax Bureau. Registration certificates are valid for three years, but still have to be renewed annually. Any change in the foreign representative has to go through the same approval procedures.

JOINT VENTURES

China passed its first law on foreign investment in 1979, and since then vehicles to channel foreign capital have steadily multiplied. The most common are an equity joint venture, joint development, limited company, cooperative joint venture, joint development, wholly foreign-owned enterprise, compensation trade and processing and assembly agreements.[1]

An *Equity Joint Venture (EJV)* is a limited liability corporation which is a legal entity in China. Each side owns a proportion of equity shares (which may take the form of equipment, cash, rights to the use of the site, factory buildings, industrial property rights, etc.). Partners together decide corporate strategy; they jointly operate the venture, share the risks, profits and losses, according to their equity share. Chinese law on Sino-foreign EJVs requires the foreign partner to take a minimum stake of 25 per cent, although there are exceptions. Once an EJV expires, it is liquidated unless the life-span has been extended, and the proceeds shared out between the partners, with the foreign side allowed to repatriate its share. The Chinese Government does not normally have the right to nationalize or expropriate EJVs. Only under special circumstances – based on social and public interest – can expropriation occur, in which case compensation must be paid.

Each party appoints its own director(s). Partners negotiate the size and composition of the board at the outset. If a Chinese-appointed director serves as chairman, the vice-chairman should come from the foreign side, and vice versa. The positions of general manager(s) – or factory manager and deputy general manager – are assumed by nominees of the respective parties. The terms of operation may differ from the norm in certain circumstances, but this depends on government approval and only on a case-by-case basis. EJVs in most industrial sectors have a fixed duration of between 15 and 30 years. If partners agree to extend the life, they must apply for an extension at least six months before expiry. The authorities must then make their decision known within a month of receiving the application.

All partners must contribute to the EJVs common registered capital. Part of the contribution must be in cash, although the foreign partners' share may also be partly in the form of technology. The government limits the value of any such contribution to 20 per cent of the registered capital or 50 per cent of the foreign partners' investment, whichever is the lower. The Chinese partner has the right to make non-monetary contributions to the registered capital in the form of use of the site, buildings or equipment, for example. The foreign side cannot withdraw its contribution while the EJV is in operation, unless another investor takes over its stake or the EJV is liquidated.

Foreign investors are allowed to set up a *limited company* in cooperation with Chinese interests. A Sino-foreign limited company is established by the sponsoring company – the sponsors comprising at least five people. An enterprise with foreign investment may be converted into a limited company.

Cooperative Joint Ventures (CJVs) involve a different division of responsibilities from EJVs. Under a CJV, the Chinese party provide the joint venture with non-liquid assets (eg: land, natural resources, labour, services, usable buildings, equipment or facilities). Foreign participants must provide either capital or technology, essential equipment, materials etc.

The terms of cooperation in the CJV contract define the distribution of its products, revenues and profits. Unlike EJVs, CJVs do not require that partners' capital contributions take the form of money. Consequently, a CJV's profits are not distributed in proportion to the partners' equity shares, but in accordance with the proportions stipulated in the contract. Again, unlike the EJV, a CJV with legal entity status does not have to be set up in China, and the Chinese and foreign parties may operate as separate legal entities. Other differences from EJVs are that there is no need for common registered capital and the equity ratio is not necessarily calculated in monetary terms. Responsibilities and rights are clearly stipulated in the contract.

Foreign CJV investors are allowed to recover their investments before the enterprise expires. Where the Chinese and foreign parties state that all of the fixed assets revert to the former, they may stipulate in the contract the method(s) whereby the foreign party first recover their investment during the lifetime of the venture. If the CJV contract states that the foreign partner may recover its investment before paying income tax, they must submit an application to the relevant finance and tax authorities. In general, if the CJV is a legal entity registered in China, foreign investors are not permitted to recover their investment by paying equipment depreciation charges. With CJVs (unlike the EJVs), the Chinese party may contribute the land use right as its share in the venture and is not required to hand over this profit to the state.

Joint Development is the term normally applied to joint exploration for offshore hydrocarbons. JDs normally have two stages: geographical exploration, and exploitation and development. During the first stage, the foreign partners take all the risk s, and they must provide all financial exploration. During the second stage, both foreign and Chinese partners contribute to the venture. Once commercial production has started, the Chinese party receives a fixed portion of the returns from the development (minus operating costs). Both Chinese and foreign parties receive a sum, with accrued interest, as compensation for their investment. The foreign side also receive an additional sum as a bonus.

A *Wholly Foreign-Owned Enterprise (WFOE)* is one set up on Chinese soil whose entire capital is invested by foreign concerns. It cannot, however, simply be a branch established in China by a foreign company. WFOEs are usually limited liability companies, although they can take other forms subject to official approval. Chinese law requires that they play an active role in developing China's economy, and should, in theory, be capable of achieving unusually large profits. The foreign investment may be in the form of free-convertible foreign currency, or machinery, industrial property rights and know-how. In order to qualify for approval, a WFOE needs to fulfil at least one of the following conditions:

- It must use advanced technology and equipment to develop new products, save energy and raw materials, improve on existing products and engage in import substitution.
- It must achieve 50 per cent or more of annual output value of all products with a balance or surplus in foreign exchange receipt and expenditure.

Chinese law forbids the setting up of WFOEs in the areas of news, publication, broadcasting, television and film industries, domestic commerce, foreign trade, insurance, post and telecommunications, and any other sectors which the authorities decide are off-limits. However, foreign companies in most of the sectors mentioned are allowed to maintain representative offices.

When wholly foreign-owned enterprises were first permitted in China, investors were attracted by the high degree of operational autonomy. Later, they became even more popular, but for a different reason – being among the cheapest and easiest ways for foreign companies to gain access to the generous incentives of the country's many special zones. According to one Western economic analyst[2]: '. . . a lot of these enterprises are just paper companies that don't involve much investment capital. They exist either to sell products on the local market or to import things duty free'. This, of course, was not what China had in mind when it made WFOEs possible. Such enterprises were meant to serve as vehicles for new production-oriented investment, not as avenues to duty-free allotments. tax breaks and the Chinese domestic market.

Investment in WFOEs has risen dramatically in recent years, in terms of both the number of ventures and the share of foreign direct investment that they represent. In 1986, WFOEs accounted for less than one per cent of foreign investment in China. By 1991, that figure was 37 per cent and nearly 8,600 WFOEs were approved the following year. For precisely the same reasons that foreigners were attracted to the WFOE option, China was reluctant to permit them as the format allowed foreign companies to both maximize their management control and protect sensitive proprietary technology. The earliest large-scale WFOEs were formed in 1984 only after their parent companies resisted heavy

Chinese pressure to accept a joint venture format. Even the dramatic rise of WFOEs in the late 1980s was not a matter of choice for China, but rather a necessary response to a severe capital shortage which meant domestic companies were unable to provide matching capital for joint-venture projects, making the wholly-foreign owned format the only way China could accommodate foreign investment.

But more and more WFOEs are being approved with only scant consideration to the legal requirements. These usually call for 15 per cent of the capital to be registered in China within three months of the enterprise's establishment, the remainder to be scheduled on very liberal terms. Some special zones required as little as £200,000 in pledged investment, meaning that for £30,000 in actual capital, a WFOE could gain access to tax holidays and duty-free allocations for imported cars and office equipment. China announced plans for more rigorous auditing of all foreign-funded enterprises in mid-1993, but initial foreign reaction was that it was debatable how effective these would be.[3]

There are drawbacks to going it alone. One Western management consultant recalled that in 1992 the Chinese government issued a statement saying that foreign companies were allowed, under certain stringent terms and regulations, to set up wholly-owned subsidiary offices somewhat different from WFOEs: 'A few companies jumped at that, including IBM. But because it was a new idea, and the Chinese were very frightened about it, they regulated the hell out of it with so many restrictions as they felt their way. Companies who had gone headfirst into that ran into a lot of problems. For example, if you're a state-owned Chinese company you are supposed to provide many benefits such as housing, medical care, schooling, just about everything for your employees. But foreign companies said obviously there was no way they were going to do that because their local employees wanted to be on an international level in terms of what they were being paid and housing provision, which from a business point of view obviously was not acceptable.' So, the wholly-owned subsidiary – the single venture enterprise as the Chinese call it – is probably not a good idea unless perhaps you are a very large company and very serious about China, and perhaps have been here for a while.

Under *Compensation Trade (CT)* deals, the Chinese side usually provide factory buildings and labour, the foreign side supplying production equipment, technology and possibly technical and supervisory personnel. Depending on the circumstances, the foreign investor may be asked to supply some of the raw materials. Repayment is normally in kind, in instalments (with the goods produced in the project), for the technology, equipment and other materials they have supplied. If it is impractical to repay the foreign investor in this way, they may be paid with other products (or by a combination of goods and cash) in a form acceptable to both parties.

There are two ways to raise capital for CT. The first is for the foreign investor to obtain foreign bank loans to pay for the capital and equipment imported by the Chinese side. The Chinese then use the goods produced to repay the equipment costs and bank interest. The second method is for the Chinese side to use export loans from foreign banks to buy production equipment. The Chinese partner then pays the bank the principal and interest in the foreign exchange earned from the sale of the finished goods.

Under *leasing*, foreign companies provide the Chinese lessees with equipment, machinery or other facilities either directly or through leasing service corporations or leasing agents. Technical and management services are usually provided. The Chinese lessees make payments by instalments according to the leading charges agreed on by the two sides. The foreign company, leasing service corporation or leasing agent, is responsible for the customs formalities on imported equipment or machines. The length of the lease varies from three to five years, although it can be longer.

Under a *processing and assembly of supplies, parts and components* arrangement, the foreign partner supplies the materials, while the Chinese enterprise processes or assembles them, according to the foreign partner's specifications. The material input from the foreign partner can include all or part of the raw materials, semi-finished products, subsidiary materials, parts or components and, if necessary, packing materials. The finished products are handed over to the foreign partner, or their agents, who are required to sell them outside China. The Chinese enterprises receive a fee for their efforts. All the machinery and equipment used must be Chinese-made, unless it is not available in the country – in which case it can be imported, and the cost deducted from the final value of the exports or the processing fee.

The main options for investing in China 151

In this case, the imported equipment is exempt from duties and taxes.

The foreign partner can settle the processing fee either by opening a letter of credit at the Bank of China, or other approved Chinese bank, or pay in cash when the goods are delivered. Alternatively, the foreign partner may fix a price for the materials or parts supplied, while the Chinese side fix a price for the finished products. The Bank of China then issues a usance letter of credit for the Chinese side when the materials supplied arrive in-country. The foreign partner's bank then issues a letter of credit at sight to the Chinese side after the finished products have been shipped.

At present, processing and assembly contracts concentrate on labour-intensive industries such as clothes-making, and textile enterprises in general, although Chinese enterprises increasingly assemble a wide range of articles such as refrigerators, vehicles, calculators, and hi-fi equipment.

Chinese factories which have surplus processing capacity and suitable technology may enter into contracts with the foreign company. The factories are regulated by the Chinese Government. Local foreign trade corporations may also take orders and sign the contracts on behalf of the factories. The finished goods generally use the foreign firms' trade mark. In addition, subject to both sides' agreement, the Chinese manufacturer's trade mark may also be used. Commodities which are regulated by quotas may not benefit from Chinese export quotas, except in specially-negotiated cases.

The Chinese government offers preferential treatment to encourage the development of the processing and assembly business. The materials, parts and production equipment imported into China, and the finished goods exported, are free from duties provided the contract has been officially approved. Profits earned by foreign firms are not taxed in China. In order to protect local enterprises against loss during the production process, the government gives them preference in foreign exchange control, finance and taxation (within certain limits). The Chinese bodies responsible for funds, materials, power and transport, insurance, settlement of accounts. and consultancy services are expected to offer as much support as possible.

UNDERSTANDING THE OPERATING RULES

It is all too easy to waste much time and money in pursuing projects that have little or no chance of approval – and discover this only at the end after, perhaps, years of fruitless negotiations. It is important, therefore, to ascertain at the outset whether the proposed project is likely to be approved, if it fits into the local, provincial or central government plan, or if it merely represents the ambition of the Chinese party whereby approval is far from certain – especially if the project could be perceived as financially wasteful or not in the public interest.

Any foreigner wanting to do business in China must clearly understand is that he or she is there on Chinese sufferance. In the first place, it is it is important ot understand that, together, the Chinese government and the business community decide that they want foreign companies within a certain category of activity to be allowed into the country. The door is then opened with a clear understanding that '. . . you may come in and do business on our terms. Maybe we haven't yet completely defined our terms. But nevertheless it will always be under our terms. You will always be the guest and we the host. We set the terms and you abide by them'.[4]

According to one management consultant: 'It can be extremely off-putting – the number of businesses who arrive and then leave again after six months is quite high because it is not a free-trading concept. You have a good product and you recognize the potential market and you come in and are supposed to be able to set up shop. But it is not a free economy in that sense. I think perhaps the foreigners who have the most problems in cracking the market are those who fail to recognize that key point that they are coming as a guest of the Chinese government or the Chinese decided they want you and you have been encouraged to come here. The foreign company will decide to come because they feel there is a market, But they must take a step back and realize that when they come to China, actually the Chinese have semi-engineered that – putting the idea in your head, previously, by, for example, shutting the door so that you couldn't come in with a certain product. Now, they have opened the door they have given you that opportunity. So you say: "I see a market and I'm going to go for it". But it only exists because the Chinese have decided it is beneficial to China that it should exist. . .the implication being that they could at any time decide that it is not beneficial to China. And then your opportunity is out the window and you're out the door and that's the end of your company.'

Summing up, the consultant stressed that any foreign businessman is part of the macro-economic plan. 'It's not a question of the Chinese consumers wanting your gadget necessarily that is driving that demand, it is on a more macro level; it's a government decision that companies such as yours and the products you provide can benefit the country as a whole. They categorize; they may make it difficult for companies selling expensive watches to come in, but companies selling heavy industrial machinery perhaps deemed important to the Chinese economy can come in much easier. One way of achieving this control is through the manipulation of import duties – heavy for the products they want to discourage for one reason or another, and low for those that are definitely needed. If they decide they don't want it, that's the end of the matter and you must always keep that in your mind you will probably go a long way towards being successful in China.'

FINDING THE RIGHT PARTNER

Where does one start to find a good Chinese partner? The businessman faces a bewildering array of choices. As the central government devolves more decision-making powers to local authorities the latter are rushing to hone their public relations skills in the scramble for foreign funds, and are going out of their way to create a good impression. In many cases the investment office has been moved out of ubiquitous gloomy concrete blocks of communist China into flashy skyscrapers; the badly-dressed party apparatchiks, bored and suspicious, have been replaced by fashionable officials armed with a permanent smile and a desire to please endless groups of investors. In Yantai, Shandong Province, the first stop for any visitor is the 'investment museum', an extensive exhibition of products ranging from cotton shirts to computers, all made in local foreign-funded factories. On the wall hangs the motto of the Yantai development zone: 'Investor is god; client is paramount'.

Around the country, however, many of the efforts continue to be spoilt by public relations brochures in bad, often incomprehensible English, boring videos that hardly rise above the banal propaganda level, and officials who are easily stumped by questions from potential investors.

Chinese English language publications are full of lists of local manufacturing companies plaintively seeking foreign joint-venture partners. Provinces take out whole-page advertisements for this purpose. But often there is a paucity of information on which to base a decision. For example, a supplement in *Business Weekly* inserted by Hebei Province in North China outlined 91 projects which required foreign investment. Project No.75, for example, was for the production of garments through a joint venture including imported equipment. Total investment would be US$1 million, half to be provided by foreign partner. Apply to the Shidai Garments Factory in Rongcheng County. Or perhaps Project No.60, for the production of quick-result pain-killing plaster, through a joint venture or cooperative agreement, and requiring $1 million in foreign funds. Applications, please, to Dongfang Traditional Chinese Medicine Factory. Alternatively, only $800,000 in foreign funds was needed by the Anguo Pharmaceutical Factory for a joint venture in the production of anti-ageing medicines.

Three opportunities taken from a list of 91, and that list being replicated by every province, and most of the counties, cities and townships all over the country, gives some of the flavour of what is happening in China today. With all of them engaged in a bitter struggle for foreign investment and know-how, and contributing to a confusing siren song of special preferences aimed at the baffled foreign investor, enthusiasm often overwhelms common sense.

There is no doubt that at present China is very much a buyer's market for those seeking a joint-venture partner. 'We used to get two or three approaches a day on average from all over China – some even came knocking on the door – before we found our eventual partner,' recalled a Japanese executive as he tried to get a new venture off the ground. But, in a complaint echoed by several others, he added: 'It's a bit like a very old-fashioned arranged marriage. There is a danger that, unless you are very careful, you don't really know what you are getting until it's too late.'

The executive recalled that when it became known his company was interested in establishing a manufacturing presence in China '... we were inundated with offers. Some were from single-component suppliers who thought they would like to expand into entire vehicle manufacture. Some were companies just starting up. In some cases they didn't even have a factory, and had nothing to show us but a piece of paper from the local government giving them permission to start operating. They would come to us waving this bit of paper and couldn't understand why we turned them down. They had no track record, nothing to show us that they had the business acumen to be a good partner'.

A Beijing-based management consultant recalled the problems faced on one occasion by an American manufacturer of feed horns, a key component at the heart of satellite receiving dishes: 'These are small, cheap things to make, but are critical components. They aren't very difficult to make, however, so the company decided it wanted to start producing them in China. Eventually, they found a factory in Shenzhen which seemed to fit the bill exactly. Top executives from the American factory flew to China to visit the plant and meet the managing director. It was a fantastic factory . . . . new, modern, beautifully-equipped, clean . . . . with obviously a lot of excess production capacity. So they ask the managing director if he can make feed horns for them and ship them overseas; and he says that, yes, he has plenty of spare capacity so there's no problem. They sign a deal and go back to the US and wait. They have two problems. First, the delivery is very slow and second, the quality of the items is terrible. So they fly back to Guangzhou and find that the guy is manufacturing these things in back alleys with old ladies and others sitting in their living rooms trying to make these things. And the factory that they saw? The businessman had rented it for one day. It seems he had gone to a local government official he knew and said: "I've got these foreigners flying in and they are probably going to sign a million-dollar deal. I'll rent your factory for a day and sign a deal". The moral of the story: if you come in raw and green to the market there is a chance you're going to be taken for a ride because no rules apply.'

A big problem in finding a suitable partner is the general lack of criteria on which to judge a Chinese company's abilities or viability. With the concept of stock markets only in the fledgling stage, and very few firms listed, there are no annual reports to be perused for key performance-related figures such as turnover and profits. Despite many improvements in recent years – and a pledge by the central government to bring domestic practices into line with international accounting norms – Chinese figures have to be treated with considerable scepticism. Every company, it seems, is always doing wonderfully well, setting new records in output and profitability each year.

As one Australian businessman commented: 'In a country as vast as China, and given the problem with communications outside the main cities, it's hardly surprising that accurate figures are hard to come by. Village and township authorities have trouble gathering correct information, which makes it hard for the provincial authorities to discover the true situation, and impossible for the central government to know exactly what is going on. At the same time, there is the a legacy of several decades of communist "need-to-know" mentality about the handling of information. Everything tends to be treated as a state property not to be divulged unless there are very good reasons. It's very frustrating when you are trying to obtain what would be considered basic public data in most other countries and find it veiled in secrecy. Only as you go up the ladder of command can one find more openness – if it suits the other side to do so.'

In trying to find a joint-venture partner, complained a Japanese executive, 'you might get little more than the company's name, address and telephone number, a list of the products it makes and how much money it wants you to invest. As a result, you often have to make decisions based on little more than intuition. You sift through the list and pick out a few that seem to be about right. And then you go and visit them to see if your intuition was right. It can be a bit like a punter picking a horse by sticking a pin in the race card. It's very primitive and unscientific, but that's China at present.'

Western companies are likely to choose state-owned enterprises because they have strong links with their supervisory bodies to get things done, and are likely to be more permanent fixtures than many of the private businesses springing up everywhere. The overseas Chinese investors discussed in the previous chapter have far more scope because of ancestral family and clan connections that provide the lubrication for the essential element in doing business in China.

The first approach for the Westerner, therefore, is likely to be through a government ministry or a state-backed industrial association who will be more than willing to produce a local partner – although there is a danger that this will be one of the virtually bankrupt enterprise left behind in the dash to a market economy, for which an injection of foreign cash may be its last hope. In this regard, be cautious of firms which are seeking to diversify out of outdated products into areas it knows little about.[5] This is likely to become more prevalent as even government agencies themselves are told to set up sideline businesses to ease the drain on central finances.

In summary, this is what various management consultants suggest is the way to find the right joint-venture partner: focus on a company that has both the technical expertise and the right connections (although these are not easy for a foreigner to discover); get a list of all the companies in China manufacturing the product required. This might be 250 potential partners, but considerations such as the need to be near a port because you are exporting or because it is a durable product and cannot afford to be on the back of a lorry from Xinjiang for four days, will weed out quite a few of these. You may then be left with 150. You can get a list of those companies with phone numbers, addresses and maybe a contact name. You call each one or send a fax or letter – 'We are a foreign company wanting to set up a manufacturing facility in China and this is our background. We will inject so-many million pounds into the operation and we expect our partner to meet certain clearly-specified requirements.' Hopefully, this will bring in about 25 responses from companies who think they are just right for you. Half of those will probably be lying or just over-optimistic after seeing the dollar or pound signs. You visit them on your screened list. Within 10 minutes you should know if they are a complete washout. You then get it down to three potential candidates, whose job is then to approach the Chinese government and ask if it's acceptable to have a joint venture with this foreign company. You don't go to the government yourself. Let the Chinese partner take care of all that. He knows a way through the maze and knows how to get things done. Of course, this selection process is rather tedious, and a much better way would be to come to us, because we have many wonderful companies on our books, say these consultants with a broad smile – which begs the question then of which management consultant to choose!

SHARED GOALS ESSENTIAL

The great need is to find a local partner with whom there is some correspondence of eventual goals. They may not necessarily be exactly the same, but they certainly should not be in conflict so as to destroy any hope of mutual cooperation. 'You need to be satisfied that the success of the venture is as important to your partner as it is to you, and that you agree on the means to achieve it.'[6]

A cautionary tale in this regard is provided by the case of the now defunct American Motor Company (AMC) – taken over first by Renault of France and eventually by fellow American car manufacturer Chrysler – which set up a joint venture in the Chinese capital known as Beijing Jeep. Any newcomer to the Chinese market would do well to study the AMC experience, and I will be referring to it several times during the rest of this book.[7]

When AMC and the Beijing Automotive Works (BAW) – formerly the 'East Is Red' plant – signed their historic deal in May 1983, press coverage contained several false assumptions and misunderstandings. First, the agreement was seen as the way forward for American companies who could team up with China, with its low labour costs, to create a base within Asia to compete on equal terms with the highly-successful Japanese. For AMC in particular it was a chance to overcome some of its financial weaknesses that relegated it to a poor fourth in its own market. Yet although the two sides had been talking to each other for almost five years when their new venture, Beijing Jeep, finally opened for business in 1984 – and at a time when Japanese salesman were fanning out across China clinching multi-million dollar deals – neither had yet decided what sort of vehicle they were going to produce.

The Chinese essentially were producing the same jeep they had introduced with Russian help in the 1950s, and what they wanted from AMC was its technology and input to help design and manufacture a completely new Chinese product (influenced largely by the PLA which was undergoing a determined modernization drive after its embarrassments in Vietnam five years earlier). The Americans, however, were not particularly interested in this idea. Development of an entirely new vehicle would have probably cost in the vicinity of a billion dollars, and neither side had that sort of cash available. What AMC wanted was a Chinese jeep which would be as close as possible to those it was producing in America, and with the primitive Chinese automobile industry hardly likely to be able to produce world-standard parts, this, in essence, meant the Beijing factory would have to produce a CKD ('completely knock-down') jeep from parts made in the United States. When the idea was first raised, the Chinese had reacted angrily, accusing the Americans of treating China as a backwater colony and of trying to find a way to control the local market. So, the idea was allowed to drift. At the same time, AMC executives knew that if they rejected outright the idea of designing a completely new Chinese jeep, the chances of concluding any deal would have been virtually nil.

'The sort of vehicle Chinese officials wanted could not be made from any of AMC's existing jeeps. But in signing the contract, the two sides glossed over this point. The Chinese intended to persuade the Americans to invest the effort and money necessary to build a completely new jeep in China. The Americans hoped to persuade the Chinese to abandon the idea of having its own unique new jeep and accept one based largely, or, better yet, based entirely on the American model.'[8]

Finally, in October 1984, the two sides agreed that from the following year Beijing Jeep would begin to build the AMC-developed Cherokee from American parts (although the joint venture would gradually replace these with Chinese-made components as justified). To the Americans this seemed the only alternative to scrapping the joint venture entirely. The Chinese side thought it was going along with a short-term expedient, and certainly did not give up the idea of a new jeep for the PLA. What they did not realize at the time was that their acquiescence shaped AMC's attitude towards the Chinese market. 'AMC would be making money by selling kits of Cherokee parts to Beijing Jeep, and inevitably it would want to sell as many kits as possible.'[9] The Americans, on their side, were also guilty of a fundamental misunderstanding. Although Beijing Jeep officials had given their reluctant blessing to the change in strategy, written approval had not been obtained from any higher authority (in this case, the State Planning Commission and State Economic Commission), even though the import of the CKD kits would require significant amounts of foreign exchange – in short supply and jealously guarded by the central government. It was a big risk and it rebounded on the venture when the money was not forthcoming, leaving thousands of ordered kits sitting in warehouses in the United States, and Beijing Jeep unable to pay its bills – including workers' salaries. The result was anguished representations in Beijing and Washington that eventually reached the highest levels in both governments before AMC got its way – in a deal which had to kept secret because the Chinese had no intention of allowing other foreign enterprises similar generous treatment (especially a provision permitting the joint venture to convert Yuan earned from continued sales of the old Chinese jeep into dollars). Beijing Jeep was getting the treatment only because of its high profile as a 'model' for Sino-foreign joint ventures.

There were further problems when American Motors officials, observing a sudden upsurge in the number of Japanese vehicles being sold in China, hurriedly tried to get into the action. The Americans told their partners they were willing to ship completed AMC jeeps to China immediately and even offered the joint venture a handsome commission for each one. But it was to no avail.

'China wanted American Motors for a different purpose [. . .] to give China the sort of technology and expertise necessary for it to develop a modern automobile industry of its own. That was, after all, what the two sides had been talking about for the previous five years. AMC had happily accepted the idea, believing it would gain, in exchange for its technology, not only entree into the Chinese market, but also a low-cost labour base from which to export to the rest of Asia.'[10]

The differences outlined over thwarted ambitions caused serious rifts in the joint management with the repercussions being felt for a number of years. And all because the two sides had decided to skate around fundamental differences in approach in their pre-agreement discussions. We will return to the Beijing Jeep story later.

MORE CAUTIONARY TALES

The signing of a contract in China, however, is not the end but merely the preliminary in establishing a successful business. The foreign businessman cannot simply go away with a piece of paper in his hand and think that all his problems are over. In many ways, they are just beginning.

As one businessman explained: 'The political element cannot be ignored. You may open your business in an aura of rosy optimism and all seems to be going well. Then, you're back in Britain or the US or wherever, and suddenly it's becoming increasingly difficult to get anything out of your Chinese partner; communications break down; you don't really know what is going on and everything begins to get woolly and cloudy. The reason may be that the power the local guy had enjoyed previously has been rescinded. He no longer has the power to act as the centre pulls in the reins. He has to hedge and pull in his horns. No amount of waving contracts under his nose is going to make the slightest difference.'

The American company involved in Dalian Western Food in the northeastern port certainly thought it had a firm contract in a joint venture with local interests that gave it a 20-year guaranteed occupancy on the ground floor of a building at the heart of the city. The fast-food venture began operating in June 1992 employing 60 people. But within three months it was ordered to quit, because the building was to be demolished to make way for a 38-storey office and apartment complex to be built with a big injection of Hong Kong capital. More than 120 families and 28 enterprises in the vicinity were relocated until Dalian Western Food was the sole occupant and it refused to move. By October, the confrontational tone had been set. Dalian city officials cut off its electricity, gas and water. Dalian Western Food claimed a conflict of interest was involved because one of the three partners in the $30 million skyscraper project was a subsidiary of the Dalian Housing Bureau, the same city government office which had ordered the company to vacate. After complaining to the US embassy in Beijing, the Chinese embassy in Washington, several American congressmen and the Dalian Mayor, the food company succeeded in little more than having its utilities restored. Negotiations then began over the amount of compensation to be paid for the forced relocation, with the American side asking for as much as $1.95 million and the Dalian side offering about $360,000. While these negotiations were underway, the builders of the office tower filed a suit against Dalian Western Food for 'long-term, unreasonable refusal to move', claiming $210,000 in damages. On 1 July 1993, the civil court notified the food company its accounts were to be sealed and that the building had to be vacated in five days. Only then did it accede to the pressure, and within hours the building had been demolished, leaving a nasty taste all round.

Another businessman discovering that a contract offered little protection was Tom Henry, who was abruptly told that his company had been unilaterally terminated as the US partner in Xinjiang Beef, a joint venture in the remote Xinjiang Uyger Autonomous Region. 'After a while, you find that the Chinese partner on the outside is showing that they have mutual cooperation, but inside they are blocking the foreign partner,' he complained. The suspicion in these and other cases is that, having learnt the ropes from their foreign partner, the Chinese concern then decides to squeeze it out of the business. This is easy since many of the firms are State-owned and have the support of local leaders, if not of the central government. The latter, however, may not be able to do much about it. According to Mr Henry, he telephoned the relevant ministry in Beijing to check if his partner had acted illegally and was told 'he can't do that'. He then telephoned a Chinese lawyer who said exactly the same. But when asked what could be done to rectify the situation, Mr Henry was told 'we don't know'.

A similar problem was faced by German businessman Anton Staudinger, when a branch of the state-run Construction Bank of China in Lanzhou, capital of Gansu Province, confiscated one of his joint ventures, Tianhe Commercial Mansion, the largest building of its kind in the northwest, and bank guards were assigned to ensure the German side's local representative could not enter his office. Staudinger immediately sued the bank and his joint venture partner, the State-run Gansu Township Service Company, but Robert Schedel, general manager of another Staudinger venture in Beijing explained: 'While he feels he has rights on paper, in effect he has no rights to be involved in this project.' At the time of writing, compromise seemed to be in the air. The Gansu provincial government, aware of the need to attract more foreign investment, removed the official who oversaw the partner of Mr Staudinger's Asde Group. The Mayor of Lanzhou also pledged the case would be handled fairly and that Gansu would do everything to protect the interests of foreign investors in the province, one of China's poorest. 'If we don't solve even the smallest problems involving foreign firms, how will we succeed in opening up?' the Mayor said.

BUREAUCRATIC BARRIER

Getting past the bureaucratic barrier can be the biggest headache for any foreign venture – even when it seems to be making an important contribution to Chinese economic efficiency and development.

Beijing Air Catering Company, China's oldest foreign-funded joint venture, was set up in 1979 to provide in-flight meals for airlines flying out of Beijing International Airport. At the start, BACC serviced only three airlines, but a decade later this had grown to 20 clients. By then, its 500 staff were preparing up to 12,000 meals a day for on antiquated equipment with a theoretical capacity of 4,000. In 1987, the company decided to embark on a second stage of development. The Chinese investor, the Beijing Management Department of the Civil Aviation Administration of China (CAAC), and its foreign partner, the Hong Kong Chinese Food Company, injected more capital to build a second production line which was supposed to be ready for the 11th Asian Games in Beijing in mid-1990. Eighteen months after the games ended, and despite more than 100 stamps of approval from various higher authorities, work had still not begun – causing the Chinese general manager to take responsibility and resign. Differences between the various government departments, including disputes over the complicated procedures required for the import of much-needed new equipment and other facilities, were the main reasons for the delay. Wu Yunqiu, the Chinese vice president, said the company was regulated not only by the Beijing Civil Aviation Administration but also by the Beijing Municipal Finance Department, Personnel Department and several others, which created a long, involved and frustrating approval process.

According to Wilson W.T. Wu, deputy general manager from

the Hong Kong side: 'It would be far better if we could escape from administrative interference. Outwardly, our company is a joint venture. But, in fact, it is controlled as if it was a state-run enterprise.' 'Foreign business management is incompatible with the low efficiency of our government,' admitted Cai Fenghao, deputy general manager of another food-based joint venture, Yili-Nabisco Biscuit and Food Company Ltd. 'I'm mortally afraid of having any contact with the bureaucrats.'

Beijing is not the only city with difficult bureaucrats. Shanghai has an equally bad reputation, according to one businessman who had wanted to set up a manufacturing operation in Shanghai, but was eventually dissuaded by the obstructionist tactics of local bureaucrats. The company faced a range of demands for everything from technology transfer to controls over exports when it looked at the city as a possible site. 'Shanghai has a way of over-regulating you right into the dirt. It's hard to get things done,' the businessmen said. Nick Norgard, who negotiated a deal for the Australian brewing giant Forster's in Shanghai described the process as 'like taking an honours degree'.

A British management adviser, commented: 'For many foreign businessmen, it's been a bit like the old children's game of snakes and ladders. You think you are getting somewhere but you eventually find yourself back at square one. You try again but in the end you go home because you are sick and tired of the whole game. In the meantime, it has taken five times as much time as you thought it was going to take you and five times as much money as you thought it would cost . . . and you still end up going home with nothing.'

Nevertheless, this consultant believed that the rapid changes which had occurred in China had created opportunities to bypass the bureaucrats. 'The situation has become extremely fluid. From a situation of all-embracing rules and total rigidity, we have virtually gone to a situation where there are no rules at all. With the right connections, there is a window of opportunity for coming in via a side entrance, a fast track which will allow you to open a business at a fraction of the prevailing costs and the minimum of frustration. I know of people who have grasped the chance and netted huge profits. All you need is cash and a good Chinese partner, with the right connections – who did they go to school with or did their father go to school with or serve in the army with? – and anything is possible. Mind you, it might not last. There's always a risk that tomorrow the government will step in and decide the whole thing is illegal. But some businessmen certainly feel that it's worth the risk.'

ENVELOPE BUSINESS

Another possibility is finding a bureaucrat who is happy to cooperate if the price is right. The government has actually encouraged this by telling its own departments that they can no longer expect to be fully-financed from state funds. They must find some way to self-finance. Everyone from the hospitals to the fire service to the economic forecasting bureau – all have to find a way to make money. As one businessman remarked: 'Here you have all these very powerful State-run organizations looking for a way to make a bit of money. The official who has got the golden chop to give you that licence you need to operate your business is now ready to listen to your proposal. That's bribery, of course, but it's always been part of the system – *guangxi*.'

The idea of self-funding government organization has led to a huge boom in corruption which has become the biggest problem facing the Chinese economy at the moment. It has made a lot of ordinary Chinese very unhappy and has led to unrest. It has also led to a growing number of officials receiving a bullet in the back of the head from the official executioner.[11]

But the so-called 'envelope business' remains prevalent as those in power decide to feather their nest while the going is good. Companies find they have to align themselves with local, provincial or national power figures to establish their business. And given China's political volatility, if a company's connections are defeated in a power struggle it could lose millions in the political fallout. 'You have terrific turf wars in China,' warns one management consultant. A Hong Kong businessman adds: 'Basically, all Chinese officials want something. It's a matter of money, but they are not going to ask you outright. You basically ask if it's possible to do this or that, and they say that anything is possible. They can make life extremely difficult or they can make it easy. It's up to you.'

Many businessmen accept this as part of the price to be paid for being in China – an in-built operating cost. It may not be as crude as an envelope stuffed with notes. Contracts might be negotiated which commit the foreign partner to paying for key figures on the Chinese side to go abroad on 'study trips', for example. When Pepsi-Cola USA bought the Kentucky Fried Chicken franchise operation from RJR Nabisco Inc. in 1986, it had to renegotiate many contracts. Visibly absent from the new ones were any commitment for Pepsi to pay for foreign travel.

Do you *have* to pay bribes? Some businessmen insist that you do not have to. Stephen Payne, managing director of the American investigative firm Pinkerton, warns that companies open themselves to blackmail if they comply with or encourage corrupt practices. Officials who take a bribe could come back for more, or tell their friends that a certain company is a soft touch. 'It's a bottomless pit – you don't know where it's going to end.'

The advice is: take the high moral ground and stay there. It may cause short-term problems, like denying your company access to vital supplies, but in the long run it will be beneficial. These tips are offered by those who have been through the mill:

- Do not go to China thinking that paying bribes is the way to go, because you will end up attracting demands left and right. Establish an ethos of integrity early in the negotiations. Talk about the importance of good business practices to your company. Wave your company's 'code of practice' at the negotiators on the other side of the table. If you haven't got a code of practice, write one. Ideally, get in first with a statement of intent to avoid being on the defensive once the requests have been made. One American manufacturer in Guangzhou began negotiations with his potential joint venture partners by producing a copy of the US Foreign Corrupt Practices Act, explaining that if he paid any bribes he would be liable to five years' imprisonment and a $2 million fine. From then on, the negotiations went smoothly with no unusual requests from the Chinese side.
- Beware of shady agents and go-betweens. If an agent tells you that corruption is the rule in China, get rid of him immediately. Agents have an incentive in telling you that bribes will have to be paid because he is going to get a cut of the payment.
- If possible, avoid areas known to be hotbeds of graft and corruption. The lesser-developed areas of the country are

likely to be easier for the foreign investor to avoid problems.
- Choose your joint venture partner with care: run a background check on the company and its officials, concentrating on their reputation for straight dealing.
- There is safety in numbers. Try to work with other companies in your industry operating in China to present a united front against corruption. Local officials can take revenge against a single company but will find it more difficult against several firms.[12]

FINDING A PLACE TO STAY

One of the first problems that any foreign investor is likely to face is where to locate the proposed operation. According to Chinese law, foreigners can only obtain the right to use land not actually own it. Before 1990, the law totally prohibited land transfers. It all belonged to the State. But recognizing the need to make life easier for foreign investors, as well as the fact that it was sitting on a valuable asset (land previously had been regarded as virtually worthless in itself) that could be traded to provide considerable budgetary revenue, the government decided to separate the use rights and ownership of land. Except for underground resources, buried treasure and public facilities, land rights can now be sold or transferred, and all companies, organizations and individuals can use and develop land in any way that is not prohibited by law. Within a legally-specified period, the usage rights can be transferred, leased, mortgaged or dedicated to other economic activities. The period ranges from 70 years for housing, 50 years for industrial, educational, scientific, and sporting uses, and 40 years for commerce, tourism and recreation. The state, in theory, cannot reclaim the land prematurely, unless it can cite overwhelming public interest. Should it do so, adequate compensation is supposed to be paid, depending on how long the land has been in use and how much it has been developed.

There are several methods for obtaining land. First is by grant, where the state assigns the right for a specific purpose and for a length of time through a signed contract. Second is through tender or auction, when sealed bids are submitted to a local land bureau. Third is through transfer, when an entity which has already received a grant from the land bureau decides to assign its rights to another party, as long as the use of the land is compatible and the terms are the same as the original agreement. Fourth, the holder of the land rights may lease them to another party, but the duties involved in the use agreement remain with the lessor (unlike the transfer where they pass to the assignee). Use of the land, again, must be in keeping with the original terms. Finally, a Chinese party to a joint-venture agreement may contribute its land-use rights as an in-kind capital contribution, assuming it has the rights to do so. The main problem here for the foreign partner is that the value of the land is arbitrarily set by the land bureau and there is no room for bargaining, encouraging the imposition of an inflated price.

Most foreign investors acquiring land rights have had to pay a higher price than that required from Chinese companies. But some coastal cities, eager to exploit their development zones, have begun offering land through auction or tender in which case there has been no discrimination between local and foreign purchaser. One of the attractions of this method is that one is dealing directly with the land bureau which makes it easier to find out who holds proper title to the land.

As in so many areas, the Chinese authorities gave with one hand and took away with the other. By the end of 1992, all provinces, autonomous regions and municipalities, with the exception of Tibet, were allowed to transfer land rights. As increasing evidence of abuse was uncovered, encouraging vast land speculation that drained off massive amounts of economic resources desperately needed elsewhere, the central government decided to impose tighter conditions on the transfer of land rights. In mid-1993, an estimated one-third of all the announced development zones were abruptly cancelled. Most existed merely on paper. In a short period of time, an estimated 1.3 million hectares was taken back by the State Land Bureau. It also halted the approval of projects occupying large areas of land, such as golf courses. In the future, it decreed, land use would be closely monitored and up to the year 2000 no more than 267,000 hectares would be allocated each year for construction purposes. Land development companies, accused of widespread tax evasion, were to be closely monitored, with the worst offenders closed down. By early 1994, a national property law was also supposed to have been implemented to replace the previous bewildering array of local rules as well as regulate some of the competing interests that have previously frustrated proper control (eg: land owned by the military which have carried out developments that are not necessarily compatible with the aims of the local administration).

Despite the reforms, obtaining land remains a major headache for foreign investors. In some parts of the country, the biggest problem is rapacious local officials who see a chance to make a fortune out of the deals by charging exorbitant prices as the following report indicates:

'Shanghai has a lot going for it: support at the highest levels from Beijing, a skilled labour force, and a 350-square-kilometre site, Pudong, on which to build a powerhouse that could drive China into the next century. Why then, do major investors describe the city as "totally unprofessional", "an ambush" and "a bureaucratic nightmare"? "Seeing Shanghai now", says Norman Givant, an American lawyer who has spent the last eight years working with multinational companies in the city, "is like seeing someone you're fond off practising self-destructive behaviour." The main problem, he says, is avarice. "Blind greed is destroying Shanghai's natural advantages."

'[. . .]In 1990, when the Pudong opening was announced, all the city had to do was manage the area's development competently and the quality foreign investment on which to rebuild Shanghai would flow in. Today, this is much less likely to happen. Instead of the long-term gains of a sound productive base, the Shanghai government has opted for the short-term rewards of an exorbitant land pricing policy that is forcing manufacturers to go elsewhere. In Pudong, four government-controlled companies that manage the area's principal development zones are demanding between $150 and $190 a square metre for land – 50 per cent more than in Guangzhou's Huangpu port area and twice as much as in the development zones of major northern cities like Tianjin and Dalian.

'Where Shanghai once had a strategy to rebuild its industrial base, today its only commitment is to the highest bidder – a fact that a well-known US multinational recently discovered. The company, a brand-name maker of homecare products, had agreed to a fixed price for land in Pudong's Jianqiao Export Processing Zone in 1991. At the time, the company was hailed as a key investor by the Shanghai government, which had asked it to go into Pudong to encourage other multinationals to follow suit. As the property market boomed through 1992, however, the Jinqiao administration tried to extort more money. First, they tried to renegotiate the land price. This was resisted and eventually a contract was signed. But prices continued to rise, and the area around where the US company had leased its land was approved for commercial development. At this point, the Jinqiao administration went back to the American company and said it was taking back the land because development was not proceeding fast enough. For several months, it looked as though the site would be taken away. It was only after appeals to the mayor and the Light Industry Bureau, that the US company was able to retain what a supposedly binding contract had guaranteed.

'"In 1991", they said, "We really need your support, so we can show we're making progress," says the company's general manager. In 1992, the economy was stronger, prices were 50 per cent over what they had given us, and they wanted to re-make. After the contract, they were looking for a loophole to get rid of us so they could resell the land for a higher price. It was totally unprofessional.

'In the same zone, Dutch multinational Unilever PLC also fared badly. The company had a reserved site and an agreed price. While company managers went back to corporate headquarters for approval, however, Jinqiao officials sold the land to a higher bidder. "They think they can get higher and higher prices, and they're breaching contracts left and right," says lawyer Givant. "When you start messing with multinational corporations, the word gets out and your reputation is soured. The folks here should know better."

'To discover the effects of Shanghai's rapacious behaviour, you need to go no farther than two hours up the road to Suzhou. There, three major multinational pharmaceutical companies – Lederle, Upjohn and Capsugel – are escaping the vagaries of the metropolis. All are high-tech "clean" manufacturers. they are the sort of businesses Shanghai is supposed to be attracting. The manager of one of the companies is quite blunt about why he is not contributing to the development of Pudong. "[It] is a place where they steal money from foreigners. It's an ambush," he says.'[13]

MISTAKES ON BOTH SIDES

To conclude this discussion of investing in China, one can say that mistakes have been made on both sides in the haste to take advantage of the new enthusiasm for foreign investment in China. Identified problems include:

- The purpose of establishing the joint venture is dubious. Some local governments have considered only the number of joint ventures they could attract, this being a key criteria by which their performance could be assessed.[14]
- Local governments in some cases do not possess the expertise to weigh the advantages or disadvantages of a specific investment proposal. Some authorities have made only a perfunctory examination of the prospective partner and done little market research. A letter to the editor of the *Business Times* newspaper, for example, said that few Chinese partners knew the situation in the market, especially internationally, and made losses when they imported equipment and raw materials.
- Cooperation between provinces is poor with the result that it is extremely difficult to take advantage of economies of scale. In one instance, a businessman wanted to ship petrol tanks for his factory in Shanghai to another similar operation in the northeastern province of Jilin. But neither the governor of Jilin nor the mayor of Shanghai would accept this. The factories, therefore, were forced to duplicate each others' efforts, to the frustration of the foreign management.
- There have been loopholes in the management of foreign investment. Often funds supplied by both sides have proved to be inadequate; some investors proed unable to put in as much as the contract stipulated, and some foreign partners even failed to offer any investment at all due to a change for the worse in the international market. According to a survey conducted by the government's Industrial and Commercial Administration Bureau in 1991, one unnamed province had only received 30 per cent of contracted amounts. Moreover failure to give proper consideration to the feasibility of using imported equipment and poor quality employees, had left advanced technologies idle. There was little evidence that the situation had improved drastically by the end of 1993.

- Most foreign funds have been invested in the processing sector, where bigger profits can be earned than in the basic industries such as energy and raw materials. To counter this, state policy is now aimed at readjusting the industrial structure, with the growth of processing industries being slowed down and much more attention paid to the development of basic industry. And, as mentioned in the last chapter, efforts are being made to channel foreign investment into infrastructural projects which will have more lasting value for the country. This, however, may not be easy to achieve.[15]
- Many areas went ahead with creating development zones without fully considering the burden that would be imposed on local transportation, telecommunications systems, water and electricity supply. Additional levies of various kinds imposed by local authorities to try and make up for the deficiencies have become a heavy burden for joint ventures in some places (eg: firms being asked to buy bonds issued by utility companies in order to ensure that they receive a 'guaranteed power supply', which some businessmen see as thinly-disguised extortion).
- The investment boom has developed so quickly that quality control systems have not been able to keep up with the influx of technology and equipment needed for China's modernization. This has tempted crooks on both sides to try and cash in, requiring the strengthening of the inspection and appraisal of imported equipment.[16]
- An immature foreign currency exchange market with big fluctuations in exchange rates resulting in some foreign-oriented enterprises losing money. In addition, many foreign businesses ran into trouble because they overlooked the fact that they had entered into deals based on the premise that they would export from China. They then discovered that, for a variety of reasons they could not do so. This might be because the quality of the products was insufficient to meet international standards, or due to an overestimation of China's ability to produce inexpensive locally-made parts, supplies and raw materials that would obviate the need to import from abroad and generating the need for the foreign exchange in the first place. The end result was to create a

serious shortage of foreign exchange and no easy way to earn an adequate supply on the domestic market – where their products were likely to come up against cheaper, if even more inferior, local products.

FOOTNOTES:

1. I am indebted to the British Embassy Commercial office in Beijing and the China-Japan Trade Group in London for assistance with this section.
2. All people directly quoted in this chapter were interviewed in China in August and September 1993.
3. *South China Morning Post*, 12 June 1993.
4. In August 1993, the State Planning Commission submitted draft proposals – Temporary Provisions on Guiding Foreign Investment and the Industrial Guidance Catalogue for 1993–95 Foreign Investment – designed to clarify China's goals. The provisions divided investment projects into four categories – those to be encouraged, permitted, restricted and forbidden. Projects encouraged by the government would receive additional preferential treatment in terms of operations, taxation, business scope, ratio of domestic to export products, and proportion of registered capital to total investment. Permitted projects, however, would have to conform to the existing approval procedures. Restricted projects would be subject to strict requirements, and divided into category A and B projects. Category A would be considered over-supplied projects that needed to be directed and regulated in accordance with economic means, including photocopiers, short fibre products and ordinary polyester filaments, machinery to produce passenger and cargo ships, marine diesel engines and certain electronic products such as video recorders, radios, monochrome picture tubes and limited capacity personal computers. Category B, involving industries requiring foreign capital to conduct limited r & d and projects subject to centralized control, included machinery for the production of cars, jeeps, motorcycles and light trucks, and electronic items such as colour televisions, colour picture tubes and camcorders. *Beijing Review*, 6 Sept. 1993.
5. Although some unlikely combination may still be the right one. Baskin Robbins, owned by the British Allied-Lyons Group, is opening a chain of ice-cream stores with the China Satellite Launch and Tracking Control agency.
6. *Financial Times* China supplement, 18 Nov. 1993.
7. The fullest account is given in *Beijing Jeep: The Short, Unhappy Romance of American Business in China* by Jim Mann, published in 1989 by Simon and Schuster. It is not easy to find these days and I was fortunate to obtain a copy in a Hong Kong bargain bookshop.
8. Ibid., pp157-8.
9. Ibid., p162
10. Ibid.,p155.
11. 'China executed seven officials over the weekend as a nationwide anti-corruption drive gathered pace. Dozens of bureaucrats have been shot recently for crimes ranging from bribe-taking to embezzlement. China launched the drive in the face of widespread grumbling among citizens about official graft and bribe-taking. A meeting of the Standing Committee of the National People's Congress charged that "corruption had reached an alarming rate in China". According to China's procurator general, one out of 10 criminal cases investigated in the first nine months [of 1993] offenders were party or government officials.' [*Financial Times*, 26 Oct. 1993] 'Nearly 30,000 Party and government officials have been disciplined in the first half of this year on charges of malpractice or irregularities. The accusations ranged from bribe-taking to neglect of duties. In one major case, three senior party officials in Henan province, who exchanged their power for private gain, were expelled and charged in court. A deputy party secretary and mayor of one town was accused of taking bribes totalling 520,000 Yuan.'[*China Daily*, 19 Sept. 1993]
12. Based on research by Harvard University doctoral student Brewer S. Stone, quoted in the

December 1993 issue of *Asia Inc.*
13. *Something is rotten in Shanghai* by Joe Studwell. *Asia Inc.* December 1993 issue.
14. 'Chinese officials recently sounded the alarm that inefficiency is occurring in overseas-funded ventures. They said the national euphoria over the flood of overseas investment in China has, in certain cases, glossed over some undesirable problems in joint ventures. These problems mainly include loopholes in project approval and losses of state property. And the glut of overseas investment has caused a shortage of Yuan for certain projects. Tong Yizhong, a government economist, said the central authorities should raise bank interest rates according to international practices which would shrink the local currency demand for immature joint ventures and encourage foreign investors to establish more wholly-owned enterprises. He said the country had become bogged down in the use of foreign capital over the past few years. For example, over-construction of development zones and the rocketing real-estate industry have outstripped market demands. Overseas investment in real estate should, in future, focus on China's older cities, he said.' [*Beijing Review*, 26 July 1993]
15. There is some foreign reluctance to become heavily involved in infrastructure development as investors rather than as mere suppliers of necessary equipment. Several bank executives, for example, pointed out that projects like railways and ports were among the least attractive in China because they rarely offered the best returns and ensuring a flow of hard currency for repayment would be difficult to arrange. 'China is an awkward place to do business and you have to be aware of the risks,' said one official. 'Infrastructure projects tended to be among the riskiest'. [*Financial Times*, 26 Nov. 1993]
16. Hainan, the largest SEZ, has been in the forefront of this effort with the creation of special investigatory bodies which led to the recovery of $1.95 million in compensation for local Sino-foreign joint ventures for the importation of sub-standard equipment in the first half of 1993. 'Among the 261 batches of equipment imported in the period, about 22 per cent were found to be sub-standard. Some of the imported equipment was old with merely a new coat of paint and new brand names. Machines, including a gilding press, a mould for high-grade plane models, and a whole set of production lines for fluorescent light and video-tape production, were found to be used without the labels of the producers and their sizes were irrelevant to the contracts. Worse, a shoe-production line purchased by a foreign businessman for a local shoe-making company was found to consist of already scrapped machines. Local commodities inspectors also discovered that some equipment was roughly made, of poor technological standard and could not reach the production capacity set by the purchasing contracts. Some foreign businessmen reportedly have taken advantage of their position and practised cheating for illegal profit by raising the equipment prices much higher than their real value. For instance, a businessman asked for $5.4 million for a multi-functional vegetable processing line, but local people found it was actually worth only $3 million on the international market.' [*China Daily*, 14 Sept. 1993]

7 Case study: the automobile industry

KEY POINTS
Previous chapters have taken a broad view of a variety of Chinese industrial sectors where foreign investment is playing a role. In this chapter, I want to focus on one industry – vehicle manufacturing – which is likely to be one of the fastest-growing sectors and which is a microcosm of all the opportunities, and attendant difficulties, for the foreign investor in China. I will look at:
- The history of the Chinese industry.
- China's future growth strategy and the role of foreign investment.
- A look at the Sino-foreign joint ventures across the country in the production of vehicles and components.
- A detailed examination of the strategy of Japanese manufacturers, belatedly pouring into China after a decade of hesitation – along with the reasons for this caution.
- The problems the foreign investors have faced in trying to make their joint ventures successful.

CHINA'S SLOW START

THE PIONEERING Chinese truck was fabricated in the First Auto Works in Changchun, capital of Jilin Province, in 1956. For various reasons, the auto industry was slow in developing, and total vehicle output remained below half a million units a year until the 1980s. For most of the first three decades, the industry could only produce medium-sized trucks; there was no capability for either light or heavy trucks, and certainly not for the mass-production of cars.

In May 1987, it was agreed that China should establish a national car industry immediately. Later the same year, the State Council held a conference in Behaide, the summer resort for the leadership, where the final decision was taken to make the automobile sector one of the 'pillar industries' of the revitalized Chinese economy, with the emphasis gradually shifting from trucks to cars. The production system was restructured to allow the production of cars, light and heavy trucks.

For passenger cars, the three largest bases are Shanghai-Volkswagen Corp., the First Auto Works-Volkswagen Corp. and Wuhan Magic Dragon Corp. (Citroën of France is the joint-venture partner). There are also three smaller projects already operating, including Beijing Cherokee Co.(involving Chrysler of the United States), Tianjin Daihatsu Co. (Japan) and Guangzhou-Peugeot Co. (France). Military enterprises in Sichuan and Guizhou are being transformed to produce mini-cars.

Beijing-Cherokee Jeep Co. Ltd, as already mentioned in the last chapter, marked the first time a foreign manufacturer had entered Chinese automobile production. In the same year (1984), the Sino-German Shanghai-Volkswagen Automobile Co.Ltd. was created and on 22 July 1985, the Sino-French Guangzhou-Peugeot Auto Corp. was registered with the China Industrial and Commercial Administration.

JAPANESE LATECOMERS

Somewhat surprisingly, the Japanese were very cautious about committing themselves to China. It took them almost a decade to recover from the so-called 'Hainan incident' that created deep distrust over the uncertainties of doing business in China. Even in the mid-1990s, companies like Nissan, Toyota and Honda were proceeding with a cautious step-by-step policy, the opposite of their previous bold penetration of the American and European markets. China is the last great undeveloped market for the automobile, they all agreed, but it is also a place where fortunes can be lost and reputations damaged.

The seeds of this caution were planted in 1983, when the local authorities on Hainan island suddenly ordered thousands of Japanese cars. Virtually every company jumped in to bid for the order which was a big breakthrough in the hitherto closed Chinese market. But it ended as suddenly as it began. One day, the companies were told: 'Order cancelled; there is no letter of credit.' The manufacturers were left with thousands of unwanted cars built to Chinese specifications which took more than a year to offload at discounts up to 90 per cent. Among those now occupying the most senior positions in these companies were a number who were closely involved in that debacle, which one executive said had 'cast a shadow on their perspective of the Chinese market'.

What had happened was that the local authorities on Hainan were using state funds to order Japanese cars at a discount which were then sold to other parts of China at a huge mark-up. According to the Communist Party's Central Commission for Discipline Inspection which investigated the profiteering scandal during a 14-month period, officials on Hainan had approved the import of 89,000 foreign cars, 2.9 million television sets, 250,000 video recorders and 122,000 motorcycles, virtually all of them for resale inland. In order to obtain the foreign exchange to buy the goods, local banks on the island charged illegal fees for granting loans, as well as soliciting money from other local governments across China. Virtually every public institution on Hainan, including a kindergarten and the local daily newspaper, set up private trading corporations to buy and resell foreign goods. The official newspaper of the armed forces, the *Liberation Army Daily*, reported that the navy had used its aircraft to transport 1,000 video recorders, 6,000 video cassettes, nearly 400 television sets and a minibus from Hainan to the inland province of Sichuan. where the goods were sold at a substantial mark-up. When this profiteering was finally uncovered, an immediate halt was ordered and the head of the local administration was dismissed (although he now occupies a senior position in another province).

The Hainan scandal was merely a symptom of the periodic overheating of the Chinese economy, with the scope of the public spending-spree catching the leadership unawares. The official media launched a campaign urging the nation not to 'blindly worship Western goods'. Japan suffered the most as bilateral trade tipped decisively its way, and Japanese companies suddenly noticed that new purchase contracts for a wide range of consumer products suddenly dried up. This was accompanied by a vitriolic campaign against the alleged shoddy quality of the Japanese goods being shipped to China, and an upsurge of public demonstrations against 'resurgent Japanese militarism' and Japan's new 'economic invasion'. The sudden clampdown on Japanese imports caught a number of prominent manufacturers and middlemen in the squeeze. In September 1985, more than a million Japanese television sets and video recorders were being held up in Chinese ports because of import restrictions. Another 300,000 television sets and 100,000 video recorders, as well as up to 10,000 cars were stranded in Hong Kong.[1]

This might have been written off to experience, as an unfortunate but not necessarily indicative experience of dealing with the fledgling Chinese market. But for the car makers an even more deep-rooted problem emerged stemming from the way the Japanese and Chinese approach negotiations.

When the European and American vehicle manufacturers decided to enter China they sent their top executives who negotiated a general agreement with high-level Chinese officials, leaving their subordinates to handle the fine details. But Japanese companies operate a 'bottom-up' approach. Middle-level managers in their early 40s take the initiative in generating new ideas which then filter upwards to senior management. The latter only become involved when everything is settled and there is no risk of an embarrassing failure. So it was the middle-level managers who visited China to conduct basic negotiations. The Chinese, however, work on the basis of 'equality of rank', so the Japanese managers ended up meeting relatively low-level officials who did not necessarily have the clout to see through the deals being negotiated.

This inevitably created problems. As one Japanese executive recalled: 'An agreement was reached and the managers reported back to Japan that everything had been settled. But then the Chinese side would come back and say: "There is a new development which must be taken into account, so we have to come back to square one". This embarrassed the Japanese managers who had taken the responsibility for the agreement and the strategy developed from it. It meant scrapping the foundations they had built on inside the company. These managers had taken a lot of time building consensus at all levels and now it was dead. They lost a lot of face and many of the managers involved suffered a serious career setback because the company thought they were poor business negotiators or didn't understand Chinese ways. Once that happens, it is difficult to do it again. It had to wait for a new generation of managers before most Japanese companies could move back into China again.'

And that is exactly what began to happen in the early 1990s. After allowing their European and American rivals to gain a long headstart, most Japanese manufacturers suddenly began scrambling for a foothold in the Chinese market. But in the initial stage, it largely involved small-scale manufacturing joint ventures – primarily trucks and buses, rather than passenger cars – along with establishment of a strong nation-wide parts supply network. The idea was to use this base to gain experience before deciding whether to commit massive investment for large-scale car production if the Chinese government agrees.

It is against this background that the caution of Japanese vehicle manufacturers has to be judged. They certainly want to be big players in what may eventually be an extremely large market, especially as it is reckoned that at least 400 million people in China will possess sufficient financial resources to purchase some sort of vehicle in the first decade of the next century. That works out at about one-third of the current population. And at a time when the mature markets of America and Europe are in decline, that is a mouth-watering figure to play with.

CHINA'S STRATEGY

China has made its motor industry a priority sector for overseas cooperation, and in order to encourage investors may allow them free rein in the rapidly-expanding domestic market, including the right to set prices in response to market forces. Li Yue, a senior official in the Ministry of Foreign Trade and Economic Cooperation (Moftec), set out the government's policy guidelines in mid-1993 as being '... the attraction of overseas capital primarily focused on heavy-duty trucks, especially container trailers, large buses and automobile spare parts. Because of the lack of variety and quality, domestic heavy duty trucks and large passenger buses have failed to meet the demands of road transportation and tourism'.

Li said at least another $25 billion was needed over and above investments already planned in the 1991-95 economic plan period. He proposed that China should establish a special bank or finance corporation and allow Sino-foreign automobile manufacturers to issue bonds at home and abroad. China should also allow automaking joint ventures to float stocks at home and abroad when conditions are right.

China National Automotive Industry Corporation (CNAIC) estimated that the country would have an annual production capacity of three million vehicles by the turn of the century, with cars making up 65 per cent of the total. In 1993, production reached 1.1 million, including 180,000 cars.

The industry has been typified until now by too many low-volume producers content with high-profit margins. There are as many as 120 manufacturers in the country, more than anywhere else in the world. Normally, vehicle production needs economy of scale and a fairly high minimum output to ensure profitability. But, to the amazement of foreign makers, in the early 1990s there was not a single factory in China capable of producing over 200,000 vehicles a year, and many turned out far less – including some with output of only a few thousand. The average output actually is only 10,000 units, compared to the 10 million vehicles that someone like Toyota Motors is capable of producing. The domestic industry has been stunted by its scattered production facilities, and only in the late 1980s did companies begin to coalesce into budding conglomerates such as the No.1 Auto Group, the Dongfeng and Jiangling groups. The motor industry gradually is being concentrated in seven major urban centres – Beijing, Changchun, Chongqing, Guangzhou, Shanghai, Tianjin and Wuhan.

Protected by high tariff barriers, with import duty up to 220 per cent, however, even the smallest factory has been able to do nicely, charging outrageous prices and enjoying high profit margins.[2] But this will all change when China rejoins the General Agreement on Tariffs and Trade (GATT) and the barriers have to come down. A Chinese-made Volkswagen Santana that costs three times the international price, for example, is going to have a hard time competing with a flood of cheap imports when the tariff barriers are very much lower.

CAUTIOUS EXPANSION

But, although the Chinese are seeking massive amounts of

overseas investment, they have been very hesitant about lifting the lid on foreign involvement in passenger-car manufacturing – even though this has resulted in growing imports of finished vehicles (at least 100,000 in 1992) which eat up valuable foreign exchange. Only eight Sino-foreign joint-venture car plants were permitted. Apart from the six mentioned in the introduction, another small Japanese manufacturer, Suzuki, managed to break into the magic circle in early 1993 with a 35 per cent stake costing $170 million in a joint venture with China North Industries Group in Chongqing. The venture was due to start production in spring 1995 with an initial output of 20,000 of Suzuki's Alto sedans, rising to 50,000 in the following year. Another Japanese manufacturer, Honda Motor Co., also gingerly tested the waters through an agreement with truck manufacturer Yangcheng Automobile to manufacture a limited number of cars under the Honda brand, with the major parts, including body and engine, being shipped from Japan. Yangcheng built 200 Civic sedans at its Guangzhou factory in November 1993. But a Honda spokesman said further production plans would be based on the market reaction, adding: 'It's a trial to see how much we can do in the Chinese market.'[3]

Two South Korean car makers, Hyundai Motors and Daewoo, are also waiting patiently in the queue for a chance to get a toehold in China as part of a broader strategy to challenge Japan throughout the Asia market. And close on their heels are the Malaysians, who are seeking permission for their own car-assembly plant either involving a derivative of the Proton, Malaysia's first national car developed in cooperation with Mitsubishi of Japan, or the second – a 660cc vehicle modelled on Daihatsu's Mira which was due to begin production in Malaysia in the spring of 1994.

For most Japanese manufacturers, however, car assembly is a distant dream.[4] They want to gain market experience through the less costly channel of pickup trucks, minivans and minibuses. There is strong logic in this, given the fact that these vehicles are a prime means of transport in the rural areas where threequarters of the Chinese population live – and where the roads and after-sales service are not developed enough for sophisticated passenger cars. But there could be a price to pay for being so tardy. 'Chinese officials always tell us that we must pay a premium for being late in the market. They say that Volkswagen took a risk and has been rewarded and that we should pay extra for starting up now', a Japanese executive explained after a high-ranking industry delegation visited China to be briefed on the growing market. But the main result of that visit was to convince the Japanese that China still is not entirely sure where the motor industry is, and should be, going – especially over the issue of how many foreign companies to allow into the passenger-car sector.

In the meantime, the Japanese companies are encouraging their major components suppliers at home to seek out potential joint-venture partners to ensure the Chinese industry has the capability to produce world standard high-quality parts at the right price. Ensuring product quality, especially in the supply of reliable components, has been a headache for most of the foreign manufacturers already working in China (of which more later). An official of the China National Automotive Industry Corporation, admitted that 'China urgently needs funds, advanced technology and equipment if the components industry is to provide support for planned expansion of car manufacturing'. By mid-1993, over 100 parts manufacturing joint ventures had been established. But Mr Liu said there was a need for a number of large-scale plants which could provide 'universal auto components'.

Taking this message to heart, Japan's number two manufacturer, Nissan Motor Company, flew over some 200 representatives from 18 of its most important parts suppliers to take part in an international components fair in Beijing. Afterwards, all of the firms travelled to Zhengzhou, central China, where the car maker has a five per cent stake in a $45-million joint venture to produce pickup trucks, to try and find suitable local partners to replicate their Japanese support operations for Nissan. The 18 companies between them manufactured air conditioners, rubber parts, small panel parts, electrical components, seats and interior upholstery, instrument panels, air cleaners, oil filters and radiators – nearly everything that Nissan might conceivably obtain locally, as it planned to provide the engines, transmissions, suspension and steering from Japan for the foreseeable future.

Nissan chose to begin with pickup trucks because they require between a third to a half less investment than passenger cars and so represent a cheaper option and lower risk (the same strategy was used by the company in the United States before it moved on to manufacture passenger cars). The first trucks were due to come off the assembly line in Spring 1994 with an initial annual output of 5,000 rising to 30,000 by 1997. Through the initial project, Nissan wanted to gain a better understanding of the Chinese working methods, level of technology, distribution and sales methods, and how the state administered the industry. Only after completion of this learning process, will car assembly be considered and that seems unlikely before the end of the century.

Learning from past difficulties experienced by others, Nissan won agreement from its Chinese partners of a free hand to ensure that the quality at the Zhengzhou plant would be as good as that prevailing in its Japanese operations. This included installing a Japanese vice-president with carte blanche to oversee all technical aspects of the project including quality control. Nissan committed itself to expanding local parts content, although without being tied to any specific timetable. According to a company source: 'We think parts suppliers will be looking to us to work out co-production or technical assistance agreements which will enhance their ability to meet our needs' – as well as winning orders from other vehicle manufacturers as the Zhengzhou venture's needs are too small to justify a big investment in components production.

This is likely to be a highly competitive sector. For example, the Automotive Components Group (ACG) of General Motors – which since 1992 has been involved in a US$100-million truck manufacturing joint venture with Jinbei (Golden Cup) Automobile Stock Co., an auto parts conglomerate based on Shenyang, northeastern China (to be discussed shortly) – established several cooperative business relationships in areas such as sparkplugs, air-conditioning and electrical wiring. GM itself is co-producing two-litre engines with the Beijing Internal Combustion Engine Factory. The future goal, company sources said, was to create a nation-wide network of parts projects across the country to underpin not only GM's own expanded vehicle manufacturing operations but the growth of a Chinese industry as a whole.

The supply of good quality, competitively-priced parts remains crucial to the successful or failure of the various foreign-invested manufacturing ventures. It was a problem that the pioneering Beijing Jeep project faced from the first day of life in the mid-1980s.

'American Motors, like other Western companies manufacturing in China, had assumed that as it found more and more Chinese parts, its costs would decline. But the common Western assumption turned out to be wrong. Finding Chinese parts was no easy feat: they were both expensive and of poor quality.[5] When Beijing Jeep could make auto parts on its own, the work wasn't too bad, but when the joint venture had to rely on outside suppliers, the quality was poor and the prices too high. [Beijing Jeep President Don] St Pierre found that, on average, Chinese-made auto parts cost approximately twice as much as those produced in the United States. Because of the low quality of Chinese steel, rubber, and other materials, the Chinese supplier had to import them; they also had to import the equipment to manufacture the parts.[6]

St Pierre also believed that some of the suppliers were charging exorbitant prices in the knowledge that the joint ventures were under heavy pressure to obtain Chinese-made parts. This can be exacerbated when there is a cosy relationship between the suppliers, Chinese joint-venture partners and local government officials. A number of the joint ventures have suffered severe production cutbacks, almost bringing work to a halt, because of this problem. Volkswagen and Daihatsu's ventures were widely described as facing severe problems in this regard, causing strains in the relationship between the venture partners, but officials of the two companies refused to confirm the reports.

'One of the underlying problems [is that] few if any Chinese factories could produce parts and components in volumes high enough to supply the nation and thus achieve economies of scale. Moreover, each enterprise purchased parts from within its own city or province: Shanghai State enterprises, for example, were pressured or ordered to buy from within Shanghai. This system was rooted in China's regional traditions, its Maoist ideology or local self-sufficiency and its antiquated transportation network.' Beijing Jeep experienced the problem when it ordered tyres from a local enterprise, but, despite political pressure from officials in the capital, it cancelled the contract and went to a company offering a superior product in Qingdao.[7]

To be fair to the Chinese, they are aware of the problem and finally do seem to be doing something about it. In May 1993, a wholly-owned subsidiary of China International Trust and Investment (CITIC) – the state concern discussed earlier – was established to develop a parts-production base to support the entire automobile industry. CITIC Automobile planned initially to strengthen ties with firms like Guangzhou Peugeot, Beijing Light Automobile and Zhengzhou Nissan, in which it owns interests. At the same time, it announced plans to convert CITIC Machinery Manufacturing Co. of Shaanxi Province – a former producer of tanks and other military hardware it took over in 1988 – into a major producer of automotive parts. The central government also said that provided they brought in funds and advanced technology, foreign businessmen would be allowed to set up wholly-owned parts manufacturing operations to serve the domestic market, subject to certain limitations. Ford Motor Company was quick to take advantage, signing a letter of intent to set up a $90 million joint venture with the Shanghai Automotive Industry Corporation to produce plastic and trim products, with a possible further investment of up to $500 million on r & d centre projects, fuel spray, air conditioning and glass systems. Ford, it should be noted, has no vehicle manufacturing presence in China.

CONTRASTING FORTUNES

The world's two largest vehicle manufacturers are General Motors of the United States and Toyota Motor Company of Japan. Each are involved, although in different ways, with the same Chinese partner, and have suffered widely differing fortunes in the short term. Their experiences sum up many of the challenges and difficulties of doing business in China.

Toyota makes vans with State-owned Jinbei ('Gold Cup') Automotive in Shenyang, northeast China, while GM produces trucks. Jinbei is a conglomerate of automotive parts makers with a work force of some 50,000. In 1986, the Japanese firm signed a technical assistance agreement with Jinbei's subsidiary, Shenyang Automotive, for mini-van assembly. In 1991, this was expanded into a licensing arrangement for the assembly of a Toyota 15-seater, air-conditioned deluxe minibus from semi- and completely knocked-down kits shipped in from Japan. Production was expected to reach 20,000 vehicles (with a possible high of 50,000 if shifts were doubled) a year by 1995, compared to 3,500 in 1992. Toyota hoped to achieve a switch to 99 per cent local content by the end of 1995, without sacrificing quality. Industry analysts thought this was probably too ambitious, meaning that the Chinese side would have to continue paying import duties of 120 per cent on the Japanese kits, ensuring the minibus remains in the deluxe bracket in price as well as quality. A price tag of $300,000 was no immediate problem as Toyota was alone at the top end of the van market, and demand among cash-rich government work units who comprised its customer base were not especially sensitive to price. As a result, the profits earned enabled Jinbei to list 'Brilliance China Automotive', a Bermuda-registered holding company, on the New York Stock Exchange in 1991. On several occasions, Jinbei approached Toyota about joint-venture collaboration, but the Japanese side demurred – even though it made it harder to impose itself on the issue of quality control.

General Motors, meanwhile, was not so coy. It agreed to a $97.5-million joint venture with Jinbei, the latter taking 70 per cent equity, in January 1992. The problem then, however, was to develop a product that would find a suitable market niche. The American side wanted to import its four-wheel driver Blazer, but the Chinese were worried that this would challenge the troubled Beijing Jeep venture only just beginning to find its feet. Instead, Jinbei asked for a truck with a four-door crew cab. GM had no such model ready in its range, so a compromise was reached on a two-door pick-up truck, the S-10. The planned annual output was supposed to reach 150,000 vehicles by 1998, but the initial market response was extremely poor, especially as the S-10 was significantly more expensive than the Beijing Jeep Cherokee. In mid-1993, production had virtually stopped, leaving the factory littered with piles of unpacked boxes with bright red General Motors markings, each containing truck parts. Zhang Defa, vice-director of Jinbei, admitted that the joint venture had assembled only 300 of 580 pick-up kits imported in the first year, while continuing to churn out the Chinese side's standard commercial van. But even these lines were running at a loss. According to industry analysts, the reason was that the truck plant's new joint-venture status had bid up the cost of everything from labour to plant and equipment leasing – items that were cheap or free when Jinbei was purely a state enterprise. And passing on the increased costs in the form of price rises was not possible, as the two trucks faced stiff competition from vehicles produced by low-overhead state-run enterprises. Others, including Beijing Jeep, have been caught in a similar bind.

According to one industry source, a key factor is '... the way these ventures are set up. Your partner is effectively the Chinese state. As a government, it regulates your prices, markets and finances. As a shareholder in the venture, it dictates your corporate policy. As owner of your supposedly arms-length suppliers, you depend on it for everything you need: components, workers, plant, equipment, foreign exchange. These things cost whatever your state sector partner says they cost. And they're perfectly happy to beggar the venture. After all, the foreigner's stake is in cash, but the Chinese contribution is in kind. The costlier things are the bigger their share and the higher their revenues'.[8]

There were recriminations, of course, as the venture got off to a bad start. The Chinese side felt the answer was for GM to invest more, particularly by providing state-of-the-art manufacturing equipment to expand capacity. But the Americans countered that this would be far more sophisticated than the Jinbei work force could fully utilize. One frustrated executive demanded: 'What is the point in boosting output when you can't even sell your present output at a profit? All some of this fancy plant is good for is to show off to the unending round of visiting delegations that come through here.' Jinbei continued to hope that GM could be persuaded to produce a new four-seater vehicle suited to Chinese conditions.

Meanwhile, other foreign companies have crowded into this sector of the market, including Iveco, the truck-making unit of Italy's Fiat, which set up a joint venture in Nanjing to produce crew-cab trucks. For Jinbei-GM the only answer might have been to import the Blazer after all, but this was not something the Chinese were keen on. In many ways it was a repeat of the Beijing Jeep story already discussed.

Nevertheless, despite this bad experience, GM was bidding – along with Toyota, having finally overcome its shyness – to be the joint-venture partner in a new van-making project proposed for Hainan Island and adjacent parts of Guangdong Province, with an annual output of 100,000 vehicles. Toyota appeared to have the edge, although executives of the Japanese firm privately conceded to having some reservations about their prospective partner, particularly over its alleged lack of openness about its financial operations. The Japanese were particularly unhappy about the way Jinbei had gone about the New York Stock Exchange listing of

Brilliance China Automotive Holdings. Toyota complained that it was not told about the listing until after the event, 'even though our name was used in some of the promotional documents'. Apart from this, the main sticking points were similar to those faced by other would-be foreign investors: differences over the value of the existing assets that Jinbei sees as its contribution to the project, composition of the work-force and the role of the imported management.

OTHER FOREIGN PLAYERS

As a pioneer in the field, *Volkswagen* has made a huge investment in creating a major car production base for the future. Shanghai-Volkswagen formerly started business in September 1985 with a total investment of 985 million Yuan, jointly divided between the two sides. According to the initial contract, the annual production capacity was to be 30,000 Santana passenger cars and 100,000 engines. The agreement was to last 25 years. Much of the early profits were ploughed back into the business and in 1992, an additional investment of $375 million was announced to upgrade the assembly lines and immediately expand capacity to 60,000 cars a year, with an eventual target of 300,000. The venture obtained a $420 million internationally-syndicated loan to help fund the expansion.

In 1991, the Yiqi (First Auto Works)-Volkswagen joint venture was established in Changchun with a total investment of 4.2 billion Yuan, split 60:40. According to the contract, in the first phase, the annual production capacity was to be 150,000 cars, 270,000 engines and 180,000 gearboxes. The car output was due to reach capacity in 1996, by which time 90 per cent of the components were to be made domestically. In the initial period, the target was 30,000 Audis and 20,000 Jettas. In 1992, output was 4,500 and 14,000 units respectively.

For France, Citroën and Peugeot are both strongly represented. Guangzhou-Peugeot Automobile Company in Huangpu was the first Sino-French cooperative project in the motor industry, a 20-year agreement being signed in March 1985 with an initial registered capital of 240 million francs. The Guangzhou Automobile Factory (now Guangzhou Automobile Corp. Holdings) took 46 per cent of the shares, Peugeot 22 per cent, and other Chinese investors the rest. The main products are the Peugeot 504-type light lorries and 505 station wagon. According to the contract, the annual production capacity for the first stage was set at 15,000 light lorries; 15,000 lorries and 15,000 cars in the second stage; 50,000 automobiles in the third stage.

The first sample lorry came off the assembly line in early 1987, after which the shareholders quickly agreed to start work on the second stage – the fabrication of 505 cars, requiring an additional investment of 325 million francs. The venture suffered, however, when Beijing launched an economic adjustment policy in the late 1980s, but vehicle output finally got back on track with almost 14,000 produced in 1991. The second phase of the project was begun the following year. Domestic content has remained below half, but with Peugeot abandoning production of the 505 car, Guangzhou was confident it could take over total assembly for the world market. By 1993, the venture was fairly profitable, producing 30,000 vehicles and optimistic of reaching 150,000 by the end of the century.

Meanwhile, in May 1992, Shenlong (Magic Dragon) Automobile Co. Ltd., a joint venture between Citroën and China Dongfeng Auto Corp. (formerly China Second Auto Works) was established, with work divided between factories in two central cities, Wuhan and Xianfeng. The cooperative period was set at 35 years, with the Chinese holding 70 per cent of the equity. In the initial period, Dongfeng assembled the 'Fukang' model from CKD kits of what Citroën calls the ZX car at home. This was intended to allow the French company to understand its Chinese partner and the domestic market before they move into development of a new product for the international market (target: 150,000 cars a year), along with engines and other components. The French Government has been most supportive and has so far provided a 1.7-billion-franc mixed loan and 1.2-billion-franc export credit.

The French presence was further strengthened when Renault signed a deal with China Sanjiang Aeronautical Corporation to establish a 45:55 joint venture producing luxury station wagons at a factory about 40 miles from Wuhan. Initial investment was $65 million. Production was due to begin in mid-1994, with output rising steadily to 40,000 vehicles in 1997 and 165,000 by the turn of the century. Renault, which also planned to open a representative office in Beijing to develop a nation-wide sales network, said it would try to persuade some of its traditional French components suppliers to establish their own joint ventures in China as a way of keeping production costs down.

Some of the Japanese involvement in China has already been discussed, especially Nissan and Toyota. Three of the smaller companies – Daihatsu, Honda and Fuji Heavy Industry – are involved in separate projects to develop mini-cars. The initial cooperative method was technology transfer rather than joint ventures.

Beginning from March 1984, Daihatsu Corp. signed a contract with Tianjin Mini Automobile Co. to cooperate for seven years. Daihatsu transferred the technology for its HIJET mini-trucks to its Tianjin partner. After two years, the two partners signed another contract for a production licence for Daihatsu's Charade for seven years. The latter vehicle has become a household world in Beijing, where it forms the bulk of the estimated 50,000 bright yellow mini-taxis – known by locals as 'locusts' or 'miandi' ('breadloaf' taxis) – that have not only brought cheap travel and a touch of colour to the capital's drab streets but also introduced residents to the delights of the daily rush-hour traffic jam. There was a time when a pedestrian could stand forlornly by the side of the road for ages looking for a taxi. These days, there are likely to be several queuing up within seconds. The Tianjin project initially could produce 20,000 mini-trucks, 30,000 Charades and 30,000 engines. According to the development programme, the production capacity for cars was due to reach 50,000 in 1995.

Two military enterprises in Chongqing and Anshun (Guizhou Province) were designated to develop civilian cars. In 1984, Honda signed a technology and trade cooperation agreement with Chongqing Changan Machinery Factory which is under the administration of China North Industrial Corp. (Holdings). According to the contract, Honda transferred the production technology of its ST90 mini-car. On the basis of the absorption of Honda techniques, Changan Machinery Factory developed a series of mini-trucks and mini-buses. In October 1991, the factory developed a new type of mini-car. In 1992, the factory produced 5,000 mini-cars, but planned to raise capacity to a total of 100,000 vehicles overall.

In 1989, Fuji Heavy Industry Corp. transferred the production technology of Subaru REX KFI cars to Guizhou Aviation Industrial

Corp. The car, developed by Fuji in the late 1970s to meet the world energy shortage, is economical and cheap. The new GHK7060 cars produced by the Guizhou company went into production after the project was approved by the State Planning Commission in April 1992. The proposed production capacity was 10,000 cars in 1995.

In September 1986, the Italian concern Iveco signed a technology-transfer agreement with Nanjing Automobile Factory involving a range of lightweight lorries. The Italian government provided a $112 million long-term, low-interest loan and after four years of development the project went into production with an initial output of 5,000 vehicles a year, hopefully rising to a full capacity of 60,000.

At the heavy end of the market, China introduced the Austrian Star, German Benz and Japanese Nissan Diesel technologies during the 7th Five-Year Plan (1986-90). Beginning from December 1983, the China Heavy Automobile Corp. (Holdings) introduced the '91' heavy lorry project from Austria Star Corp. The first China-made lorry drove away from the production line in June 1989 from Jinan, capital of Shandong Province. The output in 1990 was 1,000 lorries and by the end of the 1994 it was supposed to be 10,000 vehicles. China North Industrial Corp. began the Benz heavy lorry project in September 1989 and by the end of 1994 production capacity at Baotou was supposed to have been raised to 6,000 lorries ranging from 16 to 36 tons (1992 output was 1,000). Benz was reported to be considering further ventures in China, including production of buses. Nissan Diesel's partner is Dongfeng Automobile Corp. who produce an eight-ton lorry.

Through a corporate tie-up with Isuzu Motors, Nissan-developed truck technology is also being utilized in productive ventures at four locations in the country – Beijing Isuzu, Southwest Isuzu, with its headquarters in Chengdu, capital of Sichuan), Jiangling in Nanchang, capital of Jiangxi Province, and Qinling (in Chongqing). The latter involves investment in Isuzu, the others merely import the Japanese technology. Beijing Isuzu planned to produce 100,000 light lorries in 1995 (compared to only 5,000 in 1992), with the other three producing 60,000 vehicles between them. The Japanese presence was further strengthened in November 1993, when Hino Motors, a truck manufacturer affiliated with Toyota, set up a joint venture in Heilongjiang

Province in the northeast, to produce buses for the domestic market. Hino was to provide key components such as engines and transmissions, while the chassis was to be Chinese-made.

Not everyone needs to establish a productive presence in China. Rolls Royce, the British epitome of luxury motoring, has discovered a potential large market among the country's status-conscious nouveau riche. MD Motors, the company's Hong Kong-based sales agent for China, reported selling 20 cars to entrepreneurs and business executives in places like Beijing, Guangzhou and Shanghai, at a cost of $150,000 to $195,000 each, in the first half of 1993, and said there was a year-long waiting list. General Motors sold about 100 Cadillacs in the same period. Meanwhile, a Beijing resident became the mainland's first registered owner of a Ferrari sports car at a cost of $135,000 – although most of the roads on which such a vehicle could be given its head have yet to be built.

BEIJING JEEP

Finally in this chapter, I want to return to the ongoing story of Beijing Jeep. When the first Cherokee rolled off the assembly line on 26 September 1985 – almost six years after talks on the joint venture had begun – an enthusiastic AMC executive announced plans for production to be raised to 4,500 in the following year, and added that a domestic sales target of 40,000 jeeps in 1990 would be a 'piece of cake'.[8] As with a lot of other expectations on both sides, this was grossly unrealistic. Although the Chinese by 1986 had reluctantly given up their hopes of a new vehicle for the PLA, they were willing to guarantee foreign exchange for the import of the Cherokee kits covering only 4,500 vehicles over the following two years. The Americans, although abandoning their dreams of 40,000 jeeps in 1990, held out for 15,000 kits over a four-year period – a sharp drop in expectations! Finally, with the head of the AMC negotiating team about to depart for home, the two sides compromised on 12,500 up to May 1990 (after that time, it was assumed there would be little need for the kits because the Chinese would be producing most of the parts themselves). It was a bitter pill for AMC, sweetened somewhat by a sudden Chinese government concession to underwrite the $100 million needed for an upgrade of the operation, including development of engine, stamping and axle plants and a new paint system (which, anyway, would belong to China after the expiry of the joint-venture agreement in 2003).

All the problems really came down to one basic fact: for the Chinese the Cherokee was really a sideline operation. In 1986, Beijing Jeep produced 24,500 vehicles, but only 2,000 were the American product, and the remainder were the old stalwarts BAW had been turning out happily for many years. 'The Americans were important to Beijing Jeep not so much for their Cherokees or their knowledge of sales and markets, but because of the technology and modern equipment they brought. The Chinese would have lived without the Cherokee, but they were eager, indeed desperate, for the tools and equipment and techniques the Americans used to manufacture it.'[9]

In June 1990, the engine plant was put into operation, and by the end of 1991, almost 45 per cent of components were being made in China. After negligible profits in the 1980s, the joint venture began to earn real money – $45 million in 1991. Company officials optimistically spoke of output reaching 80,000 vehicles by 1995. For AMC, however, it was too late – in 1987 it was taken over by Chrysler Corp. and ceased to exist. It is the latter company that is finally begin to reap the rewards for all the heartaches and shattered dreams the pioneering AMC executives suffered

FOOTNOTES

1. Details of the Hainan scandal have been compiled from interviews with Japanese businessmen, Japanese newspaper accounts and reference to Beijing Jeep by Jim Mann (see bibliography).
2. These high duties have produced a lucrative smuggling business in which a number of government officials have been implicated. Several hundred thousand luxury foreign cars have been smuggled into China since 1990, with Toyota's Crown and Lexus models extremely popular, along with Mercedes-Benz, Chevrolet and Hyundai cars from South Korea. Smugglers can use containers to bring in cars disguised as something else, or ship them in on high-speed launches to remote locations along the Chinese coast using Hong Kong as the conduit. Many cars are stolen in the colony for the mainland market. Another method is falsified documents for the import of duty-free products permitted for joint ventures and some other categories. Once in the country, a car disappears into the provinces never to be seen again. In mid-1993, the central government announced a stepped-up anti-smuggling campaign and convened meetings of various experts to come up with new measures. This is not just an issue of the government missing out on import duty . According to a source at the China National Automotive Industry Corp., smuggling seriously affects sales of Chinese-built cars because without the crippling import duties, the cars smuggled in from abroad can be sold for much less and offer far better quality. A foreign executive pointed out that his company had distributors in Hong Kong, who then sold the cars to brokers and dealers: 'We cannot demand that those brokers sell the vehicles to customer A or B. So smuggling has nothing to do with us directly. We are very embarrassed.' The executive recalled visiting the northeast and seeing

thousands of South Korean cars on the roads which had bypassed official channels. Local people he questioned were quite frank – the cars had been smuggled in. But even more astonishing was to discover one of his own company's models which had never been marketed in China. The vehicle in question, in fact, had actually been shipped to the United States. 'Yet, here it was sitting in a car park in a remote part of China. Don't ask me how it got there because I cannot imagine.' In November 1993, it was reported that the Communist Party's Discipline Inspection Committee was investigating the smuggling of Korean cars through Shandong. Imports of second-hand Japanese cars have also come through a Korean minority area in northern China, with much of the profit being taken by North Korean organizers.

3. Typifying Japanese caution, Honda had actually been in the Chinese car market since the mid-1980s in a modest way. In 1984, Honda signed a technology and trade cooperation agreement with Chongqing Changan Machinery Factory under which it transferred the production technology of its ST90 mini-cars. Changan Machinery Factory used the Honda technology first to develop a series of mini-trucks and mini-buses, before moving on to create a new type of mini-car in 1991. Current output of mini-cars and mini-trucks is 100,000 a year.

4. The Japanese, however, are not holding back in production of motorcycles, which are expected to provide a buoyant market until the turn of the century when private car ownership begins to be the norm with rising income levels. Motorcycle output in China was 1.8 million in 1991, and was targeted to rise to three million in 1995 – although many experts thought this was too conservative. All the major Japanese manufacturers had a strong presence. At the time of writing, Honda's factories in China were capable of producing 560,000 machines a year, Yamaha about the same, and Suzuki 100,000 – although it also exports another 450,000 Japan-assembled machines.

5. It is a common problem. Fast food leader McDonalds, for example, was forced to cut back on opening outlets in China because of difficulty in finding local sources of high quality raw materials. In Beijing, for example, a farm set up near the capital took 10 years to produce potatoes of sufficiently consistent quality to be pulverized and reconstituted into French fries. China's size and poor transport network, however, means that a successful supplier can only provide for restaurants in the immediate area. McDonald's, therefore, has to start from scratch in each new area. [Reported in Business China, 4 Oct. 1993]

5. Beijing Jeep pp230-1.
6. Ibid., pp231-2.
7. Far Eastern Economic Review, 27 May 1993.
8. Beijing Jeep, p168.
9. Ibid., p256.

8 The Chinese art of salesmanship

KEY POINTS

Opportunities are opening up rapidly for foreign companies to sell more products to an increasingly affluent Chinese consumer base. But one should not get carried away. It is not yet that market of 1.2 billion consumers; the genuine spenders are still a small minority. But it is getting better and bigger all the time. This chapter will look at the following:
- A profile of the Chinese consumer today – what he or she is buying.
- Sales methods for the big and small trader.
- The opening up of the retail trade to foreign investment which provides the big players an opportunity to establish department store and supermarket chains for the first time.
- Customs regulations.
- Promoting the product in the marketplace.
- The growth of the advertising and public relations industries, and the promotional opportunities for foreign firms.
- A look at the changing face of the Chinese media.

CHINESE CONSUMER

FIRST, let us try and draw a picture of the typical Chinese consumer. In the mid-1970s the annual income for young people was about 300 Yuan (about $50). In 1993, the minimum income for a young factory worker was 10 times that amount – still not a great deal of money by Western standards, but a vast improvement in a relatively short space of time. Owners of private enterprises and restaurants, construction contractors and sports and movie stars are the country's wealthiest people, and there were at least a million Yuan millionaires.

At the start of the 1980s, the Chinese spent most of their money on food – mainly rice, wheat, maize, flour and vegetables; they had little extra for meat, eggs or milk. In fact, for a long period, milk was regarded as a special commodity available only for infants, the sick and senior officials. Most people could buy fish, meat and chicken only during the Spring Festival – the Chinese New Year. While city inhabitants got nearly enough to eat, some rural people often went hungry. Clothing for young and old was limited to either grey Mao-style suits or green military uniforms for almost all seasons. Fashionable and colourful clothing previously had been regarded as 'bourgeois'. One suit of clothes would serve for years.

Today, the amount spent on food has dropped to about half the monthly income and the quality has improved. Chicken and meat are now common on the dining table and eggs and milk are readily available. The consumption of rice and flour has been reduced. People have begun paying attention to nutrition: they watch carefully cholesterol and fat and eat vegetables and fruit regularly. Previously, during the long bitter winter in Beijing, virtually the only vegetable available was cabbage. In autumn, a typical sight would be great piles of cabbages on every street corner as residents stocked up for winter (piling them on balconies and in the corridors of their high-rise apartments for gradual use in various stew dishes). The biggest sign of change is the disappearance of the cabbage mountains under government decree. Now, Beijing residents can shop at private markets where farmers, some of whom have travelled a thousand miles or more from the south, offer a lush array of tropical fruits and vegetables all year round.

Foreign food is also freely available and popular. Rice from Thailand, Australian flour, Coca Cola, Nestlé coffee and M & M chocolate all sell well, though they have been on the Chinese market for only a few years. In the past, if anyone bought Coca Cola they were regarded as crazy – a dozen canned Cokes cost a monthly income. But now one will find Coke in remote small villages that have no electricity or telephones.

Clothing has become more important, too. It is no longer unusual for a villager to have several new suits. People no longer wait until their old clothes are worn out before buying new ones.

Even expensive suits which usually cost a person several months' income sell well. Many world-famous brands such as Pierre Cardin have set up branches in China's main cities and popular sports clothes such as Puma and Nike can be found in many small townships. Jewellery has also become an important part of dress. Nearly all married women have several in the form of necklaces, rings and earrings. In the small village of Shaoshan in Hunan Province, Chairman Mao's home town, a gold shop was set up in early 1993. The villagers who had not seen gold for decades, have become avid shoppers. Along with jewellery, make-up has become important for women, though only a dozen years ago make-up was only associated with the stage. Many young women spend both time and money learning cosmetics at night school, while others frequent beauty salons. Cosmetics' factories, including many Sino-foreign ventures, are increasing and advertisements for their products are regularly seen on television. The ubiquitous 'Avon Lady' has already arrived on the nation's doorsteps.

In the 1970s, watches, bicycles, sewing machines and clothes were regarded as the absolute necessities for newlyweds, and they usually cost all their savings. Today, they cost no more than one or two months' salary. There are about 400 million bicycles in China now and a new machine has become just a small wedding gift (and it would have to be a 12-speed mountain bike to get more than a passing glance). Sewing machines and watches have also become passé. The new 'four items' that all new couples want are refrigerators, television sets, washing machines and video players. There are about 200 million tv sets in Chinese homes, mostly colour in the cities, but still largely black-and-white in rural areas. Televisions are still relatively expensive, and an imported set usually costs a years' income – hence making a very nice wedding gift from doting parents. But the real status symbols are video cameras and air conditioners.

With the 'one couple, one child' birth-control policy, children have become what the Chinese call 'little emperors', able to get nearly anything they want. Even though the number of children has decreased, the market to cater for their needs has increased dramatically. In major cities, it is estimated that nearly half of family income is spent by the parents in the hope that their children will become healthy and intelligent. They buy costly electric toys for children who may soon lose interest and ask for new ones several days later. Many families have pianos and simple computers for their 'emperors'. After work, many parents accompany their offspring to night school for dancing, drawing or martial arts, or stay at home where tutors help their children with mathematics or English. Children's snacks are becoming more expensive. A packet of sweets can cost mother a day's income, but many parents buy several at one time without hesitation.[1] Believing that imported milk powders are more nutritious, some parents refuse to try domestic milk even though it's half the price.

Cars are another consumer goal. Among the half a million automobiles in Beijing, for example, nearly 10,000 are privately-owned (most are owned by state work units), and the national figure is about 40,000. This is obviously minuscule in such a large country, but is actually a rather remarkable figure considering the financial and political constraints under which Chinese have had to operate.[2] Telephones are within the reach of many, but it will be some time before every family is able to have one. In Beijing, for example, a phone can cost over 5,000 Yuan. As a result of the high costs, the number of family telephones only amounted to 2.4 million at the end of 1992, according to a survey by the Ministry of Posts and Telecommunications.[3]

CONSUMER INFLUENCE

Companies wishing to tap the consumer market would probably be well advised to direct most of their efforts for the moment to the sizeable and growing pockets of wealth in China. In 1993, there were thought to be about 60 million Chinese consumers earning at least $975 a year, a level at which substantial consumption is theoretically supposed to become apparent. Consumers in the more affluent areas of China are as rich if not richer than the average Malaysian, Thai and Indonesian. The 60 million-strong consumer market compares with an estimated 15 to 20 million in Malaysia, 25 million in Taiwan and more than 40 million in South Korea. By the end of the century, the number of affluent consumers could rise more than threefold to 200 million when China will have a market for consumer durables that is, in terms of purchasing power and population, larger than most of the present East and Southeast Asian markets today.

One of the problems with China, however, is that the affluent consumers are not concentrated in one area. The main markets are in southern China – Shenzhen and Guangzhou – Shanghai in the centre and Beijing and Tianjin in the north (by the year 2000, several other cities and provinces will have reached an average per capita income level of $975). Nor is the market unified. China is a country of regions, many of which have been encouraged by past government policy to aim for self-sufficiency. As will be discussed later in this chapter, these factors make distribution of products somewhat problematical. According to one management consultant: 'In a country with a notoriously overburdened transportation and telecommunications infrastructure, carefully planned and effectively executed distribution and sales activities will inevitably prove key factors for success.'

A major frustration for the foreign businessman has been the semi-closed door in the distribution area which has made it difficult to participate in the domestic sales market. Consumer buying power has been affected by high import tariffs (one example: the tax on foreign cosmetics is 300 per cent, but is only one-third of that for imported cosmetic materials for domestic manufacture). Many businessmen then decided that the only answer was to set up a manufacturing operation in China – only to find themselves restricted by Chinese quotas on the percentage of goods they could sell domestically. Normally, the proportion of exports must exceed domestic sales, especially goods produced in the SEZs. Generally, applications for the right to sell on the local market have to go through complicated bureaucratic procedures with no guarantee of success. High-tech products have enjoyed special privileges, as well as products regarded as 'filling a vacancy in China' or replaced imports, with the proportion of the latter two items determined by market demand. .

This, however, is the theory and not necessarily the reality. One Taiwanese businessman who set up a processing factory in Zhangzhou, Fujian Province, was allowed under his contract to sell only 30 per cent of his output in China. He was dissatisfied with the constraint, however, and astutely managed to insert a condition in an appendix of the contract that the products of his factory could be sold in the domestic market without restriction 'before the international market is fully developed'. Accordingly, the product entered the domestic market and earned big profits.

Thus, it is possible for a clever businessman, with a good Chinese partner, to get into the market without restriction or government interference. Recognizing this, as well as the fact that entry to GATT will eventually make the restrictions untenable, the Beijing authorities in 1993 raised the domestic output allowance for China-based manufacturers to 50 per cent.

There were also signs of a relaxation in the rules barring private companies from operating their own distribution networks. In electronics, for example, foreign-funded joint ventures are allowed to establish proprietary distribution and sales networks giving them direct access to consumers that enables companies to bypass the state-controlled wholesale system.

One way to participate in the market is to open a new department store or invest in an existing operation. After Deng Xiaoping's South China inspection tour in early 1992, six major cities – Beijing, Shanghai, Guangzhou, Dalian, Tianjin, and Qingdao – and the five SEZs were able to approve department store joint ventures with foreign involvement. The stores were able to import and export rights with tax exemption on a certain proportion of their commodities. Hong Kong businessmen quickly took advantage of geographic proximity to establish bridgeheads in Guangzhou. In Beijing, joint ventures were approved for Wangfujing Street, the commercial heart of the city within sight of Tiananmen Square, and Hong Kong real-estate interests were quick to scent the prospects for fat profits. Their strategy primarily has been to build large-scale commercial buildings which they then rent out to international chain-store groups. But some real estate companies have also sought to have retailing included in their permitted scope of business. Elsewhere in the capital, the Beijing-Lufthansa Friendship Store was also approved as a joint venture by the municipal government. Shanghai has also thrown open its doors to foreign retailers, including Sincere of Hong Kong, Isetan, Sogo and Yaohan of Japan and Taiwan's Sunrise. Others are not far behind. Nestlé, the Swiss food company, made a concerted push to expand its business in China, previously dominated by baby-food products, by purchasing the China assets of Dairy Farm. a Hong Kong-based dairy-products manufacturer controlled by the Jardine Matheson Group. One attraction was that Dairy Farm owned the Seven-Eleven mini-mart franchise in Shenzhen, which offered potential for a breakout into the rest of the national market. Dickson Concepts, a Hong Kong retailer of luxury goods and owner of London's Harvey Nichols department store, meanwhile, planned to manufacture and retail a line of luxury items specifically targeted at the wealthy Chinese consumer in various major cities.

'People buy, they certainly buy. Money is not a problem,' said an assistant at the Orient Shopping Centre, a four-floor Hong Kong joint venture that opened in Shanghai in 1993. Most of the serious shoppers appeared to be members of China's new entrepreneurial class: elaborately coiffeured women with portable telephones and high heels, fleshy businessmen with diamond watches, sideburns and pagers.

Katherine Bao, President of the new Sunrise Department Store in Shanghai, said her joint venture was aimed at mid-income shoppers looking for a break from the crowds, noise and slack service of state department stores: 'In Chinese stores, sometimes you cannot move as there are so many people. Here we stress service.' People begin waiting outside Sunrise long before the doors open for business, eager to begin poring over a stock selection ranging from pricey imported cosmetics to made-in-China baby strollers and colourful cups and dishes. At the Orient shopping centre where items such as the Gucci bag are for sale, Mao-suited peasants on a tourist trip seemed to outnumber the true big spenders cruising the aisles, but the store still racked up sales of about $18 million in its first six months.

With more international shopping giants opening, staid state stores have been forced to try and catch up. Just across the street from the Orient, Shanghai Number Eight Store has its own new shopping centre complete with escalators and a supermarket. And the city's television viewers are deluged with peppy rap-style advertisements urging the youth market to look for what it wants at the venerable Number Seven Department Store.

A few years ago, shoppers had no choice but to go elbow-to-elbow in the sticky July heat of Beijing's crowded state-run department stores just to buy a blouse or handbag. And, in general, people basically had to guess whether the clothes behind the counter would fit them as most stores did not have self-serve, open-plan shopping. The other obstacle was to win a bit of cooperation out of deadpan sales assistants who took out their grudges on the world in general by frustrating any attempt to get them to provide any 'service'. Post-sales service was non-existent, the buyer of a refrigerator, for example, might have to hire a tricycle to get it home several miles away through crowded streets. Times have changed. Customers now insist on service. For a start, they hate to shop in department stores that do not have escalators, open-plan trading and central air-conditioning. This has forced most of Beijing's shopping districts to pour money and time into revamping their facilities. The Beijing Department Store, the city's oldest, invested $3.6 million to renovate its decades-old shop. The Xidan Department Store, one of the city's big four, even advertised its renovation efforts on television.

Li Kuixi from the Beijing Department Store, whose sales reached a billion Yuan ($176.4 million) for the first time in 1993, admitted: 'We are feeling the pressure of competition from several modern department stores. We can no longer rest on our laurels.' Shoppers with bulging wallets like to visit stores such as the Beijing Lufthansa centre and the Civil Department Store, which provide a spacious, enjoyable shopping environment, top quality products and smiles. In 1992, Beijing signed agreements with overseas investors or real-estate companies to build modern shopping centres in the city. Xidan, one of the busiest shopping districts in Beijing, is getting a $975 million facelift that will make it the city's most modern shopping paradise with skyscraper blocks flanking an eight-lane highway – replacing the low-rise simple stores and restaurants that now flank the narrow, two-lane road.

Away from the glamorous department stores, however, the fiercest struggle in the consumer retail sector is likely to be over the establishment of no-frills chain stores. Having been given the green light, a number of foreign businessmen set up branch stores in newly-opened coastal regions, and from there sought to spread their influence inland, creating a basic sales network for popular products. Once this was in place, they moved in with a branch store. If this is still a bit too ambitious, many businessmen test the market by setting up special counters within existing department stores, or stage periodic sales exhibitions and fairs.

A new dimension has only recently been added to the retail scene with the introduction of home shopping. New services such as door-to-door sales, television and radio shopping have become popular. A centre providing door-to-door service for a fee in Beijing attracted hundreds of factories and sellers within a week of opening business. The service, which sends sales people directly to consumers' homes to market products, first met with roaring success in South China. More and more factories and stores are also looking to television to market their products. Customers need only dial the telephone number on the screen to make an order and the goods will be sent directly to their home. Shanghai and Nanjing radio stations have opened shopping hotlines, inviting sales people to department stores to answer questions and receive orders from listeners.

IMPORT/EXPORT RULES

The newcomer trying to sell a product in China has to navigate through a veritable minefield of regulations and requirements. As stressed in earlier remarks on joint ventures, one simply does not turn up in China and start selling the latest gizmo developed by the boys in the r & d department. The Chinese government wants a strong say in what comes in. Import licences are required for a wide range of products, including steel materials, natural rubber, timber, wood pulp, crude oil, sugar, tobacco products, motor vehicles, civil aircraft and computers.

One piece of good news for businessmen in 1993, however, was that customs procedures for foreign trade enterprises were in the process of being simplified. As a first step, Beijing Customs granted 24 local firms the title of 'Trustworthy Enterprises', while 96 factories gained the title of 'Highly-Reputed Enterprises'. These were either large and medium State firms or famous Sino-foreign ventures such as the Beijing Yanshan Petrochemical Corporation, the China National Aviation Technology Import and Export Corp. the Beijing Philips Co and Beijing Lido Holiday Inn Hotel (which has a large supermarket for foreign goods). The idea was to give them priority in 11 sectors as customs procedures, making customs declarations, and paying tariffs for imports and exports were concerned. To win the coveted titles, enterprises had to have normal production activities for more than two years, not be involved in smuggling deals for three years, and have paid their tariffs on time. Zhen Pu, Director of Beijing Customs, said the move was considered an experiment in borrowing foreign advanced management experience and gradually building a customs system that followed international practice.

For direct imports, the Chinese regard the dutiable value as being the normal wholesale price prevailing at the place of purchase, plus all charges such as packing, freight, insurance premiums and commissions incurred up to the place of import in China. Apart from the import tariffs – which were lowered by 8.8 per cent from 1 January 1994 'in a bid to increase foreign trade' – incoming goods are also subject to an Industrial and Commercial Consolidated Tax (ICCT), imposed at the stage of importation and again on the turnover after the goods have been sold. There are numerous classifications for industrial and agricultural products, with cigarettes (69 per cent) and alcohol (60 per cent) at the high end. Most goods tend to be in the five to 15 per cent, with the rate being much lower for materials used in production than for consumer goods. There are various potential exemptions, however, especially for machinery, equipment and other materials imported as capital investment in equity and cooperative joint ventures and wholly-owned foreign enterprises. The same can apply to materials, components and other necessary items brought in for processing and assembly when it involves products from a foreign-related enterprise for export. The authorities are also willing to listen to any hardship cases not covered by exemptions which, due to financial difficulties, have trouble paying ICCT. In addition to customs duty and ICCT, the Chinese also have an Import Regulatory Tax which is imposed at varying rates on products whose penetration of the domestic market it wishes to keep under tight rein (eg: television sets, automobiles and motorcycles, photocopiers and calculators). The rates run up as high as 80 per cent. As far as exports are concerned, China also imposes a tax if it wishes to control the amount of shipments – foodstuffs and minerals being the most obvious examples. From this brief description, therefore, it is apparent that the paperwork is complicated and time-consuming.

In order to be successful, the budding salesman (or the purchaser of Chinese goods for export), has had to establish and maintain a dialogue with key government authorities such as the Ministry of Foreign Trade and Economic Cooperation (MOFTEC), which has a large number of specialist divisions, of which the most important for the foreign businessman are the Import and Export Bureau and the Foreign Trade Administration (its responsibilities include quotas, export licences and the supervision of the representative offices set up in China by foreign trading companies) and the Bureau for Technology Import and Export. From there, it is necessary to get to the key people in State-owned banks such as the Bank of China, People's Construction Bank, Industrial and Commercial Bank (see appendices for a brief description of each bank), and the state-owned non-bank financial institutions such as CITIC, also described in chapter five. Finally, the salesman may end up dealing with one of the specialized import and export corporations set up to handle specific industrial sectors such as SINOCHEM (chemicals and rubber), MINMETALS (export of metallurgical products and other minerals and import of steel products), CHINASILK, CHINATEX and CHINATRANS (space booking, cargo allocation, customs clearance and forwarding).

In addition, under MOFTEC, there are a number of trade development bodies. One of the most important is the China Council for the Promotion of International Trade (CCPIT) set up in 1952 to promote trade and technical exchanges with other countries, promote Chinese products abroad and organize exhibitions within China of foreign goods, and provide end-users in China with the latest information on developments in foreign markets and new products likely to be of interest. Operating under its auspices is the Trademark Registration Agency which acts for both foreign enterprises wanting to register their trademarks in China and Chinese companies wishing to do the same abroad. Also active is the All China Federation of Industry and Commerce (ACFIC), which operates in a similar way to a Western chamber of commerce. It provides economic consultation services and advises foreign enterprises in their investments, as well as acting an intermediary in the case of disputes. It also has an advisory role to assist the government in the development of trade, industrial and commercial policies.

Much has changed with the open-door reforms. Provinces were granted greater independence to handle their own trade, including the right of local foreign trade companies to operate independently of their parents. Local foreign economic relations and trade commissions were also given power to issue import and export licences for a range of products and commodities. The results were to the central government's liking, however, and in the midst of chaos brought on by an inflationary buying spree in the late 1980s centralized control over foreign trade was reasserted. At the time of writing, the trend was once again towards greater freedom. There are now numerous import and export channels, many through different and often competing ministries, but also increasingly via individual companies which are given the responsibility to do their own buying and selling as outlined in Chapter Two. However, the difficulty of obtaining foreign exchange for imports does continue to act as a government-imposed constraint on open trading.

Some foreign companies get round the restrictions by employing middlemen known as 'convertors-importers', who, through networking, have import rights and hard currency to pay out for a commission of between three and five per cent. Many of them provide temporary storage and help to contract delivery to wholesalers around the country. Most of the local wholesalers do not have importing rights, but buy them from the convertors-importers. Payment terms tend to be based on a case by case basis, but are usually 30 days, with the exchange risk borne by the customer.[4]

A good sales agent would seem to be essential. But, in order to understand how the system works in selling to China – and the frustrations that it can entail – I provide the experiences of one such agent[5] dealing with low-volume, high-technology equipment.

'Tandem [an American company that makes on-line, transaction processing computers] have 14 customers in China. They know they have precisely that number because 14 of their big computers went into China. But they don't know who those customers are, where they are, or what they are using the computers for. Yet, they can see they are making money and they see China as a potentially big market for their computers, so how do they progress? They cannot get off the ground, however. The reason is that the end-user, after looking at brochures and talking to people or whatever, have decided that what they need is a Tandem computer. So then they must apply for the budget from their parent organization to allow them the necessary US dollars, even if they are maybe a revenue-generating organization such as a bank. Assuming they get this permission, they will contact a government-registered import-export company.

'In our case, we deal with the Ministry of Machine Building

and Electronics Industry, which has an import-export arm responsible for all technology items. This company will be the broker in the deal. It will purchase the equipment on behalf of the end-user. They will then make advances to Tandem, sign the contract, pay the US dollars to Tandem, receive the equipment and they are then responsible for distributing it to the end-user as requested. Tandem know their contact in the import-export firm, but they don't know who the actual user is. It could be a bank, manufacturing company, government ministry or transportation company, but there is no way of knowing or offering after-sales help. Having said this, there are now ways for end-users to raise the dollars themselves on semi-official swap markets [see Chapter Twelve] and then approach the supplier direct.

'In the computer business you sell a box, a computer; you then sell the software that runs on the computer; you sell the service and installation; you then sell the training; you sell on-site maintenance; you sell annual service contracts and upgrades, additional peripheral equipment add-ons. The whole thing spins up. What usually happens is that the computer company will go into the market soft and minimize their revenue. They sell the box very cheap and make their money on the add-on stuff. But that doesn't happen in China. What the company here will do is say we have a million dollars to spend on a computer system and we are the number one automotive parts company or whatever. They will go out and buy a box costing a million dollars. They will haggle over the price and they will just get the biggest box they can get for the money. They bring the box home and put it down and say that's the biggest computer we could get for that much money, so now what are we going to do with it guys? They will write their own software or pirate it, and develop various in-house applications. There is no money left for all the other things required. Most big computer users have an annual budget because they know they must have money to maintain the system and let it grow. But in China, you get a one-off lump sum. You buy what you can with the money and then it's gone. So the vendor will come and say: what are you going to buy this year? The user will say: no money this year but come back in five years when we might get some more budget. But for the next five years we have no money. It's a big problem. It's very difficult to make any projections of market growth revenue growth or whatever. You think you're building a big base of users...you have 150 companies in China all using your equipment, but you are still not set up because each time you sell you are dead. What vendors now do is that they double the price of the initial box. It costs twice as much as any other country because they know it is a one-off deal. It makes for a very strange business.'

COPYRIGHT PROBLEMS

Trademark piracy has long been the bane of foreign businessmen trying to sell in China. Introduce a new product to the market, and it does not take long for passable imitations to appear at a fraction of the cost. This has been a major irritant in Sino-US relations, with an exasperated Washington eventually warning of trade sanctions unless something was done. The US trade representative office has accused China of being the world's single largest pirate of American copyrights, and businessmen estimated that violations cost them about $430 million a year.

On the surface, the authorities in Beijing do seem to be doing something about curbing the practice. In mid-1993, for example, a widely-advertised exhibition was held in the capital to educate the public through a display of genuine and fake products and lectures of the dangers of buying goods which do not have the quality guarantees of the real thing. A nation-wide crusade against the manufacturers and distributors of fake and shoddy products was launched in mid-1992 and in its first year the authorities claimed to have prosecuted 68,989 cases. At least 500 people were jailed, including several who received a life sentence, while four were given the death penalty. The latter were identified as Luo Deming, producer of fake Maotai grain spirit, Han Shulin, maker of imitation Hongtashan cigarettes, Wang Lingang, producer of phoney chemical fertilizers and Bai Wusong, maker of fake medicines that caused the deaths of three children.

Over a period of several months in 1993, China entered into several international copyright conventions and tightened its copyright, trademark and patent laws. One, for example, was designed to protect the Red Cross from widespread unauthorized use of its trademark. The Red cross logo appears regularly in advertisements for medical products and health-related items. The

China Red Cross Society said nation-wide inspections would enforce the law, but little detail was given about what penalties companies would face for violations. And this seems to be the basic problem. International copyright and trademark watchdogs, while applauding the moves that have been taken, claim to detect little effort by the authorities to enforce the laws.

The US-based Business Software Alliance, for example, claimed that 90 per cent of the computer software in China was copied in violation of a copyright agreement the country had already signed. 'In China, as in other countries, it is imperative that the government on its own act to prevent software piracy. Industry and companies cannot do it alone,' insisted Robert Holleyman, head of the alliance. Individuals or companies caught pirating in China generally faced a statutory fine. 'Our experience in 80 or so countries is that if you do not have criminal penalties, you cannot begin to touch the problem. Effective enforcement includes going after a major factory, running a raid, closing it down, seizing its machines and all its property.' Foreign investment in China's software industry could slow if the problem was not solved, said Holleyman, citing the reluctance of major companies like IBM and AT-and-T to introduce their latest technology because they could not be sure it would be protected. Piracy also was widespread in book publishing[6], audio recordings and the movie industry.

DISTRIBUTION SYSTEM.

I would like to turn now to a detailed examination of the physical distribution of goods within China, which many businessmen on both sides of the fence would probably agree is far from perfect. Not unexpectedly, the Japanese retailing giant Yaohan, took the lead in establishing a large computerized distribution centre in Beijing in association with the central government for completion in 1995. Yaohan Chairman, Kazuo Wada, explained this was part of his strategy of establishing production, distribution and retail networks throughout China. '[The country] lacks proper wholesaling and distributing systems. It takes two or three months to replace a product after it has been sold,' said Mr Wada, adding that he planned to set up distribution centres in 10 provinces, and open 1000 supermarkets in China by the year 2010.

The two biggest problems are getting goods in and then

shipping them around the vast country. Mention has been made earlier of plans to expand some of the key ports to ease the long waits ships often face for unloading because demand has far outstripped capacity. Another problem, shipping companies suggest privately, can be a complex port bureaucracy which provides opportunities for graft. In Shanghai, which handles more than twice as much cargo annually as any other port in the country, only three shipping agents – two attached to the Ministry of Communications and a third under MOFTEC – are allowed to handle bunkering, provisioning and cargo-handling. Complaints are often heard of these agents wanting some financial incentive to get the paperwork done fast. Failure to pay, it is alleged, can mean a ship spending many days idle at an anchorage waiting for a pilot and a berth. Trading companies report poor motivation among the stevedore companies, especially towards the end of the month if their wage and bonus have pushed them close to the tax threshold. Again, discrete financial incentives can make a world of difference.[7]

As industrial output and foreign trade has been growing at 20 per cent in recent years, the transportation system has not been able to demonstrate similar elasticity. Freight volume in 1992, for example, grew only 3.8 per cent. The road and rail networks are operating at full capacity. One has only to drive around China to see trucks grinding along at a snail's pace due to poor roads and rapidly expanded traffic.

The railways actually carry 70 per cent of domestic freight, but it is reckoned that only about 60 per cent of the cargo being shipped arrives anywhere near its scheduled time. In mid-1993, the State Council raised the rail freight charges by 39 per cent in order to finance rail development. The Ministry of Railways estimated this would bring in an additional 8 billion Yuan in the second half of the year based on estimated transportation of 1.56 billion tons of cargo. The national rail network has raised the fee almost 100 per cent since it began levying 'railway construction funds' in 1991. To stabilize agricultural production, chemical fertilizers and pesticides were exempted from the higher freight charge.

Apart from being congested, the road and rail networks pose another threat for the cargo shipper – namely, theft. The nearer to the booming locations in southern China, the higher the risk of encountering armed robbers. So far, central and northern China have maintained low transit theft by world standards. Consumer and electronic goods are favourite targets. A truckload of children's shoes owned by a Polish joint venture was held up in Anhui Province on one occasion, but allowed to go when the choosy knife-wielding robbers decided it was not to their taste. Some of the robberies are carried out by peasants driven by hunger and poverty in general. But sophisticated theft rings also appear to have sprung up. In early 1992, for example, an American joint-venture manager found that a case of cameras had gone missing from a shipment that he personally had photographed being loaded and sealed, and which had been similarly recorded on its arrival and opening in the US. The seal appeared to be unbroken, suggesting either that the doors had been lifted off their hinges or a forged seal had replaced the original broken one. Some of the for-export-only cameras later turned up for sale on Shanghai back streets.

While transit theft is becoming more commonplace, it is important to keep the threat of highway robbery in perspective: most theft from companies is carried out by employees circumventing security and inventory systems. Nonetheless, prudence is in order. In moving goods, experts suggest that stops and overnight hauls should be kept to a minimum. Some foreign companies now operate radio-controlled convoys for extra protection. Damage to goods in transit is also on the rise. Congested railways mean goods are vulnerable to storage for days. Road transit is plagued by bad road surfaces, an increasing number of novice and unlicensed drivers and minimal traffic management. The Chinese government reports that in 1992, there were an average 31.3 road traffic deaths for every 10,000 motor vehicles. So vet your driver carefully. Goods should be packed to withstand brusque manual handling and exposure to the elements. Although there is little exterior damage to container-shipped goods, tight packing is recommended to prevent internal crushing in rough shunting. Insurance is obviously crucial, and should cover shipment from warehouse-to-warehouse rather than just port-to-port. Claimants should be prepared for a complex process which may take months to be settled unless there is a personal connection with the insurer. Photographs of the loading and unloading and the sealing of containers, along with details of all people present would be very helpful.[8]

But it is not just the goods that are being stolen off railway wagons – sometimes it is the rails themselves. There has been a huge upsurge of railway equipment which is then processed through 'scrap recycling centres' at a handsome profit. A freight train loaded with coal from Datong, Shanxi Province, to Qinhuangdao, Hebei Province, was derailed in December 1992 because track splints had been ripped out by thieves.[9] Railway police reportedly foiled 1,263 cases of attempted sabotage or theft and arrested 2,029 offenders in the first six months of 1993. This was 714 cases and 1,139 more offenders arrested than in the same period of the previous year.

'In Anhui Province, a special task force of more than 70 railway police caught 56 suspects, broke up six gangs of bandits and confiscated 78 tons of stolen track and splints in the first four months of this year. In May alone, bandits attacked the Shenyang-Dandong Railway in the northeastern province of Liaoning at least eight times, stealing fish-tail boards and bolts along sections of the railway. They were eventually caught red-handed in June by some 80 policemen who laid a round-the-clock trap to appreh end them. Meanwhile, the police also cracked down on illicit 'scrap recycling stations' along the railways to plug the disposal channel of stolen equipment. In central China's Hunan Province police closed 72 operations, among which 10 were found to be state-owned or collectively-run.'[10]

SALES PROMOTION

Having successfully passed all the various bureaucratic and physical barriers already described in getting one's products into the Chinese market, the time has now come to promote it.

The advertising industry has been gaining momentum ever since its revival in 1978, until it now carpet-bombs the consumer with an endless array of cosmetics, garments, medicines, drinks, home appliances, cars, computers and heavy machinery advertisements that the Western world is wearily familiar with from their own highly-commercialized media. Traditionally, however, Chinese manufacturers did not use promotion – the long advocated virtue of being modest and 'talk less, but do more' inspired them to concentrate on production alone. But advertisements did exist before 1949. Roadside wine shops hung signs to lure drinkers and pedlars were masters at hawking sundry goods. Advertising was a popular approach to pushing foreign goods, constantly touted articles being cigarettes and Japanese medicines (especially those claimed to cure venereal disease). By 1945, more than 90 domestic and foreign advertising agencies were in business. However, the new Communist government largely banned the advertising industry after the 1949 take-over because it was considered a tool of capitalism.

This hardly mattered, for the majority of state-owned enterprises had little need to carol their products since the government bought and marketed everything they produced. That policy began to change after 1979, and Chinese consumers were soon acquainted with such foreign brands as Rado, Nestlé, Pierre Cardin and Toshiba, and took a liking to them. With the arrival of the market reforms, Chinese companies suddenly had to sell themselves again. In the 1980s, the outlay for advertising soared at an annual rate of 50 per cent. The industry reported a business volume of 150 million Yuan in 1983, and nine years later this had swollen to 5 billion Yuan.

But advertising techniques at first were rather crude. Chinese television and radio stations produced commercials with scant imagination and advertising agencies played a weak role in the business. Even up to 1989, no professional training was available in advertising design. Hence, the local ads were overshadowed by picturesque foreign ones with vivid, easy-to-remember catchwords. To win over consumers, Chinese enterprises went to great lengths to brag about the numerous medals and certificates their products had gained. Uninspiring scenes of factories with grey gates and endless lines of machines constantly greeted viewers during prime time television. Most commercials were so bad that a 1986 poll recorded only a three per cent audience in Beijing.

But this has changed. Sophisticated skills were borrowed from advertisements devised by foreign and joint-venture ad agencies. The style softened. Jingles for Sesame Paste, Weili washing machines and Active 28 detergent provided catchphrases on everyone's lips. The advertising sector now has 11,000 companies employing 125,000 people. Meanwhile, manufacturers have been seeking to display their wares in interesting and captivating ways.

Beijing commuters, for example, discovered ads wrapped round the straps of subway cars announcing a new beverage. And ads appeared on the satellite launching pads at Xichang Launching Centre. Colourful product plugs appear on television, roadside posters, shopping bags, T-shirts, along subway passages, in and outside buses, on billboards and as flyers stuffed through private letter boxes.

Yet China remains a far cry from its sophisticated counterparts overseas in terms of image and product advertising. Many companies tend to economize on their advertising budgets believing their products can enjoy brisk sales with low-price tags. Others resort to advertising only when introducing new offerings. Few continue to advertise once their products are established on the market. Even fewer have realized the significance of image advertising. During the 1982 Olympic Games, Chinese enterprises failed to buy any of the advertising space available in Barcelona's sports arenas.

All advertising companies are controlled by the China National United Advertising Association, which, in turn, is under the State Administration for Industry and Commerce (SAIC). The association mainly handles advertising within the country for both domestic and foreign companies. Trading countries seeking export orders channel their advertising from China International Advertising Company, which is part of Moftec.

Advertising has been listed as a knowledge-intensive new technology industry, allowing it to enjoy the relevant preferential policy formulated by the state. International ad agencies were allowed back in again in 1979. The first foreign ad agency to return was Interpublic-Jardine, a Beijing-based joint venture between the American firm McCann-Erikson and Jardine Matheson of Hong Kong. Others soon followed, among them were Saatchi and Saatchi in Shanghai in 1985, Dentsu, Young and Rubicam and Ogilvy & Mather in Beijing in 1986. The chief role of these agencies is to act as a liaison between their main headquarters and local officials in the media. However, they are restricted to serving only foreign or joint-venture clients. They are also involved in marketing, research, media and public relations. They have brought new technologies and management skills to the ad business in China, introducing such concepts as market research. They also train personnel for China's publicity industry and help domestic enterprise s to launch advertising campaigns on the international market.

At last count, there were more than 40 international firms with offices in China, with Beijing having the largest number, followed by Guangdong Province and Shanghai. There were also two joint-venture advertising offices in Dalian, Liaoning Province; two in Tianjin, one in Hainan Province and one in Xian, Shaanxi Province. In return, several big mainland companies have set up shop in Hong Kong.

Television is rapidly becoming the main vehicle for advertising, with all the provinces, autonomous regions and municipalities, and a great many large and medium-sized cities, having set up their own television stations penetrating to every corner of the country. According to statistics, among the 278,880,000 households in China, there are 107.18 tv sets for every 100 urban households, while the rural penetration rate is 37.54. The most powerful station is China Central Television (CCTV). Its programmes tend to be horribly dull by Western standards, but products advertised on its channels do tend to become household names. As a result, CCTV can charge between 10,000 and 25,000 Yuan for a 30-second slot depending on the time. Advertisers queue up to pay 19,000 to 21,000 Yuan for 15 seconds immediately after the main early evening news. Conservative estimates put CCTV's advertising revenue at 700 million Yuan a year. Other national broadcasting stations are much cheaper – 600 to 1,000 Yuan for 30 seconds during break-times in well-known programmes.

Newspapers now also play an important role. Due to the fact that newsprint limited the size of newspapers (eight pages being the norm) and the fact that the newspapers were controlled by the Communist Party, advertising was almost non-existent until the 1980s. Now there are no limits. At the top end of the range, the official mouthpiece, the *People's Daily*, charges between 40,000 and 100,000 Yuan for a whole page, while the popular *China Youth News*, with a million circulation, charges between 40,000 to 70,000 Yuan.

On 15 January 1993, however, history was made when Shanghai's most popular daily newspaper, *Wen Hui Bao*, sold its entire front page for a refrigerator advertisement costing 1 million Yuan. This sparked off an intense debate over the desirability of such a course, but the newspaper's editors were unrepentant, saying they were 'challenging old conceptions about the functions of the press'. According to one executive: 'The state says it can no longer subsidize us so we have to find alternative sources of income.' Both the *Wen Hui Bao* and the previously staid *Liberation Daily* now compete fiercely to sell their front pages to advertisers, with the going rate advancing to 1.2 million Yuan and beyond. Fierce competition broke out among advertisers when the *Tianjin Evening News* printed a notice that one firm had reserved all its advertising space on 6 June – a day which in Chinese folklore is considered to be lucky. However, the firm, an unidentified joint-venture company, quickly backed out when a spring water manufacturer offered 400,000 Yuan, apparently topping the other firm's undisclosed price. After what it described as 'strenuous investigation' of the market, a Beijing drink maker offered 1 million Yuan and scared away the spring water company. The *Shenyang Daily*, meanwhile, sold its front page for a soap advertisement that cost 500,000 Yuan. The newspaper *Consumer News* has taken the concept a bit further by seeking sponsors for some of its columns, the individual stories appearing with a corporate logo prominently displayed.

For some television stations and news agencies, cooperation has replaced competition. Many local television stations have united to show each other's ads; and, headed by the *People's Daily*, dozens of major national and local newspapers signed a contract to serve as advertisement agents for each other free of charge. As a result, a foreign businessman in the provinces could ask the local newspaper office to make all the publishing arrangements for a national paper without having to go to Beijing.

THE MEDIA SCENE

This would be a good moment to digress into a brief overview of the current Chinese media scene, which has undergone drastic change in the past few years. News vendors on the streets of the capital say there is no doubt the big seller these days is the *Beijing Evening News*, which publishes a mix of gossip, and what by Chinese standards is fairly racy news. At the *People's Daily*, which for many years was virtually compulsory reading for much of the populace whose very survival might depend on tracking the shifts in the political wind that were alluded to in its drab columns, circulation has slumped from six to three million, and there are worried frowns over possibility similarities with the Soviet party organ *Pravda* which went down from a circulation of 10 million to 500,000 after the abandonment of communism. Wu Changsheng, a senior editor at *People's Daily*, admitted: 'In the past, we didn't have any competition, therefore we didn't worry much about attracting readers. Now, our task is to make the paper more attractive and appealing without losing authority.'

For much of the past four decades, numbers of newspapers had been very limited; there were perhaps as few as 100 papers in the whole country, before the reforms prompted an explosion of new titles. At the end of 1992, there were said to be 1,635 newspapers published openly, selling some 25.2 billion copies annually. Circulation growth has been rapid. The Press and Publishing Administration, which is responsible for licensing new publications, said there had been an enormous demand for new licences from newspapers and magazines. The surge in new magazine titles has been phenomenal. Some 6,400 titles, the bulk of them technical, are now published with a combined circulation of 2.3 billion.

China's establishment press and its problems were the subject of a revealing and somewhat plaintive article in 'Outlook' a magazine published by Xinhua, whose reporters had conducted an investigation into the decline of the 'big papers'. These inquiries yielded some revealing comments, including those of an anonymous *People's Daily* editor who admitted; 'The news (we) publish is not new, which is not only insulting to the word "news" but is also deceiving the readers.' The magazine also related several colourful anecdotes to reinforce the point. In one, an editor of an 'establishment' paper returning home one night to find the same old fare on the dinner table. Asked why, his wife replied: 'I learn it from your newspaper. Don't you serve up the same thing everyday?' It is the new newspapers and magazines which have departed from the 'standard' fare and that are, not surprisingly, doing best in a market that has been starved for so long of real news, plus titillating and semi-scandalous reports on all manner of subjects, ranging from the private lives of film stars and singers to fairly explicit surveys of such previously taboo subjects as homosexuality. Popular magazines, engaged in circulation wars, are using steamy cover photographs of semi-naked young ladies to market their wares.

Among the most successful new, or relatively new, newspapers in China are the *Beijing Youth News* weekend edition and its main competitor, *Southern Weekend*, published in Guangzhou. Both are giving their readers a steady diet of gossip, plus some relatively hot news. *Southern Weekend* entertained its readers for weeks with accounts of a court case involving two pop stars that arose after one accused the other of having Aids and singing badly. At the serious end of the market, however, some newspapers are doing well. Reflecting the great public interest in making money, the two national business newspapers, The *Economic Daily* and the *Economic Information Daily* are thriving. Newspapers promoting basic and popular science and technology also are doing well as more and more farmers and entrepreneurs become aware of the crucial role of science and technology. There are currently 35 provincial and 25 local science and technology journals with a total circulation of 10 million.

BUYING NEWS

Having talked about media advertising, however, it is necessary finally to mention another, cheaper way of obtaining publicity for one's product – namely, paying a journalist to write a favourable puff in the news columns. Party ideologues have made their feelings very clear about the growth of this 'unhealthy practice'.

'Some journalists and editors are using their power to make money. Some newspapers and broadcasting stations publish or air "news" that is actually advertising. These news pieces tout enterprises and their products. Some even give the addresses, telephone numbers and persons in charge of enterprises. Wise readers and listeners know that such "news" is paid with the money stuffed into the wallets of journalists and editors. And press conferences have become nearly as rampant. It is almost a set routine that gifts and money are handed out to journalists present. While some journalists are not interested in surveys and in-depth reports, they would take care not to miss any press conference. Even more intolerable is the fact that some reporters demand a price for a piece of news he or she writes. Such a bonus is called "grey income" and makes up a considerable portion of the income of these journalists and editors. Enterprises favour this kind of "news" because they are much less expensive than ads. And "news" sounds more authoritative.'[11]

The practice had become so widespread in 1993 that the party ordered editors to stop it. Xu Weicheng, deputy head of the party's propaganda department overseeing the media, called a meeting of 50 managers, editors and reporters to lecture them on the practice. 'Reporters must not solicit advertisements and no news stories should carry a fee,' he said.[12]

Foreign businessmen and public-relations firms say many Chinese journalists regularly demand payments for attending news conferences or writing articles. 'We are doing everything we can to build up our clientele without cash payments or expensive souvenirs, but it's extremely difficult,' said Paula Bennett, general manager for Burson-Marsteller, the New York-based pr firm, which stresses that it 'never pays reporters'. Journalists in Beijing often demand between 500 and 1000 Yuan for a published newspaper article, while a full-page report in a magazine goes for about 5000 Yuan. When the representative of a major US company wanted publicity for his firm, he wrote a news release and distributed it to Chinese journalists along with several hundred Yuan each. The reporters pocketed the money and his release was printed word for word, the businessman said. Chinese companies and government departments have long handed out small gifts, such as fountain pens or silk ties to reporters attending their news conferences. But now they are handing out money, too. The Sino-Hong Kong developers of a villa complex on the outskirts of Beijing reportedly gave journalists who attended their news conference two 100 Yuan notes in their press packets. The firm bussed reporters to the villas and gave them an elaborate barbecue dinner, according to one Western reporter who was there. He said that when he returned the money to the organizers they looked puzzled and crestfallen.

Foreign PR firms say Chinese clients often assume that the fees charged by the firms include paying off reporters. They say the practice is most common in Shanghai and most explicit in Guangzhou, where one Hong Kong property developer reportedly handed out 5,000 Yuan to each reporter attending his news conference. Major Chinese media organizations issued statements insisting their staff were strictly prohibited from accepting money.

But privately some reporters have argued that their monthly salary of a few hundred Yuan cannot keep pace with the rising cost of living, and that they are simply taking part in China's new money-driven economy. Some organizations, recognizing that their salaries are low, have virtually given their employees carte blanche to take on second and third jobs to make ends meet.

STREET-LEVEL PROMOTION

There was a time when the only billboards visible in Chinese cities were those exhorting the masses to keep the revolution alive, or educating them into better social habits. Now, their exhortations are more mundane – the guarantee of a better life through product X. Neon signs carrying world famous brand names have brightened up formerly gloomy skylines at night.

But Beijing embarked on an interesting experiment in 1993 when it decided to allow companies to rename the capital's bridges and overpasses after themselves. Up to 180 overpasses were theoretically available for image-conscious enterprises and big-money industries. But initially only six were sold while the government decided whether it was a good idea. Bridge names are usually associated with their locations. But three flyovers along the east Third Ring Road, a dual carriageway circling the capital's outer suburbs, were renamed after the outstanding buildings or enterprises nearby. Just before a flyover near the luxurious Yansha You Yi (Lufthansa Friendship Store) was built, the store took a bold step of suggesting they buy the right to name it after the store. The government agreed and the Yansha Flyover cost 8.03 million Yuan. And as time passes, it begins to look like a very good investment. People recognize the name on their way round the city and to and from the Capital Airport, the centre's status grows and customers flock in. Other overpasses were named after a pharmaceutical producer, a video-games maker and a washing-machine maker.

The idea was first floated in the early 1980s, but the government always said no. When the Purple Bamboo Flyover (named after a popular park) went into service on the west second Ring Road in 1992, for example, the neighbouring Shangri-La hotel offered 10 million Yuan for the name. But the move failed because there was no precedent for it. Despite the change of heart, not every bridge will be marketed – those of historical and cultural importance will keep their names forever. The government had not made up its mind whether to allow foreign-funded enterprises into a share of the bridges.

FOOTNOTES:

1. Recognizing the market potential – with 34 per cent of the Chinese population under the age of 15 – Cadbury Schweppes announced in August 1993 the establishment of a $30 million joint venture, in which it will hold a 75 per cent stake, to produce a wide range of its chocolate confectionery at a factory in Beijing. Its partner is the Beijing General Corporation for Agriculture, Industry and Commerce (BAIC), linked to the Ministry of Agriculture, which controls the milk supply and dairy processing facilities in the capital region and already has 57 joint ventures with such partners as McDonald's, Kraft and Bud's Ice Cream of San Francisco. Products were due to be shipped in from Australia and Britain for heavy promotion, pending the opening of the Beijing factory in 1995, with initial production of 5,000 tons. The project leader, Kevin Hayes, said he was encouraged by the fact that a phonetic translation of Cadbury into its Mandarin equivalent, Ji Bai Li, meant 'luck plus hundreds of benefits'. [China-Britain Trade Review, Oct.1993]
2. The Chinese dream of owning a private car became a little more realistic when a major Chinese car-maker announced discounts for private buyers in mid-1993. In a new sales campaign in major cities including Beijing, Shanghai and Guangzhou, the Tianjin Automotive Industrial Sales Corporation promised to sell 1,200 Tianjin-Charades at 91,888 Yuan ($16,000), at least 10,000 Yuan cheaper than the current market price. General Manager Song Shuxue said delivery of the special offer vehicles would be made in May 1994, but 120 customers chosen by lucky draw would obtain their cars by the end of this year. He claimed the cost of the economy-priced models from the Sino-Japanese joint venture was the 'most favourable' in the domestic market, but if prices generally had dipped by the time of delivery, buyers would be reimbursed for the difference. The company's sales slogan was 'Tianjin-Charade serving Chinese families first,' he added. Even with the discount, many market analysts felt the Charade price was still too high.
3. The information for this profile was culled from a variety of sources.
4. China-Britain Trade Review, November 1993.
5. Interview in Beijing in August 1993. The agent did not wish to be named.
6. I can recall going shopping in Beijing with a Chinese friend and entering a bookshop where, at the entrance to one section, there was a large sign declaring: 'No foreigner allowed beyond this point.' My friend went inside and bought several English-language paperback books. 'Pirated versions, very cheap,' he said on leaving.
7. Business China, 17 May 1993.
8. Ibid. 19 April 1993.
9. China Daily, 29 August 1993.
10. Ibid.
11. Liberation Daily, 27 May 1993.
12. Xinhua News Agency, 3 Oct. 1993.

9 Negotiating skills required for succeeding in China

KEY POINTS
This chapter will look at various aspects of negotiating trade and investment deals with the Chinese. It will examine:
- The differing views on the inviolability of a contract.
- What goes on behind the scenes while the negotiations are under way.
- The problems of setting a time-limit for negotiations.
- Understanding who you are dealing with and discovering whether he or she is the real decision-maker.
- The 36 Stratagems for waging war which provide valuable insights into the Chinese mentality.

THE MEANING OF A CONTRACT

EAST AND WEST hold differing views on the inviolability of a negotiated contract. Negotiations are certainly the means for nailing down detailed agreements on all aspects of a venture's business – such as the shareholding structure, product, technology transfer, local content ratios, marketing, finance, tax, access to foreign currency, management, recruitment and training. But the resulting contract will not have the weight in China as it does in the West. Virtually anything is negotiable. In that sense, the Chinese resemble the Japanese, who regard a contract as a statement of general intent but which should not be waved in their face by the other side if the situation changes. To the Chinese, topics which appear to have been closed can be reopened at any time. In countries with a strong tradition of law, a contract may be of fundamental importance in defining a relationship; in China it is more of a symbol of the harmonious relationship between the two sides. The signing of the piece of paper shows they can both get along well with each other and want to do business. They are 'friends' and, therefore, can now begin to ask for favours from the other side.

A Western business consultant explained: 'The Chinese will sign as many contracts as you want, but then they will begin the serious part of negotiating. They will come to you and say that they want to change some important clause. You may point out that it is now enshrined in print, to which both sides have put their signature, but the Chinese side will say: "Ok, but now we want to change it." The end result can be everyone getting angry and the entire business environment soured. Partly it is a cultural thing, and partly it is that many of the people you are dealing with have little or no business expertise. For a long time, politically impeccable credentials were what mattered. The right class background was vital; intellectuals, those who might have studied abroad and knew about Western business practices, were branded as reactionaries. The government would argue that this is now out-of-date, that it is old thinking and does not represent the situation in China today. But the legacy is still there and it will take a long time to eradicate.'

PATIENCE AND MORE PATIENCE

Everyone says the same thing: you need patience, and a lot of it, to carry out a successful business in China. For a start, the Chinese will want to test your powers of endurance. Are you really serious about the Chinese market? Show impatience – looking at your watch and hinting that you have a plane to catch – will raise serious doubts about whether you really want to do business. Anyone who is familiar with Japanese business practices will be well prepared for China. Like the Japanese, the Chinese place great reliance on building up a strong relationship. They set great store by people, being just as interested in who they are dealing with as in the business itself. 'One-off deals' are not too popular. The Chinese are looking for a long relationship involving mutual friendship and mutual trust. They need to develop confidence in their prospective partners before committing themselves. For this, one needs a strong head and a strong stomach, because banquets and other social occasions are a vital part of doing business in China – bonding through glasses of lethal mao tai liquor. Any foreign businessman who tries to circumvent this process is unlikely to get very far. To the 'time-is-money' Western businessman, this process may seem frustrating and old-fashioned, especially in this age of telephonic mega-deals, but that is the way the Chinese like to do things. It's congenial, and to their way of thinking, likely to create a more-lasting relationship.

Respect is very important, for the Chinese are very proud of their cultural heritage and are quick to react to anything that suggests a condescending Western superior attitude. There is a new pride in China, along with a determination not to endure again the humiliations of the nineteenth century at Western hands. Cultivating an interest in Chinese literature, painting, porcelain, Peking opera will certainly help break the ice and demonstrate that you are a worthy partner. Show irritation at having to spend a day dragging yourself around the Great Wall or the Ming Tombs, when you could be hammering out a deal in a smoke-filled room, and the negotiations are likely to prove even more difficult.

'Inevitably, relationships take time to develop and – with costs of transportation and accommodation high – not a little money [although willingness to spend money will indicate the seriousness of your intentions]. It remains true, that professionalism in the Western sense has made few inroads into China; business is not normally done on an arms-length basis, but because of an existing relationship between supplier and client. Business is done between friends and to do business you must be or become a friend. This is changing only slowly.'[1]

Richard Solomon, an American sinologist who was an Assistant Secretary of State in the Bush Administration, once wrote: 'The most fundamental characteristic of dealings with the Chinese is their attempt to identify foreign officials who are sympathetic to their cause, to cultivate a sense of friendship and obligation in their official counterparts, and then pursue their objectives through a variety of stratagems designed to manipulate feelings of friendship, obligation, guilt or dependence.'[2]

The Chinese negotiating style can be somewhat perplexing for the newcomer. One problem is determining who, exactly, is in charge of the negotiations; who has the real bargaining and decision-making power. Foreign businessmen say that they often face a large negotiating team whose composition is hard to determine. Some of the participants may seem to be taking only an indirect role in the procedures, wandering in and out of the room during the discussions, for example. The composition of the team may also change from day-to-day. Partly, this is due to the consensual style of Chinese decision-making which requires many people on different levels to have their say and participate in the final agreement.

Equally, the participants doing most of the talking are not necessarily the big players. AMC officials trying to negotiate the Beijing Jeep deal, for example, eventually discovered that the real decision-makers on the Chinese side were a small group of spectators who sat silently at the back of the room and took no part in the proceedings. They allowed their underlings to do the talking, allowing them time to listen to the American proposals without having to make an immediate commitment.

'It is often the case that the final decision-makers are not present at the negotiations. That will partly depend on the make-up of the foreign negotiating team; the Chinese are sticklers for protocol and often attempt to gauge the powers and status of the foreign negotiators and reflect these in the make-up of their own team [see chapter seven for a discussion on this point from a Japanese perspective]. They often wish to refer decisions to higher authority just as foreign businessmen may wish to refer to head office for fresh instructions.'[3]

Because of this, the negotiating process can be a drawn-out one. In the case of Beijing Jeep, it took five years to finally clinch a deal. And, whereas in Japan the negotiations may also be prolonged but then action is instantaneous once the signatures are on the piece of paper, the process has only just begun in China. Any agreement will have to be referred up the chain of command within the supervising ministry or state agency. Frustration and disappointment can be avoided if the foreign businessman bears in mind that a signed contract is not valid until it has the seal of approval from the appropriate authority.

A Rand Corporation study written by Lucian Pye, a leading American political scientist and sinologist, on Chinese negotiating tactics, stressed that the foreign businessman had, above all, to learn to be patient and be ready for repeated delays. 'The Chinese believe that patience is a value in negotiations and they frequently use stalling tactics and delays. The most elementary rules for negotiating with [them] are 1. practice patience; 2. accept as normal prolonged periods of no movement; 3. control against exaggerated expectations and discount Chinese rhetoric about future prospects; 4. expect that the Chinese will try to influence by shaming; 5. resist the temptation to believe that difficulties may have been caused by one's own mistakes; 6. try to understand Chinese cultural traits, but never believe that a foreigner can practice them better than the Chinese.'[4]

BEIJING JEEP

To show how the process works in practice, I would like to refer again to the classic case of Beijing Jeep.

On 6 January 1979, the first AMC delegation arrived in Beijing for exploratory talks only a few weeks after China and the US established diplomatic relations. After two weeks the discussions were going so well that the head of AMC's international division and the company treasurer flew in and the AMC executive in charge thought the process of doing business with the Chinese was going to be 'a piece of cake'. The reality proved to be very chewy and hard to digest.

One conflict that quickly arose was AMC's insistence on 'exclusivity' – a clause guaranteeing that it should be the sole foreign manufacturer of jeeps, or four-wheel-drive vehicles inside China. From AMC's viewpoint it was hardly an unusual request. If the company was going to start up operations in China, it wanted to be sure it had a preferred position. But the Chinese did not want the guarantee in writing; they said the word had negative connotations and would be interpreted as unfriendly by other companies with which China was dealing. At an impasse, a compromise was suggested that the document should say that China would give '100 per cent attention' to the AMC venture. Chinese officials were agreeable, but translation problems meant that the actual language was 'undivided attention'. The words sounded nice and the Chinese accepted them. An AMC lawyer might have quibbled and said this was not exactly the same sort of commitment as exclusivity, but in these first meetings, this first effort by AMC to establish a business relationship in China, the company was not going to let itself be ruled by lawyers. Second thoughts would come later.[5]

On 26 January, a vaguely-worded memorandum of understanding was signed to investigate the prospects of building a new jeep with American technology. The process was supposed to be completed by the end of 1979. Tod Clare, the head of AMC's international department, dazzled by the speed with which the initial negotiations had been settled, thought the whole thing was going to be a pushover. It was not. Firstly, there was a sudden Chinese government decision to suspend a large number of multimillion dollar contracts with foreign firms while it reassessed their need and their impact on the economy as a whole. The economy was still trying to digest projects undertaken in the 1970s which had triggered inflation. In 1980, for example, China contracts worth $1.5 billion with Japan. To those who dared complain, Chinese officials said the action was economic necessity. In the end a few companies did receive compensation and others were later rewarded with new contracts, but China had once again served notice that it would play by its own rules. A signed contract did not have the same binding effect as it had elsewhere. It was merely a statement of intentions – a general qualified agreement by which a Chinese agency agreed to try and do something, if possible, and if nothing else came up after the contract was signed.

It was some years before AMC also discovered that during the hiatus in 1979-80, Chinese officials had entered into serious discussions with Toyota Motors of Japan. China, it seemed, was using its agreement with AMC as a lever for a better deal from the Japanese. The Chinese ploy did not work. Toyota was not going to compete – at least not on the same basis as AMC. It, and the other Japanese manufacturers, wanted to play by different rules. They were eager to sell cars and trucks to China, but they had no interest in setting up manufacturing operations at the time.

At the same time, Beijing Auto Works (BAW) officials had their own problems with their government. One executive admitted afterwards that BAW had more than 10 different government sections supervising its negotiating work. At one point none of the 10 agencies was willing to give its official approval for the feasibility study necessary to get the negotiations with the

Americans going again. Arguments on the potentially destructive effects of dealing with a capitalist country were fiercely debated within government circles. Throughout this period, AMC officials were flying into Beijing and getting nowhere.

'Even when Chinese officials actually wanted to strike a deal, long delays were often part of their negotiating strategy. Just as Clare found that the Chinese put AMC on hold while they sounded out Japanese car companies, so many other foreign businesses discovered that the Chinese were adroit at playing off rival businesses against one another for protracted periods of time. At one point, executives of Westinghouse and other international companies seeking to sell nuclear power plants or equipment to China, such as General Electric and the French firm Franatome, were kept on different floors of the same hotel for several weeks, while the Chinese officials walked upstairs and down over and over again, getting different price quotations.'[6]

Some foreign negotiators have expressed a belief that the Chinese were pushing them too hard, refusing to allow them a fair profit. This may well have been true, although some authorities suggest that it could equally stem from a fear on the Chinese side that, considering themselves inexperienced and faced with foreign negotiators who are in a position to take advantage of them, they have to act tough as a matter of honour. This will be mitigated if a long-term relationship is created.

THE CHINESE – BY THE CHINESE

To balance this Western view of negotiating with the Chinese, I would now like to turn to those businessmen who would seem to have a built-in advantage through a shared knowledge of the culture and often the language of their hosts. The following paragraphs, therefore, are based on a series of interviews with Singapore Chinese businessmen actively engaged in either trade or investment projects in China.

One businessman engaged in trade in electronic goods, computer peripherals and motor vehicles, said: 'You need a good contact to break into China initially. I'd been trying to penetrate the market for three years, but I found it very difficult to make calls to break the ice. You cannot go round simply knocking on people's doors because they won't open them to you. They are very conservative. Someone who they trust must first refer you to them. I eventually got into China because someone with whom I'd been doing business in Hong Kong approached me and asked if I was interested in a business deal. China was interested in finding a Chinese businessman, but not one from Hong Kong, who could handle a deal for them. Eventually, I was able to deal direct with the Chinese officials involved, and the guy in Hong Kong now gets paid a commission for the original introduction.

'Certainly, in the first contract you have to use middlemen to develop your relations. But after a few contracts it's easy to work direct once the other side knows your capabilities and your commitment. There are a lot of companies who say they can introduce you to opportunities in China. But I don't think these people can bring you far. There were some companies who specialized in my particular area, and although I worked with them for a while I stopped because the deals weren't successful. For a start, I wasn't building up that personal relationship which is so important. Secondly, these companies work for their own advantage and everything goes to them rather than you. If I need a middleman, I work through the grapevine. I contact friends who I think can help out. If I cannot handle a deal, I'll hand it on to someone else who I can trust and get a commission for it. So, we are not talking about middlemen in the strict sense of the word. Then again, I might be dealing with one company and the manager will say that he knows of other companies who would be interested in doing business with me. He acts as the middleman and gets a commission for any deals that are struck.'

One problem the businessman faced was his age, having taken over the family firm in his 20s. 'Age is a handicap, because I am dealing with officials much older than myself. So, from the start I have got to prove that I'm experienced beyond my years. I cannot change my appearance to look older, but I have got to try and speak and act older. I have to adjust to their way of thinking. This wasn't that difficult for me because I had taken over the business from my father and had to try and understand the way he did things and the way he thought. We can introduce new ideas, but we must do it in their language and on their terms. You cannot, for instance, tell an official that he is doing things in the wrong way or that his thinking is wrong. You have to agree that, yes, that is certainly one way of doing things, but perhaps he might like to consider some alternatives.'

Another businessman offers this advice: for smooth negotiations: 'Don't act too smart. It is very important that you always act humble. Never try to prove yourself to be stronger than them because they get very offended if you do. Western businessmen some times make this mistake, particularly in bragging about their own company or their country. This doesn't go down at all well.

'In addition, you have to realize that each town has its own culture and values and you have to try to blend in and see things their way. Each area has its own idiosyncrasies that will be of value if you understand them. For example, in Guangzhou it is essential to sprinkle your conversation with vulgarities. That is the way the people are down there if you work in Guangzhou. The officials will feel very comfortable if you are speaking in the rough, earthy way to which they are accustomed. Speaking in a very sophisticated way will give the impression you are snobbish and regard yourself as superior to them. Before embarking on any negotiations, it would be advantageous if you toured the area privately with a good guide who can show you not only the bright side of the typical official guided tour but also the dark side of the locality. This will help you to get a feel for the place and its values.

'Another thing I found was that in Beijing, never try and conduct negotiations over lunch. After a hasty meal, everyone takes an afternoon nap from around 11-30 am to 2 pm, either going home or stretching out on a makeshift bed in the office. So, you must try and finish your discussions by 11-15 am and then make your excuses to leave. If you force them to work through lunch they get very edgy and they won't be happy. I found this out the hard way. I tried to have lunch with this very senior official, but he was very uncomfortable, fidgety and yawning all the time. He didn't say anything directly but I realized something was wrong. We then continued our meeting after lunch, when it was obvious that he was very angry. It was not until later that my translator told me what I had been doing wrong. The meal was a big mistake because at a later date we had to go over all the ground covered at lunch because he was conditioned to switch off and hadn't absorbed anything. If you want to have a meal with someone make sure it is in the evening.'

At some stage in the negotiations, said another businessman with long experience, the subject is going to come up of 'what's in it for me?' Once you can satisfy the other side on this crucial point, the deal is likely to go through very quickly. Failure to satisfy the questioner is likely to lead to long delays and possible abortive negotiations.

Is this bribery? In chapter six, the subject was raised mainly from a Western viewpoint. Here, then, is the oriental view. 'One reason why most Westerners cannot secure deals in China is that they are very strict about bribery. They won't commit themselves to commissions for negotiators. But in China, if there is nothing in it for the person who closes the deal with you then you won't do well. We see this not as bribery but as a commission to promote a successful conclusion of the negotiations. Three to five per cent is what I would normally pay. But it has to go the right person. It's no use starting the process bottom up, because you'll end up paying out so many commissions along the line that you end up with virtually no profit margin.

'Body language hints that you're on right or wrong track. If you see they are yawning, frowning, you're on the wrong track. But if the person you're negotiating with is hinting for a commission then you're always there. "What is the good of this contract ?" Or, "Why should we sign this deal?" are possible hints you might get. But never deal with this over the table. Take your opposite number out to a good night-club and settle it there. Next day, the contract is signed and everyone is happy. It's not a cheap process. You can spend a lot of money on entertaining – a good dinner can cost several thousand dollars. And in the end, approval may not come through and you have to write off the expense and start again. Going into China, you have to be prepared to spend money so it's no use looking for small contracts. You might be facing a hotel bill for two or three months. That's only worth it if you're talking about a multi-million-dollar deal.'

With regard to entertainment, this businessman tells another story of a mistake he made only once. 'On my first trip to China as the incoming project director, I hosted a dinner for various officials. We were getting on very well, but then I slipped up. I asked the group if they would like some liquor. They declined, although, I realized later, not too vociferously. This was where I made my mistake. I should have insisted. I should have ordered it anyway and they would have drunk it and had a better time. They couldn't openly say they wanted top quality liquor because there were a lot of minor officials around and there was a big anti-corruption and anti-conspicuous-consumption drive underway from Beijing. In the West, if people say no then you won't order. The right thing for me to have done, however, was to have ordered a range of liquor as a matter of course to create a good impression.'

Looking at the negotiating process from a broader, more philosophical perspective, all the businessmen interviewed agreed that the biggest impediment to the successful conclusion of any bargaining session was that Chinese officials essentially did not come from a background of capitalist ideas and ways of doing things, resulting in '. . . a whole lot of barriers in getting to their hearts and minds and getting them to understand your requirements and what you need and what they can do for you'.

According to one interviewee: 'There is a lack basic knowledge in how to manage an organization, how to organize for a project, how to organize for a task or how to structure financial networks. But that's really a case of lack of knowledge and training rather than unwillingness to understand. They have been used to dealing with large state-owned corporations and fixed prices. They are not used to responding to gestures and signals from the market in terms of quality, in terms of price and planning their production, product innovation and marketing. They have not hitherto had a market where prices and supply and demand forces could seek an equilibrium. That's an alien concept. When you go in they inevitably ask a lot of questions that you do not expect to be asked if you were negotiating in, say, Thailand or Indonesia, such as "What are your financing plans for the project? How do you propose to market the product?" Yes, these are questions that are asked anywhere in the world, of course; but the Chinese seem to demand a more deterministic, a more rigid, fixed step-by-step strategy than normally required. They don't see very naturally the give-and-take, the push-and-pull, the dynamics and consensus of the market, and of competition.

'One problem we encountered, and expect to continue encountering in the future, is that the Chinese, while realizing that if this investment project is to take off the basic infrastructure has to be in place, are sometimes too eager to get ahead of themselves, to put the cart before the horse. They want to have the contracts signed with foreign investors first for building factories etc. in order to justify them creating the basic infrastructure, like roads, electricity and water supply. They don't see the imperatives of providing a reasonable investment environment – that the infrastructure is basic before hard-headed businessmen will come in. It's a constant education process, trying to give them an idea how things work without being too condescending because they are very senior people in their own right. It's a tightrope we walk. But they are learning.'

Things are getting better, the businessman concedes. 'If they really want to stall they can stall for ever. Its a game of nerves and patience. They will use the most obscure regulations and laws you may not have heard of to buy time. But that's only if they want to buy time. Increasingly, we are seeing more and more Chinese groups who want a deal and want to see the negotiating process satisfactorily completed in reasonable time. There is less stalling, less trying to wear you down than before. They want to conclude the negotiating process as favourably as possible to their own side, of course. But, they are the past masters in give-and-take. They realize it has to be a win-win situation; if it's a win-lose situation then you may have a deal on paper, but, as an old Chinese saying goes, nothing written on paper is worth the paper it's written on. The spirit rather than the form of the agreement have always been more important. Having said that, however, it is becoming increasingly apparent that they also realize putting things on paper can be important.'

But in this regard, another old hand, warns that it is important not to be too legalistic. 'If you're taking your company lawyer along on the negotiations, don't identify him as such. That creates a bad atmosphere, suggesting to the Chinese that you don't trust him. By all means have your lawyer sitting at the table, keeping an eye on things. But, officially, he's merely a member of the delegation with unspecified responsibilities.'

THE 36 STRATAGEMS

Obviously when one is engaged in negotiations, and particularly when the other side comes from a different cultural background, it is important to understand their psychology and the way of thinking. Chinese use many idioms today which have been handed down over the centuries and stem from classic written works or folklore. Two books were said to have lain on Mao Zedong's bed throughout his long rule. They were dynastic works of great distinction, studied and annotated by emperors, statesmen and scholars for hundreds of years. One was the *Records of the Historian (Shi Ji)* and covered the period from the semi-mythical Yellow Emperor, China's founding father, and into the Han Dynasty a hundred years before Christ. The other, *The General Mirror for the Aid of Government (Cu Chi Tang Qian)* covered thirteen hundred years of history and had been compiled in the eleventh century. It was designed as a practical handbook for the emperor, telling him how his predecessors had handled difficult questions. Both books were well-thumbed by Mao, who regarded them as a vital guide in running the vast country he had inherited. Anyone who wants to understand the Chinese at the end of the twentieth century cannot neglect a programme of reading stretching back many centuries. In that regard, I would like to discuss an ancient work known as the *36 Stratagems* which provide an invaluable guide to the whole art of waging war both overtly and covertly. The astute businessman should be able to recognize variations of these stratagems as he negotiates with his Chinese counterparts.

Stratagems to win a war.

1. *Cross the sea by a trick.* When you think you are well prepared, you will relax your will to fight, and underestimate the enemy. If you see something or someone too often, your suspicions are lulled no matter what he might do (akin to the Western idea of 'familiarity breeds contempt'). Tricks may be hidden in something that is done in the open. The most confidential aspects are often cloaked in a common disguise. In other words: be on your guard at all times.

2. *Besiege Wei to rescue Zhao; relieve the besieged by besieging the base of the besiegers.* It is easier to conquer a separated, individual enemy than by fighting a group of strong enemies. It is better to gain mastery by striking only after the enemy has made his move. This saying comes from the Period of Warring States (475-221 BC). On one occasion, the state of Wei attacked the state of Zhao and besieged its capital. Desperate, Zhao turned to the state of Qi for help. The king of Qi asked the famous strategist

Sun Bin to mastermind the military moves. Originally Qi planned to march its forces straight to Zhao, but Sun suggested: 'It is common knowledge that to untangle a messy skein of silk, closing one's first and pulling at it will not help, and to try and mediate two fighting parties will not work. Stay clear of the enemy's main forces and strike at his weak point to create conflicts and apprehension in the enemy, then inevitably the siege will be lifted. Now, Wei is attacking Zhao. Its mobile elite troops must be fatigued, having marched so far from their homeland. On the other hand, its older, weaker forces that remain behind at home, must be under heavy strain. So, it would be wise for you to rush our troops to the capital of Wei, cut off their line of communication and attack their weak spot; then for sure, Wei will have to give up Zhao and turn to save its own capital. In this way we shall in one operation raise the siege of Zhao and at the same time reap the rewards of Wei's collapse.' The strategy was carried out. Soon Wei withdrew from the siege of the Zhao capital and on its way home its army encountered the forces of Qi and was decisively beaten.

3. *Murder with a borrowed knife; or, make use of another person to get rid of an adversary.* When the enemy is known, you should try to coax your ally, who may not be very firm, to wipe him out and thus help preserve your strength.

4. *Wait at one's ease for an exhausted opponent* if you want to force your enemy into a difficult situation, you do not have to engage in a head-on encounter. You can maintain an alert defence and gradually lower your enemy's guard and wear down his strength. In this way, you can gain the initiative.

5. *Loot a burning house; take advantage of somebody's misfortune to do him harm.* When your enemy is in difficulty or in crisis, you should seize the opportunity to launch a timely attack to defeat him.

6. *Make a feint in the East and attack in the West.* When the enemy is under the leadership of a bad commander, it is like a fly with no head, flying here and there with no aims, with no ability to predict and deal with unexpected situations. This is a sign that the commander has lost his ability to judge and act correctly. This knowledge can be used to great advantage.

Stratagems to deceive the enemy

7. *Fabricate something out of nothing.* Use false intelligence to fool the enemy, but don't make it too obvious. Tire him out with feints mixed with some truth. Try to create a false impression to mislead the enemy and then attack by surprise.

8. *Pretend to prepare to advance along one path while secretly getting along another; do one thing under cover of another.* Ostentatiously expose your actions to lure the enemy into strengthening his defences in one place, while you sneak into an area of weakness to launch a surprise attack.

9. *Watch the fire from the other side of the river; view others' troubles with indifference.* When the internal contradictions of the enemy worsen and they are in disarray, you can wait patiently for these contradictions to turn into internal revolt. When infighting begins, the enemy is doomed to defeat.

10. *Hide a dagger in a smile.* Try to convince the enemy into believing in your goodwill and, thus, to relax his vigilance. Then, you can take advantage of the opportunity to secretly plot and prepare yourself for an attack.

11. *Be ready to make sacrifices for ultimate gain.* When the situation develops to the point where it is inevitable for you to lose something, you must not begrudge partial sacrifice of your interests to gain eventual victory,

12. *Lead away a goat in passing; pick up something on the sly.* Take advantage of the enemy's loopholes or negligence to turn his minor mishaps into victory for yourself.

Stratagems to launch an offensive

13. *Beat the grass and frighten away the snake; act rashly and alert the enemy.* If in doubt, find out. Do not take any action until you are fully informed of the whole situation. Repeated reconnaissance and verification is a precondition for uncovering hidden enemies.

14. *Find incarnation in another corpse.* You cannot use those who are capable and uncontrollable. Those who are weak and

incapable have to rely on other people to survive and thus be controlled by you.

15. *Lure the tiger out of the mountain.* Do not besiege the enemy until natural conditions become favourable for it. Try to deceive the enemy with well-designed schemes. When it is too risky to attack, try to provoke an attack on yourself.

16. *Allow someone more latitude at first in order to keep a tighter rein later.* A cornered beast will do something desperate. When you act too hard in pressing the enemy into a corner, he will risk everything in a single attack to escape. But if you let the enemy go, you can dampen his morale. Chase him but do not press too hard. Allow him to become exhausted and downhearted; then, when he feels utterly despondent, you can capture him without shedding a single drop of blood.

17. *Cast a brick to attract a jade.* Offer a few commonplace remarks by way of an introduction so that others may come up with possibly more valuable opinions. Do the same with your enemies (get him talking so that he will reveal more than he wants).

18. *Capture the leaders to destroy the enemy.* The backbone of any force is its commander. Capture or destroy him, and his forces will disintegrate.

Stratagems to confuse the enemy

19. *Take away the firewood from under the cauldron.* When two armies are pitted against each other, do not attack at the strongest point. Find other ways to weaken the enemy's morale and fighting capability. (This phrase was used by the Beijing leadership in 1993 when it imposed a credit squeeze to stop illegal bank loans that were fuelling land- and stock-market speculation).

20. *Fish in troubled waters.* When chaos erupts in the enemy ranks you can exploit its weaknesses and lack of judgement that is produced, melding it to your own desires. Another way of looking at this is encapsulated in the expression, *when the snipe and clam grapple, the fisherman profits.* This is taken from *Zhanguo Ce (Warring States Record).* According to the story, 'The state of Zhao was going to assault the state of Yan. Su Dai came to see

King Hui of the state of Zhao and said, "On my way here I was crossing the Yishui River when I saw a clam, just coming out to take the sun on the shore. A snipe came over to peck at the exposed flesh of the clam, which quickly closed its shell to clamp the bird's bill. 'If no rain comes today or tomorrow, there'll be a dead clam,' said the snipe. 'If you can't get your bill free today or tomorrow, there'll be a dead snipe,' riposted the clam. None of the two would budge. Then along came a fisherman who easily caught them both." After a pause, Su Dai continued: "Now that Zhao is ready to attack Yan. But, if both states were locked in a long stalemate with neither side ready to yield, then both peoples will be equally worn out. I'm afraid that the powerful Qin will turn up as the fisherman. Therefore, I do hope that your highness will give the matter careful consideration before you act." "Well said," nodded King Hui. And he gave up his military plan.'

21. *Slip out of a predicament like a cicada sloughing its skin.* Keep your defensive positions looking intact to create an impression that you are still maintaining a strong combat-ready force to discourage the enemy from attacking your weak points. Transfer your main forces while the enemy remains confused about your intentions.

22. *Bolt the door to catch the thief.* Besiege the weak enemy to wipe it out. Enemies in small groups, though weak in overall might, are more surreptitious and free in their movements and thus are more difficult to guard against. Therefore, you cannot be too rash in chasing them afar.

23. *Befriend distant states while attacking those nearby.* When military targets are restricted by geographical conditions, it is first desirable to attack your nearest enemy rather than bypassing him to attack someone far distant. Though the distant foes may hold conflicting political views, we can still form a temporary alliance with them to facilitate our future strategy to destroy them one by one.

24. *Borrow a path to attack the state of Guo.* When a small country sandwiched between two big powers is threatened, you must extend an immediate helping hand. This will allow you to build up your military strength in it. For a country in difficulties, it is hard to win its trust by paying mere lip service to assistance

without concrete help. *Lushi Chunqiu (Master Liu's Spring and Autumn Annals)* expands on this concept from the viewpoint of the poor state in the middle. 'Duke Xian of the state of Jin, bade Xun Xi launch an expedition against the state of Guo by way of the state of Yu [located in Shanxi Province]. Thereupon Xun Xi ventured to suggest: "To secure Duke Yu's promise to let our army pass when we come to Yu, the surest way is to buy him over with our Chuji Jade and Quchan steeds ‹[›Quchan was at the time famous for its fine horses]." "But the stone is a treasure by inheritance and the horses are for my own use," said Duke Xian. "Suppose Duke Yu accepted our gifts but refused our request, what is to be done?" "Well, if he didn't mean to let us pass, he wouldn't accept them; if he did and accepted, we'd only be allowing a temporary shift of the jade from our own house to be stored in someone else's," answered Xun Xi. "What is there to be worried about?" Duke Xian nodded with approval and readily sent Xun Xi to the state of Yu to achieve his purpose of attacking Guo by way of Yu. The horses were soon displayed in the courtyard of Yu, with Xun Xi holding the precious stone in his hand. Duke Yu, greedy for the fine gifts was about to make the messenger a promise when his subject Gong Ziqi came forward to protest: "There shall be no promise of any kind, Your highness. Yu is to Guo like gums to cheek. Gums are closely related to cheeks and cheeks to gum, which exactly represents the situation in Yu in relation to Guo. Our ancestors had a saying, If the lips are gone, the teeth will be exposed to cold. That Guo is able to subsist depends on Yu while Yu's ability to survive hinges on Guo. If we make way for Jin, then the day will see Guo perish in the morning to be followed by Yu in the evening. Why should we ever let Jin pass?" Duke Yu, however, refused to listen and gave Jin troops access to Guo. Thus, Xun Xi attacked Guo and conquered it, and on the way back attack Yu and conquered it, too. Xun Xi triumphantly returned the jade and the horses to Duke Xian, who, greatly pleased, said in good humour: "The jade remains the same, but the horses have got more teeth!" The lesson is: "Seek a small gain, only to harm vital interests".'

Stratagems to annex the enemy.

25. *Steal the beams and pillars and replace them with rotten*

timber (perpetrate a fraud). Set designs that will encourage the enemy to change its defensive positions frequently so as to debilitate the combat capability of the enemy's main force. Wait for the enemy to degenerate towards defeat and then seize the opportunity to control or annex his forces. Likewise, after you tug the wheels of a cart, you can control its movement.

26. *Point at the mulberry and abuse the locust (make oblique accusations)*. When a strong country cows a weaker state into submission, it often resorts to admonition although it does not have be done directly or in forthright language. But a correct tough line can be supported and maintained. Act resolutely to get your subordinates to respect and observe your orders.

27. *Pretend to be silly, but make sure you stay wise and sober.* It is better for you to play the fool and take no action than assume a wise man and act recklessly. Devise your strategies without exposing them beforehand.

28. *Remove the bridge after crossing the river, kick down the ladder after climbing upstairs.* Expose your weak points purposely to the enemy to give it an opportunity to be lured deep into a trap. Then, you can cut off its vanguards and back-up forces and lead it into your pre-set snares.

29. *Decorate the bare tree with artificial flowers to make it appear exuberant (make an empty show of strength).* Make a spectacular display of strength by means of others' resources. Although your real power is weak, it looks strong judging from appearances. A formation of fully-fledged swans or geese always attracts attention.

30. *Reverse the positions of the host and guest.* Take advantage of any opportunity to plant your agents into key positions or in the headquarters of your enemy.

Stratagems to defeat the enemy

31. *Use a sex trap.* Facing a strong enemy, you have to set traps to control its commander. As a wise, resourceful enemy commander, you must erode his fighting will. With the will of the commanders blunted and morale of the soldiers dampened, the enemy loses its fighting ability. To exploit every weak point of

the enemy, every human weakness, to divide and demoralize is a means for you to preserve your own strength.

32. *Empty city stratagem* (bluffing the enemy by opening the gates of a weakly-defended city). Confound the enemy by offering no defence. This strategy has special value when your enemy is strong and you are weak.

33. *Stratagem of sowing distrust or discord among your enemies.*

34. *Ruse of self-inflicted injury to win the enemy's confidence.*

35. *A set of interlocking stratagems.* When the enemy forces are strong and powerful, and you cannot match them in a tit-fot-tat engagement, you should set them up to kill each other to weaken their strength.

36. *Retreat in order to advance.* Facing an invincible enemy, you should retreat to avert the no-win situation, and wait for a chance to launch your own attack when conditions are right to do so.

The *Warring States Record (Zhanguo Ce)* already referred to offers another example of how a wily person can turn weakness into strength. It tells, for example, of a tiger who caught a fox. '"Don't you dare eat me!" said the fox. "The Emperor of Heaven has made me king of the beasts. You eat me and you will be going against His orders. If you don't believe what I say, just let me lead the way and you follow close behind. Then we'll see if they flee at the sight of me." The tiger agreed to the idea, so the two of them set off together. When the other beasts saw them coming, they all turned tail. Not realizing that it was he that was the cause of their panic-stricken flight, the tiger thought they were afraid of the fox.'

I have quoted the stratagems and ancient stories at some length because Chinese friends assure me they are still valid and provide valuable insights into the Chinese mentality. The common theme is an admiration of the wily strategist who uses subtlety and subterfuge to gain his ends. In preparing for business negotiations in China, it would be no harm to read the Chinese classics now available in English translation. The businessman who spent a few weeks reading the three volume-sets of *The Dream of Red Mansion, Journey to the West, Outlaws of the Marsh* and *Romance of the Three Kingdoms*, before jetting off to Beijing would be well rewarded with greater insights into his 'opponents' (even if they are to become business partners, because they are seeking to gain the best possible advantage out of the deal whether they are negotiating from weakness or strength). I do not wish to labour the point, but I would invite the diligent reader to keep the 36 Stratagems in mind when studying not only the other parts of this chapter but the rest of the book.[7]

FOOTNOTES

1. *China Perspectives*. Third Edition. Arthur Andersen and Co.
2. Richard H.Solomon. 'China: Friendship and Obligation in Chinese Negotiating Style,' in *National Negotiating Styles*, Foreign Service Institute 1987.
3. *China Perspectives*.
4. Lucian Pye, *Chinese Commercial Negotiating Styles*, the Rand Corporation 1982.
5. *Beijing Jeep* by Jim Mann, pp46-47.
6. Ibid p71.
7. I am indebted to a Chinese friend for the translation of the 36 Stratagems and other stories.

10 Management and labour

> **KEY POINTS**
>
> Any foreign sales, service or manufacturing operation in China is largely going to stand or fall on the quality of its local personnel. In this chapter I wish to examine:
> - The Chinese approach to management and how it might differ from Western concepts.
> - How local staff are hired.
> - Pay scales and the problem of welfare benefits.
> - The changing climate in career selection, allowing more freedom of choice and job-switching.
> - The role of trade unions – under pressure to change.
> - Labour disputes.
> - Staff training.

MANAGEMENT CONTRASTS

MOST of a foreign businessman's dealings still are likely to be with the state sector. But, despite all the enthusiasm over capitalist-style reforms, the progress of state-owned enterprises towards the adoption of market-oriented management practices seems to be painfully slow. This emerges quite clearly from a research project led by the University of Lancaster Management School which compared practices in China with those of British private-sector companies in similar fields. In particular, it examined how companies made decisions on strategic investments and management of human resources. Some caution is needed in evaluating the results because the research was conducted largely in 1991, although not released until late 1993. Changes have begun to occur, but broadly the project's findings remain valid. If nothing else, they provide an historical backdrop for the foreign manager in understanding where his Chinese counterpart has come from.

The researchers did find some similarities between the two countries – for example, the process of winning the support of colleagues, managers and eventually the board for a new project, as well as the inordinate length of time taken to complete the procedures. The efforts of Chinese managers, however, were mostly directed outside the company. The relationships they needed to build were with supervisory ministries and other authorities, with the aim of securing the many approvals needed for a project to go ahead. At the same time, Chinese companies inevitably take a far broader range of considerations into account, including conformity with central plans, social responsibilities and technological progress. This would suggest that the contract responsibility scheme, discussed in chapter two, has not shaken off the tight hand of the bureaucrat. It is likely to be some years before the market-place is able to break down the uniformity which the research team found in the approaches of the Chinese companies. Standardized behaviour – which does at least help foreigners to know what to expect – derives from the structure of the ministries which draw senior staff from the enterprises, and from a system designed to manage the entire country from top down.

The Communist Party's role in the management of companies helps to perpetuate a common approach, the Party secretary within an enterprise generally forming a balance of power with its director. Nevertheless, there are signs that the former's role is tending to be limited to monitoring personnel decisions and that professional managers are on the rise. At Beijing Yanshan Petrochemicals, for example, the researchers found the Party secretary to be more important than the director, whose appointment he had recommended. But in Nanjing Chemical the director had worked his way up over 30 years, had strong links with the supervising ministry and controlled all business decisions including personnel, while the Party secretary's role was limited.

Although there had been some devolution of authority, the researchers found that all important investment decisions had to be approved by the state or national government. Once the nod came from the minister concerned, approvals would follow in rapid succession from all other relevant authorities. One company established an office in Beijing for six months to lobby for its new chemical plant. Its executives repeatedly telephoned key officials to ensure they had all the information. Proposals were still being driven less by the sensing of a market opportunity than by a need identified in central planning – for example, shortage of a specific petrochemical. Managers said projects were becoming more market-directed and that proposals needed to contain more detailed market analysis, particularly as the state had ceased to provide grants and financing must be negotiated with banks. However, '. . . managers' understanding of the market and, in fact, the market itself, was still dominated and distorted by the continued strong planning-base of the system'.

Procedures for individual performance evaluation and promotion, though sophisticated, are also homogeneous. Under an annual appraisal system, specialist units within companies interview some 15 to 20 of a manager's peers and a large number of subordinates about his or her performance. Criteria for promotion are, in order, good moral and political practice, competence and motivation in the present job, quality of relationships with others in the company, and performance record. Senior managers are chosen from production posts and will have deep knowledge of operations. Dismissals are rare. However, changes are beginning to be forced upon companies: graduates are no longer automatically assigned to their first jobs by ministries, and the growth of non-state industry means that a large part of the labour market is outside the planners' control. In the fast-growing province of Guangdong, directors operate with more autonomy and have to offer higher salaries and benefits to attract staff. I will return to the job market later in this chapter.

Differences in management approach were quickly apparent in the Beijing Jeep joint venture to which I have referred on several occasions. American executives, dedicated to getting the job done in the shortest possible time, were frustrated at the difficulties they encountered in persuading their Chinese counterparts to demonstrate the same single-mindedness.

'The Americans felt the Chinese leaders inside the factory just weren't tough enough. The Chinese factory managers were intimately involved in every aspect of their workers' lives – their pregnancies, their children's education, their housing assignments and recreation. The Chinese managers spent far more time with workers on the factory floor than management people did in

American plants. Yet all these other responsibilities tended to take the Chinese managers away from running an efficient factory. [...] At Beijing Jeep the Chinese leaders were so busy solving problems of mothers-in-law having to share bedrooms with daughters-in-law that they couldn't understand the role the Americans wanted them to play.'[1]

Cultural differences emerged in a variety of ways both big and small. For a start, the Chinese side were baffled that there could be any relationship between good management and cleaning toilets. But, as a somewhat bemused local press report[2] indicated, the American side certainly thought so.

'The American insistence on clean bathrooms is a good example of the cultural chasm that sometimes separates overseas business people from Chinese partners. The Chinese side have questioned such tactics: "Is cleaning the toilets part of the good management?" "Sure" says one of the American managers. "If we can't run our own toilets well, how can we run a large company." When the American general manager decided to spend 200,000 Yuan to rebuild and sanitise the toilets, the decision was greeted with dismay by Chinese managers. They asked: "Is this the best way to spend our money?" The general manager instructed each American executive to take charge of one toilet, write a status report and come up with a renovation plan. Then, to the astonishment of Chinese workers and managers, the Americans filed into the filthy toilets to investigate and, sometimes, to clean up. As a result all 58 toilets were fitted with mosaic-tiled floors, ventilation fans and windows.'

Differences in the approach to discipline also caused problems in the joint venture. Again, to the Americans, the management was too soft and did not enforce discipline. The Chinese leaders would do nothing to control the workers. If the latter did not want to do something, nothing on earth could make them do it – and the considerable difficulty in sacking anyone removed that disciplinary leverage. 'No Chinese leader wanted to play the role of disciplinarian; if the Chinese workers didn't like one of their supervisors, they could often get rid of him.'

There was considerable laxity about the start and finish times as well as the various breaks. In theory, the Chinese workday began at 8-30am and ended at 5-30pm. But in practice production started late, stopped for a long lunch and ended early, perhaps an hour and a half before closing time. Fuming American managers calculated that the average Beijing Jeep worker put in four-and-a-half to five hours a day.

The Americans always wanted the work-force to move faster, be more alert and dedicated to the job on hand. One worker who took a shower during the work day was fined 60 Yuan, about four days' wage, while another who was seen eating an apple during work was given a three-month reduction in wages. One of the rules is: 'During the work day, nothing should be done except for work.'[3]

A photograph of a worker sleeping on the assembly line, published in 1986 along with Western news accounts of troubles at the joint venture, was for the American side a perfect example of Chinese lassitude. 'But to the Chinese, the same photograph showed a good guy and, ironically, a good worker, too. On the afternoon that the picture was taken there had been nothing more for workers to do on the assembly line. In fact, most of the workers had quietly slipped off and gone home. The worker in the photo had been too conscientious to leave early. Instead, with no tasks to perform, he had decided to take a quick nap while remaining on the job. Most factories in China were overstaffed and workers took it for granted that there would be little if anything to do.'[4]

Chinese managers recognize this and allow considerable leeway. With both husband and wife usually working, it is often necessary for one of both of them to slip away for an hour or two to attend to domestic chores, whether it be taking a small child to nursery school, shopping or dealing with the paperwork involved in the many bureaucratic demands of daily life in China – even something as mundane as paying a utilities bill (no direct debit arrangements in China, just long waits in queues at cheerless offices to try and get the better of surly clerks). Knowing this, a good manager has had to turn a blind eye to absenteeism.[5]

Contemplating the overall indolence, the Beijing Jeep executive in charge of production and maintenance decided it was not a cultural trait but simply a reflection of the Chinese system – too many workers with too little work. The answer, he decided was to cut the working week. The assembly line was running six days a week. The executive decided that a reduction to a five-day week would not only benefit the work-force but also result in considerable savings (eg: reduced electricity bills). With more time off, the workers would have higher energy levels and be able to produce the same number of vehicles in a shorter time. The extra day off would reduce the high level of absenteeism and make for happier, better-rested workers with more free time. 'The employees will gain more time for their housework and still have time for rest and social activities,' he said, making it sound as though Chinese workers, like Americans had big houses with lawns to mow and leaves to rake.

In practical terms, the idea made sense. But it also called for a fundamental change in the entire rhythm of Chinese life. Chinese officials liked the idea of the energy savings, but not giving workers an unprecedented extra day off. Compromise was suggested: close the assembly line on Saturday, but the workforce would still come in for 'training'. This, of course, would negate the idea of giving workers more free time. Gradually the American executive realized that Chinese leaders did not like the idea of giving workers more free time being nervous about the social consequences. In the US, factories were merely for production, but in China, where apartments were tiny and streets overcrowded, the factories also served the purpose of social control. Having workers in the factories kept them off the streets.[6]

Another management problem that has emerged is creating an acceptable wage structure. According to a study of Sino-foreign joint ventures in Tianjin, for example, the foreign managers widened the salary gap between different grades of workers in accordance with international practice, in contrast with Chinese firms where there is very little such disparity (Chinese employers making up for low pay by providing various perks such as heavily subsidized food, housing and medical care). Many foreign managers rejected these ideas when the joint ventures were established in the interests of creating incentives for brighter employees. What they succeeded in doing was to create jealousy and dissatisfaction among those employees being paid less who then protested by becoming even more slack in their work.

LABOUR-MANAGEMENT RELATIONS

Managers of foreign-funded and wholly Chinese-owned companies are going to have to pay greater attention in future to labour relations. There is little doubt that social unrest is on the increase. The end of state subsidies for daily necessities and a rapidly-rising cost of living encourages workers to demand higher wages. They are also becoming more aware of their rights to a decent working environment. Meanwhile, a shake-out in the state sector means millions of workers will have to find new jobs or swell the growing ranks of the unemployed. This is not a prospect that makes for a peaceful night's rest for the leadership.

Details of industrial unrest are rarely given in the official media, Like demonstrations, strikes are in effect illegal, because they are seen as a threat to public order. But they do occur and foreign-funded enterprises are not immune. Beneath the surface there is often a simmering undercurrent of resentment that, having been exploited for 40 years by their Communist rulers, a fresh layer of exploitation is being added by the influx of profit-seeking foreign entrepreneurs.

Sweat shops do exist, some of them Dickensian in the appalling environment in which employees must work. Industrial safety is lax. This was emphasized by the tragedy in November 1993 when 81 workers died as fire swept through a two-storey toy factory in Shenzhen – a joint venture with a Hong Kong company. In order to prevent theft (some accounts suggested it was to ensure that the staff did not slip away before the appointed finishing time), the factory kept all its doors and windows locked. When fire broke out, apparently among cotton cloth and other stored materials, there was no escape. Most of the victims died from suffocation. Virtually all were young women who had flocked to Shenzhen from poor rural areas in search of a better life.[7]

Earlier in the year, the *Beijing Youth News* reported at least 10 strikes had occurred in the port city of Tianjin, mainly due to poor pay and bad working conditions. The paper said one stoppage began after bosses at a South Korean factory forced slow workers to kneel before them, sometimes kicking their legs to make them comply. At another strike-hit factory, also South Korean-owned, 1,200 women were making shoes for eight hours a day for a wage of about 100 Yuan a month, low even by Chinese standards. The workers had the use of only one small, filthy toilet, while the foreign managers had one of their own with all mod cons, the newspaper said, adding that foreigners could not expect to match the high standard of Chinese managers in being concerned about the welfare of their workers.

This is an important issue. Foreign managers involved in manufacturing operations often come under pressure to match their Chinese counterparts in providing a complete welfare package, which, particularly in the state sector, includes housing. This was one of the issues in a strike which occurred at a Japanese-owned camera factory in Zhuhai SEZ. The entire 800-strong factory floor workforce walked out to demand substantial increases in their monthly pay averaging 600 Yuan. The management of Canon Zhuhai said the demands were confused, with some workers asking for 20 per cent and others 50 per cent. The company offered only seven per cent and the workers immediately downed tools. The pay was negotiable, but the dispute was complicated by a further demand for housing. 'We cannot provide that. Our losses would be very serious,' said a spokesman.

A typical example of the unhappiness that can exist on both sides of the labour-management divide – especially when the Chinese partner is from the state sector – is provided by BACC, the Beijing-based airline catering firm mentioned in a previous chapter. The Deputy General Manager Wilson Wu complained that it was virtually impossible to dismiss unqualified workers because the local authority opposed it, because 'it would cause social instability' (even though the Regulations on Labour Management, allow joint-venture companies to terminate the employment of any local staff in certain circumstances, including unsuitability and breaches of discipline)

Wu went on: 'The staff earn higher salaries than state-run enterprises and enjoy two free meals a day. Yet they only think about making money not of working hard to earn it. They lack a sense of responsibility and initiative.' The secretary of the manager's office, Li Jingxue, admitted that it was difficult to control the staff because they knew they could not be fired and even if the company fined them for rules infringements they had enough money to pay without pain.

But a foreman, Zhao Jiaqiang, disagreed with the management. Chinese workers could bear hardship, he insisted, because the workshop in which they worked was very crowded and the equipment was difficult to maintain: 'In developed countries, workers would not tolerate such conditions on our wage levels. We're producing three times the designed capacity of the equipment so I don't think our worker's are any less efficient or technologically proficient than those in other countries. The only reason they do better than us is that their equipment is more up-to-date.'

One company that has gone out of its way to satisfy all its employees' welfare needs is Beijing Matsushita Colour CRT Company (BMCC) a 50-50 joint venture between Japan's Matsushita Electric Industrial Company and four Chinese companies, situated in the Beijing suburb of Chaoyang. The factory, producing picture tubes for colour televisions, is the largest single foreign-funded joint-venture company in China. In an effort to build up worker loyalty, the company built two high-rise blocks of flats on the factory site to house 300 families, a bachelor dormitory and a kindergarten for 60 children.

A senior company official, who wished to remain anonymous, explained: 'The Chinese government holds down salary levels [in order to avoid causing too much jealousy with the state sector] so that we have to stress the welfare side to get the best workers. Even though we pay a good salary by Chinese standards, the workers are complaining that the work is very heavy and they should be paid more. But we tell them that they must work hard in order to reach international standard.'

The staff at BMCC work in bright, clean conditions with modern equipment, with two free meals a day and wage levels well above state-sector levels. Yet, some workers are still dissatisfied. Zhang Zhongwen, a Chinese vice-president, said 10 to 20 workers quit every month for a variety of reasons, but the most important was their belief that the work was too hard considering the pay on offer. Most of those who quit are from the workshop where the work admittedly is the hardest. 'They go to find more comfortable places to work, such as foreign-funded hotels,' one official said. Another worker grumbled that the factory rules were 'too strict and working is too hard. If I can find a better job I will go'. According to Zhang: 'The biggest problem we face is to train workers not only in operating skills but also in their work attitudes. They have to realize that labour is a duty and a responsibility.'

The perception that foreign managers are hard taskmasters is also reflected in the story, reported by a Shanghai newspaper, that workers at a ball-bearing plant sought certificates to show they were mentally ill rather than work for a Hong Kong company they feared would demand greater efficiency and hard work. Workers began leaving the state-owned Harbin Ball Bearing complex pleading mental illness when the plant signed a joint-venture agreement with an unnamed Hong Kong firm. 'This incident seriously affected the plant's normal work. Later investigation showed that of the 260 people holding mental illness certificates only 40 really warranted it.' Harbin city's mental hospital sold the certificates to people for 200 to 500 Yuan, the price rising with increased demand, the newspaper said.

For foreign investors, however, the reports of industrial disputes are at present a minor problem, the threat of occasional strikes being outweighed by the attractions of cheap labour and a huge market. But what worries the Beijing authorities is the prospect of industrial unrest caused by reforms of state-run industry. For years, unemployment has been seen as a Western capitalist phenomenon. China's state factories simply spread the work thinly so that there was something for everyone to do. But now, the government is urging enterprises to cut costs and staff. A Chinese sociologist says this new group of redundant state workers 'is the most unstable factor in China'. In 1992, an arbitration system was set up by the Labour Ministry because of the 'sharp increase' in disputes as a result of reforms. The government aims to move some 17 million workers off the payroll of state industries, with seven million jobs being created, mostly in new industries, but 10 million will have to find their own jobs. Officially, the urban unemployment rate is only 2.5 per cent, but this does not include millions 'waiting for work', or who are still on the payroll of a loss-making enterprise. There is little welfare in China, although this is gradually changing – as I will discuss shortly. But, in most instances, when workers are laid off they can expect only a gradually decreasing percentage of their wage being paid for a few months. Then they are on their own.

Although the official media has concentrated on strikes at foreign-funded enterprises (perhaps because it is a slightly less volatile issue politically), there is evidence that state-owned firms are not immune. In early 1993, for example, hundreds of workers at a Beijing factory went on strike. The dispute at the Beijing

Cooling Machinery Factory, which employs more than 1,000 people, centred on alleged abuses by the factory's parent company, Beijing Building Materials (Group) Corp. The company was formerly the Beijing Building Materials Bureau which oversaw but did not run the factory. After the bureau was corporatized it assumed full managerial powers. The strikers claimed that the new company had allowed one of its subsidiaries to occupy the plant and adjoining office building paid for by the workers, which had 'severely affected the Communist Party's image and caused considerable harm to the interests of workers'. The workers were also informed that because the existing site was going to be redeveloped with office buildings and blocks of flats, they would have to move to an affiliate factory in a Beijing suburb where they said conditions were far worse. 'If an outsider comes into your home and tells you to get out, would you just leave?' asked one worker. Eventually, however, the strikers had to accept defeat, only slightly sweetened by compensation payments.

TRADE UNIONS

The plight of workers, particularly in joint ventures and private Chinese enterprises, prompted union leaders to press for early promulgation of a long-discussed labour law. Union sources claimed that there was little control over working hours so that some factory hands were required to work 10 to 12 hours a day, and there were even examples of workers having to toil for 18 hours. Equally, a lack of laws on wages allowed many enterprises to deliberately delay paying salaries, some for several months.

The government tried to head off trouble by improving the work of the official trade union organization, the All-China Federation of Trade Unions (ACFTU). One possibility was to give local branches more authority in bargaining for subsidies from individual firms to help blunt the impact of inflation. Conservatives who were instrumental in purging unions active in the 1989 pro-democracy movement were replaced. But while the unions might lobby harder for labour welfare, there is unlikely to be any relaxation of political control. Security departments stepped up surveillance of members of disbanded 'wild cat' unions which were active in early 1989. Workers in cities such as Shanghai and Zhuhai had been demanding the right to form non-official trade unions. What was particularly worrying for the government was that unionization moves appeared strongest among workers in joint-venture concerns, presaging possible political embarrassments in future.

There are provisions within the Regulations For The Implementation Of The Law On Joint Ventures for the establishment of labour unions within individual firms. The regulations assert that unions have the right to represent the work-force in signing labour contracts and overseeing their implementation. They are also allowed to participate in board meetings as non-voting members. In practice, negotiations on important company matters are handled by the Chinese representatives on the board, restricting the unions to the arrangement of recreational activities. Nevertheless, the unions do have some say in the dismissals or disciplinary actions against any worker, including the right to make representations to the board. And there is a growing argument that as factory managers are given more authority in the management of the operations, including hiring and firing, so there is a need for a strong trade union role to prevent abuses.

Seeking to assuage some of the growing militancy, several cities announced pioneering job insurance schemes, but with a nation-wide credit crunch it is likely to be difficult for most local governments to find the necessary funds for a meaningful insurance programme.

Reflecting on the changing situation, the authoritative newspaper *Economic Daily* declared that it was better for the state to represent the general, long-term and fundamental interests of the workers; the enterprises to care about their collective and public benefits; and the trade unions to stand for the interests of individual employees. The union system was developed in accordance with the planned economy and was not totally capable of meeting the needs created by the market-oriented reforms. Trade unions should become real workers' organizations to negotiate with management and to protect individual workers' interests, the newspaper said.

SOCIAL SECURITY

A possible increased role for unions is very much tied up with the development of a nation-wide social security system for both the public and private sectors, including unemployment benefit and a pensions scheme funded by contributions from the government, employers and the individual worker. The government is estimated to be paying out more than 50 billion Yuan a year in welfare subsidies to 150 million urban workers in the state sector. Traditionally, each work unit has had to bear the costs of medical care and retirement pensions, and although no formal unemployment insurance existed. Public employees in reality were fully covered against job loss. Mergers and annexations involving state-run enterprises has not been encouraged by the fact that the work unit taking over a less-than-successful operation had to assume all its social responsibilities, including housing, food subsidies and pensions.

Businesses, however, have been pressing the government for changes, mainly because of the increasingly heavy burden of pensions. This is particularly true of the older companies with a large number of retirees living longer because of improved life expectancy. Statistics show that in 1988 pensions accounted for 14.2 per cent of the total national wage bill, compared to 3.5 per cent a decade earlier. Over the same period, the number of active workers supporting one retiree fell from 26 to six. The system overall tended to bind workers to the bloated state sectors and discouraged them from transferring to private enterprises where skilled manpower is desperately needed.[8]

Experiments with a reformed social security system were undertaken in the early 1990s leading some economists to suggest that the way forward was to create a minimum basic pension, unemployment and medical insurance scheme for state employees to allow the bankruptcy law to work efficiently, and then extend it to private-sector urban workers. New enterprises, it is argued, would find this relatively painless to start due to a young work-force and no pension liabilities at this stage. Such a scheme would allow a worker to transfer to the private sector without any loss. Central and local governments should cooperate in the provision of a minimum base pension for all urban workers based on the standard wage and funded by a social security tax. Enterprises, both public and private, would then be required to provide an additional pension through private insurance companies, which individuals could top up on their own initiative.

More than 72 million urban workers in the state sector are

already participating in an unemployment fund launched on a trial basis in 1986, with the government initially playing the lead role in financing it, but eventually hoping to step back and rely on contributions from the employers and their work-forces, with the private sector also included. A recent report shows that more than 650,000 members who lost their jobs had received benefits while seeking new jobs. At the same time, some 85 million workers had joined the national pension scheme.

A related issue is the possible end of free medical treatment available to all workers in the public sector. Since the economic reforms began, the cost has risen by 550 per cent, adding substantially to business costs. When the system was started, only four million people were eligible; now there are 130 million. Medical costs also soar with age. In Beijing, for example, 'aged cadres', or retired officials at various levels, account for a quarter of the city's total spending for free medical treatment, although in number they only account for some 3.3 per cent of those entitled to the benefit. The range of medical treatment has also expanded as a result of changes in outlook towards health. Formerly, people went to hospital only when they fell ill, but many now go to see the doctor for routine physical check-ups, or just maintain fitness. At the same time the use of high-grade medical equipment has increased and the price of medicines has soared.

All these factors will increase the cost of doing business in China. A great number of people have enjoyed a wide range of free or low-cost benefits for a good many years and are reluctant to part with them. At the same time, there are rising welfare expectations all round, which companies will have to meet in the years ahead.

FINDING STAFF

How do foreign companies go about finding staff in China? Traditionally, these have been supplied by the government through the Foreign Enterprise Service Corporation (FESCO), which sets their wages and working conditions (a standard FESCO contract is provided in the appendices). Enjoying a monopoly position, the corporation tended to foist staff on foreign businesses with little or no choice. In recent times, other service organizations have sprung up around the country, and there is now a little more leeway allowed for some sectors. Joint ventures and wholly-owned operations, for example, can now go out into the open market to look for staff, many of whom are now recruited through newspaper advertisements. A new craze which began in 1991 is 'job fairs', where foreign companies can set up booths to meet job-seekers. Representative offices do not, as yet, have the same hiring freedom. In theory, incompetent staff can be sacked, but this has to be handled carefully if there are not to be difficulties with the service corporation over finding replacements.

FESCO wage rates vary from city to city. However, a chief representative, consultant or senior engineer might expect to earn 2,500 Yuan a month, a businessman manager or translator 1800 and a driver about 990 Yuan a month. Salaries are calculated on a 13- month basis including a one-month bonus. Many businessmen say an extra bonus is often sought as an under-the-table payment for the Chinese New Year.

The salaries are relatively generous by Chinese standards. But a word of warning: the employee does not get anything like this amount. The money is paid to FESCO which for many years handed over only 10 or 20 per cent of the amount, but increased this to between 40-45 per cent in August 1992. FESCO justifies the retention of the bulk of the pay as being necessary to pay for the employee's housing, medical care and pension. But when the percentage increase was announced, the organization took away some of the previous benefits and subsidies, including food and transportation allowances.

Some foreign businessmen see the wage system as a way for the Chinese side to obtain additional funds in disguise. For example, when the Beijing Jeep joint venture was being negotiated, AMC was staggered by a demand that it pay the Chinese executives the same salary as its own top managers were paid – at the time about $40,000. The Americans were willing, as long as all the money actually went to the Chinese executive. But they knew from experience that he would only be receiving no more than one per cent of that amount. Where was the rest of the money going to go? That was never made clear. It seemed to be part of a general principle that foreigners should always pay more for everything in China than their local counterparts because they can afford it. Foreign businessmen say they repeatedly face demands for payment of additional charges, some of which seem designed merely to test how much they are willing to pay to do business in China.

There is little doubt that labour costs are rising steadily for foreign companies employing local staff. In 1993, salaries for Chinese nationals rose 22 per cent on average, compared to a 15 per cent increase in 1992. If the authorities cannot keep the lid on inflation, companies will face demands for further big increases. Foreign managers say it is increasingly difficult to hang on to good Chinese staff because newly-established enterprises tend to lure them away with offers of higher salaries. One business man recalled: 'My secretary walked out without any advanced warning. She reckoned I was underpaying her and that she could do better elsewhere. It's difficult to make any sort of plans when you don't know if you will have the staff around to carry them out.'

JOB HUNTING

There is a good and bad side to this. Job mobility – the freedom not only to seek out a prospective employer without bureaucratic hindrance, and change workplace at will – is one of the most important changes brought about by the economic reforms. Increasingly, in theory at least, it will allow foreign enterprises to compete for the cream of China's educational system rather than accepting what are sometimes second-raters fobbed off on them by the government. But the price will be high because the battle for talent is becoming heated.

In July 1992, the Shandong provincial government held a press conference in Beijing to try and entice talented workers to work in the region. Those who accepted were to be granted a relocation fee of 10,000 to 30,000 Yuan. If their work achievements produced more than 8 million Yuan in tax and profit, they would be given a Volkswagen Santana car. Government offices in Shanghai and Shenzhen have gone even further afield, sending official missions to Europe and North America to canvas young Chinese studying there.

Nearer home, witness the scene outside the International Exhibition Centre in Beijing in October 1993. Hours before the doors open, thousands of young people are milling around the entrance. Half an hour after the event began, thousands more were still jammed up against the ticket desks, each person thrusting out a two Yuan note in the hope of getting a precious entry pass – and being refused because the hall was already wall-to-wall people. A rare rock concert, perhaps? No such thing; rather the country's first National Talented Personnel Fair, a four-day opportunity for the professional classes and academic elite to try a bit of match-making with employers from all of the mainland's 30 provinces, autonomous regions and municipalities. Nearly 1,000 companies and state organizations set up stalls where job applications disappeared as fast as they could be laid out.

The reforms of the employment system have created a nation-wide grab for talent which poses serious problems not only for domestic firms but foreign-funded enterprises. For the best-qualified workers, there is now a chance to choose where and how one wants to work and live. Less-attractive areas, such as the under-developed inland provinces, have to offer powerful inducements now to get good people. One engine manufacturer in Guangxi Zhuang Autonomous region was reported to have paid out $18,000 to hire 11 graduates from the capital's highly-rated Qinghua University.

Under the old system of central planning, graduates were allocated jobs when they left university or college. The strict household registration system which required government permission for a move from one place to another also discouraged any form of job switching. And even if the permission was given, once a job was assigned it could not be easily abandoned without the payment of a substantial fine. It was like an arranged marriage. People had no right to choose their spouses, knew nothing about their partners and had little possibility of obtaining a divorce if the relationship was not happy. The system did have a positive role in that, with the state giving every graduate a job, the situation which had prevailed before the Communist take-over of 'graduation means unemployment' no longer prevailed. But it also left a lot of resentment on both sides.

In the late 1970s, when Zhang Gang was facing graduation, he did not know where he would go and what sort of job he would take. 'We were told to pack our bags and wait,' he recalled. 'We were playing cards every day speculating on our future. Then, one day shortly before the deadline for us to leave university, I received a card telling me I would work in an engineering factory in Beijing, although my speciality was theoretical physics.'

Wang Xiayou had a similar experience. She studied history in the People's University in Beijing, and after graduation in 1986 was assigned to work at a broadcasting station in a small town in Gansu Province where her parents lived. But the station already had two broadcasters, so there was no work for her. She asked the head of the local county administration to give her something to do, but he replied: 'What can a person who studied history do in our small county?' Finally, she became a cook in the county government headquarters' dining-room. To escape, and gain a residence card for Beijing once again, she had gained admission back to her old university for post-graduate study.

In the first two decades of communist rule, the assignment work was led directly by the late Premier Zhou Enlai, and was a 100 per cent state-controlled. The government issued a plan to colleges, who decided which student should go to which work unit on the plan. There was no choice. The government justified this by pointing out that the youngsters had received a completely free education. They did not pay any tuition or dormitory fees; their medical expenses were also met out of official funds. Many students also received other subsidies to help them with their living and study expenses. Therefore, it was only right for the state to decide where they should go after graduation. And many idealistic young people were quite happy to respond to the clarion cry of 'Go wherever the country needs you most'.

Zhang Dofa, an engineer graduate in the 1960s, recalled: 'We did not care whether our new jobs paid well or not, did not care whether we would stay in Beijing or be sent to a remote area. We just thought about the nation's needs.' In contrast, his son refused to work at the company assigned by his college, and got his own job with a private computer firm. 'We are a new generation living in an environment completely different from my father's era. We have new ideas,' he commented.

The old system certainly was not always efficient and there were many cases of trying to push square pegs into round holes. It was estimated that up to 20 per cent of the college graduates' jobs were not suited to their academic training up to the early 1980s, when the government finally began stressing the need for change.

Finally, in April 1989, the Education Ministry issued the 'plan for the reform of the job assignment system of colleges and universities'. Central to the proposed reform was a 'two-way selection system', allowing graduates to choose jobs more freely through the recommendation of their schools. But not long after the system was tried in a few key institutions, complaints arose that the measures did not go far enough. In addition, they opened the way for corruption, since the power of employing graduates had been transferred to each 'work unit', enabling personnel officers to offer jobs to those with whom they had good 'guanxi' regardless of academic performance or behaviour at college. This was a severe discouragement to those from the countryside with little good contacts in the city, giving rise to the comment that: 'study doesn't matter if you have powerful parents'.

The government gave schools the overall responsibility to find jobs for their students, but many teachers complained about the additional burden which meant they spent more time calling up prospective employers than on traditional classroom activities. Nevertheless, the schools realized they had a valuable asset sitting at their desks. A new system then evolved whereby either the graduate or the enterprise (or both) had to pay to $1,500 to the university or college if both sides wanted to come to their own employment arrangement. About a tenth of the graduates from Beijing's higher education facilities in 1993 admitted they had paid to find their jobs.

At the time of writing, the system seemed to be something of a halfway house between freedom and control. Take the 1993 graduates of the Beijing Polytechnic University. Out of the 1,100 students going out into the world, the 110 most outstanding were permitted to chose their own occupation without any limitation by the school. Another 146 students, with slightly lower academic qualifications, were able to do the same after paying $885. The rest had to choose their occupation from a range set by the institution. Youngsters from other areas of China attending schools in big cities like Beijing or Shanghai continue to be at some disadvantage. Schools in Beijing, for example, are given government quotas for students from other provinces allowed to stay in the capital after graduation to prevent over-concentration in a few areas. Beijing Broadcasting Institute set a 15 per cent proportion based on academic achievement and 'integrity'. Amid the climate of reform, the government said it was looking at new ways to induce graduates from big cities to work in another areas, so as to avoid a regional imbalance.

For those free to decide where to live and work, a thousand 'talent-exchange centres' have sprung up across the country to act as a bridge between labour supply and demand. And these have, in turn, created a new trend of *'taiocao'* – job-switching – which I will discuss in more detail shortly. Most cities now have a local jobs market, typified by the one held every Sunday in Beijing's Xianwu district, which claimed that in its first year of operation after opening in August 1992 it was visited by some 100,000 applicants, of whom a fifth had found new jobs. Yang Chuan, the market's head, said most of the applicants already had jobs and were looking for something better. Each Sunday, around 70 joint-venture operations, local factories, shops and hotels set up desks at the Xianwu Workers' Club to deal with the flood of prospective employees. The manager of a trading company, looking for management, personnel and electronic appliance maintenance men, explained: 'In the past, if the company needed some employee, we would submit an application to the Labour Bureau who would send us someone. Now we can choose, we can employ the people who meet our demands.'

It has largely become a seller's market, although some foreign companies possess a definite advantage in the struggle for talent. On university campuses, it is said that the ambitions of China's modern youth is to join a joint venture which offers opportunities for overseas travel, along with 'gold and power'. In Shanghai, it is estimated that more than half of the staff recruited by foreign companies have come from personnel exchange activities.

JOB SWITCHING

With the iron rice bowl and the job-for-life being scrapped, it is no longer unusual for a Chinese worker to switch jobs. Nevertheless, when a number high-level staff from a large state-owned enterprise did so – moving to a private company which offered not only more money but more responsibility – it caused a considerable stir in early 1993. The columns of the prestigious *Economic Daily* were filled for some weeks with readers arguing the pros and cons of the event. I would like to tell the story here in some detail because I believe it is a good illustration of the changes taking place in the Chinese labour market-place about which any foreign businessman needs to be aware.

Dalian Machine Tool Factory is China's largest combination machine-tool factory. Located in the north-eastern city of Dalian, it had 7,000 employees. Among its clients were the country's biggest automotive manufacturing companies, including Beijing Jeep, for whom it provided an estimated 90 per cent of their needs in precision combination tools. In September 1992, the heads of the design, finance and business management departments quit and accepted an invitation from a village-run enterprise in the Dalian suburbs to set up a rival machine-tool factory. Another 50 DMTF technical staff followed them, and within two months a series of new products had been designed and were winning new orders – promising to make deep inroads into DMTF's revenue in 1994.

DMTF Director Zhou Kui was enraged at the resignations which he said had undermined the foundation of the factory. He agreed with the theory of encouraging a flow of talent, but this had to be regulated. He said it was unfair that after DMTF had spent a lot of money on their training and overseas trips, they had departed. Moreover, they took the blueprints with them, which Zhou believed infringed intellectual property laws. As for competition among enterprises, the director complained that the two machine-tool companies were competing under unequal conditions. The new factory had only 90 – mostly young – employees while DMTF had to take care of thousands of retired workers. As a high-tech township-run enterprise, the new factory enjoyed tax deductions or exemptions which DMTF could not enjoy but must instead meet the increased annual production targets set by the state. Zhou said he could not keep people at DMTF because he did not have the right to raise their salaries or provide them with more comfortable apartments the way the new factory could. The job-switchers had betrayed the interests of the country, he complained bitterly.

Sun Yinhuan, former manager of the village-run enterprise, admitted he had lured the specialists with attractive offers, However, he argued that the non-state-run enterprises could not have developed so quickly in the past few years if they had not invited technical personnel from state enterprises. Anyway, DMTF would not suffer great losses because 90 per cent of its technical staff remained and most college graduates would be assigned to work there. He had tried to talk to DMTF about compensation for expenditures on their former staff but was rejected.

One of the three original defectors, Li Fuxi, now director of the new factory, explained why he left DMTF where he had worked for more than 30 years. He said there were too many restrictions in state enterprises and it was impossible for him to accomplish what he wanted. At the age of 52, he had eight years to go before retirement and wanted to accomplish something before then. Li admitted he had been offered a higher salary and a better apartment by the village-run enterprise, but the more attractive aspect had been that he would have decision-making powers over the factory's management, investment and income distribution.

Many readers of the *Economic Daily* agreed that a free flow of labour should be allowed and that spread of knowledge should be respected. State enterprises should improve the treatment of their employees, especially the technical staff, because competition among enterprises was actually competition for talent. However, many agreed there should be some regulations concerning the flow of professionals such as paying compensation for the losses suffered by former enterprises which had spent money on the domestic and overseas training of their employees. One reader criticized some state enterprises for their inertia and arrogance, nurtured by long-time government control. They were not used to asking for favours, the reader claimed, resulting in their weakness in market competition. However, others argued that it was not the firms but the government which was at fault for controlling the enterprises for so long and making them totally dependent like over-protected children.

In 1992, nearly one million technical and managerial employees registered at local personnel exchange centres across the country looking for opportunities to change their work unit. Many others are thought to have done so without registering. According to a sample survey by the China Scientific and Technical Personnel Exchange Centre, 30 per cent of the country's workers in these fields indicated an intention, or at least a desire, to change jobs. The actual transfer rate at the time was 2.6 per cent.[9]

TRAINING COSTS

After that digression, I would like to return finally in this chapter to the foreign-funded venture and its need for staff, particularly well-trained staff. Training can be a big hidden cost of labour in a joint venture. Even well-educated Chinese staff frequently lack management sales and technical skills essential to a Western business. Some joint ventures content themselves with poaching talent from other joint ventures. The more ethical alternatives, however, are on-the-job training, bringing in experts from the overseas head or regional office, using training courses offered by a service company, sending staff abroad, investing in a training centre.

One somewhat limited survey of joint-venture labour costs[10] found that firms in Beijing were spending an average of 3,000 to 5,000 Yuan for the training of each recruit in the first year of employment, while management training costs tended to start at around 10,000 Yuan a year. One Shanghai joint venture brought in experts from overseas several times a year, costing more than $5,000 a year per employee trained. Using outside service companies is not necessarily a cheaper option. Firms can expect to pay 10,000 to 15,000 Yuan for a two-week course in computers or finance at a Chinese-owned training centre, while foreign-funded management training firms charge substantially more. Large companies can afford to send their Chinese staff abroad, either to regional offices or to the home country, enabling them to exercise greater control over training quality and introduce staff to the company culture. It is also a highly desirable employment perk. But aside from cost, bureaucratic hurdles sometimes impede overseas training. Just before opening its China factory, one big multinational food company sent six Chinese line supervisors to one of its plants in Thailand for six weeks at a total cost of $10,500. The company wanted to send more staff but was unable to secure exit visas. Some joint ventures, however, manage to arrange overseas training so it is virtually cost-free. One Beijing engineering firm sends new staff to affiliates abroad for six to nine months that are planning to export projects to China. These affiliates can get enough work out of the trainees to justify them picking up all their transport and living costs.

For companies with big investments in China, financing a training centre makes sense. The German firm Siemens, for example, used to spend tens of thousands of pounds a year sending employees of its joint venture Beijing International Switching Company to Germany for training. But in 1989 it opened its own training centre in the capital. Siemens provided the equipment, teachers and construction funds, but the centre is effectively owned and operated by the Beijing municipal government. A typical two-week course costs about $300 per person. BISC now sends several hundred employees and customers there each year at substantial savings. Computer makers Digital Equipment and Compaq have both opened centres in Beijing which offer computer courses to staff from institutions, government offices and Chinese and joint-venture companies.

The overseas training option was taken a step further by the Japanese-funded Beijing Matsushita Colour CRT Company (BMCC) mentioned earlier. Almost from the start of production, it was able to export picture tubes to Japan and to export-oriented factories in Malaysia, accounting for a third of its output. Matsushita said this had been made possible because of stable quality levels. The factory has a reject level averaging 1.5 per cent, the same as the company's plants in Japan. Productivity between the two countries is almost the same.

How was it possible to achieve such high quality so quickly, given China's known deficiencies in this area? During the plant construction, the first 250 Chinese workers recruited, a mixture of line personnel and management trainees, were sent to Japan for training varying from three months to a year. But this was no ordinary training programme. They worked with the very production facilities they would take back to China. Eventually, they attained such a high level of quality production that Matsushita was able to accept 5,000 picture tubes they had made for its Japanese television plants. Then, the Chinese disassembled and packed all the production machinery for shipment back to China. They returned home and were waiting at the port when the containers arrived. These were unpacked and the same workers then assembled the machinery in the BMCC factory.

'As a result,' said BMCC President Chikayoshi Ninagawa, 'they had great confidence in doing this because it was their own equipment they had been working on and which they had taken to bits, numbered and packed themselves. So, they had no excuse for failure. After we began operations we were able to move to full mass-production very quickly because all these original trainees had great confidence. The original 200 Japanese-trained workers then trained the remaining 1,000 line personnel when they were hired. This was the first time Matsushita had ever attempted such a training operation and it was the key to success.'

Ninagawa admitted the idea emerged from his experiences more then decade earlier when he was responsible for the supply of black-and-white picture tubes to a factory in Shanghai. 'So many contracts did not run smoothly and the Chinese had so many excuses – wrong equipment, poor equipment, outmoded technology, poor training etc. I was determined when BMCC was set up that there would never be an opportunity for any such excuses.'

FOOTNOTES:
1. Beijing Jeep, p203.
2. Supplement by the Publishers Auxiliary in China Daily, November 1992.
3. ibid.
4. Beijing Jeep, pp199-200.
5. It is very easy to obtain medical leave from sympathetic doctors. I experienced some of these frustrations during my own working stints in China, where it was a rare day when there was not at least one absence due to a sudden, unexplained fever. Other excuses: having to help grandmother pack for a trip, meeting a friend or relative arriving unexpectedly from the provinces, family illness, having to queue for a rail ticket, having to fill out an application form (a task which could have been completed in 10 minutes but somehow occupied a whole day) etc. For some reason, it was never possible to anticipate any of these things so that I could be warned in advance. Someone on the Chinese side would merely inform me that so-and-so had sent to message to say he or she could not come to work today because...
6. Beijing Jeep, p258.
7. In 1993, for the first time, the Ministry of Labour released the figures for industrial accident fatalities. The toll was 15,146, which the ministry said was 3.13 per cent over the deaths in the previous year. The casualty figures had been kept confidential in the past, according to official sources, 'to avoid undesirable social reaction'. The mining industry has the worst accident record of all, with 9,683 deaths. Another 7,152 workers died at township enterprises. Sun Lianjie, Director of the Labour Safety Bureau, blamed the high casualties on negligence at some enterprises which tried to gain higher output by disregarding worker safety. Current laws and regulations were not sufficient because they failed to specify many of the obvious violations of labour safety. As a result, the government has begun introducing regulations for insurance and compensation for industrial accident victims, Sun said.
8. The insecurity of the private sector is illustrated by the case of Dai Yan, a woman in her early 30s who quit her job with the state-run Beijing Machinery Institute in 1989 to join a Japanese company, Yamafuku Trading, partly because of her desire to travel abroad. She earned about 1,000 Yuan a month, a relatively good salary but not enough to give her security if problems

arose. And this is exactly what happened in 1990 when she was hospitalized for two months, which cost her the equivalent of half a year's wages. 'If I'd still been with Beijing Machinery Institute it wouldn't have cost me a cent,' she said regretfully.
9. *Beijing Review*, 1 Feb. 1993.
10. *Business China*, 22 March 1993.

11 China's financial system

KEY POINTS
Some of the most radical changes in the move from a centrally-planned to a market economy are taking place in the financial sector. The government is overhauling its entire fiscal and monetary policy, and a new legal structure is being created to provide the necessary back-up. This chapter will look at:
- Moves to strengthen the powers of the central bank, the People's Bank of China (PBOC).
- The transformation of the four specialized banks – who work closely with the PBOC and government in carrying out State policy – into commercial ones.
- The creation of new banks to take over the specialist role in high-risk, low-profit State projects.
- Moves to create a new interest rate structure related to market needs.
- The role of foreign banks in China.
- How foreign businesses can obtain loans from Chinese banks.
- Raising capital via the stock market.
- The creation of a vast network of futures markets across the country.

BANKING STRUCTURE

THE SYSTEM is dominated by the central bank, four specialized banks and eight other commercial banks.[1] The People's Bank of China, founded in 1948, was given central bank status in 1984. The push for financial reform, however, means a proliferation of new financial institutions, greater freedom for existing ones and decision-making based on economics not politics – all of which requires a strong central bank that can regulate in fact as well as in theory. But there have been many complaints that the PBOC has actually exercised very little control over the state banks it is supposed to supervise, and has had no control whatsoever of the new banks, often set up by existing state institutions to circumvent the existing restrictions and constraints, or the new non-banking financial institutions which have been pouring money into various speculative instruments. In addition, it has not had control over the money supply. Monetary policy has been the prerogative of the State Council and State Planning Commission not the People's Bank. Every ministry has a voice in shaping monetary targets, with the goal of balancing the voracious appetite of the state enterprises for funds and the need for a strict diet to keep a lid on inflation. The People's Bank, in consultation with its masters, decides on targets, but it appears that nobody, including those officials takes them seriously. 'It isn't a major bureaucratic player. It is a printing press. It is the government cashier,' insisted one Western diplomat.[2]

Monetary policy in China exhibits a bottoms-up pattern. Provincial banks submit to the regional branches of the PBOC provisional plans for the districts, specifying their funding requirements. Upon receiving proposals from the branches, officials from the central bank, the specialized banks and other financial institutions, meet and try to finalize the overall plan based on the following factors: the planned GNP; the targeted inflation rate, money-supply growth during the past five years, and specific requirements from the State Planning Commission and the State Council.

Immediately below the central bank are the four specialized or the so-called 'comprehensive' commercial banks:

Industrial and Commercial Bank of China founded on 1 January 1984 as a special state bank operating industrial and commercial credit and savings business for cities and towns. Its work covers deposits of industrial and commercial enterprises, agencies and organizations, the issuance of loans to state-owned industrial and commercial firms, and personal savings.

Agricultural Bank of China set up on 1 March 1955 to handle rural finances. Its main tasks are the provision of credit to rural areas, leadership of rural credit cooperatives and development of rural financial structures.

Bank of China, specializing in foreign exchange and trade, works closely with the central bank in the macro-regulation of state finances; it conducts state policy-linked business, organizes the use and accumulation of foreign capital, and deals in foreign currency and Renminbi.

People's Construction Bank of China, established in October 1954, has assumed responsibility for administration of investments in fixed assets, business credit and investment, and appropriation for capital construction.

Traditionally, the specialized banks have not made loans on commercial considerations. Instead, they function as a direct arm of the government and lend according to government instructions. Like the central bank, they are primarily intermediaries, cashiers that provide funds to the state enterprises at the behest of the State Planning Commission. The World Bank estimates that at least 70 per cent of the loans are what it calls 'policy-based'. The comprehensive banks can lend on commercial terms, but since the government fixes the interest rate structure, they cannot effectively manage risk and allocate credit according to market forces. Foreign exchange supervision is undertaken by the State Administration of Exchange Control. Its main duties are to oversee the operations of regional swap markets and determine official exchange rates (more on this later).

Reviewing the current state of affairs, Zhang Xinze, an official in the PBOC's Research and Statistics Department, agreed that fiscal and credit system reform was not keeping pace with the development of a market economy. The ambiguous dual role of specialized banks in supporting state-owned firms while at the same time trying to maximize profits left them in an awkward position. Deficit-ridden companies relied on loans from the specialized banks for their survival. But about 30 per cent of the banks' funding was provided by the central bank. That meant the banks' balance sheets were very fragile and they could not stand on their own. Should the banks stop lending to the public enterprises, they would run into financial trouble and thus make a smaller tax contribution, which would, in turn affect the central bank's funding activities. In other words: a classic vicious cycle.

On the other hand, once the investment frenzy began, banks stretched their credit limits beyond breaking point to lend in the booming property market and investment projects. With the banks used as blank cheque writers, indirect monetary instruments such as interest rates and reserve requirements were blunt to the point of uselessness. There was, for a start, little relationship between deposits and lending. At the People's Construction Bank, for example, total deposits amounted to 210 billion Yuan ($37 billion) at the end of the 1991 financial year, but loans outstanding totalled 260 billion Yuan ($46 billion), with the authorities making up the shortfall. And, since much of the lending targeted at national projects was made far below the going interest rates at the behest of the Ministry of Finance, the bank had to be compensated for that also.[3] In many cases, banking regulations made lending through official channels difficult, so the money flowed out through unofficial channels. With financial institutions other than banks are not subject to a lending limit, some borrowed heavily from specialized banks to grant loans and engage in investment. Some banks even set up subsidiaries to invest directly in projects as an equity partner.

This was one of the contributory factors in the explosive inflation that so alarmed the central government in the first half of 1993. Tight control had to be restored, and fast. The result was the appointment of Vice President Zhu Rongji as central bank governor in July. He immediately read the riot act to the banking community, ordering managements that they would face 'severe punishment' if they did not immediately institute three basic steps: (1) Immediately stop all interbank lending in violation of state regulations and recall such outstanding loans within a prescribed time; (2) no financial institution allowed to independently raise their interest rates on bank deposits or loans in disguised forms or compete with each other for bank savings by raising interest rates. They were also prohibited from requesting or receiving commissions on bank loans; (3) all banks immediately to cut their links with business firms run by them and no credit to be offered to these firms.

There was an immediate response. The heads of the Industrial and Commercial Bank and the Bank of China pledged to recall their high-risk loans to other banks within five weeks, with lending to non-bank financial institutions to stop within six months. ICBC President Zhang Xiao identified his biggest problem as finding ways to increase saving deposits and expand reserves in light of the shortage of funds for key projects. Zhang admitted that in the first six months of 1993, the bank had attracted 40.7 billion Yuan ($7.2 billion) less than the same period of the previous year, as investors with cash found more attractive vehicles for their funds. To increase the number of savings accounts, the bank would open more branches, encourage the use of credit cards, act as a broker for stocks and bonds, to earn commission for the bank and draw in potential savers. Every branch manager would be given a quota for attracting new accounts. The bank president pledged that in future ICBC loans would go for the purchase of agricultural products, the support of profitable enterprises and key state construction projects, and money would no longer be leant to factories whose products did not sell or for real-estate projects or speculation in securities.

By the middle of August, Zhu's warning had achieved some results, as banks reported a total of 72.7 billion Yuan ($12.8 billion) in illegal loans had been recalled. A central bank circular at the time said that any outstanding funds had to be recalled immediately if they were used for the construction of holiday resorts and villas, for processing industry construction projects that fell outside central planning or as working capital loans for stockpiled products, and funds used in trading real estate, securities and foreign exchange.

This, of course, was only a short-term measure, dealing with the symptoms rather than the source of the disease. For that, floating interest rates were seen as the key to banking reform. China introduced such a policy in 1984, when the PBOC's provincial branches were given the right to determine the floating margins of interest rates. However, head office revoked this power in 1988 when the country launched a three-year austerity programme.

Five years later, a PBOC official was quoted in the official *China Daily*[4] as saying: 'The next wave of banking reform will make some fixes in the rate policy. For instance, the right to decide fluctuating margins will be delegated to specialized banks. In the end, the market will decide rate fluctuations.

'Under the old planned economy, the role of interest rates was not significant because it was the central planners who decided the rate. Neither the government nor producers actually paid much attention to the functions in the rate in regulating the economy. Capital is in great shortfall in China and, even worse, it usually does not float to where the mouth is. For example, infrastructure projects starved of funds while the real estate market is crammed with speculative money. Administrative measures will inevitably lead to inadequate decisions in allocating such rare resources. In fact, besides official interest rates, there are market rates for funds not included in the state plans. This is the so-called "double track" system which can also be found in other sectors. Since demand for funds has greatly surpassed the supply and the state is prudent in extending loans to avoid inflation, it is difficult to get bank loans within the state's plan at the official rate. So more and more enterprises have to borrow loans outside of the state's plan.

'As a result, the interest rates are pushed much higher than the official rates. The big margin which reached as high as 30 percentage points in the south before July [1993] was one reason for financial disorder. By offering higher interest rates various fund-raising companies lured many depositors away from the state banks. At the same time, some employees at state banks have pocketed the big interest margins. To let markets regulate interest rates can enhance the central government's control over the economy, because the current rate is too rigid to make responses to changes in the market.'

An indication of how the banking reforms would proceed was provided by Chen Yuan, Vice-President of the People's Bank of China. The first step would be to '... expand money and capital markets, breaking down regional barriers and establishing a unified market'. This would be followed by allowing interest rates of the money markets to float freely and by cutting off direct links between money markets and capital markets, with the central bank regulation designed to retain a basic balance between the two. 'The money market itself will become the base on which the central bank uses monetary policy tools to regulate the money supply. On the capital market, there should be strict supervision over the amount of capital issuance. No price controls will be imposed on the secondary market.'

Chen said that to reach the desired goal, China planned to establish a number of short-term capital markets in big cities throughout the country to meet enterprises' capital needs, along with a national unified and orderly inter-bank lending market to standardize capital lending in the country. A short-term commercial bills market should also be developed, the PBOC official stressed.

At the time of writing, several new laws were being drafted for possible implementation in 1994 to strengthen the powers of the central bank, and give more freedom to the major commercial banks. Three new 'policy-oriented' banks were to be set up, one to look after the needs of agriculture, and the other two being a long-term development credit bank and an import and export credit bank. The development credit bank would provide capital for construction projects vital in sectors like energy and transportation which need long-term and low-interest loans that commercial banks are reluctant to offer because of high risk and low profit. The third new bank would offer import and export credits, export credit financing insurance and project financing. This was expected to give a strong push to China's external trade by stimulating exports of large machinery and electronics products. The major source of funding for all three specialized banks will come from their own capital, and they will be able to float bonds at home to bolster this.

The establishment of these three new institutions will then liberate the present four specialized banks which will then be able to transform themselves into commercial entities, assuming risks and becoming responsible for their own profits and losses. On a lower tier, the present urban and rural credit cooperatives will then gradually be turned into urban and rural cooperative banks to serve the local economy and small and medium-sized businesses.

But while bank lending is still hopelessly entangled with government industrial policy, symbolized by the continued commitment to state-owned enterprises, many economists feel that true reform of the banking system will be extremely difficult to achieve. Two possible ways to achieve a breakthrough have been proposed by economists at Stanford University in California. The first, outlined by Qian Xingyi, is for China to adopt a version of Japan's 'main bank' system. Decisions about loans would be more commercialized, but banks would remain closely involved with their corporate borrowers, helping them with their investment decisions and watching their performance. Qian argues that this suits China's conditions and its aim of gradual industrial reform combined with fast economic growth.

The other way would be to force all firms to heed market signals, making them go to the capital markets for their finance. This seems hard to achieve when the capital markets are still so small. Ron McKinnon, also of Stanford, offers a solution based on his assessment that the non-state rural enterprises have been such an outstanding success because they were financed almost entirely out of owners' funds and retained earnings, and thus subject to market discipline. He suggested insulating the financial system that served the reformed firms, whether state-owned or otherwise, from the system serving the traditional juggernauts. Unreformed firms would still have access to bank credit, but their cash balances and investment decisions would be under tight bank control to ensure a gradual weeding out of the unprofitable ones. Reformed firms could do what they wanted with their earnings but could not borrow from banks.

FOREIGN BANKS

Where do foreign banks fit into this picture of troubled reform? The opening up of new business areas may be an exciting prospect in the long term, but for the moment the commercial activities of foreign banks is confined to foreign currency lending, trade settlements, leasing, advisory services and financial derivatives. There has been talk of allowing the foreig banks into local currency business, but even if this is eventually permitted, there are certain to be considerable restrictions.

Local banks have looked on the increased liberalization with some concern, but can see that the arrival of the foreigners does mean the introduction of a whole new range of banking products and services and new technology which can only create a larger pie for everyone to share from.

Since the early 1980s, more than 220 bank offices have been opened around the country, although only a fraction of them have been granted full branch status. The strongest presence, perhaps unsurprisingly has come from the two banks with a long history of China contact – Standard Chartered and Hong Kong & Shanghai Banking Corporation. Standard Chartered actually opened its first office in Shanghai in 1858. The two rivals have spread their representation into most of the SEZs and several of the coastal open cities where the bulk of inward investment and foreign trade flows have been focused.

One frustration for everyone has been the Chinese insistence on allowing only one branch per city. As a Standard Chartered spokesman commented: 'Shanghai is a very big city, but if you have a branch in Puxi, you cannot have another at the other end in Pudong. I don't see why that should be. If McDonald's can have more than one branch in a city, why can't we?'

Generally, foreign bankers say one of the biggest problems is that China does not have a clearing system and therefore no cheque accounts. People normally have to carry cash around in bulk when making large purchases. Many local banks actually refuse to provide a personal cheque service because outside the big cities clearance still has to be done manually rather than through computers, and staff do not want to be troubled by numerous small transactions. The government and the leading banks, however, are now trying to popularize the concept of both cheque books and credit cards as part of the banking revolution.

Foreign banks are not allowed to provide Yuan-based services, and that limitation is unlikely to disappear for some time. This gives domestic banks a big advantage in holding on to Chinese customers. As one banker explained: 'Domestic banks attach conditions on their Yuan loans to keep us at bay. So, even though the clients might prefer other services from foreign banks, they have to use the domestic ones because that is part of the deal.'

As more foreign banks are allowed in China, however, the government is also encouraging domestic financial institutions to open their own overseas subsidiaries as conduits for raising investment capital. At present, the Bank of China is the main operator of overseas subsidiaries, its London operation having started in 1924, but the People's Construction Bank is operating in Japan and Singapore, and the Industrial and Commercial Bank is also active in the latter. The Singapore connection is line with a government desire to see a well-balanced overseas spread – so that, apart from the obvious major financial centres like London, Frankfurt, New York and Tokyo, the banks also move into areas where trade and investment links with China are growing fast, such as South Korea and Russia.

BORROWING FROM CHINESE BANKS

Having discussed the banking structure, the question then arises: can foreign businesses operating in China obtain loans from domestic banks? And the simple answer is, yes. They can borrow from the Bank of China and the specialized banks. Loans can be granted in the name of the enterprises or in the name of the foreign or Chinese investors. The interest rate of the loans and the procedure fee are almost the same as that for state enterprises. Should a company decide to borrow money overseas and bring it into China, it has to be placed with the State Administration of Exchange Control and its provincial branches.

All foreign-funded enterprises approved by the Ministry of Foreign Trade and Economic Cooperation and its authorized organs, registered with the State Administration for Industry and Commerce and holding valid business licences, can apply for loans from the Bank of China. The conditions are:

1. The enterprise has got a business licence issued by the local bureau for industry and commerce and has opened the account in the local branch of the Bank of China.

2. It has paid in the registered capital and this has been confirmed by the government departments concerned.

3. The company's board has made a decision to seek a loan and issued an authorization certificate.

4. The fixed assets investment projects by the enterprise have been approved by the relevant planning organs.

5. The enterprises have the capability to repay the loan and have provided reliable guarantee for repayment of the loans and interest.

Capital can be provided in the following ways:
- Fixed assets loan. This includes construction expenditure for capital projects and technical innovation and the purchasing and installation fee on buying technology and equipment. It can be a short to medium-term or medium to long-term loan, or a buyer's credit. The amount of the loan generally does not exceed 85 per cent of the amount of the commercial contacts involved.
- Circulating fund loan – the capital used by the enterprise in production, circulation and operation. The means of the loans are production reserve funds and operating loans; temporary loans and overdrafts.
- Spot foreign exchange mortgage.
- Reserve loans.

In accordance with state policy, the Bank of China provides

priority loans to the following foreign-funded enterprises: (a) export-oriented enterprises – the products are mainly exported overseas and the enterprise can achieve a balance in foreign exchange ; (b) technically-advanced enterprises which introduce advanced technologies, develop new or update old products or create import substitutes, and including state enterprises transformed with advanced techniques by foreign investors; (c) key enterprises encouraged by the state.

REVIVAL OF STOCK EXCHANGES

Perhaps one of the largest indicators of change in China has been the return of stock exchanges, abolished soon after the founding of the People's Republic to eliminate speculation and profiteering. All that was forgotten when the central leadership realized what a handy device bond and share issues could be in raising foreign capital for financially hard-pressed state enterprises and relieving the central government of the funding responsibility. Now there is no stopping the craze. In 1993, there were at least a dozen books on display in Beijing shops explaining the operations of a stock exchange and how to play the market. The capital's first school geared specifically to the stock market was also opened with great fanfare. In southern China, large crowds gather outside brokerage firms to monitor electronic displays of stock-price movements. In Shanghai, anyone with a telephone can dial a local number to obtain the same information.

China started to issue State Treasury Bonds in 1981 to make up for insufficient government revenues. Other types of bonds and shares followed in the ensuing years. The first experiments met a very cautious public response, understandable after decades of being bombarded with propaganda about the evils of capitalism. Faced with such reluctance, staff of the first enterprises offering shares had to go from door to door trying to promote them, but were still only able to sell about half the total issues. But the situation changed when it was announced that interest and dividends being paid by the Development Bank, the first institution to sell stocks in Shenzhen, had reached 30 per cent, four times higher than bank savings deposits. The news spread like wildfire through the country and business picked up almost overnight – the price of Development Bank stock rising from 20 to 180 Yuan in a very short time. It is acceptable under socialism to own shares, people began to tell each other; 'a stock system does not mean privatization', became the catchcry.

In 1988, the authorities gave the green light to the trading of securities at officially-controlled exchanges. Some 800 million Yuan ($120 million) worth of securities was swapped in that year and the volume soared to 2.5 billion Yuan in 1989 and 10 billion in 1990. These securities, however, were circulated only among Chinese groups with foreigners specifically denied access. A report in an official newspaper declared: 'The stock market concept has filtered throughout the country. It not only helps to bring cash back into circulation and trim the country's budget deficit but also improves the distribution of resources.'[5]

Shanghai, which typified the twin sins of speculation and profiteering more than any other city in China under the old regime, was first in the field with its own stock exchange although only a handful of companies were officially listed. By August 1991 it had grown enough to launch its own index. Shenzhen began in December 1990 in a humble way with shares in five local companies being quoted, but after a rocky few months, it began to outshine Shanghai perhaps due to the dazzling performance of the local economy.

When it finally decided to open up to foreign investors, the central government moved in a typically cautious way by creating two types of Yuan-denominated shares — A-class available only to Chinese citizens, and B-class available only to foreigners and paid for with foreign currency. The two were not interchangeable, but provided equal rights to their holders. B-shareholders were allowed to take hard currency out of the country at exchange rates set by official foreign exchange swap centres if they sold stocks through domestic securities dealers. Shanghai Vacuum was the first to be opened up to foreign investors in this way.

To trade in B shares, investors have to use a foreign brokerage house or a Chinese securities firm approved by the Shanghai and Shenzhen branches of the PBOC. Foreign brokers originally could not deal direct but were required to execute transactions through a local agent. In 1993, Shanghai permitted a limited number of major overseas dealers to trade directly as long as they took over a seat of Chinese brokers. A total of 23 firms were admitted: Jardine Fleming, Standard Chartered, Baring, Hung Kai Securities, Tung

Shing, Peregrine and Hoare Govett Asia from Hong Kong, Kim Eng Securities, OCBC Securities and Sasoon of Singapore, Nomura International (HK) Ltd, Kankaku Securities and Yamaichi International of Japan, Barclays, Credit Lyonnais, Morgan, Smith New Court and Wardley James Capel of Britain, PEI Securities of the Netherlands, Pacific Capital of Taiwan, Bockook of South Korea, SCBI Securities of Switzerland, and Merrill Lynch of the United States. Hoare Govett Asia also became the first foreign dealer on the Shenzhen Stock Exchange, and a great many more were reported to be queuing up for early admission.

All are really investing in the future because there is not much business to be done at present. Shanghai had only 13 B-class shares on its board, and Shenzhen 19, and trading volume on most days has been very thin. One of the key factors in this poor performance was the difficulty investors experienced in obtaining adequate information on a company's financial performance to make a considered judgement. Some enterprises still use a financial and accounting system that is incompatible for international practice, making it very hard for foreigners to read their financial statements. Some enterprises are also accused of presenting false reports. Webs of graft and corruption have been uncovered tying officials and banks involved in issuing stocks. This problem, however, is now being tackled with a temporary new law to ban insider trading by anyone working in securities or regulating the industry either directly or indirectly through third parties. The offering or receiving of bribes was also outlawed, with any organization found offering a bribe being banned from issuing bonds or conducting any securities-related business. Two new securities watchdogs were set up in 1993 – the State Council's Securities Policy Committee and the China Securities Regulatory Commission – armed with impressive powers on paper to punish wrongdoing. But at the time of writing, permanent regulations on the operation of the securities industry were still bogged down in the bureaucratic morass.

In an effort to promote more enthusiasm in the B-share market, the securities industry was considering the possibility of allowing companies to launch American Depository Receipts (ADRs) – bank-issued negotiable certificates for shares of foreign-based corporations held in a custodian bank (they are a popular financial tool used to attract foreign capital because the investors do not have to go abroad to buy foreign-issued shares). Shenzhen, meanwhile, began quoting its B shares in US dollars rather than Yuan to help overseas investors hedge foreign-exchange risks.

Another possibility is that the government will open B shares to domestic investors. Li Yining, who heads the government committee drafting the permanent law, has said that '... I cannot see why Chinese investors should not buy B shares with foreign currency, since one of the purposes [for issuing them] is to raise much-needed hard currency for construction'. If the government took the step it would only be legitimizing what already takes place, as many Chinese have found ways (eg: though relatives overseas) to bypass the restrictions. Analysts foresaw mixed blessings of an opening. The increased liquidity of the B shares would benefit foreigners holding stakes in the listed companies, but it could also introduce increased volatility given the free-wheeling behaviour demonstrated by domestic investors in A shares.

On the domestic side, stock fever led to bizarre and chaotic scenes. At first, because of the release of pent-up demand, stocks defied gravity – soaring into space and never coming down again. When reality finally returned and certain shares did slump, some unlucky investors lost heavily. A spate of suicides were reported. One such was Liu Xiaodong, 39, found dead with electric wires binding his wrists and a multi-functional socket on his chest. Two months before, Liu had used about 20,000 Yuan – including 13,500 Yuan borrowed from his father-in-law and neighbours – to buy shares issued by three companies, in the hopes of making a fortune. But the stock market plunged, resulting in the loss.

Meanwhile, Shenzhen, facing a situation were demand far outstripped supply, came up with the idea of making a lottery out of the allocation of the new shares up to a ceiling of $75 million permitted during the financial year. They printed five million application forms for sale at $15 apiece – the proceeds to go to local 'welfare spending' – with up to 10 forms available per customer on a first-come-first-served basis. Eventually, one-tenth of the applications chosen by lot would be entitled to buy up to 1,000 shares per form in the 14 companies that were being floated on the exchange during the year. The fact that the unlucky 90 per cent would lose their money, or that the identity of the 14 companies was not disclosed – thus making it impossible to determine their performance or prospects – did not seem to blunt the appetite of would-be investors, who poured into Shenzhen from across the nation. It was estimated that the city's two million population was temporarily swelled by another million as queues grew outside the numerous designated application points on the weekend of 8–9 August 1992. The result was chaos.

'Clutching wads of cash and dreaming of overnight riches, hundreds of thousands of would-be capitalists from across China engulfed the southern boom town for a slim chance of playing its new stock market. Exasperated police flailed away with electric cattle prods, bamboo canes and leather belts to try to control the huge crowds that gathered over two days outside 302 Shenzhen banks and brokerages.'[6]

'Tens of thousands of speculators rampaged through Shenzhen to denounce alleged corruption over share allocations. In some of the worst violence to hit China's brief but turbulent flirtation with stock market capitalism, protesters chanting 'down with corruption' kicked and beat plain-clothes police, set a van ablaze and overturned several vehicles. They were angry at reports that certain city officials were giving preferential access to share application forms to family members and friends. Near hysteria has gripped the industrial city ... invaded by a million potential capitalists trying to buy share application forms, egged on by official media reports of ordinary Chinese making fortunes in stock trading. Riot police fired at least 10 teargas shells in one part of the city... Police reported one person was crushed to death in the mayhem, although the authorities later denied anyone had been killed or seriously injured in the stampede for forms. Shanghai [stock exchange] trading has been marked by several stampedes, while two men were murdered earlier this year in Shenzhen as gangsters fought over positions in queues of share buyers. Shenzhen authorities later launched a series of swoops to arrest hundreds of gangsters in the special economic zone.'[7]

This demonstration of capitalism in action was further tarnished in the middle of 1993, when the central authorities revealed evidence that what the rioting mob had suspected – namely that the whole lottery process had been rigged by local officials smoothing the way for potential investors in return for a handsome golden thank-you – were true. Undeterred, however, Shanghai decided that it, too, would adopt a lottery system for the allocation of new share issues. But, learning from the Shenzhen experience, there would be no limit on the number of application forms offered to would-be investors, and strict measures were promised to ensure that the forms were not transferred or traded on the black market.

The uncertainties of dabbling in Chinese stocks and bonds was amply demonstrated by what journalists dubbed the 'Great Wall Bubble'. The scandal in mid-1993 rocked the Chinese establishment and provided a horrifying reminder to an estimated 100,000 swindled investors, including some top officials, that money can be lost just as easily as it can be made. It raised serious questions about the flimsy laws and regulations covering the capital markets, along with weak enforcement and virtually no protection for investors. The Great Wall affair certainly hastened the departure of Li Guixian as central bank governor and his replacement by Zhu Rongji.

The scandal involved an estimated one billion in 'junk bonds' offering a stunning 24 per cent interest rate, twice the rate of government bonds. At the centre was a 39-year-old businessman, Shen Taifu, who raised the money by issuing bonds in his Great Wall Machinery and Electronics High Technology Corporation and allegedly squandered all the money on fast-living, including expensive houses, luxury cars and good food. In addition to Great Wall executives, more than 100 government officials were implicated, and some journalists were also arrested on accusations they had received payments or favours from the company in exchange for writing friendly articles in the official press.[see chapter eight for a discussion of this phenomenon.]

Several hundred companies had raised money by issuing private bonds, so that Great Wall was not doing anything unusual. The investment plan was officially approved through a licence from the State Administration of Science and Technology. Shen's bonds, in fact, did not attract much public interest at first. But then, he began selling them through dance hall girls and salesmen working on commission. In January 1993, Fei Xiaotong, a former vice-chairman of the National People's Congress, wrote a long commentary praising Great Wall. 'I feel their methods are novel, and the company has given me inspiration,' Fei gushed in the *People's Daily*. Bond holders, some of whom invested their entire life's savings, made much of official responsibility when the bubble burst. 'We believed the government. We believed the party newspaper. We didn't invest blindly but because the *People's Daily* told us it was a good idea,' said a retired electrician who had lost about $1350.

According to the government in a subsequent report, Shen had no intention of paying anyone back for their investment. Instead, money was transferred into his own and his wife's private bank accounts. He opened 120 subsidiaries across the country and ordered each to buy expensive cars, houses and carpets. He reportedly rented six hotel suites on a permanent basis and hired bodyguards for himself and his young son. In March, the government finally began suggesting that Shen's bonds were fraudulent. He was arrested at an airport just as he was trying to flee south under a false identity. When banks in Beijing froze the company accounts they discovered only a fraction of the raised capital still remained. The government subsequently promised irate investors partial repayment of the bonds, although it was unclear how much this would be.

Despite the concerns these scandals raise, a growing number of 'China Funds' have sprung up around the world to seek equity investment opportunities in China, and the Chinese themselves have not been slow to recognize the possibilities. An earlier chapter described the operations of CITIC, the Beijing-based investment conglomerate. In November 1993, one of its subsidiaries CITIC Australia joined with Hambros Australia in Sydney to launch a quoted investment vehicle to make direct equity investments in China. The new company will start in a modest way with the issue of 35 million A$1 shares. Twenty per cent of the capital raised will be invested in the Shanghai and Shenzhen markets, and another 30 per cent in Hong Kong, where an increasing number of mainland companies are seeking a listing.

Another possibility was offered by the China Aeronautical Technology Fund, with an initial capital of $111 million, established by China Aerospace Industrial Corp., an investment arm of the Ministry of Aeronautical and Aerospace Industries, to seek investments in various unlisted mainland enterprises. A spokesman said the fund was established initially to invest in 19 promising joint ventures supervized by the ministry. Capital gains would be realized through public listings and sales of stakes to corporate investors or direct investment funds after the enterprises had matured, the spokesman said.

To sum up: foreign interest in the fledgling stock markets is definitely growing. By the end of 1993, Western merchant banks alone had raised some $975 million to invest in shares in Shanghai and Shenzhen, accounting for about 13 per cent of the market capitalization of the two bourses. But it pays to be wary. Lack of acceptable accounting standards and a regulatory framework which offers protection to minority shareholders – which foreigners are by law – certainly requires caution.

'The law in China is still somewhat disorganized. The National People's Congress, the fairly tame parliament, passes laws; the State Council issues "decisions"; and government departments and agencies promulgate regulations. All have force of law, but their administration is capricious – party officials are wont to dabble – and their means of interpretation are far from clear. All this leads to an opaqueness in decision-making. One Western diplomat, talking about the way companies are chosen for [market] listing, observed: "Often it appears to have as much to do with the strength of a company's political connections as it does with the intrinsic nature of the business".'[8]

ACCOUNTANCY REFORMS

According to the Ministry of Finance, reform of China's accounting system is now in full swing. A red letter day was 1 July 1993, when the new Business Accounting Standards and the General Rules of Financial Affairs for Enterprises came into effect. This '... ended the time when the country had tens, if not hundreds, of accounting systems for enterprises managed by different government departments'.[9] Take the example of Shoudu Iron and Steel Co., an industrial group embracing many different sectors. Because each one of the supervisory ministries or agencies had different accounting requirements it proved impossible to produce a consolidated account and annual report. It also created numerous difficulties in gathering the accurate data on the various business activities to enable Shoudou to plan ahead. This problem surfaced in Shanghai in 1991 when the stock exchange there wanted to issue several B shares in Hong Kong. The plan had to be postponed as the statements and reports the Chinese side presented were '... incomprehensible to the Hong Kongers. The enterprises concerned had to spend a lot of money paying international accounting companies to re-make the statements and reports in an internationally-accepted form'.[10]

'One of the biggest changes brought by the new system is in allowing enterprises to be autonomous in setting their individual accounting items. They were no longer required, as for example, to have separate accounts for different government allocations or bank loans, and will be able to make their own decisions on how to use the funds. Enterprises will be strengthened as more money will be left with them for further development. For instance, accelerated depreciation rates will be adopted and the heavy levies on depreciation funds stopped. Interest on long-term loans for fixed assets will be included in production costs so that enterprises will be more capable of repaying bank loans. Enterprises may also have enlarged reserves for bad debts, business expansion, innovation and employees' welfare. These measures have greatly increased the cost accounts of enterprises.

'Shortage of funds is a major obstacle against the development of state firms as the government used to pay little attention to leaving sufficient money for them under the old system. Enterprises had to rely heavily on bank loans for their capital investment and even working capital. But the heavy interest burden usually prevents them from expanding production and being technically innovative. Although the new system, by increasing cost accounts, is expected to solve the problem in the long run, it will create a big difficulty of hidden losses during the transition period. Currently, about one-third of state firms are suffering from losses. But as the new system will raise production costs on a large scale, the number of loss-incurring companies will increase dramatically.

This is a left-over problem from the old system. 'Since production cost used to be artificially reduced in the books, the profit rates were usually exaggerated, which affected the state revenues,' said Ding Xuedong, a Ministry of Finance official. 'The new system may dramatically increase production costs of enterprises by billions of dollars.' The hidden losses are also revealed as huge amounts of asset losses failed to be taken into account in time due to the old way of accounting, such as unsaleable products, wasted equipment and bad debts.

'State enterprises tend to provide employees with cradle-to-grave welfare without considering their economic returns, and this has resulted in huge deficits in welfare reserves. Uncovering hidden losses is extremely unacceptable to managers, especially those contracted to achieve a certain amount of profit each year. The most important thing for them may be their "achievements", measured by the amount handed over to the government. In fact, a big proportion of the hidden losses result from the manager's pursuit of achievements. Many even choose to complete a contract at the cost of the firm's future development. Although the Ministry of Finance has made some compromises, such as allowing contracted firms to continue calculating their taxes and profits in the old way until their contracts end in 1995, the risk is still there of the new system failing to reach its goal.'[11]

Along with these reforms, a cadre of qualified chartered public accountants was in the process of being created. The profession only returned to China in 1981 after an absence of 30 years. By the end of 1992, there were an estimated 10,000 CPAs nationwide, but the government predicted a 10-fold increase by the end of the century. Vice Premier Zhu Rongji admitted that without the presence of registered CPAs, talk about changing governmental functions 'can only be empty verbiage'.[12]

Foreign accountancy firms began to return to China in the mid-1980s and most of the leading international names are now present in the various big cities. One difficulty they encountered, however, was their inability to open auditing and assets evaluation businesses. They were restricted to providing consulting services or doing business in cooperation with their Chinese counterparts. However, the final auditing verification report had to be signed by a Chinese CPA.

That was in the process of changing as this book was being written. A new law went into effect on 1 January 1994, allowing foreigners to obtain Chinese accountancy qualifications. But this will be based on reciprocity. If the home country of the foreign CPA allows the qualification of Chinese accountants, China will do likewise.[13]

FUTURES MARKETS

Finally in this chapter, I would like to look another part of the financial revolution – the growth of futures trading. By the end of 1993, China had established 12 'State-class' futures markets adhering to international operating practices. Some had already linked themselves with the international market. In east China's Jiangsu Province, the Nanjing Petroleum Exchange has become part of the world market through the dissemination of quotations provided by the internal news agencies Reuters and AP-Dow Jones (the exchange is one of three in the country – along with Beijing and Shanghai – dealing in crude oil, gasoline and gas-oil; Beijing, however, is concentrating more on forward contracts than futures trading). Members of the Shanghai Metals Exchange can also directly trade metals futures internationally through links with London and New York. Fifty Chinese brokerage firms have been established nation-wide to provide an international service in farm produce, metals, energy, foreign exchange and options. Meanwhile, the Shanghai Cereals, Oils and Foodstuffs Exchange, the first in the country to deal in oils and foodstuffs, is not only linked internationally through Dow Jones' Telerate Financial Information Network and Reuters' financial services, but has also established its own domestic satellite communications network to promote more efficient internal dealing.

The Shanghai Foreign Exchange Futures Market has a large number of foreign-funded domestic and foreign financial institutions as members. Most of the 200-plus futures brokerage companies in the east and south China coastal areas have foreign participation .

In November 1993, a comprehensive futures exchange began operating in Beijing in a bid to standardize the fast-growing market. It was divided into four 'pools' covering agricultural products, metals, fibres and energy and chemical products, with a capacity in each of 100 members. Exchange President Qiao Gang said it had applied for permission to conduct trading in financial products. Trading of futures options, was also under consideration. The exchange would release its quotations via the Associated Press and Reuters, and was seeking wider cooperation and exchange of information with foreign futures exchanges and companies. The latter would be welcome to become exchange members when the time was ripe, Qian said.

Exchanges are being opened up rapidly to cover most major commodities. These include a non-ferrous metals exchange in Shenzhen, a timber market in Harbin and what is claimed to be the world's first exchange exclusively devoted to coal in Shanghai. The explosive growth, however, has, as in other areas of financial development, led to fears of confusion and underhand dealings. In late 1993, therefore, the government began preparing for the establishment of a futures regulatory body probably modelled on the Securities Regulatory Commission, set up to strengthen control over the fledgling stock markets. At present the overstretched State Administration for Industry and Commerce is responsible for the registration and supervision of futures companies.

In late 1992, 12 state-owned commodities and materials companies got together to form China International Futures Corp. (CIFCO) in Beijing to begin operating as a trading consortium. The corporation now dominates the plethora of small domestic exchanges and actively trades futures in the United States, London, Singapore, Japan and Hong Kong. In December 1993, it applied for membership of the three biggest American exchanges – the Chicago Mercantile Exchange, the Chicago Board of Trade and New York Commodity Exchange – and indicated that it would also like a presence on the London Metals Exchange.

FOOTNOTES
1. For more details on the roles of the different banks, please see appendices.
2. *Far Eastern Economic Review*, 14 Jan. 1993.
3. Ibid.
4. Aug. 24, 1993.
5. *China Daily*, 5 May 1991.
6. *London Times*, 10 Aug. 1992.
7. *Financial Times*, 10 Aug. 1992.
8. *Financial Times*, 19 Sept. 1993.
9. *China Daily*, 1 July 1993.
10. *Beijing Review*, 7 Dec. 1992.
11. *China Daily*, 1 July 1993.
12. *Beijing Review*, 7 Dec. 1992.
13. *Beijing Review*, 29 Nov. and *Business Weekly*, 28 Nov. 1993.

12 Taxes and taxation policy

> **KEY POINTS**
>
> This chapter will briefly look at:
> - What kinds of taxation do foreign businesses have to pay on their investments in China?
> - What tax-related preferential policies are available for the foreign-invested enterprise?
> - What changes are underway in the tax structure at both the national and local level?

WHAT DO I HAVE TO PAY?

FIRSTLY, let us deal with the types of tax the foreign investor is expected to pay. Basically these are:

(a) *Foreign-funded Enterprise income tax*, applicable to all operations other than joint ventures, begins at 20 per cent on the first 250,000 Yuan of taxable income and rises by five percentage points over the following 750,000 Yuan, with 40 per cent being levied on income remaining beyond one million Yuan. There is also a local tax of 10 per cent, although small-scale production operations (taxable income below one million Yuan or in what may be considered low-profit occupations may be exempted. FEIT returns are filed quarterly and tax payments made within 15 days of the end of each quarter. The returns may be filed on the basis of actual profits in the quarter or estimated either by taking one quarter of the budgeted profit for the current year or one quarter of the taxable income of the preceding year.

(b) *Joint Venture income tax* is 30 per cent assessed on worldwide net income after deduction of costs, expenses, depreciation and losses; there is also a local income tax of three per cent. The tax returns and payments are handled in the same way as FEIT.

(c) *Personal income tax*. All foreigners should pay income tax, as long as they reside in China for a full year, for income gained within China as well as that remitted to China from a foreign source. For any period from 90 days but less than a full year, tax is paid only on Chinese-source income. Basic rates start at five per cent, after a deduction of 800 Yuan, and go up to a maximum of 45 per cent. Wages, a daily living allowance including meals, cost of living allowance, foreign service premium, royalties, interest, dividends and bonuses from investments, income from property leasing are all taxable. An individual must register with the Tax Bureau within 30 days of entering China and make monthly tax returns and payments.

(d) *Customs duties*.

(e) *Industrial and Commercial Consolidated Tax*. This is a turnover tax levied on all firms and individuals who engage in industrial production, purchase of agricultural products, communications, trade, retail business, transportation and services. It is imposed on agricultural products at the stage of production and is imposed on imported goods at the stage of importation. When the goods are subsequently sold, the tax is imposed again on turnover. For those engaged in communication, transport and other services, the tax is imposed on revenue received. There are about 40 different tax rates, the top rate being 69 per cent on cigarettes. Most other goods are taxed at rates ranging from five to 15 per cent.

(f) *Real-estate tax*.

(g) *Licence fee for cars and ships*.

Foreign Enterprises income tax is levied on establishments set up in China by foreign entities for independent operation, including wholly foreign-owned enterprises, foreign entities engaged in cooperative production or operation of business with Chinese entities, and foreign entities that do not have establishments in China but are receiving dividends, interest, rentals, royalties or other income originating in China. In paying the tax, the foreign-funded enterprise may enjoy some preferential treatment. In general, the government encourages enterprises who adopt advanced technologies and equipment, or exports all or most of their products. The preferential policies are as follows:

(i) The enterprise income tax of the following enterprises which are operated in the SEZs or ETDZs, and are productive enterprises with foreign investment are levied at a reduced rate of 15 per cent (rather than 24 per cent). They should be engaged in machinery, electronics, energy industries (excluding oil and gas exploitation), metallurgical, chemical and construction materials; light industries; textiles and packaging; medical equipment and pharmaceuticals; agriculture, forestry, animal husbandry and water conservation; construction, transportation (excluding passenger transportation); information and consultation industries; maintenance of sophisticated instruments; and any others approved by the State Council.

The enterprise income tax of the following foreign-funded enterprises is also levied at 15 per cent for productive enterprises with foreign investment in the coastal economic regions or in the old urban areas of the SEZs and ETDZs who are engaged in the following projects: technology and knowledge-intensive projects; projects whose investment exceeds US$30 million and whose repayment period is long; projects involving energy, transportation and harbour construction. Sino-Foreign joint ventures engaged in the construction of harbours and ports. Second, foreign-funded banks, Sino-foreign joint venture banks and other financial institutions set up in the SEZs and regions approved by the State Council. The condition is that the capital poured by the foreign investor or the operational capital of the branch bank allocated by the general foreign bank exceeds US$10 million and the operational period is longer than 10 years. Third, productive enterprises with foreign investment set up in the Pudong New Economic Zone and those engaged in energy and transportation projects, such as the construction of airports, ports, railways, expressways and power-generation plans. Fourth, enterprises with foreign investment who are confirmed as high-tech enterprises and located in the new technical industrial zones approved by the State Council. Fifth, the foreign-invested enterprises who are engaged in projects encouraged by the State.

(ii) For the productive enterprises with foreign investment whose period is longer than 10 years, they are exempt from income tax for the first and second years when they gain profit, after which they pay a half-rate in the third and fourth years.

(iii) For Sino-foreign joint ventures who are engaged in the construction of harbours and ports and whose operational period is longer than 15 years, when they begin to make a profit are, with tax bureau approval, exempt from income tax for the first five years; their liability is reduced to half from the sixth to 10th years.

(iv) In the Hainan Special Economic Zone and Shanghai Pudong New Economic Zone, foreign-invested enterprises who are engaged in infrastructure facilities, such as the construction of airports, ports, harbours, railways, expressways, power plants and water conservation projects, can enjoy the same preferential treatment as described in the previous paragraph.

(v) For foreign-invested enterprises engaged in the service sector of the SEZs, with an investment exceeding $5 million and an operational period of 10 years or longer, tax exemption is available for the first year, with a half-rate operating in the second and third years.

(vi) In the high-tech industrial development zones approved by the State Council, if Sino-foreign joint ventures are confirmed as high technical or new technical enterprises and their operational period is longer than 10 years, they can apply to the local tax bureau for tax exemption in the first two years they begin to make profits.

(vii) For export-oriented enterprises, after the lawful period of exemption and reduction of income tax, the tax rate is reduced to half if the export value is more than 70 per cent of annual output value.

(viii) Technically-advanced enterprises operated by foreign investors can also qualify for three years of half-rate tax after the lawful period of exemption has expired.

(ix) For foreign-funded enterprises engaged in agriculture, forestry and animal husbandry, or who are set up in economically backward inland regions, can, after the lawful period of exemption and reduction of enterprise income tax, apply for their income tax liability to be reduced by 15-30 per cent for the following 10 years.

Benefits are also available as regards payment of the General Industrial and Commercial Tax.

(a) In joint ventures, the machinery, equipment, components and other materials needed for the construction of plants and the installation and fixing of machinery which is invested by foreign investors, and the imported machinery, components and other materials within the quota of investment, are free of commercial and industrial tax. Vehicles imported for self-use or as part of the productive operation, and office materials, plus machinery and equipment for undersea oil exploration are also exempt.

(b) The export of their own products, except for crude oil, finished oil products and other products prohibited by the State Council, are exempt. However, if the products are for domestic sale, the enterprise may still apply for a reduction of the tax for a certain period during the initial operating period if it faces some financial difficulties.

(c) Most products made by foreign-funded enterprises in SEZs for sale within the zones are tax free. However, mineral oil, cigarettes and wine are taxed at half the normal rate. If companies have difficulty paying the tax in the initial operating period, the SEZ administrators have the right to decide on exemption and reduction for a certain period.

(d) For enterprises engaged in commerce, transportation and other service industries in SEZs, their industrial and commercial tax liability is levied at three per cent.

PAST TAX STRUCTURE

To understand the changes being introduced to the tax system, it will be helpful to look back at the old structure. In a nutshell, it was complicated, multi-tiered and a mess. When the switch to a market economy was decided, an attempt was made to reform taxation, but they only served to add to the complications.

Prior to 1978, under a planned economy, life was fairly simple. All enterprises were owned by the people. Incomes were turned over to the state largely in the form of profits, and only a small proportion was tax. The State kept a tight control on revenues and expenditures in what was known as the 'big pot' distribution system. But once the market reforms began to take effect, the industrial structure splintered into publicly-owned corporations, private and individually-operated concerns, exclusively foreign-owned and Sino-foreign joint ventures. With even the state firms gradually assuming management independence, the 'big pot' concept was under threat. Between 1979 and 1982, the central government tried out a new system of taxation in 456 state-owned companies in 18 regions of the country. They began to pay taxes instead of profits to the state and were able to retain their after-tax profits for use as they saw fit. After 1984, the new industrial and commercial tax system was introduced nation-wide, with 30 different taxes being assessed.

Major changes brought about by the reforms included:
- The original industrial and commercial tax was sub-divided into product, value-added and business taxes.
- A resource tax was collected for the extraction of crude oil, natural gas and coal.
- An urban maintenance and construction tax was added, and taxes on real estate and land use, driving licence tax on vehicles and boats were restored.
- Income and regulatory taxes began to be collected from profitable state-owned firms.

China also signed agreements to avoid double taxation with more than 30 countries including, Britain, Japan, the United States, France, Germany, Belgium, the Netherlands, Italy, Malaysia, Thailand and New Zealand.

Officials argued that the new system had had a positive impact on the Chinese economy, but gradually weaknesses began to appear. Eventually, it was conceded that the tax structure had not been well thought out and was, in fact, an inefficient way of raising revenue. There was also a great deal of inequality which actually hurt the state enterprises, the backbone of the economy. For instance, large and medium-sized firms were expected to pay a tax rate of 55 per cent, which, coupled with the handover of a portion of their profits, meant these companies were shouldering an inordinate share of the taxation burden and hindering their growth. Finally, the ability of taxation to adjust income inequalities and the overall scope of the system were inconsistent with the overall development of a market economy. What was needed was a simple, unified tax system that allowed everyone to compete on an equal basis.

In June 1993, Jin Xin, Director of the State Administration of Taxation, set out the basic steps of tax reform to be undertaken over the next year or so. The key characteristics were to be:

1. Turnover and income taxes will continue to be the main sources of tax revenue. Turnover will be taxed at a high rate for a considerable length of time.

2. A unified income tax law will be applied to all domestic state-owned, collectively-owned, private, cooperative and shareholding enterprises.

3. A unified turnover tax will be gradually implemented for both domestic and foreign-funded enterprises, and the Industrial and

Commercial Consolidated Tax will be abolished. Individual income tax will be the same for Chinese, foreigners and all enterprises, regardless of whether the funding comes from domestic or overseas sources.

4. The distribution of earnings between the state and enterprises will be standardized via income tax. The present form of contract responsibility will be phased out.

5. Turnover tax will be collected with tax included in prices. Taxes not included in the calculated prices will not be implemented.

6. The enterprise income tax will be proportional, while the individual income tax will be progressive on income in excess of specific amounts.

7. Value-added tax will be collected at various stages from production to circulation and from wholesale to retail markets. A product tax will be levied. These two taxes will be collected together, the value-added tax functioning as a general regulator, and the product tax as a special regulator.

8. The tax base will be expanded and freed from any reductions. The rates stated in taxation rules and regulations shall apply to all taxable income.

9. The tax rates will be raised or lowered in a timely manner according to the demands of the market economy so as to reduce the gap between the nominal tax rate and the real tax-bearing capacity. This will improve the tax authority's ability to control the market and will ensure that the burden on individual taxpayers is reasonable.

10. The tax system will be simplified and the number of taxable items reduced. The number of industrial and commercial taxes will be reduced from the present 30 to about 20.

Taxes for state-owned, collective and private enterprises will be combined into a single income tax collected equally for all companies using domestic funds, with a basic rate set at 33 per cent. A new tax system will be introduced made up of value-added tax, product tax and business tax. It will be adjustable at two levels. the present individual income tax law will be amended so that it applies equally to all individuals, regardless of nationality. Finally, Jin reported, the tax management system will be reformed, especially through the expansion of the scale of local taxation. Taxes on land and property, and a considerable part of the business and resources taxes will be left with local authorities. This is designed to channel huge amounts of cash from the developed coastal areas to the underdeveloped inland provinces, and from the manufacturing to basic industries.[1]

Having set the new taxes, however, Beijing still has to collect them. The central government lacks the sophisticated mechanisms and manpower required to impose a strict collection regime. Another problem, as outlined in the previous chapter, is a shortage of trained accountants. Tax avoidance and evasion is widespread. Competition between the centre and provinces in tax collection – the two are often engaged in a struggle for a share of the revenues – is another factor bedevilling efforts to bolster central coffers.

The authorities appear to be targeting foreign-funded operations in particular. According to an official report,[2] the State Auditing Administration planned to use new powers to catch tax cheats and '... chart a healthy direction for foreign investment. State auditors are going to get tough with Sino-foreign joint ventures and cooperative firms that are linked with State enterprises.' The report said that blatant tax evasion and squandering of state-owned capital were common occurrences in such joint ventures. Some foreigners acted out of ignorance, but others were 'determined to exploit the loopholes in China's imperfect legal system'. The Commission planned to check whether state capital was appreciating in the enterprises, on the ratio between assets and liability, and on profitability or losses. Beijing's taxation authority, meanwhile, announced a new special registration system for the city's 7,000-plus overseas-funded firms as a means of filtering out those that had 'cheated the government under the preferential tax policies.'[3]

Another report stated: 'China has launched a crackdown on tax cheats, targeting fraudulent foreign investors, dishonest exporters and corrupt tax departments who deprive the government of millions of dollars. The government has cracked a major case of tax evasion by exporting companies that conspired with dishonest tax offices to gain illegal refunds that cost the state 200 million Yuan. In the first half of the year [1993], more than 40 companies conspired with 30 provincial tax administrators to get false tax receipts involving two billion Yuan. Last year, 151 companies issued false sales receipts worth more than five billion Yuan, defrauding the government of 200 million Yuan in wrongly issued refunds [introduced in 1985 to encourage trade growth]. An investigation shows that enterprises and foreign trade companies participating in this kind of crime are spread all over the country.' The report said that one particular worry is the overstating of the value of equipment imported by foreign investors as their contribution to a joint venture. An investigation of 1,000 different pieces of equipment, for example, had found that their value had been overstated by 23 per cent on average – inflating the subsidies and other preferential treatment they might receive. This can be crucial as it is estimated that 70 per cent of foreign investment in a dozen key sectors was in the form of goods and equipment.[4]

FOOTNOTES
1. Culled from the *People's Daily* and *Beijing Review*, 21 June 1993.
2. *Business Weekly*, 14 Feb. 1993.
3. *China Daily*, 20 Aug. 1993.
4. Xinhua News Agency, 13 July 1993.

13 The challenges that lie ahead

KEY POINTS

This final chapter will look at the challenges facing China, namely:
- What sort of society is likely to emerge in the dash for economic modernization.
- The prospects of Communism withering away. But will it be replaced by what the West would call 'democracy'?
- The difficulties the central government faces in maintaining control over the country at large.
- The prospects for preventing the economy overheating.
- The difficulties in creating a domestic trade regime that would allow China to enter GATT.
- The challenge of the Yuan – how to develop it into a convertible currency.
- Finding China's rightful place in the world. The challenge of locking it into an enduring, stable international order.
- The new diplomatic alliances that could shape China in the twenty-first century.

THE CEMENT CRUMBLES

THIS BOOK is intended primarily as a business guide and not one that examines the Chinese political system. Nevertheless, anyone wishing to have any sort of dealings with China has to understand something of the political complexities that have emerged in the 1990s. China's development as a safe place in which to invest will be determined by a number of domestic and international political factors which need to be examined, at least in brief.

The first thing to be understood is that the cement which has held modern Chinese society together, whether it be party edicts from the centre, blind faith in Maoism or whatever, has begun to crumble. According to Singapore's elder statesman Lee Kuan Yew, who has excellent contacts with the Chinese leadership, the country's present rulers are 'only nominal' Communists. 'Very few believe in Marxist-Leninism as the way to the future. Their legitimacy for being in power is the progress they are achieving for China through their open-door policies and free-market reforms.'

So, if the leadership does not believe in Communism, there is little need for the rank-and-file to pay more than lip service to it. In private, many Chinese will not tell you that they believe the progress that has been made in recent years occurred *despite* the Party not *because* of it. 'Think where we would have been without it,' muttered one critic I met in a Beijing park. Yet, in some ways, this collapse of belief has created a unhealthy moral vacuum. In the absence of religion, there is a need for some sort of code of ethics. Confucius once filled this requirement, but was one of the victims of the Cultural Revolution. China today is essentially an amoral country. The surface egalitarianism that prevailed during the Mao years has been abandoned in a headlong rush towards acquisition. Those whose business it is to follow the undercurrents of Chinese life closely say there is rampant abuse; blatant corruption that has always existed at the top has now filtered down to the general public.

Even organs of law and order are involved. There have been widespread tales and rumours of police forces which have become a law unto themselves. There have been executions without trial, people who have been shot within minutes of being charged with a crime. There was, for example, a hotel worker who was accused of stealing from a guest. Three hours after his arrest he was shot and his picture was posted in the staff room as an example to others. There was also the case of a Hong Kong businessman who had no passport and only travel documents showing his right to live in Hong Kong, who was kidnapped by the provincial security organization in northern China while on a business trip. At the time of writing, the man had been held for more than two years because his family insisted it could not pay the demanded ransom of $1 million. A family member who went to the town where the businessman was being held to try and negotiate his release was warned that if he returned he would be killed. This is purely anecdotal evidence which suggests that anarchy is developing. In some ways it is reminiscent of the 1920s and 1930s when warlords emerged in various parts of China to bring great misery to the countryside. The cases mentioned inevitably are snippets because Communist China does not go into for a great deal of public self-flagellation unless there are strong political reasons to do so. Nevertheless, the leadership has admitted the existence of widespread corruption as discussed briefly in an earlier chapter.

'There are laws in China but no law,' is a well-known saying among Westerners reflecting a real problem foreign lawyers have in trying to pursue cases where companies or government bodies have abused some sort of agreement or contract they find it very difficult indeed to gain any sort of redress. According to one senior lawyer: 'In my own experience, certain bodies have lied blatantly. They delay and obfuscate. They transfer assets out of a company if it is being challenged so that if a legal action is brought it has no way of offering redress. The day after the case is abandoned the money is likely to be back in the company accounts.'

Above all, it should be understood that government power is absolute only in theory. It is true that, in many matters, a one-party central government can be implacably determined if thwarted, particularly if an individual or relatively small group is involved (hence the alleged individual cases of human rights cases involving dissidents which have been given so much publicity in the West).In major matters it can force everyone into line and can even control a great many aspects of its citizens' everyday lives with considerable success. But the government of a sprawling country such as China, or any other which is run by an entrenched and largely unaccountable bureaucracy, may have a difficult time indeed in securing day-to-day obedience from its civil servants. Things becomes even more pronounced the further one moves away from the capital, as petty functionaries were very much aware under Imperial rule.

Regulations are misunderstood, intentionally or not; a particular rule is conveniently considered not applicable because of supposed special conditions. A friend in higher office will protect against troubles if rules are not followed; and, with no agency outside the jurisdiction of the party to blow the whistle in any decisive way, the chances are slim that anyone can object successfully to subversion of official orders for the purpose of gaining personal power or profit. The freewheeling wilfulness of officials is seen in many other aspects of life as well. The combinations and permutations of personalities, interests, opportunities, loyalties and objectives, and so on can be dizzying.

Decentralization in recent years has drastically reduced the central government's monopoly of economic power and weakened its power to control. Localities are forging ahead eager for profits – typified by Shanghai, with 13 million people, determined to become an economic hub of the new Pacific era and bitterly resentful of having to send too much of its money to Beijing. When the economy threatened meltdown in early 1993, the centre had to send out hit squads of ministerial enforcers to try and persuade recalcitrant provincial authorities to toe the line and accept a Beijing-imposed credit crunch. As far as the latter were concerned, there was no economic overheating in their area, so why should they slow down? They have been encouraged in their resistance by the fact that much of the feverish investment activity which led to overheating was perpetrated by corporations affiliated with senior cadres, military officers and their offspring.

But despite all the criticism of the Communist party, one still has to ask: what, for the moment, is the alternative? And the answer is that in a vast country like China, with so many regional rivalries (at least eight distinct markets with differing dialects, climate, culture, diet and ways of life), there simply is no alternative. There is, in fact, probably a very good case to be made for a strong government. This was certainly the thrust of a report produced by two leading scholars to chart the nation's future path.[1] Well, they would say that, wouldn't they? Indeed they would; but there is a lot to be said for the arguments put forward by the two scholars to back up their contention that giving the provinces their head has caused more problems than it solved.

'By their nature, unregulated market systems pay little or no heed to such strategic areas as basic industries, health and education, scientific and technological research, and the preservation of the environment and natural resources. China has reasons for requiring a strong central government. These include such problems as a bloated population, environmental deterioration, poor infrastructure, increasing unemployment and the widening income gaps between regions, individuals and urban and rural areas.'[2]

The fiscal responsibility system adopted in the 1980s invigorated local economies, but at the expense of the central coffers. The revenue element of gnp fell from 31 per cent in 1978 to 14 per cent in 1992 as a result of this, as well as massive tax evasion, cheating and 'the wanton promises made by local governments to attract foreign investors'. The scholars warned that, '... it would cost the country dear if people believed the market economy cleared them to indulge in tactics like undisciplined speculation in real estate and securities, tax fraud, regional protectionism and bad local tax policies'. They stressed they were not advocating a return to a planned economy, but merely that China could not afford to drift into a market economy without a strong hand on the tiller.

According to the Beijing-based *Guangming Daily*, the economic reforms have revealed that what is really lacking in China at present is a sound legal system that provides a set of rules and norms to which people in various sectors could work under public supervision. It cited some examples of the problems that had arisen through the development of a market economy that have created an unhealthy worship of money.

'More brand-name and quality products have entered the marketplace. But more counterfeit and inferior ones have also appeared to reap quick profits. The increase in moonlighting has enabled many people to make full use of their skills and increase their income. However, some workers have become less efficient on their main jobs and some only put in half-hearted effort, reserving their talents for their second, more lucrative jobs. Hospitals have improved service. Today, people can request respected specialists for operations providing they can pay what the doctors demand. As a result, many people are excluded from high-quality medical care because they are unable to afford the extra charges. Some members of the media are paid to carry reports that mislead the public. And a few state schools are enrolling as many self-financing students as possible, while paying little attention to improving teaching standards [the teachers are also moonlighting]. Seeing such unfamiliar problems in the country, some people are warning that the economy is booming but professional ethics are sliding.'[3]

WHITHER DEMOCRACY?

Trying to make sense of modern Chinese politics, one writer commented:

'There are no easy ways to characterise politics in China as "democratic" or "totalitarian" or as a struggle between "revolutionaries" and "pragmatists", or see the realm of politics as limited only to the institutions, procedures or personnel of government and party. Politics as the Chinese experience it is the complex reality of a people with a long tradition and intense revolutionary experience and still living through a process characterized by personal and group conflict as well as by sudden swells of mass imput. It is a drama that links every-day life to history, personal values to public behaviour, and public behaviour to an actively pursued vision of the ideal community.'[4]

This is certainly applicable when it comes to the question of whether or not there is a factional struggle underway in China. Many Chinese insist that the breakdown of the Beijing leadership into 'conservatives' (the black hats) and 'reformers' (the white hats) has more meaning for foreigners, who prefer arguing personalities to examining policies, than it does for them. Not only is it difficult to tell what colour the hats really are, but some in the bureaucracy seem to switch them frequently [if some reforms are in trouble]. And this has very little to do with whether the reforms in question are under attack from mean-spirited conservatives, but a lot to do with the fact that the policies are seen not to be achieving the desired results. This largely stems from the fact that the economy, being neither market nor planned but a peculiar amalgam of the two, creates strains that are tolerable to some in the ruling group as growing pains but are seen by others as signs of serious trouble. Some Chinese commentators argue that the differences of opinion within the Communist Party of China are no greater and no more damaging than the wide differences that often appear between the so-called 'wings' of the political parties in Britain and the United States, for example.

'As in many other countries, officials who wear black hats on one issue may wear white on another; or they may change their views or change sides completely on a given issue without being factionalists or villains. The Chinese have a great traditional preference for consensus wherever policy, so they see only normal differences within the leadership concerning the concrete steps to be taken in the process of reform, such as the appropriate speed of reform of the priorities of development. Given the painful lessons of the Cultural Revolution and the flat failure of the leftist economic policies before that, only the most die-hard old-line communist would oppose economic reform.'[5]

Looking at the rapid pace of capitalist-style reforms, one might be tempted to think that, despite the desire of the Beijing leadership to maintain the political status quo, things will have to change. But will the end result be democracy – or what the West regards as democracy? Any businessman entering the Chinese market today believing that this is the case, would do well to listen to the words of caution offered by Singapore Prime Minister Goh Chok Tong at a 1993 international seminar in Tokyo on developments in the Asia-Pacific region. One key interest for the Chinese leadership was certainly the preservation of a culture which emphasized strong political control, blending nationalism with self-interest, Goh observed. This applied both to the old and new leadership:

'The new generation of Chinese leaders, like the previous generation, will want a strong government that can maintain stability and order. The new leaders are better educated, more market-oriented and pragmatic. But they are not closet democrats. They do not want China to descend into chaos, and neither does the rest of Asia. China will evolve; change is inevitable. As Communist ideology withers away in the consciousness of the Chinese people and leadership, and the economy becomes more complex, a looser more differentiated political system may develop. But it will not be 'democracy' as the West hopes. Unlike the Russians, East Europeans or Latin Americans, the Chinese have never had any wish to be considered Westerners.

'As China's economy develops, with better communications, education and openness, I believe that conditions will improve, as they already have. We must encourage this with patience, sophistication and realism. We should understand, however, that Chinese leaders suspect that the West wants to use human rights as a tool to pressure them to change their political system. If the West gives them cause to believe that this is true, it will give a sharper and more xenophobic edge to Chinese nationalism. The

Chinese leaders could react in many ways that would make life extremely uncomfortable for all of us.'

A demonstration of insecurity in high places emerged in October 1993, when members of the Standing Committee of the Politburo attending a conference on state security in Beijing were told that despite a relaxation of international tensions, there was no peace under heaven and instability was on the increase. Because China had been at peace for a long time, some Chinese did not understand the need for vigilance and turned a blind eye to spies and foreign enemies. A few even became traitors. A commentary in the *People's Daily* explained to readers why they needed to worry:

'The hostile forces outside our country have never stopped endangering the safety of our country. They take advantage of our policies of reform and openness to get hold of our political, economic and scientific secrets through different channels and try all means to infiltrate, split and damage us. If we lose vigilance and let them succeed, the safety of our country will not be ensured.'[6]

In the spirit of vigilance, the party acted to protect its long-standing monopoly on information – regarded as a key element in retaining power. New regulations were published banning the sale of the satellite dishes that had been bringing into the homes of so many Chinese the subversive news broadcasts of CNN and the BBC World Service, not to mention seamy pop videos on MTV. Receiving foreign satellite broadcasts had been forbidden since 1990, but the authorities neglected to ban the sale of dishes. People bought them in droves, and dishes began to adorn buildings even in the poorer provinces. In many blocks of flats, families pooled their money to buy a dish. The new regulations banned ownership of satellite dishes, except for those who can prove that they need one to boost their television reception and those required to watch satellite transmissions for their work (eg: state-run news organizations and foreign affairs departments). In the improbable event that these regulations are rigorously enforced, unlike so many others in China, they will condemn the Chinese once more to stultifying evenings of China Central Television. They will also present countless people with the problem of what to do about an embarrassingly large lump of illegal metal on their balconies or rooftops. The regulations did not make clear what will happen to existing dishes, nor to the many prosperous dish salesmen, who were hoping for the removal of the 1990 ban on receiving foreign broadcasts, and were unprepared for this new act of censorship. The authorities, of course, did not use the nasty word 'censorship'. One official told *China Daily* that 'the dishes are detrimental to the environment'. The *People's Daily*, more frankly, said the ban was intended to 'further the construction of socialist spiritual civilization'.

But the Party was not united on the issue of continued tight controls. A confidential Communist Party document prepared by a senior cadre in Beijing argued that a crackdown on satellite dishes was justified because they could be used to import pornography or reactionary programmes. But at the same time, another briefing paper prepared by the Shanghai authorities took the opposite view, arguing that if China was to achieve development goals it must give its people access to instant information and embrace new technologies like satellite television. There was also the paradox posed by the fact that the Army General Staff Department and the Ministry of Radio, Film and Television both turned a good profit by selling satellite equipment to the public, while the Ministry of Electronics operated a factory in Gansu province that had only, weeks before the ban, announced plans for production of 70,000 dishes a year. This typifies the ideological schizophrenia that exists in China's ruling circles today.

It is hard to see how the Party could keep the lid on the information revolution without damaging the very process of economic development. Fax machines are everywhere, even in private homes and direct-dial international telephones are multiplying much more quickly than the number of state security employees who bug such calls. The number of long-distance calls doubled from 1989 to 1991 when 1.7 billion were recorded. Computers are spreading as well, so that a growing number of people can communicate via electronic bulletin boards and electronic mail. Young people exchange information with Chinese students studying in the US – like the one developed a couple of years ago that appears on a screen to ask whether the computer operator likes Prime Minister Li Peng. If the person at the keyboard says no, regular work can continue. If the person says he likes the prime minister, the virus wipes out all the computer's memory. In Guangdong, families watch Hong Kong television sometimes with the convenience of officially-run cable systems. In Fujian province, millions of Chinese aim their antennae eastward and tune into Taiwan television news and other programmes. Short-wave radios have proliferated and are now an important source of news for dissidents and Communist officials alike, Chinese listen not only to the BBC and VOA but also to broadcasts from Australia, France and Taiwan.

THE DIPLOMATIC EQUATION

This concern about security confirms that China's place in the international community still has to be worked out. The two most important relationships will be with Japan and the United States. Interaction between Beijing, Tokyo and Washington increasingly will shape developments in the Asia-Pacific region. Management of this trilateral relationship will become a major focus of international concern, just as East-West alignments were crucial during the Cold War era. On it will stand or fall the region's chances for the stability that will allow it to play the vital leading economic role envisaged for it in the twenty-first century. In the mid-1990s, there remains an adversarial element to contacts between the three countries which will require delicate diplomacy and active statesmanship. Foreign policy in Tokyo and Washington in future will have to be governed by the realization that, like it or not, China wants to be and is going to be a great power. China has not forgotten (and probably never will forget) the suffering inflicted on the people by rampant Japanese militarism in the first half of this century. The Japanese will have to accept this, but hopefully both countries can find ways to file the past away in a draw where it will not continue to bedevil efforts to achieve future rapprochement. At the same time, China must find ways to assure Japan that its growing economic strength is not eventually going to pose a security threat (if it does, we will have the dangerous prospect of a nuclear-armed Japan possibly repeating past mistakes). The two countries inevitably are going to be rivals, especially once China achieves its predicted position as the world's leading economy in the twenty-first century. It is hard to imagine Japan gracefully accepting second place (or worse, given the rapid development of the South Korean economy).

China's neighbours in North and Southeast Asia, in particular, have a common interest in keeping China peacefully engaged. For this purpose, they are currently building economic, political and other links aimed at giving Beijing a deep and enduring interest in maintaining international order.

In this regard, great thought is being given to the creation of a number of economic alliances involving individual regions of China and adjacent foreign territory. One that has already been much discussed if the Northeast Asian common market encompassing northeastern coastal China, adjacent areas of the former Soviet Union, Mongolia, North and South Korea and Japan. With an eye to this, the prospering port cities along the Bohai Gulf and Yellow sea, such as Tianjin and Qingdao – already discussed in chapter four – have developed free trade zones and developed air and sea links with the neighbouring states. Mutually complementary resources and industrial structures work in favour of greater economic cooperation and integration. China has rich labour resources and increasingly advanced technology, but lacks funds with which to develop them; Japan and South Korea lead the region in capital and technology, but are hampered by the rising cost of labour, the eastern part of the former Soviet Union is rich in timber and oil, but chronically short of labour, capital and technology; and North Korea and Mongolia both have plenty of resources, but lack funds and technology. China certainly recognizes that economic relations with Japan are pivotal to a resolution of old tensions. But it is wary of domination by its powerful neighbour, and sees increasing Korean industrial strength as a useful counterweight, while a wider regional grouping would also guard against Japanese 'bullying'.

The emergence of an economic bloc along these lines in northern Asia would be only one of a series of interlinked blocs stretching all the way down into Southeast Asia. Among the ideas that have been discussed in recent times have been:

- Sea of Japan Rim Economic Zone, made up of the former Soviet Far East, northeast China, the Korean peninsula and Japan – a huge economic bloc combining about 290 million in population (not far short of the current European Community) and about $3 trillion in gross national product.
- Yi Men Jiang Economic Zone, comprising various cities in the Yi Men Jiang river estuary on the borders of China, North Korea, and the former Soviet Far East, such as Nahodka,

Vladivostock, Yenji (Jilin Province) and Chinjin (North Korea).
- Yellow Sea Rim Economic Zone, covering South Korea's West Coast, China's Shandong and Liaoning Province.
- South China Economic Zone centred around Hong Kong and parts of Guangdong province like Shenzhen and Guangzhou and extends as far as Taiwan and Hainan Island. Its economic growth is characterized by the inflow of foreign capital from Hong Kong and Japan and is export-driven.
- Baht Economic Zone: Thailand's economic might dwarfs that of the countries of Indochina like Laos, Cambodia and Vietnam, but together they form a giant market of 120 million people. The growth rate in the southern area of Vietnam is particularly high. In the long-term there would be possibilities of extending cooperation over the border into southern China, linking up with provinces like Sichuan, an important centre of Chinese industry and its most populous area with another 120 million people.
- Growth Triangle Concept, aimed at bringing foreign investment to a zone comprising Singapore, the neighbouring Malaysian state of Johor and nearby Indonesian islands like Batam and Bintang where free trade industrial zones have already been created.

All these disparate elements could then be drawn together under the East Asian Economic Grouping Concept proposed by Malaysian Prime Minister Dr Mahathir, aimed at counteracting such economic blocs as the EC and North America. It would cover Japan, China, the six countries in Asean (Association of Southeast Asian Nations) and those of Indochina.

Examining China's foreign economic strategies for the rest of the decade, one official suggested:

'The US and West European countries are without question important trade partners of China and sources of advanced technology. The former Soviet Union and East European countries are large markets for China's textiles and light industrial products. Africa, the Middle East and Latin America are markets with great potential. [But] while developing economic and trade relations with these countries, emphasis will be laid on the Asian-Pacific region and East Asia in particular, because 70 per cent of China's commodities are sold in Asia and 60 per cent of its capital comes from [there]. The region has become China's base for further developing its foreign economic and trade relations.

'The Asian-Pacific region in particular and Europe will enjoy the most rapid economic development in the 1990s and offer plentiful economic and trade opportunities. But Europe is faraway from China and has closer relations with America. China, on the contrary, has closer relations with Asian and Pacific countries. Many of these have a long-standing relationship with China [and] were influenced by Chinese culture; overseas Chinese have a strong influence on industry and commerce in this area and enjoy harmonious relations with local people; all these can be of assistance in developing trade and economic relations with these countries.

'In the great Asian and Pacific economic sphere, China will actively promote and take part in the development of the East Asian Economic sphere and participate in the activities of the region's economic cooperative organizations. China will seriously study the Malaysian proposal to establish an eastern Asian Common Market. China will work out feasible methods to undertake cooperation with an awareness that Asian countries from north to south, differ in their progress towards economic development. With its vast territory, China is connected to both North and Southeast Asia. In accordance with this situation, China may develop a closer and smaller regional economic cooperation.'[7]

Huang Fanzhang, Deputy Director of the State Planning Commission's Economic Research Centre, has proposed a triangular concept for China's trade strategy. The largest triangle comprises China, Japan and the United States, a medium-sized one involves the six members of the Association of Southeast Asian Nations, Taiwan and Hong Kong, while the smallest triangle covers only the latter two entities. China's best strategy, Huang suggests, is to '... rely on the small triangle, win over the medium system, and jockey for position within the larger one'. At the same time, it should not neglect any opportunities further afield, including Europe, Latin America and Oceania.

HONG KONG'S FUTURE

The small triangle involves the concept of 'Greater China' discussed in the opening chapter, reflecting the increased interaction between the markets of Hong Kong, China and Taiwan which has a potential to become a significant force in the world economy in a very short time. This, of course, raises immediate questions about the future of Hong Kong after it reverts to Chinese control in July 1997.

One insider has no doubts that even after the take-over it will be business as usual for the former British colony as it becomes a Special Administrative Region under the 'one country, two systems' principle. 'Hong Kong will continue to evolve as the International Division of China Inc. managing China's exports and importing foreign goods for re-export to China. This role will increase as China continues to open up to the outside world. Hong Kong's established business and social connections with China and the rest of the world, its excellent telecommunications and transport facilities and its financial sophistication make it uniquely suited to be China's entrepot. The economies of Hong Kong and Guangdong are closely interlinked. Some 25,000 enterprises in Guangdong produce goods for Hong Kong companies. [. . .] An estimated 20 per cent of Hong Kong's currency circulation takes place in Guangdong. Hong Kong investment and influence are also spreading north to Shanghai, Beijing and many other Chinese cities. China is increasing its stake in Hong Kong. It is now the largest investor in the territory. It is estimated that mainland investors will control one-fifth of the real-estate market by 1997.

'Some question Beijing's intentions toward the territory. But if China is not committed to Hong Kong, why should it buy in now at current market rates? Why not wait for the take-over when prices might be lower? The answer is that China sees Hong Kong as a good investment now and in the future.'[8]

Nevertheless, Singapore Prime Minister Goh Chok Tong, in the speech already referred to, sounded a note of caution. '[T]he fundamental approach for the Chinese leadership toward Hong Kong is political, not economic. Chinese leaders are keenly aware of Hong Kong's social and cultural influence on contiguous regions of China and are concerned about it. They will not allow political arrangements for Hong Kong beyond those that they are eventually prepared to accept for the rest of China. Beijing wants to pre serve Hong Kong's prosperity, but it will not sacrifice its own political survival to do so.'

The Chinese government has shown itself capable of great pragmatism. But it can also move to the other extreme. The foreigner approaching China has to understand the weight of history that influences many attitudes and decisions. Even ordinary Chinese are imbued with a sense of outrage at the way foreign countries took advantage of China's weakness in the dying years of Imperial rule to extract concessions and territory – including Hong Kong. The reversion of the colony to Chinese control, therefore, is not just of rectifying a past injustice but also demonstrating that China has stood up and is not going to be dictated to again.

There was a time when the main argument was that China needed Hong Kong and, therefore, would do nothing to damage its international standing. But it seems to me that the positions have now been reversed. With so much capital flowing northwards, it is now Hong Kong that needs China. With all the development going on up the Pearl River, and developments along the coast and into the Yangtse valley, Hong Kong's former unique role as China's entrepot port has been weakened. Thus, there would seem to be less reason for the Chinese to make what they consider 'unreasonable' concessions to preserve Hong Kong in the way the British might prefer.

RESOLVING TRADE WORRIES

A burning issue for China – and the West which has an acute interest in liberalization of Chinese trade – is Beijing's steps towards rejoining the General Agreement on Tariffs and Trade (GATT). Progress has been slow not only because China has a long way to go to meet the membership requirements, but also because the West wants to ensure that a new trade juggernaut in its midst plays by the rules. This has become more pressing since it finally reached the elevated plateau as one of the world's top 10 traders. The World Bank exposed the task confronting China in its efforts to conform with the minimum standards required by Gatt signatories as far as tariff and non-tariff barriers are concerned, pointing out that in 1992, more than 50 per cent of China's imports were subject to some form of administrative control. China's tariffs, according to the bank, remained higher, more numerous and more dispersed than most other large developing countries. In 1993, Europe, Japan and the United States all faced large trading deficits with the Chinese that made them even more determined to make sure that this disadvantage did not last.

The United States spelt out the minimum conditions for entry to GATT as: a single national trade policy common to all provinces and regions; full transparency of trade regulations; the gradual removal of non-tariff barriers ; a commitment to move to a full market economy; and acceptance of safeguards to protect GATT signatories from a possible surge in Chinese exports. It is the latter concern, given China's enormous strides recently as an export power, that is weighing most heavily with the West. An EC official said in Beijing the Commission's principal requirement was a strong safeguard clause and it was most unlikely to accept anything less. According to the EC representative, in spite of China's claims to have embarked on a concerted process of trade liberalization, barriers to entry to the Chinese market abound. Many are derived from bureaucratic interference, such as the difficulties EC dairy products faced overcoming the sometimes arbitrarily applied health requirements.

A decade or so ago, China ranked 20th among trading nations with exports of about $21 billion which represented less than one per cent of world trade. Projected exports in 1993 of $100 billion would account for more than 2.5 per cent of world trade. The range and quality of products are also showing marked improvement, with a continuing shift towards more sophisticated manufactured items, including machinery and transport equipment – sectors where there has been high foreign investment. Exports of these items has risen sharply and last year accounted for 16 per cent of the total, compared to six per cent in 1988. China's trading partners have not overlooked the fact that much of the foreign investment pouring into the country is, by Beijing's design, going in to export-generating industries.

At the beginning, Chinese officials were predicting that GATT entry was a mere formality, and were taken back by what they saw as an unhelpful posture adopted by the West. They have resisted American pressure to agree to a safeguard clause, which would enable individual signatories to impose import quotas on items such as textiles and electronic products. They were impressed by an American observation that China's situation was unique because 'GATT was not written with a socialist market economy in mind'. This, Washington said, was why it was necessary to negotiate a 'boutique protocol aimed exactly and uniquely at the Chinese system'. The Chinese, who have been anxious to resolve the GATT issue quickly to reduce bilateral trade pressures, said it was unfair to impose a special safeguard system on them when other recent signatories, such as several of the former Eastern bloc states, have not been obliged to accept the same conditions.

GATT membership involves pluses and minuses for China. With the Uruguay Round successfully concluded, the World Bank estimates that reduced protectionism in the Europe, Japan and the United States could boost Chinese exports by a respectable 38 per cent, partly due to the relatively high share of textiles and clothing products in its total exports. Conversely, the vastly improved opening of the domestic market to foreign products which Beijing would be obligated to allow poses a real threat to many inefficient industries. This is one reason why China is trying to attract vast amounts of high-tech foreign investment for modernization. In the long run, however, GATT membership is considered desirable in giving China a more respectable image in world trade.

CONVERTING THE YUAN

Another hold-up to GATT entry was a two-tiered exchange rate regime. Sales and purchases of foreign currency in the official market were regulated by a complex system of quotas, with the rate adjusted on a weekly basis. Many transactions, however, have in recent times taken place in a network of swap centres at a more depreciated exchange rate determined by supply and demand. The swap centres were the closest thing China had for some time to a market mechanism for setting the Yuan's exchange rate. They were a semi-official black market and typified the concept of 'one eye open, one eye closed'. Essentially, the government was saying: 'We know that a black market exists, but rather than trying to stamp it out (forcing it underground where it will be even more difficult to control) we are going to semi-legalize it without actually publicly announcing that it is acceptable.' The swap centres were used by companies who needed to buy or sell foreign currency; individuals continued to use the lady on the vegetable stall in the local street market who kept a close eye on rate changes. The existence of a two-tier system allowed the government to keep the official exchange rate of the Yuan remarkably stable, good for the country's image, while allowing the reality of a volatile market play itself out through the swap centre rates.

Until the end of 1993, companies had to sell 20 per cent of their foreign exchange earnings to the government at the official rate. The government also had the right to buy another 30 per cent at the swap rate. This control over 50 per cent of the exchange deals enabled the government to exercise some influence over the swap rate.

Vice Premier Zhu Rongji made it clear when he took over as governor of the People's Bank of China that he wanted to see the dual system abandoned. The goal was to unify the two rates during 1994, as a first step towards making the Yuan fully convertible. As a first step, citizens of Hong Kong, Macao and Taiwan were be allowed to freely convert their foreign currency into RMB. Rate unification has been on the agenda for some time. In 1991 and early 1992, the rates were fairly close together, but they began to diverge again from the middle of the year. As the economy overheated in the first half of 1993, the authorities tried to cap the exchange rate at about 8 Yuan to the US dollar (compared to the official rate of around 5.7 Yuan), but had to abandon the effort in June. As a result, the unofficial rate soared to around 11 Yuan for a while, amid fears of financial chaos, before it could be stabilized at round 8.5 Yuan again.

To achieve this, the People's Bank of China used its limited muscle as the central bank to send signals to the market. But just how limited this effort was is indicated by the fact that it only spent $20 million from the foreign reserves to boost the Yuan's value on the Shanghai swap market – small change compared to the vast amounts the Bundesbank or Bank of England, for example, would pay out in a matter of minutes in currency support operations. According to an official of the Shanghai Branch of the State Administration of Exchange Control, 'the buying or selling [of hard currency] by the central bank is but a signal for the market. Its influence is still limited and it is not as powerful as expected'. This was the first admission, however, that the bank had used policy-driven sales to rescue the Yuan. Bank deputy governor Chen Yuan said the PBOC would resort to 'indirect open market operations' again to stabilize the Yuan if necessary. But economists were quick to point out that China's limited foreign exchange reserves (reported at around $28 billion in mid-1993) meant the central bank could only nudge the market, with prolonged and large-scale intervention unsustainable.

Amid pessimism that exchange rate unification would be hard to achieve, the government then took virtually everyone by surprise by announcing at the end of December that from 1 January 1994, the official exchange rate would be abandoned and the Yuan allowed to float. This was really an acknowledgement that it was the swap centres which were really 'calling the shots'. Even state enterprises, heavily subsidized in being able to use the artificial rate to import goods more cheaply, were increasingly being told to use the swap market rate. At the time of writing it was hard to determine the precise implications of the change. In general terms, however, it is clear the state sector will suffer. Inflation will also probably worsen. Among the beneficiaries, however, will be foreign investors, who will no longer have to register the capital in their joint ventures at the official rate but repatriate their profits via that set by the swap market.

The government also eliminated the ubiquitous Foreign Exchange Certificate – the special domestic currency received by foreigners in return for their dollars and pounds etc., which also had an official and black-market rate (local people who could get their hands on FEC could use it to buy imported goods not available for Renminbi due to foreign currency restrictions).

LONG WAY TO GO

In conclusion, one has to say that China has a long way to go before it has worked out a modern economic structure capable of supporting its grandiose ambitions. Throughout this book, I have discussed some of those problems in detail, so I do not wish to repeat myself here. Just how far China has to go was illustrated by a meeting of the Party Central Committee held in November 1993 in Beijing which had been heralded by the official press as the most important since the 1978 Party plenum launched the reform drive. The bland communiqué that was issued at the end of the four-day meeting provided little of substance, devoting itself largely to repeating well-established positions strongly linked to what elder statesman Deng Xiaoping had said years ago. A 50-article manifesto of reform provided a few titbits, including proposed reforms of the tax structure, as already discussed in the last chapter.

There are obvious differences at various levels of government and party. Provincial leaders are wary about allowing Beijing to strengthen its grip on the purse strings after all their efforts over the years to achieve some loosening. A state enterprise lobby is nervous about all the reforms of the public sector, fearing that additional pressures on faltering industries will drive many into bankruptcy and cause widespread unemployment and social unrest. Many officials owe their status to the association with industries, which are having a difficult time adapting to the demands of the market economy. These officials are fighting to preserve their fiefdoms.

Above all, there is a central dilemma for the present rulers as they try and dampen down the raging fires sparked by their own economic reform programmes. If they turn the tap down and the flow of goods dwindles, the people will be aroused. If they do not turn down the tap, the people will become progressively more independent. The Communists cannot remain on top unless they can win hearts and minds, or at least pacify the populace, with the fruit of economic progress. But such progress will be slow unless provinces, municipalities and even individuals are allowed autonomy to make their own decisions. It is a difficult choice, and it portends trouble for China in the years ahead.

There are so many contradictions to be resolved. How can China commercialize a state enterprise sector in which at least a third of which is loss-making without the widespread bankruptcies that officials reject? How, without an end to subsidies to these enterprises, can the banking sector run along commercial lines or the central bank run a market-based monetary policy? If the subsidies are to be paid through budget allocations, how is Beijing to raise the necessary taxes from unwilling provinces? Woolly commitments to market-based reforms cannot disguise the fact that the hybrid monster that has so far been created leaks at all the seams.

The government has yet to find solutions to the growing inequality being created by the reform process or how to create macro-economic stability if development is to continue at a breakneck pace. China does not have the social or physical infrastructure in place to sustain the growth rates that have been seen in recent years. But without sophisticated monetary and fiscal levers, the central government does not have the means to create sustained and stable growth. As mentioned elsewhere, the economic reform programme has been described as opening the cage and allowing the bird inside to learn how to fly. The trouble is that '... each time the bird has soared higher, it has fallen back to earth with a bigger, reform-threatening thud'.[9] Whenever things threaten to get out of control, there has in the past been no subtlety. All the brakes are slammed on hard (eg: a total credit freeze) and the economy comes to a juddering halt.

The Dengist reforms have left China on a knife-edge. Nowhere was this more apparent than in the area of price controls on basic commodities. Having been abandoned in a fanfare of publicity, they had to be reimposed as Christmas 1993 approached – symbolizing the core problem for a nation that needs to become 'rich and powerful' through the introduction of capitalist techniques, coming face to face with the greater need of the Communist Party to retain absolute control. The price ceilings, removed in May 1993 from 27 commodities including rice, cooking oil, pork and eggs, were reimposed after inflation reached 30 to 40 per cent on basic foodstuffs in November.

The action was taken as the Organization for Economic Cooperation and Development (OECD) gave a warning that China was in a vice: its anti-inflationary measures might bring down the growth too jarringly, but relaxing austerity measures might result in greater dangers. In Beijing, rumours that inflation would soar and that stocks of basic foodstuffs were dwindling resulted in panic buying.

For the Party, there is a dilemma that ensuring its survival will ultimately mean upsetting some of the increasingly powerful vested interests in the country. 'If enriching east-coast investors and regional bosses makes them happy, and pulling on their reins makes them recalcitrant, the Party will do what is necessary, even relaxing control of loans and printing mountains of currency. If urban residents grumble at inflation and short supplies, the Party will order trains loaded with food to the main cities, and deal with the peasants later.'[10]

The need to develop more sophisticated policy levers will require some re-centralization of economic power which, as already discussed, the richer provinces are reluctant to accept. At the same time, the task is complicated by the fact that, as the economy has developed, it has made it more difficult to deal with one sector at a time because all have become closely interrelated. For example, the central bank cannot do its job until the banking sector is totally reformed; but the banks cannot perform properly while they have to wet nurse the state enterprises; the state enterprises cannot stand on their own, unless the state takes over their primary welfare functions like housing, health and pensions. The state, however, does not have the means to create a comprehensive welfare structure unless there are major changes in the political structure. One has to have a lot of sympathy for reformers like Vice Premier Zhu Rongji in trying to tackle this accumulated mess.

But despite all the criticisms, China has achieved remarkable progress in a very short time. It is going to achieve much of the predicted growth potential, although there will probably be a few blips on the way. It is going to be a major player in the world stage in the coming years. No matter how much some Party stalwarts and entrenched bureaucrats may grumble, the market reforms now seem unstoppable. And, over time, they are going to create some new freedoms and some semblance of greater democracy. The market of 1.2 billion eager consumers has not yet arrived, but by the year 2000 annual retail sales are widely predicted to reach $600 billion (a 300 per cent increase over 1992). What businessman is going to turn his back on a share of that mammoth pie? The overwhelming argument is in favour of jumping on the bandwagon now. The ride may be rocky for a while, but those with strong nerves and a firm grip ultimately should bless their foresight.

The final question to be asked, therefore, is: could it all go wrong? Could all the economic reforms be reversed in some Maoist-style U-turn? Nothing is impossible, but it seems highly unlikely – although there will be many a rough passage ahead. In this regard, two of the businessmen I interviewed in researching this book offered contrasting views of the risks and the opportunities involved in doing business in China which I think are worth quoting.

According to one: 'I agree there are a lot of opportunities, but there are also a lot of risks. You cannot go into China in a strictly professional way because there is no professionalism to speak of at present. When a rule is made, and you find it is not to your advantage, you can change it if you have sufficient influence with the right people. There are no hard and fast rules in China, which is why I've never invested there. I will not set up a factory and put hard cash into the economy. So far I have only traded with China. I don't have a single cent invested there because I still don't trust the Communist rule. Things can change overnight. You don't know where you stand and what the government will do next. For example, when it decided to recall loans overnight as part of the credit squeeze in mid-1993, many foreign companies suddenly had to repay their loans and had a hard time to find the cash. I think that could happen again any time. There are a lot of chiefs in the central government. Someone can make an announcement, then someone else can revoke it. I don't feel comfortable with that environment.'

But the other businessman offered a more upbeat assessment: 'I don't gloss over the problems China is facing but if I was a betting man I would be prepared to put money on it being able to solve those problems – and others that are not yet foreseen. Because it's the biggest economic and business opportunity all over the world, there will be a lot of vested interests overseas who will help China avoid the pitfalls that have faced many developing countries as well as the Soviet Union. I predict success in the long run. It will not be clear for quite a few more years, and it might be another 30 or even 40 years before we can declare it a success.

'I hope the West will show wisdom in this regard. There are some people who think it is not in the West's interests to help China because it will be creating a fresh challenger who could make life very uncomfortable, especially if it united, in spirit at least, with other parts of Asia to challenge Western dominance of the global system. I don't accept that. I think that business will win the day, making money will win the day ... pragmatism will triumph. A unified, peaceful growing superpower-to-be like China will greatly benefit the world. The benefits will be not only for the big multinationals but also for the little back street trading or manufacturing operation. Nobody should want to hold China back because it is going to be the next driver of the world economy. I know there are some who fear possible Chinese hegemonistic ambitions. But, from my long observation, I believe the Chinese would rather trade with you than go to war. They are not naturally hegemonistic. They'd rather make money. They are very materialistic. You can do good business with people like that. And my long-term investments in China say that I'm right.'

One encouragement for the future is provided by the fact that the Beijing-based People's University has abandoned courses in Marxism in favour of business studies. Some 14 new business subjects, including real-estate management and marketing, are available at the university, which was established by the Communist Party to train young revolutionaries before the People's Republic was founded. The new business subjects replaced 17 courses related to communist dogma which were said to have been abandoned due to lack of student interest. The Communist Party School, main centre for training high-level cadres, is also for the first time teaching courses in stock-market operations. The People's University, a hot-bed of Red Guard activity during the Cultural Revolution, has disbanded its Planned Economy Department and replaced it with a Department of National Economic Management. Mere straws in the wind, perhaps, but surely indicative that China has come too far down the capitalist market road to turn back now.

FOOTNOTES

1. Wang Shanguang and Hu Angang submitted a 140,000-word report to the government in June 1993 on the progress of economic reform and the problems created.
2. *China Daily*, 21 July 1993.
3. *Guangming Daily*, 25 July 1993.
4. *Changing China*, pp21-2.
5. Ibid., pp36.
6. *People's Daily*, 11 Oct. 1993.
7. Mai Liben, a senior official in the All-China Federation of Industry and Commerce, writing in *Beijing Review*, 5 May 1991.
8. Paul M.Chung, Chairman of the Hong Kong General Chamber of Commerce, writing in the *International Herald Tribune*.
9. *Financial Times*, 18 Nov. 1993.
10. 'China fixes prices to prevent unrest.' London *Times*, 22 Dec. 1993.

APPENDIX 1

AN INTRODUCTION TO THE CHINESE GOVERNMENT STRUCTURE

Form of government: one-party rule by the Chinese Communist Party (CCP), although there are eight ostensibly non-Communist parties represented on the National People's Congress (NPC).

The Executive: 15-member State Council elected by the NPC.

Head of state: A president elected for a renewable five-year term by the NPC.

National legislature: Unicameral NPC; 2,970 delegates elected for a five-year term by provinces, municipalities, autonomous regions and the armed forces; apart from electing the president and State Council, it selects members of the Standing Committee of the NPC which meets when the full congress is not in sitting. The NPC's prime functions are to amend the constitution, enact laws, elect the Chairman of the State, elect the Chairman of the Military Commission and approve candidates for the State Council.

National government: the Politburo, currently 20 members, of the Chinese Communist Party which sets policy and controls all administrative, legal and executive appointments; its six-member Standing Committee is the real focus of power.

CHINA'S POLITICAL SYSTEM

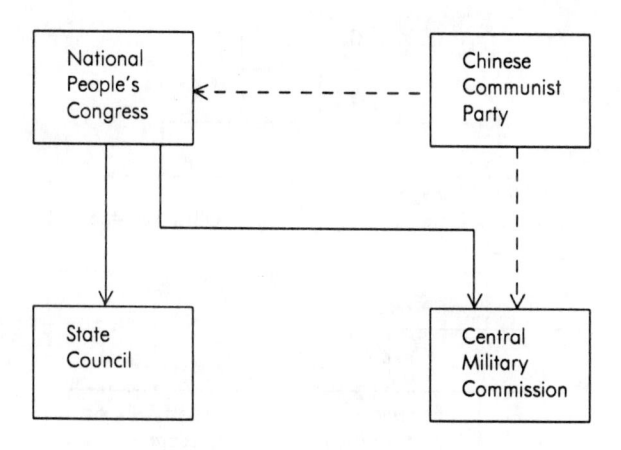

```
┌──────────────┐              ┌──────────────┐
│ National     │ ←----------- │ Chinese      │
│ People's     │              │ Communist    │
│ Congress     │              │ Party        │
└──────┬───────┘              └──────┬───────┘
       │      └──────────────┐       │
       │                     │       │
       ▼                     ▼       ▼
┌──────────────┐              ┌──────────────┐
│ State        │              │ Central      │
│ Council      │              │ Military     │
│              │              │ Commission   │
└──────────────┘              └──────────────┘
```

CHINA'S ADMINISTRATIVE SYSTEM

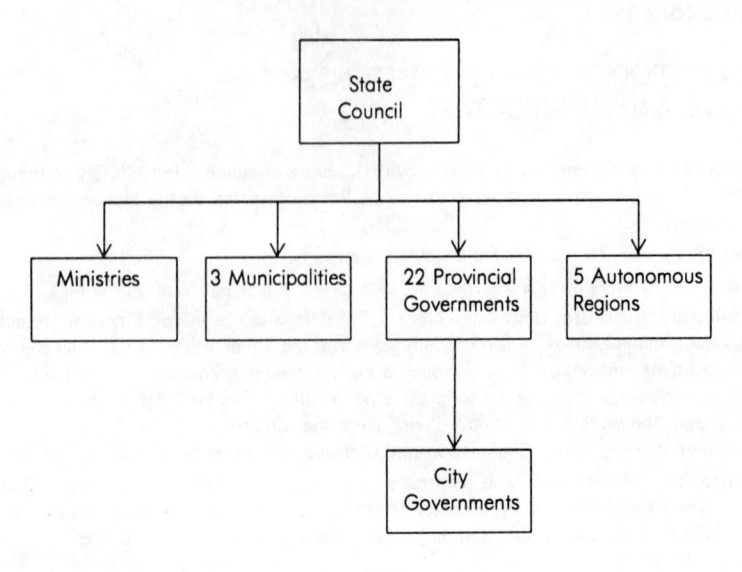

```
                    State Council
                         │
   ┌─────────────┬───────┴───────┬──────────────┐
Ministries  3 Municipalities  22 Provincial  5 Autonomous
                              Governments      Regions
                                   │
                                   ▼
                                 City
                              Governments
```

FOREIGN TRADE SYSTEM

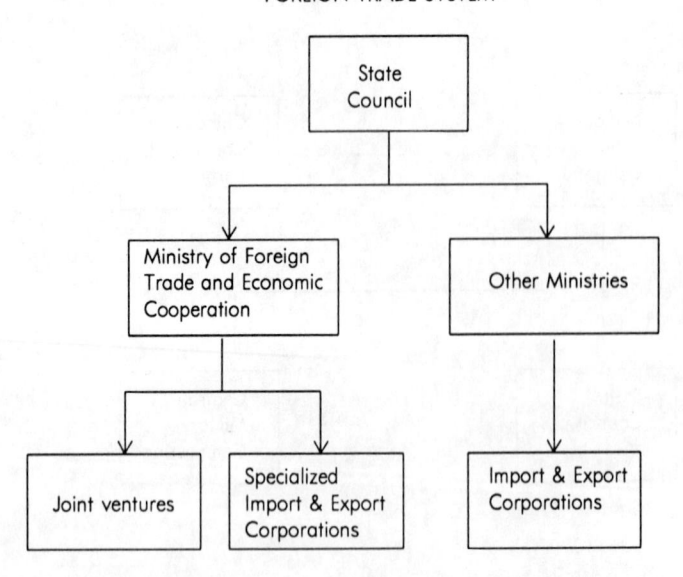

```
                    State Council
                         │
          ┌──────────────┴──────────────┐
   Ministry of Foreign              Other Ministries
   Trade and Economic                     │
      Cooperation                         ▼
          │                       Import & Export
   ┌──────┴──────┐                 Corporations
Joint ventures  Specialized
                Import & Export
                 Corporations
```

APPENDIX 2

CHINA'S BANKING SYSTEM.

BANKS.
(a) The People's Bank of China (the central bank).
(b) National specialized banks:
The Industrial and Commercial Bank of China
The Agricultural Bank of China
The Bank of China
The People's Construction Bank of China.
(c) Other banks:
The Bank of Communications
The Industrial and Commercial Bank of CITIC
Other regional banks
(d) Foreign-capitalized banks, Sino-foreign joint-venture banks and banks with capital of overseas Chinese.

NON-BANKING FINANCIAL ORGANS
Trust and investment companies.
Securities companies
Financial companies
Lease companies
Rural credit cooperatives
Urban credit cooperatives
The People's Insurance Co. of China and other insurance companies.

ROLE OF THE PEOPLE'S BANK OF CHINA
1. Research and formulate the national financial policy and carry out the policy after approval by the State Council.
2. Carry out monetary policy under the approval of the State Council.
3. Be responsible for the issue and distribution of the national currency, the RMB; adjust the demand for cash.
4. Draft the financial laws and legal regulations.
5. Formulate the basic system and methods for the administration of the financial business and implement the system.
6. Draft the national credit programme, foreign exchange credit programme and social credit programme, and implement these after the approval of the State Council; administrate RMB and foreign exchange credit capital; manage the circulation of funds for state enterprises; compile statistics; supervise, analyze and predict social credit activities; control the scale and structure of credits.
7. Formulate rediscount and reloan policies and provide such facilities to financial enterprises.
8. Draft policy on interest rates and foreign exchange rates and implement the policies after approval by the State Council.
9. Administer the circulation of gold and silver; administer the national foreign exchange

and gold reserves.

10. Administer international commercial loans and supervise foreign debts; participate in international payments; formulate the programme for the use of foreign investment.

11. Examine and approve the establishment, withdrawal and merger of domestic financial enterprises; examine and approve the establishment, withdrawal and merger of foreign-funded joint-venture financial enterprises in China as well as Chinese-invested joint-venture financial enterprises in other countries.

12. Examine and approve the establishment, withdrawal and merger of insurance enterprises; administer the insurance business.

13. Formulate policy on the issue and circulation of negotiable securities with other governmental departments concerned and implement the policy after approval by the State Council.

14. Administer the financial markets in bonds and stocks.

15. Manage the national treasury and the issue of government bonds.

16. Lead capital clearance among financial enterprises.

17. Lead, administer, coordinate, supervise and examine the business activities of financial enterprises.

18. Formulate the personnel, employment and salary systems of financial institutions; appoint and dismiss leaders of financial institutions; hold overall training responsibility.

19. Participate in international financial activities on behalf of the government.

ROLE OF INDUSTRIAL AND COMMERCIAL BANK OF CHINA

1. Four fields: industrial production, commodity circulation, technological innovation, and accepting deposits from residents.

2. Main clients: state and collective enterprises, self-employed people and individuals.

3. Loans are provided for circulating funds, technological innovation, industrial and commercial construction, scientific development and individual economic needs.

4. Other domestic banking activities include developing trust businesses, investment, leasing, consultation, and real-estate development.

5. Gathering economic information and producing various business surveys.

6. Beginning from 1984, ICBC was allowed to conduct foreign currency business at some of its branches. This included savings and loans, currency remittances, trade and non-trade settlement for import and export, foreign exchange and foreign currency bills, foreign currency guarantees, outbound foreign exchange borrowing, discounting bills of foreign exchange, issuing or acting as agents for the issue of negotiable securities in foreign currencies, consultation and credit information services, and handling the transfer of loans provided by international financial organizations and foreign governments.

BASIC FUNCTIONS OF THE BANK OF CHINA

1. The bank is responsible for the management of the national foreign exchange reserve, revenue and expenditure of the national foreign exchange, and raising funds on behalf of the state

2. The bank is allowed to operate in all areas of foreign exchange and RMB business, such as: trade and non-trade international settlement, operating FEC (Foreign Exchange Certificate) credit, loans for export-oriented enterprises, loans for foreign-invested

enterprises, and foreign exchange loans; operating buyer and seller credit for import and export; managing loans of international banking groups and commercial loans; managing trust investment and lease business; managing or being entrusted to operate outlets for the purchase and sales of foreign exchange, international bonds and gold; issuance of foreign currency, RMB bonds and other negotiable securities; absorption of foreign exchange and RMB deposits; managing information services.

3. The bank is allowed to operate branches abroad.

MAIN BUSINESS OF THE PEOPLE'S CONSTRUCTION BANK OF CHINA

1. Entrusted by the Ministry of Finance with the responsibility for the management of capital construction expenditure budget, operating the allocations and loans for capital construction and technical innovation projects and allocations for geological prospecting; examining and approving the financial programmes and final accounts of governmental organs in charge of capital construction, the actual construction units and the geological prospecting units and development enterprises; formulating a national financial system for capital construction.

2. Operating banking settlement.

3. Absorbing self-raised funds of enterprises, institutions and self-producers, and other savings, to be put to use for capital construction and technological innovation.

4. Managing cashier business, deposits of residents and household savings.

5. Issuing various kinds of national, financial, construction and enterprise bonds and negotiable securities; operating a stock exchange facility.

6. Providing medium and long-term loans for capital construction and technological innovation projects, loans for equipment and housing construction.

7. Providing circulating capital for construction, industrial and commercial enterprises.

8. Managing international financial business, including: foreign exchange deposits, loans, remittances, outbound foreign exchange loans, transfer of loans from foreign governments and international financial organizations, transfer of export credit provided by the afore-mentioned organs, international settlement, exchange of foreign currencies and bills, issuance of negotiable securities in foreign currency, foreign exchange guarantees, credit information and consultancy services.

9. Operating trust, lease, consultation, guarantee and proxy businesses, and other financial activities.

10. Managing real estate business, and classifying the capital reliability of construction enterprises.

11. Operating other businesses approved by the government.

ROLE OF THE BANK OF COMMUNICATIONS

This was set up under the direction of the State Council and is styled as a 'national comprehensive bank'. Its business scope is:

1. Absorbing various kinds of RMB savings, individual deposits, foreign currency savings, and savings of overseas Chinese.

2. Managing RMB loans for circulating capital, RMB discount and fixed assets loans, managing loans, overdraft and discount of foreign currencies.

3. Operating domestic and international settlement, and remittance business.

4. Issuing bonds in RMB or foreign currencies, and other negotiable securities.

5. Operating international and domestic inter-bank saving, loan and discount businesses.

6. Managing the purchase and sales of foreign exchange, and foreign exchange stocks and bonds.

7. Operating investment banks, joint-venture banks, financial companies and other enterprises in Hong Kong, Macao and elsewhere in the world.

8. Organizing international syndicated loans and loans from banking groups.

9. Operating domestic and international businesses for trust, insurance, investment, lease, consultation, guarantee and proxy.

10. Setting up financial and non-financial branch economies.

11. Managing real estate businesses.

12. Issuing various kinds of stocks and bonds, managing the transfer, purchase, sales of various kinds of negotiable securities.

13. Operating businesses entrusted or approved by the People's Bank of China.

14. Participate in international financial activities determined by the state authorities.

CHINA'S BANKING SYSTEM

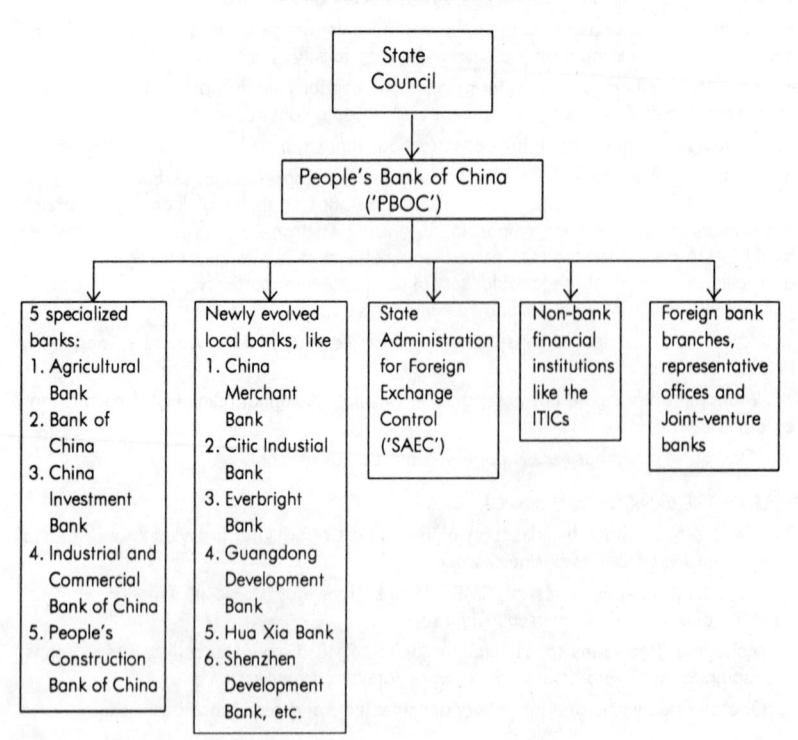

```
                        ┌──────────────┐
                        │    State     │
                        │   Council    │
                        └──────┬───────┘
                               │
                               ▼
                   ┌────────────────────────┐
                   │ People's Bank of China │
                   │       ('PBOC')         │
                   └───────────┬────────────┘
                               │
   ┌──────────────┬────────────┼────────────┬──────────────┐
   ▼              ▼            ▼            ▼              ▼
```

5 specialized banks:	Newly evolved local banks, like	State Administration for Foreign Exchange Control ('SAEC')	Non-bank financial institutions like the ITICs	Foreign bank branches, representative offices and Joint-venture banks
1. Agricultural Bank	1. China Merchant Bank			
2. Bank of China	2. Citic Industial Bank			
3. China Investment Bank	3. Everbright Bank			
4. Industrial and Commercial Bank of China	4. Guangdong Development Bank			
5. People's Construction Bank of China	5. Hua Xia Bank			
	6. Shenzhen Development Bank, etc.			

APPENDIX 3

LAW OF THE PEOPLE'S REPUBLIC OF CHINA ON FOREIGN-CAPITAL ENTERPRISES

(Adopted at the Fourth Session of the Sixth National People's Congress, promulgated by Order No. 39 of the President of the People's Republic of China and effective as of 12 April 1986)

Article 1 With a view to expanding economic cooperation and technical exchange with foreign countries and promoting the development of China's national economy, the People's Republic of China permits foreign enterprises, other foreign economic organizations and individuals (hereinafter collectively referred to as 'foreign investors') to set up enterprises with foreign capital in China and protects the lawful rights and interests of such enterprises.

Article 2 As mentioned in this Law, 'enterprises with foreign capital' refers to those enterprises established in China by foreign investors, exclusively with their own capital, in accordance with relevant Chinese laws. The term does not include branches set up in China by foreign enterprises and other foreign economic organizations.

Article 3 Enterprises with foreign capital shall be established in such a manner as to help the development of China's national economy; they shall use advanced technology and equipment or market all or most of their products outside China.

Provisions shall be made by the State Council regarding the lines of business which the state forbids enterprises with foreign capital to engage in or on which it places certain restrictions.

Article 4 The investments of a foreign investor in China, the profits it earns and its other lawful rights and interests are protected by Chinese law.

Enterprises with foreign capital must abide by Chinese laws and regulations and must not engage in any activities detrimental to China's public interest.

Article 5 The state shall not nationalize or requisition any enterprise with foreign capital. Under special circumstances, when public interest requires, enterprises with foreign capital may be requisitioned by legal procedures and appropriate compensation shall be made.

Article 6 The application to establish an enterprise with foreign capital shall be submitted for examination and approval to the department under the State Council which is in charge of foreign economic relations and trade, or to another agency authorized by the State Council. The authorities in charge of examination and approval shall, within 90 days from the date they receive such application, decide whether or not to grant approval.

Article 7 After an application for the establishment of an enterprise with foreign capital has been approved, the foreign investor shall, within 30 days from the date of receiving a certificate of approval, apply to the industry and commerce administration authorities for registration and obtain a business licence. The date of issue of the business licence shall be the date of the establishment of the enterprise.

Article 8 An enterprise with foreign capital which meets the conditions for being considered a legal person under Chinese law shall acquire the status of a Chinese legal person, in accordance with the law.

Article 9 An enterprise with foreign capital shall make investments in China within the period approved by the authorities in charge of examination and approval. If it fails to do so, the industry and commerce administration authorities may cancel its business licence. The industry and commerce administration authorities shall inspect and supervise the investment situation of an enterprise with foreign capital.

Article 10 In the event of a separation, merger or other major change, an enterprise with foreign capital shall report to and seek approval from the authorities in charge of examination and approval, and register the change with the industry and commerce administration authorities.

Article 11 The production and operating plans of enterprises with foreign capital shall be reported to the competent authorities for the record.

Enterprises with foreign capital shall conduct their operations and management in accordance with the approved articles of association, and shall be free from any interference.

Article 12 When employing Chinese workers and staff, an enterprise with foreign capital shall conclude contracts with them according to law, in which matters concerning employment, dismissal, remuneration, welfare benefits, labour protection and labour insurance shall be clearly prescribed.

Article 13 Workers and staff in enterprises with foreign capital may organize trade unions in accordance with the law, in order to conduct trade union activities and protect their lawful rights and interests.

The enterprise shall provide the necessary conditions for the activities of the trade unions in their respective enterprises.

Article 14 An enterprise with foreign capital must set up account books in China, conduct independent accounting, submit the fiscal reports and statements as required and accept supervision by the financial and tax authorities.

If an enterprise with foreign capital refuses to maintain account books in China, the financial and tax authorities may impose a fine on it, and the industry and commerce administration authorities may order it to suspend operations or may revoke its business licence.

Article 15 Within the scope of the operations approved, enterprises with foreign capital may purchase, either in China or from the world market, raw and semi-processed materials, fuels and other materials they need. When these materials are available from both sources on similar terms, first priority should be given to purchases in China.

Article 16 Enterprises with foreign capital shall apply to insurance companies in China for such kinds of insurance coverage as are needed.

Article 17 Enterprises with foreign capital shall pay taxes in accordance with relevant state provisions for tax payment, and may enjoy preferential treatment for reduction or exemption from taxes.

An enterprise that reinvests its profits in China after paying the income tax, may, in accordance with relevant state provisions, apply for refund of a part of the income tax already paid on the reinvested amount.

Article 18 Enterprises with foreign capital shall handle their foreign exchange

transactions in accordance with the state provisions for foreign exchange control.
Enterprises with foreign capital shall manage to balance their own foreign exchange receipts and payments. If, with the approval of the competent authorities, the enterprises market their products in China and consequently experience an imbalance in foreign exchange, the said authorities shall help them correct the imbalance.

Article 19 The foreign investor may remit abroad profits that are lawfully earned from an enterprise with foreign capital, as well as other lawful earnings and any funds remaining after the enterprise is liquidated.

Wages, salaries and other legitimate income earned by foreign employees in an enterprise with foreign capital may be remitted abroad after the payment of individual income tax in accordance with the law.

Article 20 With respect to the period of operations of an enterprise with foreign capital, the foreign investor shall report to and secure approval from the authorities in charge of examination and approval. For an extension of the period of operations, an application shall be submitted to the said authorities 180 days before the expiration of the period. The authorities in charge of examination and approval shall, within 30 days from the date such application is received, decide whether or not to grant the extension.

Article 21 When terminating its operations, an enterprise with foreign capital shall promptly issue a public notice and proceed with liquidation in accordance with legal procedure.

Pending the completion of liquidation, a foreign investor may not dispose of the assets of the enterprise except for the purpose of liquidation.

Article 22 At the termination of operations, the enterprise with foreign capital shall nullify its registration with the industry and commerce administration authorities and hand in its business licence for cancellation.

Article 23 The department under the State Council which is in charge of foreign economic relations and trade shall, in accordance with this Law, formulate rules for its implementation, which shall go into effect after being submitted to and approved by the State Council.

Article 24 This Law shall go into effect on the day of its promulgation.

APPENDIX 4

PROCEDURES FOR THE REGISTRATION AND ADMINISTRATION OF RESIDENT REPRESENTATIVE OFFICES OF FOREIGN ENTERPRISES IN CHINA

(Promulgated by the State Administration for Industry and Commerce and Effective 15 March 1983)

Article 1 In accordance with the Interim Regulations for Control of Resident Representative Offices of Foreign Enterprises in China (hereinafter referred to as the interim provisions), the present procedures are formulated to carry out the registration and administration of resident representative offices in China of foreign enterprises and other economic organizations and to protect their legitimate business interests.

Article 2 Resident representative offices in China of foreign enterprises and other economic organizations (hereinafter referred to as resident offices of foreign enterprises), which have been approved in accordance with Art. 4 of the interim provisions, shall go through the registration procedures prescribed in the present procedures.

Article 3 Resident offices of foreign enterprises shall be understood as those engaging in non-direct-profit-making operations. Those provided for in inter-government agreements shall be dealt with in accordance those agreements.

Article 4 The State Administration for Industry and Commerce of the PRC is the organ of the authority for the registration of resident offices of foreign enterprises. It shall empower the administrations for industry and commerce in various provinces, municipalities, and autonomous regions to handle registration procedures.

Article 5 The main items to be registered for the resident office of a foreign enterprise are: name of the office, address of residence, number of representatives and their names, business scope, and duration of residence.

Article 6 Foreign enterprises and other economic organizations shall go through the prescribed registration procedures at the administrations for industry and commerce in the provinces, municipalities, and autonomous regions where the said offices are to be located within 30 days from the date when their applications for setting up resident offices within the territory of the PRC are approved.

Article 7 A foreign enterprise or economic organization shall submit the following documents in applying for registration of a resident office:
(1) The approval document issued by the competent authorities of the PRC.
(2) The documents and materials as listed in Art. 3 of the interim provisions.

Article 8 If the documents submitted by a foreign enterprise or economic organization for registration are established, through examination, to meet the requirements set forth in the present procedures, the registration office shall grant permission to register and issue a certificate of registration and certificates for the representatives after a registration fee is paid.

The resident office of a foreign enterprise shall, upon the strength of the document approval, certificate of registration, and certificates for the representatives, register with the public security bureau, the bank, and the customs and tax authorities and other departments for residence permits and other related matters.

Article 9 The resident office of a foreign enterprise is deemed as officially established from the date of its registration and the legitimate activities of the said office and its representatives shall thereafter be protected by the laws of the People's Republic of China.

A resident office that has not been approved and registered shall not proceed with its business activities.

Article 10 In engaging the service of Chinese personnel, the resident office of a foreign enterprise must follow the provisions prescribed in Art. 11 of the interim provisions and promptly report this to the registration authorities for the record.

Article 11 The registration certificate for the resident office of a foreign enterprise is valid for a period of one year. The said office must, upon expiration of the period, renew the aforesaid document if it wishes to continue its residence.

To renew its registration, the resident office of a foreign enterprise must, within 30 days before the date of expiration, submit to the registration authorities an annual report of its business operations (in Chinese) and an application for renewal. In cases where the term of residence approved for a resident office expires, the document of approval for renewal issued by the same authorities must also be submitted at the time of renewing the registration and a form for renewal shall be filled out. After examination by the registration office, the original certificate shall be turned in and a new certificate of registration shall be issued.

Article 12 When the resident office of a foreign enterprise wishes to make alterations with regard to the name of the office, the number of representatives and their names, the scope of the business, and the address of the resident office, an application for alteration shall be filed with the registration office together with the document of approval issued by the competent authorities before going through the prescribed procedure for alterations in the register.

In cases where there is a change of representatives, a power of attorney issued by the foreign enterprise or economic organization shall be submitted together with the resumés of the new representatives.

Article 13 If the resident office of a foreign enterprise desires to terminate its business operations upon or before the expiration of the term of residence or the enterprise represented by the office declares bankruptcy, it shall go through the deregistration procedures at the registration office.

In going through the deregistration procedure, documents issued by tax authorities, banks, and Customs to certify the clearing up of taxes, debts, and other related matters shall be produced before approval is granted for cancellation and the certificate of registration is revoked.

Should the aforesaid office leave any matter unsettled, the foreign enterprise or economic organization the office represents shall be held responsible for the settlement of that matter.

Article 14 The State Administration for Industry and Commerce of the PRC and the administrations for industry and commerce in the provinces, municipalities, and autonomous regions are entitled to supervise and inspect the business activities of the resident offices of foreign enterprises within the jurisdiction of the present procedures.

In carrying out inspection and supervision, staff members of the aforesaid administrations should present identification cards specially issued for that purpose. The resident offices must report honestly and provide such information and materials as required. Refusal to report or holding back of information is not allowed.

Article 15 Any one of the following cases in violation of the provisions in the present procedures shall be punished by the State Administration for Industry and Commerce according to the seriousness of the case:

(1) The resident office of a foreign enterprise proven to have engaged in direct profit-making operations in violation of the provisions of Art. 3 of the present procedures shall be ordered to stop its business operations, with a fine of less than *Rmb* 20,000.

(2) The resident office of a foreign enterprise proven to have altered any item in the register without going through the required procedures or fail to deregister when it should have shall be given a notice of warning for circulation. For more serious cases, a fine of less than *Rmb*5,000 shall be imposed or the registration certificate may even be cancelled.

When the resident office of a foreign enterprise is found to have engaged in speculation, swindling, and other unlawful activities, all proceeds and properties thus obtained shall be confiscated in addition to a fine or even the cancellation of the registration certificate as the case may be. Cases that violate the criminal code of the PRC shall be brought before the court and punished according to that law.

Article 16 A foreign enterprise or other economic organization engaging, without authorization, in business operations only allowed for resident offices shall be ordered to stop such activities and a fine of less than *Rmb*10,000 shall be imposed.

Article 17 The present procedures also apply to foreign enterprises and other economic organizations applying to post their resident representatives within the boundaries of the PRC.

Article 18 Companies and other enterprises run by overseas Chinese or by compatriots from Hong Kong and Macau, when applying for the establishment of resident offices, shall go through registration procedures in reference to the present regulations to obtain registration certificates for the resident offices of overseas Chinese enterprises and enterprises from Hong Kong and Macau.

Article 19 PRC-foreign joint ventures operating outside China which have been approved to establish resident offices in China shall also go through registration procedures in reference to the present procedures.

APPENDIX 5

CONTRACT FOR EMPLOYMENT OF CHINESE EMPLOYEES
FOREIGN ENTERPRISE SERVICE CORPORATION (FESCO)

The Personnel Department of Foreign Enterprise Service Corporation, Beijing (hereinafter referred to as Party A) and _____ (hereinafter referred to as Party B) after friendly consultation have concluded this agreement respecting the employment of Chinese employees, with terms and conditions as follows:

Chapter I

Employment and Employment Recipience

Article 1 Party A shall select and provide Chinese employees in accordance with the requirements of Party B. Party B has the right to choose whomever it wishes to employ and shall provide the Chinese employees with necessary facilities for carrying out their tasks.

Article 2 Party B has the right to recommend candidate(s) for its employment, but those it recommends must be approved by Party A. For a person employed in this way, there shall be no probation period. If the employee is dismissed after working for less than a year, Party B should pay him/her two month's salary/wage as a severance pay. If he/she has worked for one year or longer, the provisions of Article 9 shall apply.

Article 3 Party B has the right to take probation for an employee, but the period of probation must not exceed three months. During the probation period, Party B has the right to terminate the probation if it finds that the probationer is not suitable for the job. If on completion of the probation the probationer is accepted as a regular employee, the period of his/her employment shall be reckoned from the first day of probation.

Article 4 Salaries/Wages of Chinese employees should be determined through consultation between Party A and Party B. On completion of each year's service, the employee should be granted salary/wage increments, the amount of which shall be determined through consultation between Party A and Party B.

Chapter II

Rights and Obligations of Party A

Article 5 Party A demands that the employees abide by the following stipulations:
(1) In addition to the laws, regulations and decrees of the PRC, employees should strictly observe the office rules and regulations of Party B, keep Party B's business secrets, and conscientiously perform their duties.
(2) In case of sickness and sick leave is needed, Party B shall be notified in time. If

the sick leave exceeds two days, a doctor's certificate must be produced. In case of compassionate leave, prior consent should be sought from Party B.

(3) Employees should, when Party B's business requires, work overtime and take business trips.

Article 6 Party A has the right to withdraw an employee, but prior notice should be given to Party B and a decision made through consultation between Party A and Party B. If an employee should be withdrawn by Party A for his/her personal reasons, no severance pay will be required of Party B.

Chapter III

Rights and Obligations of Party B

Article 7 Party B shall ensure that its employees are entitled to the following:

(1) A work day shall not exceed eight hours and a work week shall not exceed five-and-a-half days. Saturday afternoons shall be reserved for studies and recreational activities sponsored by Party A. Whenever overtime is required, overtime pay should be given by Party B. Party B should pay nightmeal allowance for overtime work extending to 9:30 p.m. and allowance for missed meals when the employee is unable to take them in the internal cafeteria because of overtime work in the morning or evening. Party B should pay employees a certain sum of lunch subsidy, the amount of which may be decided by Party B. The overtime pay per hour for an employee should be calculated in the following way:

Monthly pay divided by 30 days divided by 8 (hours) × 1.5 = overtime pay per hour

All overtime payments are doubled for work on public holidays. Overtime pay for typists, drivers and househelps are stipulated in the Appendix to this Contract. Party B should pay a special nutrition subsidy to employees engaged in work that involves radioactivity or pollution harmful to health.

(2) In addition to public holidays in the PRC, employees who have been employed by Party B for half a year or longer are each entitled to an annual vacation of 15 consecutive days with full pay each calendar year. Those who have been employed for less than half a year are to be given an annual vacation with full pay within the calendar year for as many days as the number of months he/she has worked with Party B. To employees who cannot take their annual vacation or part of it because of their indispensability from work, an overtime pay for as many days as have not been used as vacation shall be paid in lieu.

(3) At the end of each calendar year, Party B undertakes to pay an extra month's salary/wage to an employee who has been engaged for half a year or longer. for those who have been engaged for less than half a year, the extra pay should be 1/12 of his/her monthly salary/wage times the number of months he/she has worked with Party B. As a gesture of encouragement, a bonus can also be given directly to those employees who have performed outstanding work.

(4) Party B should pay full salaries/wages to employees whose accumulated sick leaves do not exceed one month, accumulated compassionate leaves do not exceed 15 days, and/or maternity leaves do not exceed 90 days (in special cases 105 days)

in one calendar year. When an employee is on sick leave, compassionate leave, maternity leave or annual vacation, Party B should pay separate salary/wage to a temporary replacement should Party B deem it necessary to have one. The salary/wage for the replacement should be the same as that of the employee on leave or vacation.

(5) In addition to meal, accommodation and travel expenses, Party B should pay incidental expenses for employees who are on business trips within China but outside Beijing. To employees who go on business trips in remote areas, a special subsidy should be paid.

(6) Party B should take out a personal accident insurance for its employees with the People's Insurance Company of Beijing. The insured amount is Rmb 40,000 for each employee. In case an employee who has not ben insured against accidents is injured while on duty, Party B must pay the expenses of the employee's medical treatment and nutrition up to but not exceeding Rmb 10,000 in addition to his/her salary/wage for the entire period of medical treatment. If an employee injured while on duty does not recover after six months' treatment, the total expenses for which Party B is liable shall be discussed between Party A and Party B and paid by Party B in a lump sum not exceeding Rmb 30,000. In case of disability or death resulting from injuries sustained by an employee while on duty, Party B must pay in a lump-sum a pension of Rmb 30,000.

Article 8 In case of traffic accidents caused by drivers, the damages shall be borne by Party B if the authorities concerned judge that the responsibility falls on the driver employed by Party B.

Article 9 Party B has the right to dismiss an employee, but prior notice should be given to Party A and a decision made through consultation between the two Parties. Party B shall give a dismissed employee who has been employed for over half a year a severance pay calculated in the following way:

For an employee who has been employed by Party B for more than half a year but less than one and a half years, the severance pay shall be one month's salary/wage.

For an employee who has been employed by Party B for one and a half years or longer but less than two and a half years, the severance pay shall be two months' salary/wage.

For each additional year of employment thereafter, an additional one month salary/wage shall be paid. However, the maximum severance pay shall not exceed six months' salary/wage. If Party B decides to terminate the engagement of an employee on the expiry of the present contract, the severance pay for the employee shall be calculated on the same basis as mentioned above.

Article 10 Party B can sign individual contracts with its Chinese employees in accordance with its needs, provided the individual contracts do not contravene laws, regulations and decrees of the PRC, nor the provisions of this Contract.

Chapter IV

Settlement of Payments

Article 11 Party A shall, before the 25th of each month, submit a settlement statement of the employees' monthly salaries/wages, overtime pay, etc. for the current month to Party B who, upon checking and finding it in order, shall pay the amount due to Party A's Accounting Department within the same month. All accounts should be paid in foreign currency or in Foreign Exchange Certificates of the PRC. If payment is not made in due time, a 1%, 2% and 3% surcharge shall be added for arrears of ten, twenty and thirty days respectively. If the arrears exceeds 30 days, the case shall become one of dismissal of the employees by Party B, and shall be dealt with per the provisions for dismissal contained in Article 9 of this Contract, which means that apart from paying the employees' salaries/wages, overtime pay, allowances, etc., Party B must also pay the severance pay and the above mentioned surcharges.

APPENDIX 6

MAJOR OVERSEAS AGREEMENTS SIGNED BY CHINESE INVESTORS 1990–93

Investor	Country	Investment (Date)	Price	Purpose
Shougang (Capital Steel Corporation)	Peru	Hierro-Peru, (state mining co) Dec '92	US$312 million	Natural resource
CITIC	Hong Kong	10% in Yaohan Int'l of Japan ('93)	US$25 million	To develop supermarket business in China selling food sourced by CITIC Australia
	Australia	JV stockbroker with Hambros Australia ('93)	under negotiation	Financial services – tapping Australian institutional investors
	Australia	100% in egg carton manufacturing plant ('90)	US$1.4 million	Investment
	Australia	100% in Metro Meats, a meat packer ('93)	under negotiation	Investment
	Australia	100% of Portion Control Foods, an arm of Metro Meats, which supplies food to airlines. (Held by Pacific Asia Merchandise of which CITIC has 51%) ('93)		
CITIC Canada	Canada	Celgar pulp mill expansion project: JV with Stone Container Corp and Venepal of Venezuela ('91)	US$265 million (total investment US$530 million)	Natural resources
China Resources Holdings	Hong Kong	10% in Hong Kong Int'l Terminals ('90)	US$154 million	Investment
	Thailand	Office and residential complex in Bangkok ('90)	US$200 million	Investment
Shanghai Bicycle Corp	Brazil	Bicycle and bicycle chain factory ('92)	Total investment US$2 million and US$700,000 respectively (SBC will put in 40% in technology and equipment)	To sell to South America
Anshan Iron & Steel Complex (China)	Australia	JV with Portman Mining to develop the Koolyanobbing iron ore deposits ('93) (Anshan has 40% equity)	US$13 million	Natural resources. Percentage of iron ore to be shipped to China. This is the first time a contract has been made with a regional steel mill in its own right

SOURCE: ASIAN BUSINESS, Dec. 1993

APPENDIX 7

LEARNING MANDARIN IN CHINA

Speaking Chinese is a major challenge, not least because it is a very tonal language and to the untutored Western ear many words with radically different meanings sound exactly the same. Apart from Mandarin and Cantonese, there are numerous regional dialects (eg: Shanghaiese, Hokkien) to baffle the beginner. The Chinese government offers scholarships to the serious student of Mandarin at 17 universities and institutes listed below. They can be contacted direct, or via the Education section of the Chinese Embassy.

Name	City	Zip Code	Fax	Tel.
Beijing University	Beijing	100871	861-2564095	861-2501230; 2501231
People's University	Beijing	100872	861-2566152	861-2566454
Fudan University	Shanghai	200433	8621-5491669	8621-5483962
Nankai University	Tianjin	300071	8622-344853	8622-358825
Nanjing University	Nanjing	210008	8625-316747	8625-300550
Wuhan University	Wuhan	430072	8627-712661	8627-722712 ext. 2209
Zhongshan University	Guangzhou	510275	8620-4429173	8620-4425465
Xiamen University	Xiamen	361005	86592-286402	86592-286211; 286139
Sichuan University	Chengdu	610064	8628-582844	8628-582844
Jilin University	Changchun	130021	86431-823907	86431-825787 ext. 2680
Shandong University	Jinan	250100	86531-802167	86531-803860 ext. 2501
Liaoning University	Shenyang	110036	8624-652421	8624-643356; 643428
Beijing Language Institute	Beijing	100083	861-2017249	861-2017585
Beijing Foreign Studies University	Beijing	100081	861-8428140	861-8422587
Tianjin Foreign Languages Institute	Tianjin	300204	8622-312410	8622-312410
Shanghai International Studies University	Shanghai	200083	8621-5420225	8621-5423229
Beijing Institute of Economy	Beijing	100026	861-5001706	861-5006091

APPENDIX 8

HOW RELIABLE ARE CHINESE STATISTICS?

This book contains many statistics, many of them from Chinese sources. There has been good cause over the years to treat such numbers with considerable caution. Examples have been given of the way figures were inflated. In the politically supercharged atmosphere of most years from liberation through the Cultural Revolution, statistical data could be used as ideological ammunition, and in many periods and places was compiled and published with an eye to political advantage.

It has often been very difficult to obtain accurate figures because of the Chinese attitude towards information of all kinds – not only statistical data but even things like official biographies of leaders – which is much more cautious than in most other countries. Material which would be publicly distributed elsewhere might be highly classified in China. In the early 1990s, a high official said of data regarding the progress of the special economic zones: 'The figures aren't secret, but there is no imperative need for the public to know them.' This means not only that the information would be withheld from the public but that it also might not be available for use even by statisticians or responsible managers in related bureaus or areas of interest, or even in the same bureau.

Also, in many subject areas there simply is not much data. A public health researcher working in China noted: 'The limited information demands a near-addiction to making estimates and interpretations based on a sense of context, general principles and incomplete data.' When the Great Leap got under way, such little statistical information as had been coming from the People's Republic quickly became useless as everyone from units in the countryside to ministries in Beijing vied for the most impressive production records and reported statistics which would have been unbelievable in any other milieu and were not credited among foreigners. There is now a greater appreciation that such behaviour does not help China's international image, and many of the old shortcomings have been eliminated – although, statistically speaking, there is still a tendency to emphasize the good and play down the bad.

The biggest problem today is with numbers. The reason is the Chinese numeration is less flexible than decimal numeration. For example, the unit *wan* stands for 10,000 and there is no convenient expression for larger quantities before 100 million called *yi*. One million, for example, must be expressed as 100 wan. It is understandable that decimal points may float bewilderingly. Sometimes the problem is clearly with the decimal points, but the source of the difficulty is not so obvious. Problems may exist simply due to lack of knowledge as to the difference between kilowatts and kilowatt hours, for example. The danger can lie in the fact that the rest of the translation from Chinese to English may be impeccable which lulls the reader into acceptance of the figures when a little thought would indicate that they simply do not add up.

BIBLIOGRAPHY

Chang, Jung. *Wild Swans. Three Daughters of China.* London, Harper Collins.
Ching, Frank. *Ancestors. 900 Years in the life of a Chinese family.* London, Harrap.
Ethridge, James M. *Changing China. The New Revolution's First Decade 1979-1988.* Beijing. New World Press.
Grant, Pamela. *Celestial Empire. China In The 20th Century.* London, Queen Anne Press.
Keown-Boyd, Henry. *The Fists of Righteous Harmony. A History of the Boxer Uprising in China the Year 1900.* London, Leo Cooper.
Lui Guogang and others. *China's Economy in 2000.* Beijing, New World Press.
Mann, Jim. *Beijing Jeep. The short, unhappy romance of American business in China.* New York, Simon and Schuster.
Murray, Geoffrey. *The Rampant Dragon. China's Long March To A New Economic Dynasty.* London, Minerva Press.
Roberts, J.A.G. *China Through Western Eyes. The Nineteeth Century.* Stroud, Alan Sutton Publishing Ltd.
Salisbury, Harrison. *The New Emperors. Mao & Deng, A Dual Biography.* London, Harper Collins.
Siu See-Kong. *The Simplest Way To Learn PRC Business.* Simple Books.

Other reference sources:

China Daily and *Business Weekly, Beijing Review, China Pictorial.* All may be obtained through China International Book Trading Corp. (Guoji Shudian), PO Box 399 Beijing China or via Guanghua Co. 32 Parker Street, Covent Garden, London WC2B 5PH.
Business China. The Economic Intelligence Unit, 20th Floor, Luk Kwok Centre, 72 Gloucester Road, Hong Kong.
China-Britain Trade Review. Monthly newsletter published by the China-Britain Trade Group, 5th Floor, Abford House, 15 Wilton Road, London SW1V 1LT.

Index

Academy of Social Sciences 39, 47
Accountancy reform 286-288
Advertising 212
AEG 135
All China Federation of Industry &
  Commerce (ACFIC) 205
  Trade Unions (ACFTU) 253
Aged cadres problems 256
Agents 150, 166, 210, 216, 240
America see United States
American Motor Co. (AMC) 158-160,
  192, 226
Anhui 86, 87, 90
Asia-Pacific Economic Cooperation 4
  Forum 134
Asia-Pacific Region 312
Asia Brown Boveri 136

Basan 61
Baht Economic Zone 311
Bank lending 277-279
Bank of Communications 88
Banking reform
  structure 269-276
Bankruptcy 47, 319
Barter trade 107
Beihai 57
Beijing-Kowloon railway 88
  - Shanghai 88
  - Guangzhou 88
  - Cherokee Jeep Co. 176
  - Lufthansa Friendship Store 200
Beijing Jeep 159, 183-185, 192-193,
  225, 226, 246
Beijing Review 25
Bonds 18, 33, 41, 76-77, 92, 132, 140,
  172, 180
Border trade 106-109
BOT (Build, Operate, Transfer) 115
Bribes see envelope business
Brilliance China Automotive 186, 188
Britain 91, 134, 166, 305

Bullet train 65, 88

Canada 91
Canton 2
Capital market 18
Capitalism, attitude to 23, 306
Central bank, role of 16, 18
Central Committee 318
Central planning 10, 22-23, 26, 34, 76,
  245, 259, 273
Chain of debt 45
Chaozhu-Shanton Railway 67
Chen Yun 30
Chengdu 15, 96
China Daily 31
Chinese Economic Area 4
Chinese multinationals 139
  CATIC 141
  CITIC 139, 184, 205
Chongqing 3, 96
Chongqing 87, 99
CIS 95
Citroën 188
CNAIC 180, 182
CNN 307
Coca Cola 196
Communist Party of China 53, 303, 305,
  308
Competition, role of 10, 26, 33, 61, 81,
  135, 186, 202, 216-217, 232,
  263-264
Contract, meaning of 222-223
'convertors-importers' 206
Copyroght problems 208-209
Corporate Law, lack of 19
Coupon system 44
Crude oil 44
Cultural Revolution 20
Customs duty 204

Daewoo 133, 181
Daihatsu 190

345

Daimler-Benz 135
Dalian 54, 130, 161
Daqing 105
Dashing Electronics Co. 62
Debt, chain of 45
    National 45
Decentralization 59, 303
Defence industry see also military factories
Democracy, future of 305
Deng Xiaoping 1, 8, 9, 29, 36, 110, 126
    on economic reform 29
Department stores – foreign involvement 2, 15, 75, 201–203
Diplomatic policy 309
Distribution system 209–212
Dong Furen 40
Dongfeng Automobile Group 42
Dongguan 61
Du Pont 90
Dutiable value 204

Economic and Technological Development Zones 57, 71
Emperor – 'Little Emperor' 197
Envelope business 165
Europe (trade) 134–135, 179, 312, 315
European Community 4, 6
Everbright Holdings 141
Exchange rate 318

Factory Director Responsibility System (FDRS) 36
Factory manager, role of 47, 245, 254
Featherbedding 47
Fengdu 94
FESCO 256
Fiat 187
Five-Year Plan 48
Ford Motor Co. 185
Foreign banks, position of 276–277
Foreign exchange 14, 33, 58, 75, 83, 108, 113–114, 122, 129, 148, 150–151, 160, 172–173, 177, 181, 187, 192, 206, 270, 273, 278–280, 289, 317–318
    see also swap markets
Foreign Exchange Certificates (FECs) 14, 318

Enterprise Service Corporation (FESCO) 256
Foreign investment 8–10, 12, 25, 27, 111
    Investment Administration 86
Foreign Trade Administration 204
Fuji Heavy Industry 190
Fujian 63
Futures markets 288–290
Fuzhou 54, 64

Gas Shangkun 47
Gansu 103, 162–163, 260, 308
GATT 180, 199, 314
GEC Alsthom 136
General Motors 183, 186
Germany 4, 91, 135
Gold 104, 118
Gong Yuzhi 28
Grand Canal 88
Growth Triangle Concept 311
Guangdong 8, 10, 56, 63, 308, 313
Guanggao 66
Guanghan 12
Guangxi Zhuang Autonomous Zone 104, 107, 259
Guangzhou 2, 57, 137 199
Guanxi 120

Haicang ('Ethylene City') 66
Hainan 58, 59, 177
Hangzhou 2
Hebei 154, 212
Hefei 91
Heilongjiang 109, 191
Hitachi 130
Honda 131, 190
Honda Motor Company 176, 181
Hong Kong 4, 28, 63, 64, 65, 66, 91, 96, 101, 312
    future of 313–314
    investment in China
Huafa Electronics Co. 62
Huan Xiang 35
Hubei 86
Huizhou 61
Human rights 306
Hunan 87, 94–96, 197
Hyundai Motor Co. 133, 181

Illegal loans 273
Import and Export Bureau 204
Import/export rules 203
Income (per capita) 2
Industrial and Commercial Consolidated Tax (ICCT) 204
Inflation 13, 15
Infrastructure 136
Institute of Economics 54
Inter-provincial rivalry 10
International Monetary Fund 5
Investment Methods
   Compensation Trade 149
   Cooperative Joint Venture 146, 154
   Equity Joint Venture 145
   Finding the right partner 153-158
   Joint Development 147
   Limited Company 146
   Processing and assembly of supplies, parts and components agreement 150
   Representative Office 143
   Wholly-owned Foreign Enterprise 147
Iron Rice Bowl 49, 50
Italy 134
Iveco 187, 191

Jakarta 65
Japan 4, 5, 91, 95, 96, 126-132, 312
   Investment patterns 126
   Trade relations 315
Jialing River 97
Jiang Zemin 9, 25, 28, 33
Jiangsu 86, 89
Jiangxi 86, 87, 94-96
Jilin 175
Jinmen 62
Jinqiao 170
Jiujiang 94
Job hunting 258
Job switching 262
Joint ventures 19
   see also investment methods
Junan 86

Kentucky Fried Chicken 124
Kuala Lumpur 65
Kuwait 65

Labour contract system 50
   management relations 248-253
   Unions 253-254
Labour Ministry 50
Land Use 11, 12
   ownership 167
Law and order 302
Leasing 40
Lee Kuan Yew 119, 301
Legal system 304
Li Langqing 112
Li Peng 24
Li Yining 40, 44
Lianyungang 54
Liaoning, province 45
Light industry 43
Little Japan 79, 130
   see also Dalian
Liu Jipeng 41
Liu Zhifeng 51
Liu Zhongli 15
Lunghu 66

Macao 28, 57, 63, 96, 101
Macro-economic control 28
Management style 243-248
Manila 65
Mao Zedong 1, 8 26, 49, 234
   Great Leap Forward 3
Market economy 8, 15, 22, 28-30, 32, 39-40, 52, 54, 114, 139, 157, 269, 271, 295-297, 304, 315-316, 319
Maoism 47
Matsu 62
Matsushita 130
McDonalds 124
Media 216-218, 304
MFN (Most Favoured Nation) status 125
Mianyang 99
Military factories 99, 153
   converted to civilian products 98-102
Millionaires 56
Minerals 103
Ministry of Agriculture 12
Ministry of Foreign Trade and Economic Cooperation (MOFTEC) 113, 131, 179

Mistakes (problems identified) 171–173
Mitsubishi 90, 130
MOFTEC 144, 204, 205, 210, 214
Monetary policy 16
Monetary taps 16
Mongolia 310
Monopoly on information 307
Motor industry 130, 179–80, 182, 188
Motorola 113
Multinationals, Chinese 139

Nan'ao Island 67
Nanchung 94
Nanjing 2, 87
Nantong 54
Napoleon 3
National Panasonic 100
National People's Congress 53
Negotiations 223–226
    Process 224
    Tactics 228–233
    The 36 Stratagems 233–242
Nepal 108
Nestlé 200
News – 'buying' 218–219
Newspapers 217
Ningbo 57, 88
Ningxia Hui Autonomous Zone 79
Nissan Motor Company 176, 182, 191
Nonferrous-metal industry 53
Norinco 100
North Korea 310

OECD 6, 320
Oil exploration 72, 95, 294
One country, two systems 28, 313
'Operating rules' 152–153
Overseas Chinese 115–121

P & O 93
Partner – finding the right one 37, 40, 93, 100, 106, 114, 117, 125, 127, 132, 137–140, 143, 145–147, 15—151, 153–158, 160–164, 166–168, 171, 176, 182–185, 187, 189–191, 200, 221, 224, 242, 246, 250, 259, 272, 311, 315
Pearl River 2, 93

Penang 65
People's Bank of China 17, 317, 318
People's Construction Bank of China 205, 271–272, 277
People's Daily 24, 215, 307
People's Liberation Army Daily 17, 98
Personal income tax 17
Peugeot 93, 188
Philips 90, 113
Planned Economy 10, 16, 27–29, 48, 97, 254, 273, 295, 304
Power struggle 165
Pricing (policy) 31ff
Private business sector 52
Privatization 29, 34, 40, 280
Production targets
Property law 168
'Prospecting Treasure Plan' 103
Public ownership, concept of 25–27, 29–31, 40–41
Public sector 22, 25–26, 34, 40, 54, 73, 256, 319
Public Security Bureau 145
Pudong 61, 169
    see also Shanghai

Quaidam Basin 106
Qarhan Salt Lake 106
Qianjiang Beer Group 50
Quindao 57, 310
Qinghai 105–106
Quinhuangdao 57

Railway network – congestion and expansion 210
Red Cross 208
Reform (bi-monthly) 27
Renault 189
Renmimbi (RMB) 14, 317
Robbers/Robbery 211
Rolls Royce 192

SAIC 214
Sales promotion 212
Savings habit 15
Sea of Japan Rim Economic Zone 310
Seagull Watch Factory 47
Shangdong 8, 36, 40, 57

348

Shanghai 2, 8, 12, 15, 37, 96, 169
   Steel works 45
   Stock Exchange 41
Shantou 12, 56, 66-68
Shenzen 2, 5, 12, 15, 56, 59-62, 199
   Stock Exchange 41
Shougang 39
Sichuan 11, 12, 15, 86, 94, 96-98
Siemens 135
Singapore 4, 65, 112
Sinopec 105
Smitth, Adam 8
Social Security 254-256
Socialism 22ff, 25, 26, 28, 40, 52
   with Chinese characteristics 25, 26
Socialist construction 25
Socialist market economy 8, 23ff
Socialist modernization 22
Sony 130
South China Sea Economic Zone 311
South Korea 4, 5, 95
   growing investment 132-134, 310
Soviet Union 98, 110, 310, 311
Special Administrative Region 313
Special Economic Zones (SEZs) 12, 56ff
Staff hiring 256
Staff training 265
State Council 12, 15-16, 37, 46, 53, 106, 129, 139, 141, 176, 210, 270, 281, 286, 293-295
State Economic Commission 37
State Planning Commission 160
State planning, restructuring of 30, 47
   economy 51
   pricing 31
State sector, role of 43
State Statistics Bureau 5, 44
State-owned enterprises 10, 15, 18, 48, 156, 213
Stock markets 279-282
Stock speculation 282-285
Suzhou 89
Suzuki Motor Company 181
Swap markets 14, 207, 271
Swire 140

Taishan Iron and Steel Corporation 36

Taiwan 4, 25, 54, 63, 98, 101, 121-124, 309, 312
Tandem 206
Tax Bureau 145, 292
Taxes 58
   foreign investor 291
   historic structure 295
   industrial & commercial 294
   reform 296
Telecommunications 137-138
Telephone (lines) 137, 198
Television 14
   advertising 215
   per household 3
Thailand 4, 96
Three Gorges Dam 86
Three Gorges Dam Project 93, 137
Tiananmen 47, 200
Tianjin 2, 8, 12, 47, 57, 310
Tibet 9, 108
Toyota Motor Company 176, 180, 191
Trade disputes 248ff
   unions see labour
Trademark piracy 208
transit theft 211

Unilever 170
United States 4, 5, 6, 13, 91, 98, 101, 124-126, 184, 305, 312, 315
Uraguay Round 316

Value-added tax 297
Volkswagen 135, 181

Walt Disney 124
Wang Bingqian 18
Wang Zhongya 15
Wenzhou 57
Wharf Holdings 92-93
Workers' Congress 51
World Bank 4, 6, 64, 65
Wuhan 3, 91-94
Wuhan Cityford Dyeing and Printing Industry 91
Wuhu 87
Wu Yi 114

Xiamen 12, 57, 62-66

Xinjiang Uygur Autonomous Region 9, 162

Yamaha motorcycles 100
Yangpu 69-70, 124
Yangtse 86, 133
Yangtse River Economic Development Company 88ff
Yantai 57
Yantian 59
Yellow River 102-105, 133
Yellow Sea Rim Economic Zone 311
Yi Men Jiang Economic Zone 310
Yiehang 86
Yuan convertibility 316
Yueyang 87

Zhangjiagang 87
Zhangzhou 65, 182, 199
Zhanjiang 57, 87
Zhejiang 50, 86
Zhou Shulian 39
Zhougshan 61
Zhu Rongji 13, 40, 46, 53, 317, 321
Zhuhai 2, 57